LinkedIn®

FOR

DUMMIES®

2ND EDITION

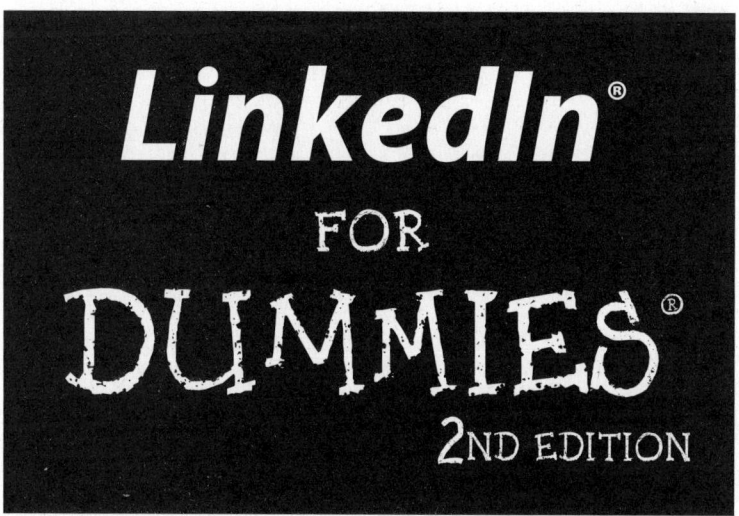

LinkedIn®
FOR
DUMMIES®
2ND EDITION

by Joel Elad, MBA

WILEY

John Wiley & Sons, Inc.

LinkedIn® For Dummies®, 2nd Edition

Published by
John Wiley & Sons, Inc.
111 River Street
Hoboken, NJ 07030-5774
www.wiley.com

Copyright © 2011 by John Wiley & Sons, Inc., Hoboken, New Jersey

Published by John Wiley & Sons, Inc., Hoboken, New Jersey

Published simultaneously in Canada

For general information on our other products and services, please contact our Customer Care Department within the U.S. at 877-762-2974, outside the U.S. at 317-572-3993, or fax 317-572-4002.

For technical support, please visit www.wiley.com/techsupport.

Wiley publishes in a variety of print and electronic formats and by print-on-demand. Some material included with standard print versions of this book may not be included in e-books or in print-on-demand. If this book refers to media such as a CD or DVD that is not included in the version you purchased, you may download this material at http://booksupport.wiley.com. For more information about Wiley products, visit www.wiley.com.

Library of Congress Control Number: 2011920887

ISBN 978-0-470-94854-5 (pbk); ISBN 978-1-118-03857-4 (ebk); ISBN 978-1-118-03858-1 (ebk); ISBN 978-1-118-03859-8 (ebk)

Manufactured in the United States of America

10 9 8 7 6 5

WILEY

About the Author

Joel Elad, MBA, is the head of Real Method Consulting, a company dedicated to educating people through training seminars, DVDs, books, and other media. He holds a master's degree in Business from UC Irvine, and has a bachelor's degree in Computer Science and Engineering from UCLA. He also operates several online businesses, including NewComix.Com, and is launching a new blog.

Joel has written seven books about various online topics, including *Facebook Advertising For Dummies, Starting an Online Business All-In-One Desk Reference For Dummies, Starting an iPhone Application Business For Dummies,* and *Wiley Pathways: E-business.* He has contributed to *Entrepreneur* magazine and Smartbiz.com, and has taught at institutions such as the University of California, Irvine. He is an Educational Specialist trained by eBay and a former Internet instructor for the Learning Annex in New York City, Los Angeles, San Diego, and San Francisco.

Joel lives in San Diego, California. In his spare time, he hones his skills in creative writing, Texas Hold'Em poker, and finance. He is an avid traveler who enjoys seeing the sights both near and far, whether it's the Las Vegas Strip or the ruins of Machu Picchu. He spends his weekends scouring eBay and local conventions for the best deals, catching the latest movies with friends or family, and enjoying a lazy Sunday.

Dedication

To my best friend Magda, who faces life and adversity as strongly as she values our friendship. You amaze and inspire me, and I hope you never give up on anything! Friends Forever

— Joel

Author's Acknowledgments

First and foremost, I have to give the BIGGEST thanks to the great team at Wiley who made this book project possible. Thanks to Bob Woerner for pushing this project forward and having the confidence to put me in place. An absolute, huge, bear-hug thanks to Paul Levesque for putting up with my fast and furious submissions; he definitely kept me on track to make this book happen. And where would I be without copy editors like Teresa Artman; she made me sound so clear and grammatically correct!

Secondly, I want to acknowledge the absolutely terrific folks at LinkedIn for being open, eager, and absolute quality professionals to work with on this project. The big shoutout goes to CS, you know who you are! Adam Nash, Kay Luo, Mario Sundar, and Jay Thomas, thank you so much for your time, advice, stories, and access. You definitely made this book a better read because of your help.

I have to give a special thanks to Scott Allen, who was instrumental in getting this book project started, and I appreciate your help and support, as well as your infinite knowledge on the subject.

Thanks, as always, goes out to my friends and new LinkedIn contacts who provided me with stories, examples, and endless amounts of encouragement. I especially want to thank Cynthia Beale, Michael Bellomo, Janine Bielski, Hal Burg, Eric Butow, Anthony Choi, Joan Curtis, Lynn Dralle, Steve Hayes, Chuck Hester, Rob Keller, Kyle Looper, Carol Mendolsohn, David Nakayama, Kristie Spilios, Jan Utstein, and Michael Wellman.

Lastly, thanks to my family for putting up with my late-late-night writing sessions and frequent seclusion to get this book ready for publication. Your support is always invaluable.

Publisher's Acknowledgments

We're proud of this book; please send us your comments at *http://dummies.custhelp.com*. For other comments, please contact our Customer Care Department within the U.S. at 877-762-2974, outside the U.S. at 317-572-3993, or fax 317-572-4002.

Some of the people who helped bring this book to market include the following:

Acquisitions and Editorial

Senior Project Editor: Paul Levesque

Executive Editor: Bob Woerner

Senior Copy Editor: Teresa Artman

Technical Editor: Melanie Nelson

Editorial Manager: Leah Cameron

Editorial Assistant: Amanda Graham

Sr. Editorial Assistant: Cherie Case

Cartoons: Rich Tennant (www.the5thwave.com)

Composition Services

Project Coordinator: Patrick Redmond

Layout and Graphics: Joyce Haughey, Laura Westhuis

Proofreaders: Lindsay Amones, Toni Settle

Indexer: BIM Indexing & Proofreading Services

Publishing and Editorial for Technology Dummies

Richard Swadley, Vice President and Executive Group Publisher

Andy Cummings, Vice President and Publisher

Mary Bednarek, Executive Acquisitions Director

Mary C. Corder, Editorial Director

Publishing for Consumer Dummies

Kathleen Nebenhaus, Vice President and Executive Publisher

Composition Services

Debbie Stailey, Director of Composition Services

Contents at a Glance

Table of Contents

Introduction

● ●

Relationships matter. Ever since the dawn of time, when caveman Fred asked caveman Barney whether there was any work down at the quarry, human beings have always networked. We're social creatures who like to reach out and talk to someone. As the Internet developed and grew in popularity, people rapidly took advantage of this new technology for communication, with e-mail, instant messaging, personal Web pages sharing voice, video, and data with each other, and lots of other applications to keep everybody connected. But how can the Internet help you do a better job with your professional networking? I'm glad you asked. Welcome to *LinkedIn For Dummies,* Second edition.

LinkedIn was founded in 2003 by a guy named Reid Hoffman, who felt that he could create a better way to handle your professional networking needs. He saw lots of Web sites that let you build your own page and show it to the world, extolling your virtues and talents. But a lot of the popular Web sites that Hoffman came across focused more on the social aspects of your life and not that much on the professional side. LinkedIn changed all that with its approach of augmenting all the professional networking you do (or should do) on a daily basis. You don't have to be looking for a job to use LinkedIn, but if you're looking, LinkedIn should be a part of your search.

In short, LinkedIn allows you to coordinate your professional identity on the Internet and make you more effective in your career. The site is designed to make the aspects of networking less time consuming and more powerful, so you can open doors with your professional connections and tap the connections of people you know who make up your extended network. LinkedIn doesn't require a huge amount of time or usage to be effective, and is focused only on providing tools that help your professional career.

Perhaps you've heard of LinkedIn, but you don't understand fully what it is, how it works, and most importantly, why you should care about it. Maybe you got an Invitation to join the LinkedIn Web site. Perhaps you've gotten multiple Invitations, or you keep hearing about it and want to find out more. Well, you're taking the right first step by reading this book. I talk about the Whys as well as the Hows. If you're looking to enhance your professional life, I truly believe you need to look at LinkedIn. If you want to go straight to the beach and retire, maybe this isn't the book for you!

This book covers LinkedIn from start to finish. In case you haven't already joined, I show you how you can sign up. If you're already a member, this book is also very useful because I show you how to build your identity and take advantage of LinkedIn's functionality. This book is useful regardless of your skill level, whether you want to join or you've been on LinkedIn for years but feel stuck.

About This Book

This book covers all aspects of using the LinkedIn site: from signing up and building your profile, to growing your network of contacts, to taking advantage of some of the sophisticated options, and everything in between. I include a lot of advice and discussion of networking concepts, but you also find a lot of step-by-step instructions to get things done. In this second edition, I revisit some of the newer facets of LinkedIn, including its Groups and Companies sections, and have updated all the core processes, from creating your profile to looking for a job.

This book is organized as a guide; you can read each chapter one after the other, or you can go straight to the chapter on the topic you're interested in. After you start using LinkedIn, think of this book as a reference where you can find the knowledge nugget you need to know and then be on your merry way. Lots of details are cross-referenced, so if you need to look elsewhere in the book for more information, you can easily find it.

How This Book Is Organized

I divide this book into six handy parts:

Part I: LinkedIn Basics

This part starts with the basics; I talk about the benefits of LinkedIn, how to sign up, and how to build your online profile.

Part II: Finding Others and Getting Connected

In Part II, I go a step further and discuss your network of connections. I go through how to search the LinkedIn database of tens of millions of professionals, how to introduce yourself to other people, and how to grow your own personal network.

Part III: Growing and Managing Your Network

This part starts to heat things up a bit by covering some of LinkedIn's built-in functionality, like getting and receiving Recommendations, adding LinkedIn toolbars to your e-mail and Web browser, and importing and exporting your network to other applications, such as Microsoft Outlook.

Part IV: Finding Employees, Jobs, and Services

Part IV takes everything I cover in the first three parts of the book and applies it to the top reasons why people use LinkedIn: namely, searching for a job, finding an employee, and finding a reputable service professional.

Part V: Using LinkedIn for Everyday Business

In this part, I continue on the trend of showing the real application of LinkedIn by applying the site's capabilities to different professions. I talk about how to use LinkedIn for marketing, sales, venture capital and startup, and even some creative uses you may have never thought of doing with LinkedIn.

Part VI: The Part of Tens

Part VI is the traditional *For Dummies* Part of Tens — this part contains lists that detail a number of LinkedIn functions and resources you can find on the Internet to help you with your LinkedIn experience.

And Just Who Are You?

I assume that you know how to use your computer, at least for the basic operations, like checking e-mail, typing up a document, or surfing the great big World Wide Web. If you're worried that you need a Ph.D. in Computer Operations to handle LinkedIn, relax. If you can navigate your way through a Web site, you can use LinkedIn.

You may be utterly fresh on the idea of social networking, or the specific ins and outs of a site like LinkedIn. LinkedIn allows you to do some really cool stuff and enhance your professional life. There's more to it, and this book is here to show you the ropes — and help you take full advantage of what LinkedIn has to offer.

This book assumes that you have a computer that can access the Internet; any PC or Macintosh line of computer will be fine, as well as Linux or any other operating system with a Web browser. All the main Web browsers can access LinkedIn just fine. In some parts of the book, I discuss specific applications such as Microsoft Outlook; if you have Outlook, I assume you know how to use it for the purposes of importing and exporting names from your address book.

Icons Used in This Book

As you go through this book, you'll see the following icons in the margins.

The Tip icon notifies you about something cool, handy, or nifty that I highly recommend. For example, "Here's a quicker way to do the described task the next time you have to do it."

Don't forget! When you see this icon, you can be sure that it points out something you should remember, possibly even something I said earlier that I'm repeating because it's very important. For example, "If you are only going to do one of my bullet point suggestions, do the last one because it's the most powerful."

Danger! Ah-oo-gah! Ah-oo-gah! When you see the Warning icon, pay careful attention to the text. This icon flags something that's bad or that could cause trouble. For example, "Although you may be tempted to go into personal details in your profile, you should never post anything that could embarrass you in a future job interview."

This icon alerts you to something technical, an aside or some trivial tidbit that I just cannot suppress the urge to share. For example, "It would be as ludicrous for me to recommend the 802.11q standard as it would be for me to insist that 1 is a prime number." Feel free to skip over this book's technical information as you please.

Where to Go from Here

You can start reading this book anywhere. Open the Table of Contents and pick a spot that amuses you or concerns you or has piqued your curiosity. Everything is explained in the text, and important details are cross-referenced so that you don't waste your time reading repeated information.

Good luck with LinkedIn. Happy networking!

Part I
LinkedIn Basics

The 5th Wave   By Rich Tennant

"This is getting downright annoying. He updates his profile every time he's about to go down a chimney."

In this part . . .

*I*t's like they say, "You gotta start somewhere." Well, of course you have to start somewhere, where else would you be? So, when you're ready to make that first step, that great leap for all of mankind, this is the place you want to be. And any other inspirational saying I can squeeze into this paragraph. . . .

This part covers the basics of using the LinkedIn Web site. I start with some background on the site and outline all the different features covered in this book. Then you move into the sign-up phase, where you can create your LinkedIn account, and end with building your LinkedIn profile, a Web page that details your professional and educational experience for all who want to see it — depending on who you want to see it, that is.

Chapter 1

Looking into LinkedIn

*W*hen I hear the terms "social networking" and "business networking," I always go back to one of my favorite phrases: "It's not *what* you know; it's *who* you know." Now imagine a Web site where both concepts are true, where you can demonstrate *what* you know and see the power of *who* you know. That's just one way of describing LinkedIn, one of the top Web sites today where you can do professional networking and so much more. Social networking has gotten a lot of attention over the years, and the two sites that everyone talks about are Twitter and Facebook. Let me state right now, in the first paragraph of the first chapter, that LinkedIn is *not* one of those sites. You can find some elements of similarity, but LinkedIn isn't the place to tweet about what you had for lunch or show pictures of last Friday's beach bonfire.

LinkedIn is a place where Relationships Matter (the LinkedIn slogan). When you look at the mission statement, LinkedIn's goal "is to help you be more effective in your daily work and open doors to opportunities using the professional relationships you already have." This is not a Web site that requires a lot of constant work to be effective. It's designed to work in the background and help you reach out to whomever you need while learning and growing yourself. The key is to set up your online identity, build your network, and steadily take advantage of the opportunities that most affect you or greatly interest you.

In this chapter, I introduce you to LinkedIn and the basic services it has to offer. I answer the question "What is LinkedIn?" and, more importantly, "Why should I be using LinkedIn?" I talk about how LinkedIn fits in with the rest of your online activities, and then I move into the tangible benefits that LinkedIn can provide you, regardless of your profession or career situation. I discuss some of the premium account capabilities that you can pay to use, but rest assured, LinkedIn has a lot of features that are free. The last part of the chapter covers basic navigation of the LinkedIn site. I show you the different menus and navigation bars, which you use throughout this book.

Discovering Your New Contact Management and Networking Toolkit

When describing how people can be connected with each other, think of a tangible network. For example, roads connect cities. The Internet connects computers. A quilt is a series of connected pieces of fabric. But what about the intangible networks? You can describe the relations between members of your family by using a family tree metaphor. People now use the term "social network" to describe the intangible connections between them and other people, whether they're friends, co-workers, or acquaintances.

People used to rely on address books or contact organizers (PDAs) to keep track of their social networks. You could grow your social networks by attending networking events or by being introduced in person to new contacts, and then you would continue to communicate with these new contacts, and eventually the new contacts were considered a part of your social network.

As people began to rely more and more on technology, though, new tools were created to help manage social networks. Salespeople started using contact management systems like ACT! to keep track of communications. Phone calls replaced written letters, and cellular phones replaced landline phones. E-mail has replaced phone calls and letters, and with the mass adoption of cell phones, text messaging increasingly handles short bursts of communication.

Internet tools have advanced to what people refer to as Web 2.0 systems, where online communication within your network is much more automated and accessible. Sites such as LinkedIn have started to replace the older ways of accessing your social network. For example, instead of asking your friend Michael to call his friend Eric to see whether Eric's friend has a job available, you can use LinkedIn to see whether Eric's friend works for a company you want to contact, and you can then use LinkedIn to send a message through Michael to Eric (or in some cases, send a message direct to Eric's friend) to accomplish the same task. (Of course, this is all dependent upon the fact that you, Michael, and Eric are all members of LinkedIn.)

In the past, you had no way of viewing other people's social networks (collections of friends and other contacts). Now, though, when folks put their social networks on LinkedIn, you can see your friends' networks as well as their friends' networks, and suddenly hidden opportunities start to become available to you.

This means you can spend more time doing research on potential opportunities (like finding a job or a new employee for your business) as well as receiving information from the larger network and not just your immediate friends. This makes the network more useful because you can literally see the map that connects you with other people.

However, just because this information is more readily available, that doesn't mean there's no work anymore in networking. You still have to manage your connections and use the network to gain more connections or knowledge. But because LinkedIn works in the background to guide the way, you spend your time more productively instead of making blind requests and relying solely on other people to make something happen.

Keeping track of your contacts

Does this situation sound familiar to you? You made a connection with someone — say, your roommate from college. It's graduation day; you give him your contact information, he gives you his information, and you tell him to keep in touch. As both of you move to different places, start new jobs, and live your lives, you eventually lose track of each other, and all your contact information grows out of date. How do you find this person again?

One of the benefits of LinkedIn is that after you connect with someone you know who also has an account on LinkedIn, you always have a live link to that person. Even when that person changes e-mail addresses, you'll be updated with that person's new e-mail address. In this sense, LinkedIn always keeps you connected with people in your network, regardless of how their lives change. LinkedIn shows you a list of your connections, as shown in Figure 1-1.

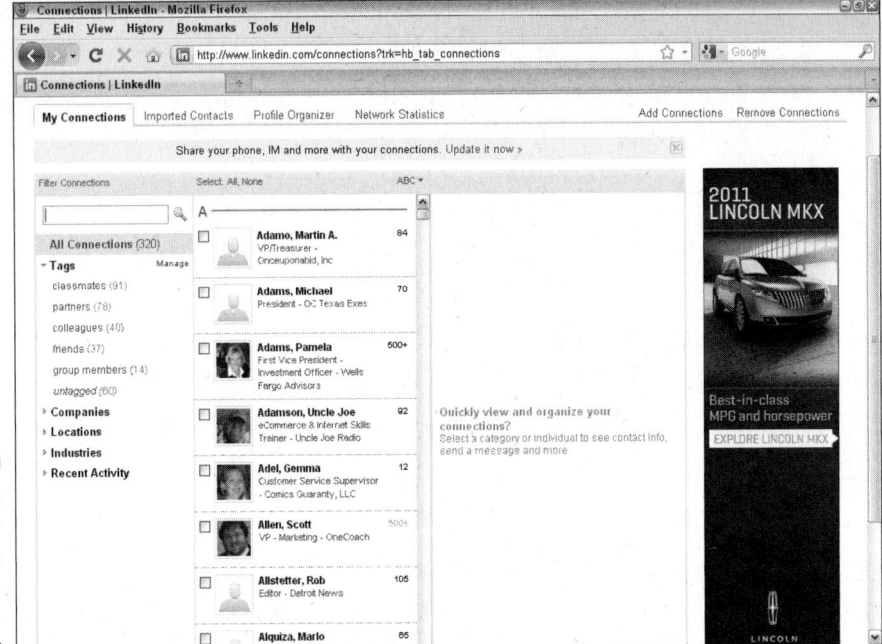

Figure 1-1:
See all your
connections
in one cen-
tralized list.

The different degrees of network connections

In the LinkedIn universe, the word *connection* specifically means a person who is connected to you through the site. The number of connections that you have simply means the number of people that are directly connected to you in your professional network.

Specifically, though, here are the different degrees of how you're connected with people on LinkedIn:

✔ **First-degree connections:** People you know personally; they have a direct relationship from their account to your account. These first-degree connections make up your immediate network and are usually your past colleagues, classmates, group members, friends, family, and close associates. Unlike Facebook, where everyone you connect to is a "friend," on LinkedIn, you can connect to friends who don't necessarily have work, school, or group connection to you, but are people who you know personally outside those criteria.

✔ **Second-degree network members:** People who know at least one member of your first-degree network connections: in other words, the friends of your friends. You can reach any second-degree network member by asking your first-degree connection to pass along an Introduction from you to his or her friend. (I discuss Introductions more in Chapter 5.)

✔ **Third-degree network members:** People who know at least one of your second-degree network members: in other words, friends of your friends of your friends. You can reach any third-degree network member by asking your friend to pass along an Introduction from you to his or her friend, who then passes it to his or her friend, who is the third-degree member.

The result is a large chain of connections and network members, with a core of trusted friends who help you reach out and tap your friends' networks and extended networks. Take the concept of Six Degrees of Separation (there is, on average, a chain of six people that can connect you to anyone else on Earth), put everyone's network online, and you have LinkedIn.

So, how powerful can these connections be? Figure 1-2 shows a snapshot of someone's network on LinkedIn.

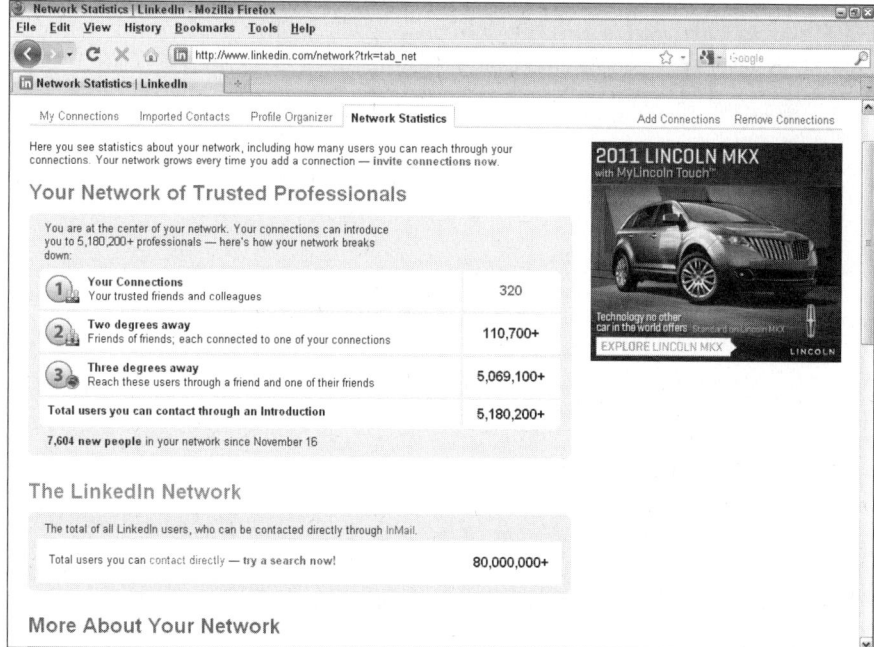

Figure 1-2:
Only three degrees of separation can give you a network of millions.

The difference between a user and a LION

Given all this power and potential to reach people around the world, some people — LinkedIn open networkers (LIONs) — want to network with anyone and everyone who's eager to connect with them. Their goal is to network with as many people as possible, regardless of past interaction or communication with that person.

One of your most prominently displayed LinkedIn statistics is the number of first-degree connections that you have. After you surpass 500 connections, LinkedIn doesn't display your current count of first-degree connections but just the message 500+. (It's kind of like how McDonald's stopped displaying the running total of hamburgers sold on its signs. Or am I the only one who remembers that?) Part of the reason LinkedIn stops displaying updated counts past 500 is to discourage people from collecting connections. Many LIONs have thousands or even tens of thousands of first-degree connections, and the 500+ statistic is a badge of honor to them.

LIONs encourage open networking (that is, the ability to connect with someone you have never met or worked with in the past) by advertising their e-mail address as part of their professional headline (for example, John Doe; Manager >firstname@lastname.com<), so anyone can request this person to be added to their network. You can find more information at sites such as www.mylink500.com. (Read more about this in Chapter 3.)

LinkedIn offers a formal program — OpenLink — for people interested in networking with the larger community. You can sign up for this premium service any time after you establish a premium account. When you enable the OpenLink feature, you can send and receive messages with any other OpenLink member. I discuss this in upcoming the section, "Understanding LinkedIn Costs and Benefits."

I've been asked many times whether it's okay to be a LION: if there is any meaning or benefit to having so many connections. My answer is that I don't endorse being a LION, *at all!* Although some people feel that they can find some quality hidden in the quantity, LinkedIn is designed to cultivate the real quality connections that people have. Not only does LinkedIn heavily discourage a user being a LION to the point of almost banning them, but also the random connections make it next to impossible to tap the real power and potential of LinkedIn.

The account in Figure 1-2 has 303 direct first-degree connections. When you add all the network connections that each of these 303 people have, the user could reach more than 103,800 different people on LinkedIn. Go one step further and add in the third-degree network members, the user of this account could have access to almost 4.9 million members, part of a vast professional network that stretches across the world into companies and industries of all sizes. Such a network can help you (and you can help them) advance your career or professional goals.

The Things You Can Do with LinkedIn

Time to find out what kinds of things you can do on LinkedIn. The following sections introduce you to the topics you need to know to get your foot in the LinkedIn door and really make the site start working for you.

Build your brand and profile

One of the best ways to think about what you can do on LinkedIn is to recognize that LinkedIn can help you build your own brand. Hmm. Are you going to create a fancy cursive logo of your name like Coca-Cola and slap it on everything you own? No. (But hey, that does sound like fun if you have absolutely nothing else to do.) What I mean by *brand* is that your name, your identity, is like a brand in terms of what people think of when they think of you. It's your professional reputation. Companies spend billions to ensure you have a certain opinion of their products, and that opinion, that perception, is their brand image. You have your own brand image in your professional life, and it's up to you to own, define, and push your brand.

Most people today have different online representations of their personal brand. Some people have their own Web sites, others create and write blogs, and others create profile pages on sites like Facebook. LinkedIn allows you to define a profile and build your own brand based on your professional and educational background; I use my profile as an example in Figure 1-3.

Your LinkedIn profile can become your jumping-off point where any visitor can get a rich and detailed idea of all the skills, experiences, and interests that you bring to the table. Unlike a resume, where you have to worry about page length and formatting, you can detail as much as you want on your LinkedIn profile, including any part-time, contract, nonprofit, and consulting work in addition to traditional professional experience. You also have other options to consider; for example, you can

- ✔ Write your own summary.
- ✔ List any groups you belong to.
- ✔ Show any memberships or affiliations you have.
- ✔ Cite honors and awards you have received.
- ✔ Give and receive Recommendations from other people. (I discuss Recommendations in greater depth in Chapter 8.)
- ✔ Indicate your professional interests.
- ✔ Upload presentations for others to view.
- ✔ Post Web site links to other parts of your professional identity, such as a blog, a Web site, or an e-commerce store you operate.

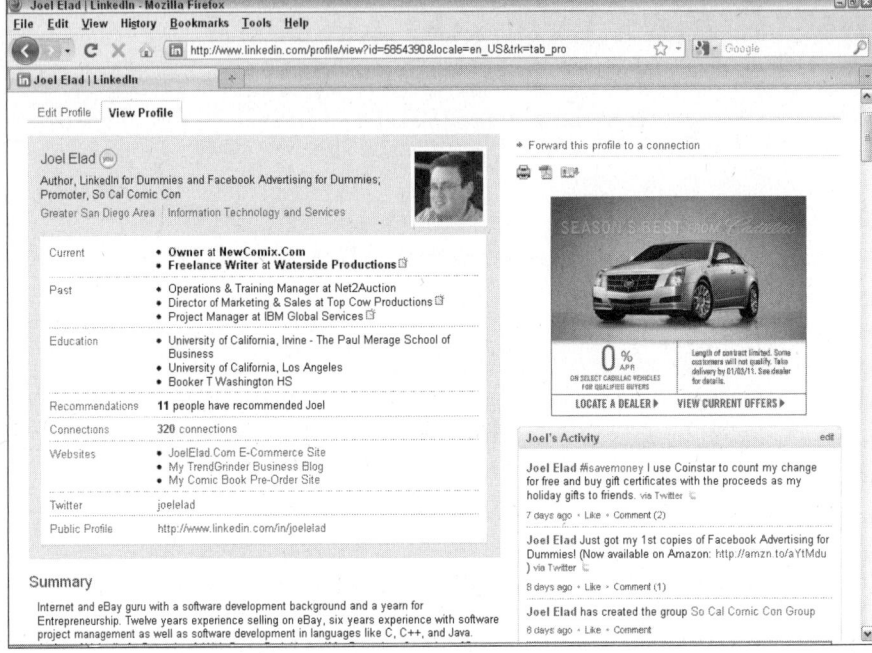

Figure 1-3:
Create a
unified pro-
file page to
showcase
your pro-
fessional
history.

The best part is that this is your professional identity, and *you* control and shape it, not other people. You decide what the content should be. You decide what you emphasize and omit. You can decide how much information is visible to the world and how much is visible to your first-degree network connections. (I talk more about the power of your profile in Chapter 3.)

Looking for jobs now and later

Face it: At some point in your life, you'll probably have to look for a job. It might be today, it might be a year from now, it might may be ten years from now. The job search is, in itself, a full-time job, and study after study shows that 60 to 80 percent of all jobs are found not through a job board like Monster.com or a newspaper classified ad, but rather by a formal or informal network of contacts where the job isn't even posted yet. LinkedIn makes it easier than before to do some of the following tedious job search tasks:

✔ **Finding the right person** at a target company, like a hiring manager in a certain department, to discuss immediate and future job openings

✔ **Getting a reference** from a past boss or co-worker to use for a future job application

✔ **Finding information** about a company and position before the interview

✔ **Searching posted job listings** on a job board like the one on LinkedIn

The hidden power of LinkedIn is that it helps you find jobs you weren't looking for or applying to directly. This is when you're a *passive job seeker,* currently employed but interested in the right opportunity. Currently, hundreds of thousands of recruiters are members of LinkedIn, constantly using the search functions to go through the database and find skilled members who match their job search requirements. Instead of companies paying big money for resume books, they now have instant access to tens of millions of qualified professionals, each of which has a detailed profile with skills, experience, and recommendations already available.

This practice of finding passive job seekers is growing quickly on LinkedIn, mainly because of the following reasons:

✔ **Companies can run detailed searches** to find the absolute perfect candidate with all the right keywords and skills in his or her profile, and they then contact the person to see whether she is interested.

✔ **LinkedIn users demonstrate their capabilities** by answering other people's questions on the site, which gives companies insight into the passive job seeker's capabilities. LinkedIn hosts an extensive network of discussion boards on its site called LinkedIn Answers, where LinkedIn users can pose a question in dozens of categories, and other LinkedIn members can provide short or detailed answers for that question. I cover this in greater depth in Chapter 7.

✔ **Companies can review a person's profile** to do reference checks ahead of time and interview only people they feel would be a great match with their corporate culture.

✔ **Currently employed individuals can quietly run their own searches** at any time to see what's available, and they can follow up online without taking off a day for an in-person or phone interview.

LinkedIn research shows that "People with more than 20 connections are 34 times more likely to be approached with a job opportunity than people with less than 5 connections." Therefore, your connections definitely influence your active or passive job search.

Finding out all kinds of valuable information

You can use LinkedIn to find out more than just information about your job search. You can use this immense database of professionals to find out what skills seem to be the most popular within a certain industry and job title. You can learn how many project managers live within 50 miles of you. You can really learn more by finding past employees of a company and interviewing them about their previous job. LinkedIn now has thousands of detailed Company Profiles that not only show company statistics but also recent hires, promotions, changes, and lists of employees closely connected with you.

Imagine if you could pick the brains of tens of millions of professionals around the world about almost any topic. Well, now you can, using a system called LinkedIn Answers. With LinkedIn Answers, you can post a question about a certain topic, mostly business- or LinkedIn-related. Other LinkedIn members can browse the questions by category and write free responses — from the one-line response to the three-page essay — to share their thoughts and answer your question the best they can. There's no think-tank to pay, no prequalifications or lag time in your data gathering. Typically, you start to see people responding within one to two business days. I talk more about LinkedIn Answers in Chapter 7.

Best of all, LinkedIn can help you find specific information on a variety of topics. You can do a search to find out the interests of your next sales prospect, the name of a former employee you can talk to about a company you like, or how you can join a start-up in your target industry by reaching out to the co-founder. You can sit back and skim the news, or you can dive in and hunt for the right facts. It all depends on what method best fits your goals. I discuss search in greater depth in Chapter 6.

Expand your network

You have your network today, but what about the future? Whether you want to move up in your industry, look for a new job, start your own company, or achieve some other goal, one way to achieve these goals is to expand your network. LinkedIn provides a fertile ground to reach like-minded and well-connected professionals who share a common interest, experience, or group membership. The site also provides several online mechanisms to reduce the friction of communication, so you can spend more time building your network instead of searching for the right person.

First and foremost, LinkedIn helps you identify and contact members of other people's professional networks, and best of all, you don't have to contact them via a cold call, but with your friend's Recommendation or Introduction. (See Chapters 8 and 5, respectively, for more information.) In addition, you can find out more about your new contact before you send the first message, so you don't have to waste time figuring out whether this is someone who could be beneficial to have in your network.

You can also meet new people through various groups on LinkedIn, whether it's an alumni group from your old school, a group of past employees from the same company, or a group of people interested in improving their public speaking skills and contacts. LinkedIn Groups are ways for you to identify with other like-minded members, search for specific group members, and share information about the Group with each other. I cover LinkedIn Groups in Chapter 14.

Understanding LinkedIn Costs and Benefits

Signing up for LinkedIn is free, and many of its functions are open to all account holders, so you can take advantage of most of the opportunities that LinkedIn can create. You don't have to pay a setup or registration fee, but you can pay a monthly fee for a premium account to get additional functions or communication options. Finally, tailored solutions are available for corporations that want to use LinkedIn as a source for hiring quality candidates.

Free versus paid accounts

There's not much difference between a free account and paid account on LinkedIn. And the basic account is anything but basic in usage.

Your free account with LinkedIn allows you to use most of LinkedIn's most popular features, including

- Building a network of connections with no limits on size or numbers
- Reconnecting with any member of the LinkedIn network, provided that he knows you and agrees to connect to you
- Creating a professional and detailed LinkedIn profile on the Web
- Giving and receiving an unlimited number of Recommendations
- Posting up to ten questions (and answering an unlimited amount of questions) on LinkedIn Answers
- Joining or creating up to 50 different LinkedIn Groups
- Requesting up to five Introductions at one time. (After someone accepts an Introduction, you can request a new Introduction in its place.)
- Performing an unlimited number of searches for LinkedIn members in your extended network

If you want to step up to a paid account, some of the main features include

✔ Sending a message to anyone in the LinkedIn community — regardless of whether she is in your extended network — through an InMail messaging service

✔ Sending more Introductions out at any one given time than the basic account allows

✔ Viewing more LinkedIn profile information of people not in your LinkedIn network when you do Advanced searching

✔ Seeing more LinkedIn network profile information when you do Advanced searching

✔ Seeing exactly who has viewed your profile and how they arrived at your profile

✔ Performing a Reference Search on someone (explained in Chapter 11)

✔ Membership in the OpenLink program and unlimited OpenLink messages. (See the sidebar elsewhere in this chapter, "The difference between a user and a LION.")

✔ Premium customer service channels with guaranteed response times

Comparing the paid accounts

LinkedIn offers a few levels of paid accounts, each with a specific level of benefits. For the most up-to-date packages that LinkedIn offers, check out the Compare Accounts Type page

```
www.linkedin.com/static?key=business_info_more
```

which should look like what you see Figure 1-4. You can also click the Account Type link at the top left of your screen, next to the LinkedIn logo, to see a comparison of the paid accounts.

Every premium account comes with certain benefits regardless of the level you choose. These benefits include

✔ Unlimited one-click reference searches

✔ OpenLink network membership

✔ Unlimited OpenLink messages

✔ Access to premium content

✔ One-business-day customer service for your LinkedIn questions

Compare Account Types

	Basic	Premium Business	Premium Business *Plus*	Premium Pro	Enterprise LinkedIn Talent Advantage
Cost per Month/Year	FREE	$24.95/month or $249.50/year *(Get 2 months FREE)* Upgrade	$49.95/month or $499.50/year *(Get 2 months FREE)* Upgrade	$499.95/month or $4,999.50/year *(Get 2 months FREE)* Upgrade	Recruiting Solutions Learn More
Receive Requests for Introductions (?)	Unlimited	Unlimited	Unlimited	Unlimited	Over 900 companies are already hiring hard-to-find passive candidates with LinkedIn Talent Advantage:
Send Requests for Introductions	5 at a time ¹	15 at a time ¹	25 at a time ¹	40 at a time ¹	• Widest Search Available
Send InMails™		3 per month	10 per month	50 per month	• Enhanced Messaging • Collaboration Tools
Receive InMails™ (?)	Unlimited	Unlimited	Unlimited	Unlimited	• Ultra-Precise Targeting
Profile Organizer (?)		5 folders	25 folders	25 folders	And much more »
Receive OpenLink Messages (?)		Unlimited	Unlimited	Unlimited	*'LinkedIn is one of the most valuable recruiting tools available in targeting high quality, passive*
Reach over 80 million					

Figure 1-4: Compare different paid account features on LinkedIn.

As of this writing, LinkedIn offers three premium packages targeted at individual users: Business, Business Plus, and Executive (formerly Pro) accounts. Each account level comes with a specific level of benefits:

✓ **Business:** $24.95 per month or $249.50 per year. This account includes

- Three InMails per month, with a seven-day response guarantee that states that if you don't receive a response to your InMail within seven days, you will receive that InMail credit back. (Unused InMail credits roll over each month, up to a maximum of 9 credits. I discuss InMail specifically in Chapter 5.)

- Expanded Profile views and a total of 300 search results outside your network when you search.

- Five folders to save LinkedIn user profile information and notes in your Profile Organizer.

✓ **Business Plus:** $49.95 per month, or two months free when you pay for 10 months. This account includes

- Ten InMails per month, with a seven-day response guarantee (Unused InMail credits roll over each month, up to a maximum of 30 credits. See Chapter 5 for more on InMail.)

• Expanded profile views and a total of 500 search results outside your network when you search.

• Twenty-five folders to save profiles and notes in your Profile Organizer.

✔ **Executive:** $99.95 per month, also reduced when purchased on an annual basis. This account includes

• Twenty-five InMails per month, with a seven-day response guarantee (Unused InMail credits roll over each month, up to a maximum of 30 credits. I discuss InMail in detail in Chapter 5.)

• Expanded profile views and a total of 700 search results outside your network when you search.

• Fifty folders to save profiles and notes in your Profile Organizer.

Upgrading to a premium account

To upgrade to a premium account, I highly recommend starting by creating your free account and using the various functions on LinkedIn. If you find that after some usage you need to reach the larger community and take advantage of some of the premium account features, you can always upgrade your account and keep all your profile and network information that you previously defined.

If you're in charge of human resource functions at a small, medium, or large company and you are interested in using the Talent Advantage functions for your company, don't follow the steps in this section. Instead, visit the following URL for more information:

```
http://talent.linkedin.com
```

To subscribe to a premium account, just follow these steps. *Note:* You must have created a LinkedIn account already (see Chapter 2).

1. **Go to the LinkedIn home page at www.linkedin.com. Roll your mouse over your name near the top-right corner of the home page, then click the Settings link.**

2. **At the Account & Settings page (see Figure 1-5), click the yellow Upgrade button from the Account section to bring up the premium account options, as shown in Figure 1-6.**

LinkedIn accepts Visa, MasterCard, American Express, or Discover to pay for your premium account. Make sure the billing address you provide matches the credit card billing address on file.

3. **Scroll down and select the check box to agree to automatic billing every month and LinkedIn's Terms and Conditions.**

4. **Click the Buy Now button to upgrade your account.**

   That's it! LinkedIn will prorate your first month's charge based on how many days are left in the billing cycle, and it will automatically charge your credit card each month afterwards for the full amount, unless you bought a yearly plan, for which the charges renew every 12 months.

5. **Click the Upgrade button for the premium level to which you want to upgrade.**

6. **Fill in the appropriate billing information, as shown in Figure 1-7.**

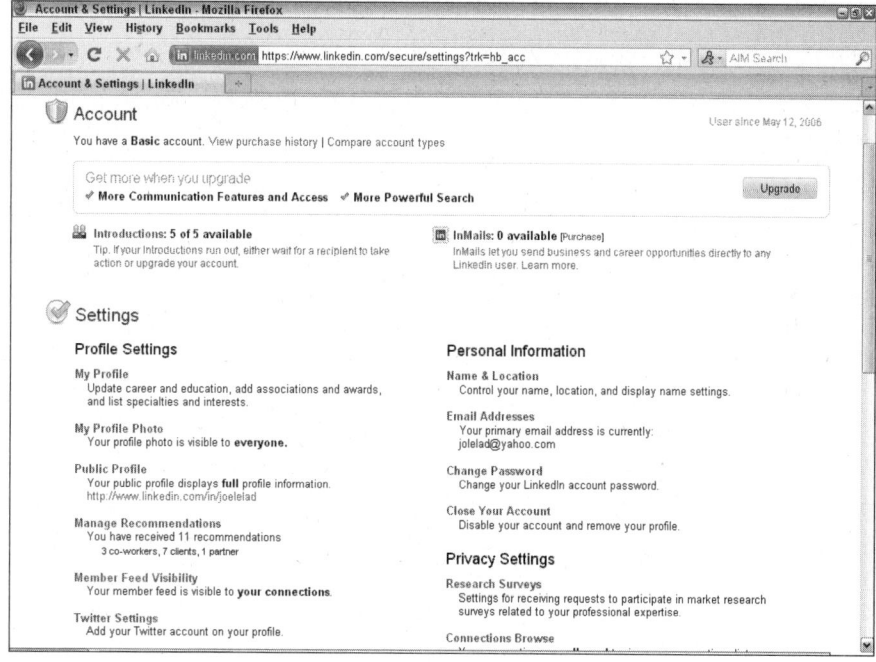

Figure 1-5:
Upgrade
your
account
from the
Account
& Settings
page.

Figure 1-6:
Choose the
premium
account
that's right
for you.

Figure 1-7:
Enter your
billing
information.

Navigating around LinkedIn

When you're ready to get started, you can sign up for an account by checking out Chapter 2. Before you do, however, take a look at the following sections, which walk you through the different parts of the LinkedIn Web site so you know how to find all the cool features I discuss in this book.

After you log on to your LinkedIn account, you see your personal LinkedIn home page, as shown in Figure 1-8. There are three important areas on your LinkedIn home page, which you'll use a lot, and I cover those areas in the following sections.

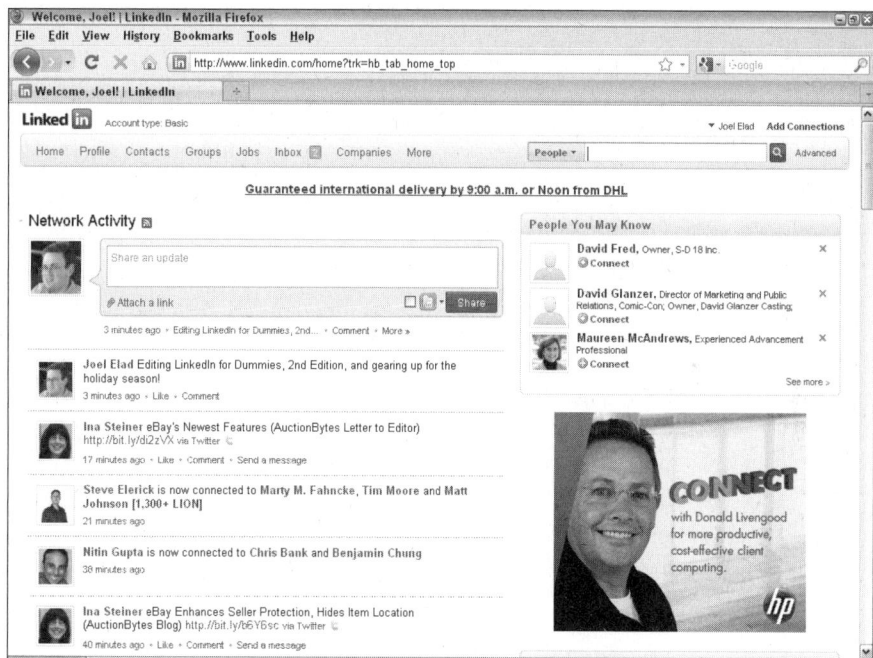

Figure 1-8:
Your
LinkedIn
home page.

The top navigation bar

Every page on LinkedIn contains certain links to the major parts of the site, and I call this top set of links the "top navigation bar" throughout this book. As of this writing, the major parts of the top navigation bar are

- ✔ **Home:** Link to your personal LinkedIn home page.

- ✔ **Profile:** Links to the profile and Recommendations part of LinkedIn

- ✔ **Contacts:** Links to view your connections on LinkedIn or add/import new connections

- ✔ **Groups:** Links to the different LinkedIn Groups you belong to or administer on LinkedIn

- ✔ **Jobs:** Links to the different job searches and postings you can do on LinkedIn

- ✔ **Inbox:** Links to read or manage your LinkedIn messages

- ✔ **Companies:** Links to search LinkedIn Company Pages or keep track of companies you can follow using LinkedIn

- ✔ **More:** Links to the rest of the LinkedIn functions, such as LinkedIn Answers and the Application Directory

When you roll your mouse next to any of these words, you can see the various options within each section, like the Profile options shown in Figure 1-9.

Figure 1-9:
Roll your mouse over each menu element to see options for each section.

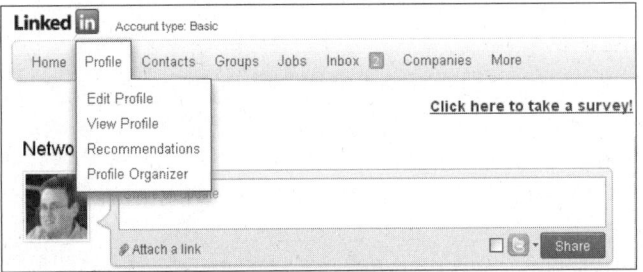

If you simply click the word, like Profile or Jobs, you're taken to the main page for that section. You can also click the Advanced link to the right of the top navigation bar and Search box to bring up an Advanced People Search, or you can click the drop-down list before the Search box to search for Jobs or Answers from any page on the site. If you already changed the search criteria to another function, like Jobs or Answers, clicking the Advanced link brings up the appropriate search page.

The Account & Settings page

If you ever need to update any aspect of your LinkedIn account, go to the Account & Settings page; see Figure 1-10. You can always find a link to this page at the top right of any page within LinkedIn by rolling your mouse over your name, and then clicking the Settings link.

At the Account & Settings page, you first see the settings for your particular account level, especially if you have a premium account. I cover this earlier in the chapter, in the section "Upgrading to a premium account."

- ✔ **Profile Settings:** Update any part of your profile, add a profile photo, change your status and public profile settings, and manage your Recommendations.

- ✔ **Personal Information:** Update personal information that LinkedIn has on file for you, including name, location, e-mail addresses, and pass-words. This section also contains the link for closing your LinkedIn account permanently.

- ✔ **Email Notifications:** Set how you receive various communications from other LinkedIn members, such as Introductions, InMail, Invitations to Connect, and OpenLink messages, if applicable.

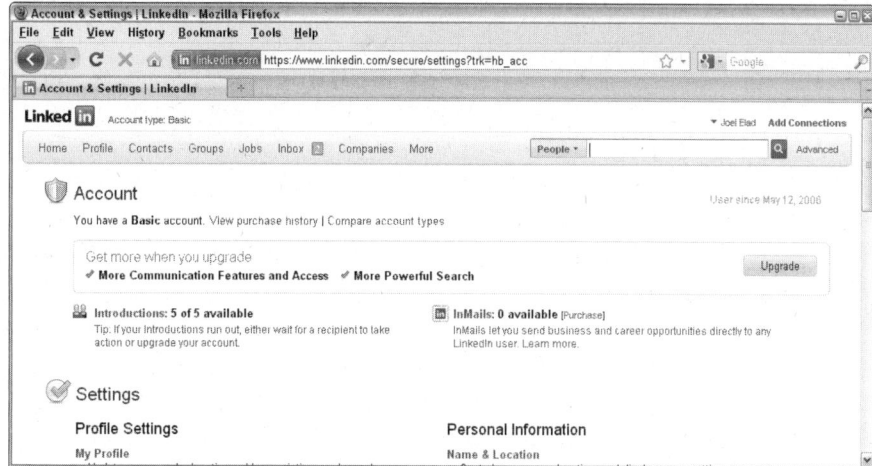

Figure 1-10:
See the
details
of your
LinkedIn
account.

Scroll down to see all the different settings you can update for your LinkedIn account, as shown in Figure 1-11.

The categories you can access from this page are

- ✔ **Privacy Settings:** Set how much of your profile is accessible by your contacts, and also how much information you want to make available to your network in terms of profile or status updates.

- ✔ **Home Page Settings:** Set how Network Updates and News articles are displayed on your LinkedIn home page.

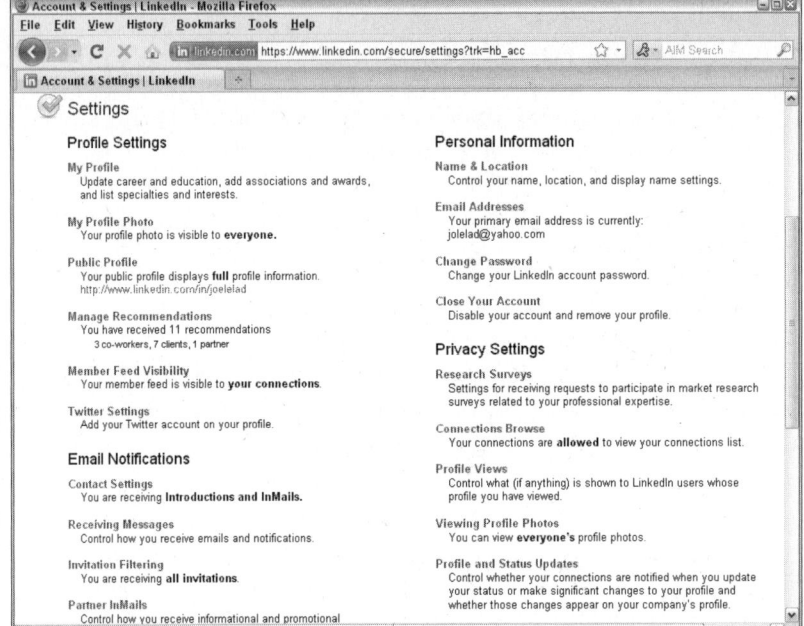

Figure 1-11: Update your account settings for LinkedIn here.

Settings

Profile Settings

My Profile
 Update career and education, add associations and awards, and list specialties and interests.

My Profile Photo
 Your profile photo is visible to **everyone**.

Public Profile
 Your public profile displays **full** profile information.
 http://www.linkedin.com/in/joelelad

Manage Recommendations
 You have received 11 recommendations
 3 co-workers, 7 clients, 1 partner

Member Feed Visibility
 Your member feed is visible to **your connections**.

Twitter Settings
 Add your Twitter account on your profile.

Email Notifications

Contact Settings
 You are receiving **Introductions and InMails.**

Receiving Messages
 Control how you receive emails and notifications.

Invitation Filtering
 You are receiving **all invitations**.

Partner InMails
 Control how you receive informational and promotional

Personal Information

Name & Location
 Control your name, location, and display name settings.

Email Addresses
 Your primary email address is currently:
 jolelad@yahoo.com

Change Password
 Change your LinkedIn account password.

Close Your Account
 Disable your account and remove your profile.

Privacy Settings

Research Surveys
 Settings for receiving requests to participate in market research surveys related to your professional expertise.

Connections Browse
 Your connections are **allowed** to view your connections list.

Profile Views
 Control what (if anything) is shown to LinkedIn users whose profile you have viewed.

Viewing Profile Photos
 You can view **everyone's** profile photos.

Profile and Status Updates
 Control whether your connections are notified when you update your status or make significant changes to your profile and whether those changes appear on your company's profile.

✔ **RSS Settings:** Enable RSS feeds, which is a collection of any updates you make to your profile that you can subscribe to and read without visiting LinkedIn.

✔ **Groups:** Update settings for your memberships with different LinkedIn Groups. You won't see this category until you join at least one group.

✔ **My Network:** Update settings that tell LinkedIn how you plan to use the site. LinkedIn uses this information to customize the messages you see when using the site to help fit with your stated goals.

Chapter 2

Sign Me Up!

. . . .

. . . .

*W*hen LinkedIn first launched, it grew primarily through invitations —
you joined only if someone who was already a member invited you
and encouraged you to join. However, membership is now open to anyone
18 years or older (as long as the user hasn't previously been suspended or
removed from LinkedIn, of course). You can have only one active account,
but you can attach multiple e-mail addresses, past and present, to your
account so that people can more easily find you.

You'll be presented with some configuration settings during the signup process that you might not know what to do with until you get more familiar
with the system. Fortunately, you can customize all those settings later, but
for now, I suggest some initial settings. In addition, based on your initial settings, LinkedIn will recommend people to invite to your network. In Chapter
6, I discuss the ways you can grow your network more extensively, but this
chapter touches on this initial Recommendation process.

Joining LinkedIn

Many people join LinkedIn because a friend or colleague invited them. You
can join just as easily without receiving an invitation, though. Everyone joins
at the basic level, which is free. (You can opt for different levels of paid membership, as spelled out in Chapter 1.) Being able to start at the basic level
makes the signup process quite straightforward.

Joining with an invitation

When a friend or colleague invites you to join, you receive an e-mail invitation. The e-mail clearly identifies the sender and usually has `Invitation to connect on LinkedIn` as its subject line. (There's a chance, though, that the sender came up with a custom header, but hopefully that message will have the word LinkedIn in the subject line.)

When you open the message, you see an invitation to join LinkedIn, like the message in Figure 2-1. There might be some extra text if the person inviting you personalized the message. You'll also see a button or link that takes you back to LinkedIn to create your account, such as the Confirm That You Know Joel button shown in Figure 2-1.

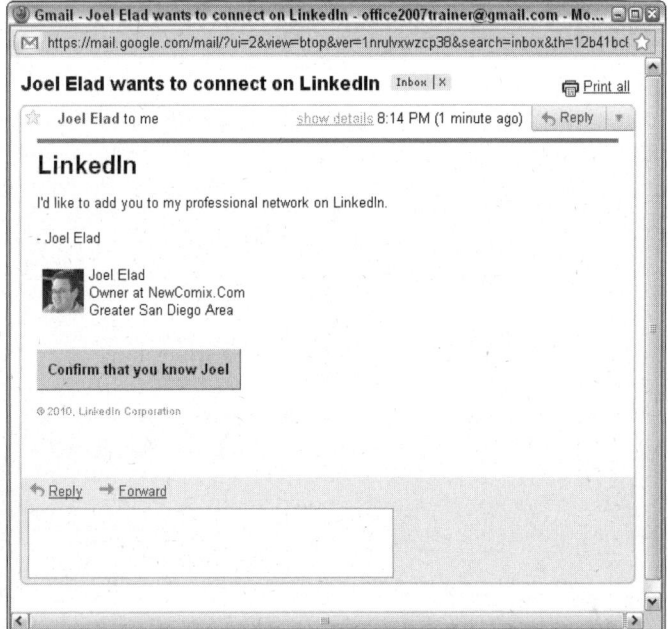

Figure 2-1: An invitation to connect on LinkedIn.

When you're ready to join LinkedIn with an invitation, just follow these steps:

1. **Click the button or link from your invitation e-mail.**

   You should see a new window open that goes to the LinkedIn Web site and asks to verify your name and e-mail address, as well as enter a password for your new LinkedIn account, as shown in Figure 2-2.

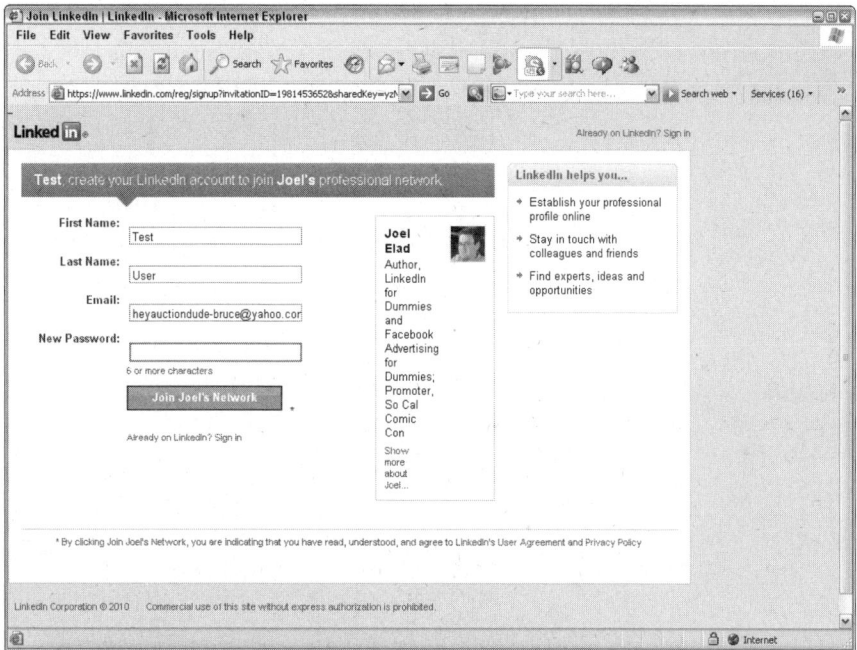

Figure 2-2:
Confirm
your name
and create a
password.

TIP

If you want to be known on LinkedIn by another version of your name (say a nickname, maiden name, or proper name), or if you want to use a different e-mail address from the one used for your invitation, you can change the details now in those fields — First Name, Last Name, Email.

2. **Enter your correct first name and last name, and create a new password for your account. Then click the Join *Name's* Network button.**

   You'll be taken to the Create a LinkedIn Profile Like (the name of your inviter), as shown in Figure 2-3. At this point, LinkedIn wants to collect some basic information it will use when it creates your account.

3. **Complete the fields presented on the Create a LinkedIn Profile page to tell LinkedIn your current employment status, company name, job title, industry, country, and ZIP code.**

   In the first drop-down box, you can choose between these five options to identify your current employment status:

   - Employed
   - A business owner
   - Looking for work
   - Working independently (like a consultant)
   - A student

Figure 2-3:
Start to give
LinkedIn
some basic
information
about
yourself.

In the next box, enter the name of the Company where you are currently employed, and then your Job Title in the third field provided. Depending on your employment status, LinkedIn may reload the page with a new field, Industry, whose drop-down list you can then use to identify which industry you feel you belong to, as shown in Figure 2-4 below.

Confirm your country of residence by selecting your country from the drop-down list provided, and then enter your ZIP or postal code in the box provided.

4. **Click Continue to proceed.**

   LinkedIn offers to import your contacts from your e-mail program, as shown in Figure 2-5. If you see your e-mail system among the choices, select the radio button next to that system and then click the Login button. LinkedIn will walk you through the steps of importing your address book, offering you the chance to connect to existing members of LinkedIn. At this point, you can also just click the Skip This Step link and then come back and take care of this after you create your account.

   It might be tempting to start inviting friends and colleagues to connect with you right away, but you might want to work on your profile or think of a strategy first before flooding people's e-mail inboxes with Invitations. You can always invite people to connect with you at any time.

5. **Decide who you want to connect with using your new LinkedIn account.**

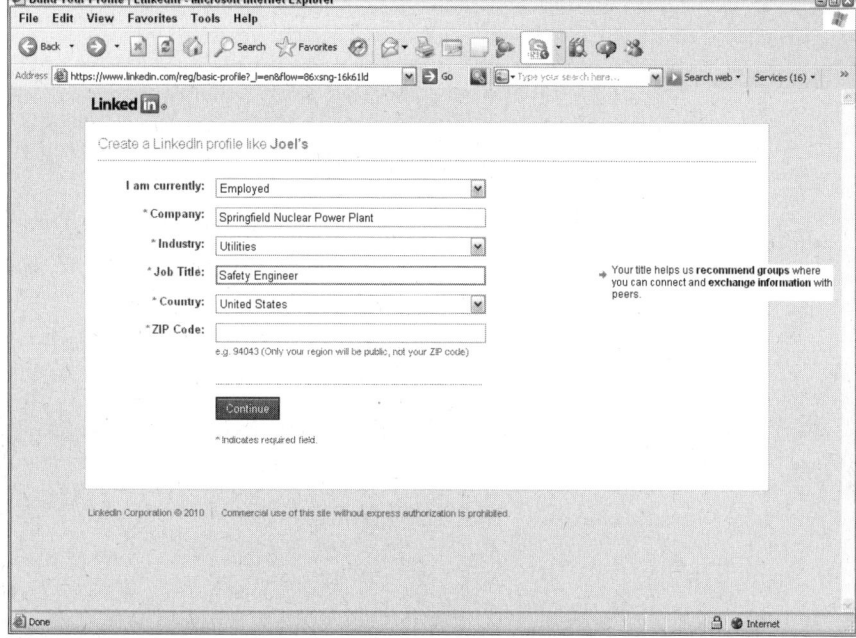

Figure 2-4:
Pick the
industry
that best
matches
what
your job
belongs to.

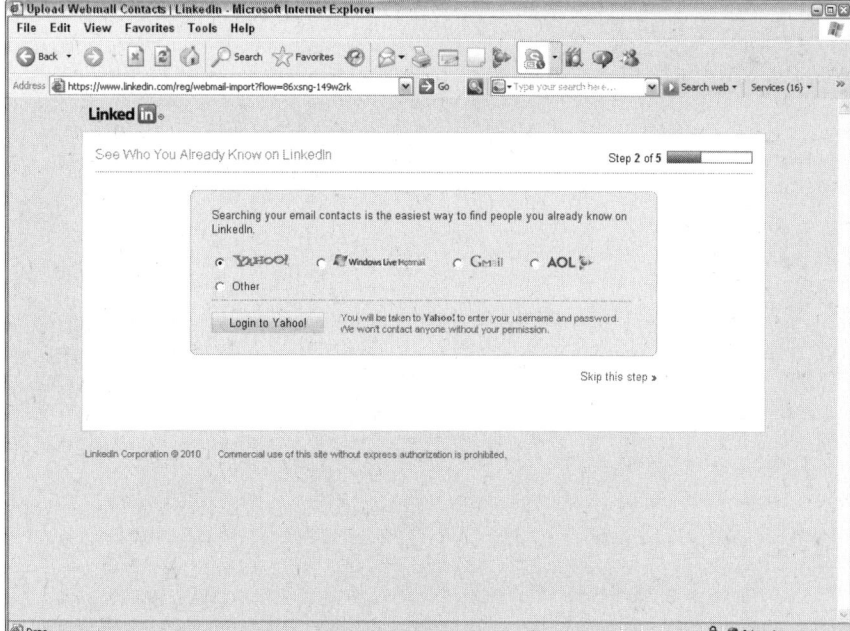

Figure 2-5:
LinkedIn
can help
you identify
who to add
to your
network.

After you import your e-mail contacts or skip that step, you get to the final step of the invitation process, where LinkedIn confirms your connection to the person who invited you, and asks you whether you want to invite anybody else, by entering their e-mail addresses into the Connections box, as shown in Figure 2-6. You can enter addresses now or you can click Skip This Step and invite people later. (I discuss this process also in Chapter 6.)

6. **Click either the Send Connections button or the Skip This Step link.**

At this point, LinkedIn has created your account and will take you to your home page, as shown in Figure 2-7.

In the meantime, if you want to take a break to check your e-mail, you'll find a nice Welcome to LinkedIn! message there from LinkedIn Updates, assuring you that you're now a registered LinkedIn user. The e-mail (as shown in Figure 2-8) has some useful links to explore later, including a tour of LinkedIn and how it works. The e-mail also offers some ways to find contacts, and I will discuss these methods in the section "Starting to Build Your Network" later in this chapter.

Figure 2-6:
You have got your first connection; LinkedIn offers you a chance for more.

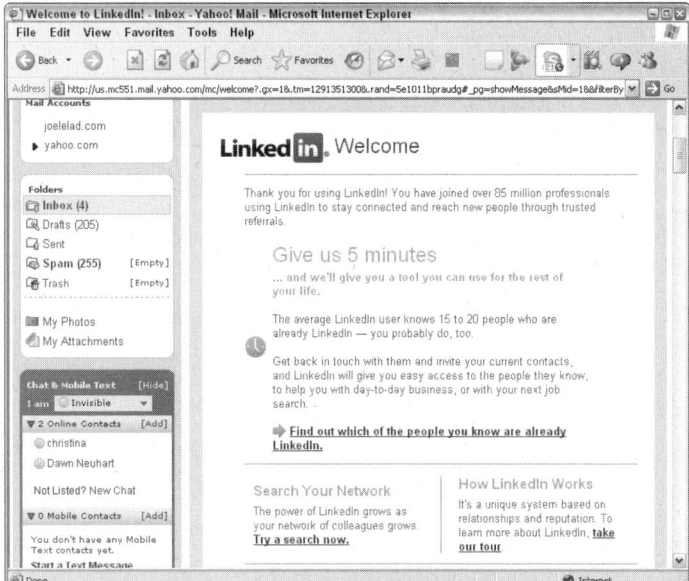

Joining without an invitation

If you haven't gotten an invitation, don't let that turn you into a wallflower. You can join LinkedIn directly, without an invitation from an existing user.

Open your Web browser and make your way to www.linkedin.com. You see the initial LinkedIn home page, as shown in Figure 2-9. Click the What Is LinkedIn? link, in the top-left corner, to read more information about LinkedIn. Otherwise, when you're ready to join LinkedIn, just follow these steps:

1. **In the Join LinkedIn Today section in the top-right corner, provide your first name, last name, e-mail address, and a password in the boxes provided, as shown in Figure 2-9.**

2. **Click the Join Now button to continue.**

   You're taken to the next step, where LinkedIn starts to build your professional profile by asking about your current employment status and location, as shown in Figure 2-10.

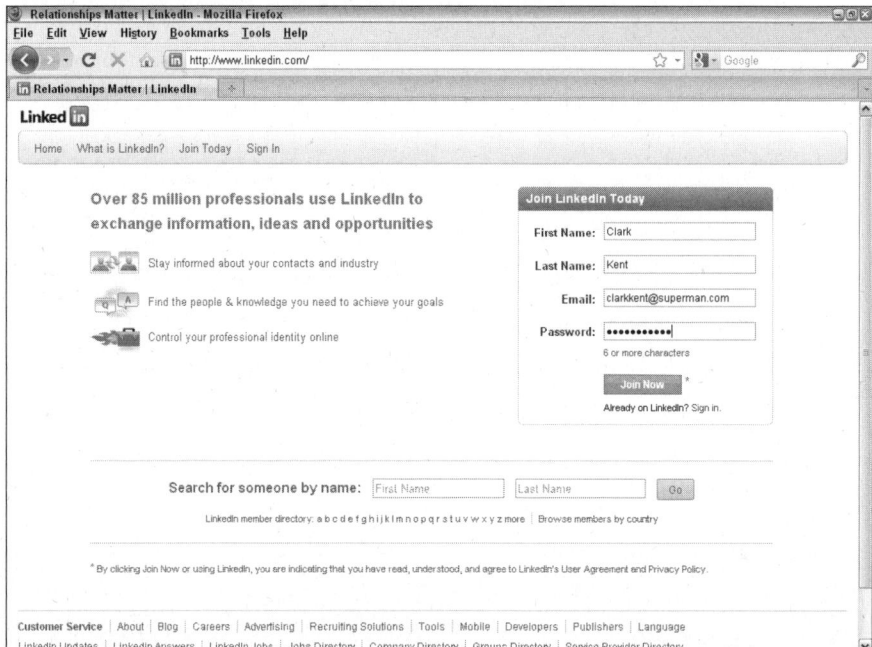

Figure 2-9:
Join
LinkedIn
from its
home page.

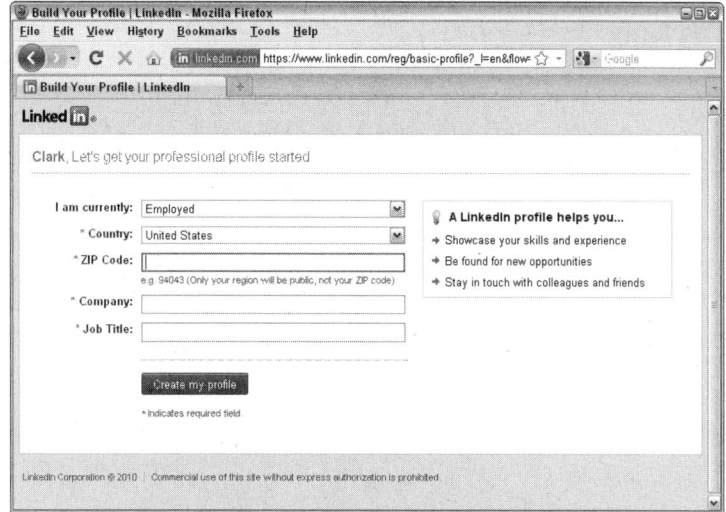

Figure 2-10:
Tell LinkedIn
a little about
yourself to
create your
account.

3. **Complete the fields regarding your current employment status and location from the drop-down or text boxes provided.**

   Specifically, you need to provide the following information:

   - **I am currently:** Indicate whether you're employed, a business owner, looking for work, working independently (like a consultant), or a student.

   - **Country and postal code:** LinkedIn won't display your ZIP code, but it does use it to assign a Region to your profile so others know the general area where you reside.

   - **Details about your status:** Depending on your status, LinkedIn will ask for a Company, Job Title, and Industry if you are employed, or ask for Industry focus if you're looking for work, as shown in Figure 2-11.

   If you find it difficult to choose an industry that best describes your primary expertise, just choose one that's closest. You can always change the selection later. If you're employed but looking for another job, you should still pick the industry of your current profession.

4. **Click the blue Create My Profile button to continue.**

   LinkedIn will then offer to import your contacts from your e-mail program, as shown in Figure 2-12. If you see your e-mail system among the choices, you can pick the radio button next to that system and then click the Login button. LinkedIn will walk you through the steps of importing your address book and offering you the chance to connect to existing members of LinkedIn. You can also do this after account creation by clicking the Skip This Step link.

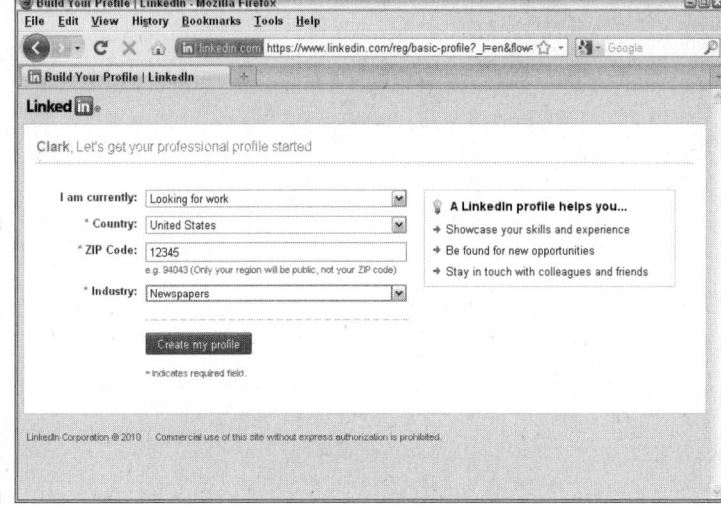

Figure 2-11:
Depending on your work status, LinkedIn asks different questions.

Figure 2-12:
LinkedIn can help you identify who to add to your network.

5. **LinkedIn will ask you to confirm the e-mail address for your account.**

Depending on the e-mail account you used to register the account, LinkedIn may be able to log directly into that e-mail account and confirm your e-mail address. (For example, I can click the Confirm My Yahoo! Account button illustrated in Figure 2-13 to confirm this sample account I'm creating.) Otherwise, LinkedIn will e-mail you a confirmation e-mail, which you can choose to receive instead of using LinkedIn to log directly into your e-mail account.

If you choose (or have) to receive a confirmation e-mail, open your e-mail program and look for an e-mail from LinkedIn Email Confirmation with the subject line Please confirm your e-mail address. When you open that e-mail, you should see a request for confirmation, as shown in Figure 2-14. Either click the Click Here (to Confirm Your Email Address) link or copy and paste the URL provided in the e-mail into your Web browser.

When you click the link, you're taken back to LinkedIn and asked to confirm your address, as shown in Figure 2-15. Click the Confirm button to confirm the e-mail address for your account. You'll then be asked to log in to your account, so simply provide your e-mail address and password when prompted.

If you skip this step of confirming your e-mail with LinkedIn, you won't be able to invite any connections, use functions like LinkedIn Answers, apply for jobs on the LinkedIn job board, or take advantage of most other LinkedIn functions.

Figure 2-13:
LinkedIn may be able to confirm your e-mail address directly with your e-mail provider.

Figure 2-14:
Confirm your e-mail address with LinkedIn.

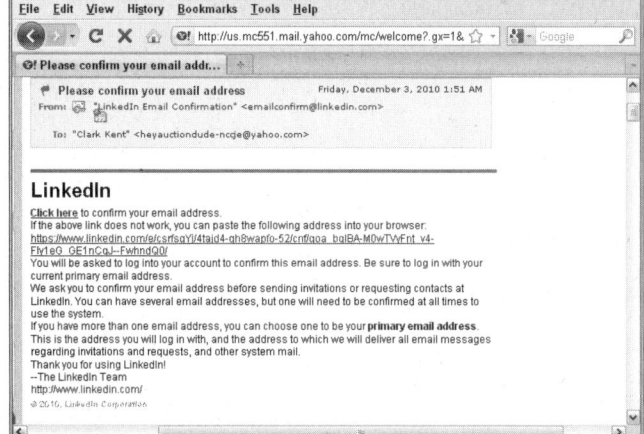

6. Your account is created, and you are now free to start building your network and updating your profile!

You'll be taken to your home page, as shown in Figure 2-16, with a confirmation message that your e-mail address is confirmed.

In the meantime, if you want to take a break to check your e-mail, you'll find a nice Welcome to LinkedIn! message there from LinkedIn Updates, assuring you that you're now a registered LinkedIn user. The e-mail has some useful links to explore later, including a tour of LinkedIn and how it works. The e-mail also offers some ways to find contacts, and I will detail some of these steps in the next section, "Starting to Build Your Network."

Figure 2-15:
Click the
Confirm
button to
confirm
your e-mail
address
with
LinkedIn.

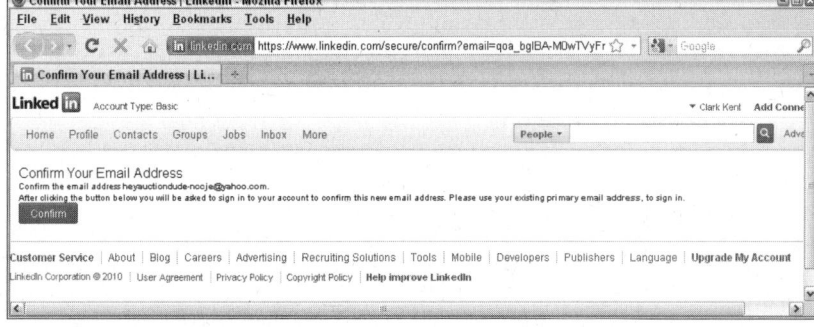

Figure 2-16:
Welcome to
LinkedIn!

Starting to Build Your Network

You're ready to look at how to build your network, with tools and forms provided by LinkedIn. Your first step is to decide who you want to invite to connect with you on LinkedIn.

Your profile is so important it gets its own chapter (Chapter 3 if you really must know). Be sure to completely fill out your profile before you start inviting people to connect. Having a complete profile makes it easier to find former colleagues and classmates. After all, if you invite someone whom you haven't spoken to recently, he will take a quick look at your profile before responding. If he doesn't see a part of your professional history where he knows you, he will most likely ignore your invitation.

Your best bet now is to start using LinkedIn with some thought and planning, which is where I come in (along with this book, of course) with some advice. Here are some common pitfalls after signing up:

✔ You feel compelled to start inviting friends and colleagues to connect with you right away, before working on your profile or thinking of a strategy.

✔ You get nervous and decide not to invite anybody beyond one or two close friends or family members.

✔ You wonder about the value of LinkedIn and leave your account alone for a long period of time with no activity.

I will admit, I have seen all three situations occur with various people who have joined LinkedIn, so don't feel bad if one of these is your natural reaction.

When you want to start using LinkedIn, start by navigating to the home page and clicking Sign In. You will be asked for your e-mail address and LinkedIn password, which you provided when you joined the site. Once you are logged in, you can access any of the functions from the top navigation bar.

In order to build your profile, roll your mouse over the Profile link in the top navigation bar and then click Edit Profile. You will see your Edit Profile page, as shown in Figure 2-17. Simply click the links marked Add and follow the instructions to fill out your profile. I will discuss this in greater detail in Chapter 3.

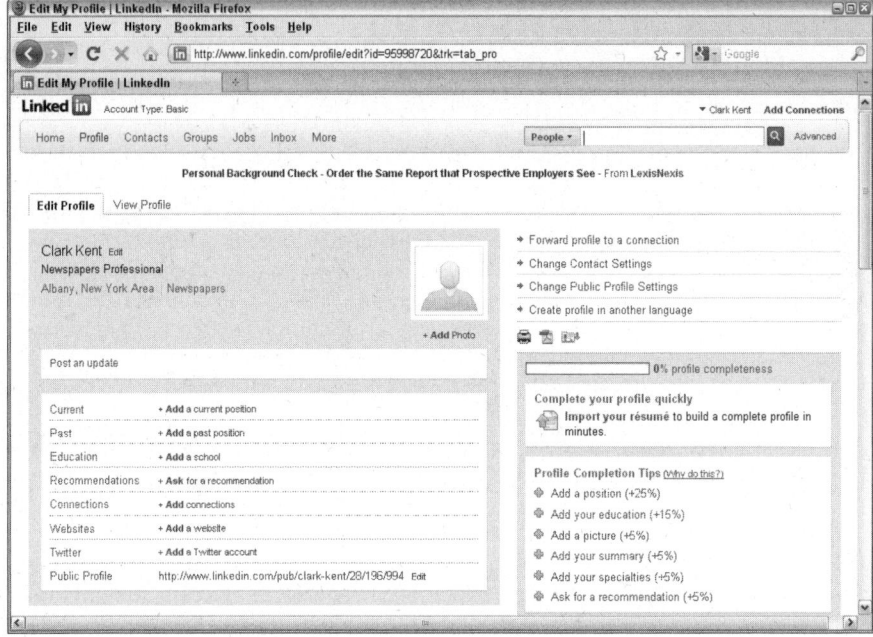

Figure 2-17:
Start build-
ing your
profile on
LinkedIn.

Next, start thinking about who you'd like to invite to your network. LinkedIn provides some neat tools to help you identify, in your existing networks, people you know and trust well enough to feel confident about inviting them and expecting that they will accept.

The multi-faceted Add Connections section of LinkedIn, as shown in Figure 2-18, is always available from the Add Connections link at the top right of any LinkedIn page, and it is worth studying for a moment. The Add Connections section, with four distinct tabs (Add Connections, Colleagues, Classmates, and People You May Know) incorporates some basic options to identify and grow your network, which we cover in more depth in Chapter 6:

✔ Check the address book for your Web-based e-mail system, like Yahoo!, Gmail, and AOL.

✔ Check your address book for contacts to invite with options for systems like Microsoft Outlook and Apple's Mail app by importing your desktop e-mail contacts with the link provided.

✔ Reconnect with past colleagues by clicking the Colleagues tab.

✔ Find former classmates by clicking the Classmates tab.

I cover these techniques in greater detail in Chapter 6, and I definitely recommend that you first spend a little time thinking about who you want to invite. Then focus on getting your profile set up, and then invite people.

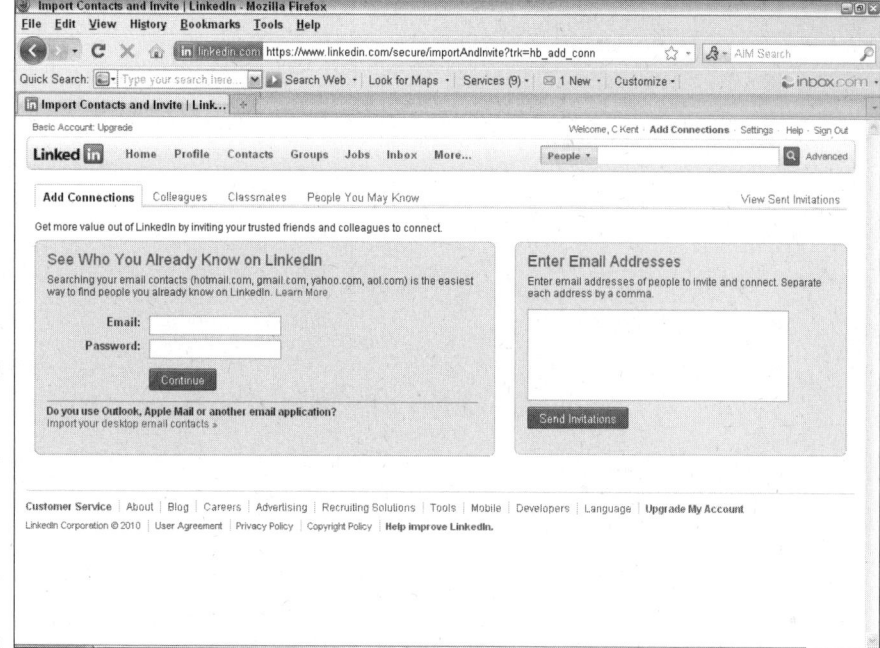

Figure 2-18:
Use this handy section to add connections to your network.

Privacy confidential

When you provide LinkedIn with access to your existing contact lists (such as on Gmail or Yahoo! mail), rest assured that LinkedIn respects your privacy.

LinkedIn is a licensee of the TRUSTe Privacy Program. In its Privacy Policy, LinkedIn declares its adherence to the following key privacy principles:

✔ LinkedIn will never rent or sell your personally identifiable information to third parties for marketing purposes.

✔ LinkedIn will never share your contact information with another user, without your consent.

✔ Any sensitive information that you provide will be secured with all industry standard protocols and technology.

Chapter 3

Building Your Profile

After you register with LinkedIn and work to build your network by looking outward, it's time to look inward by focusing on your profile. Think of your LinkedIn profile as your personal home page to the business world: This profile exists to give anyone a complete picture of your background, qualifications, and skills as well as paint a picture of who you are beyond the numbers and bullet points.

In this chapter, I walk you through all the different sections of your profile and explain how to update them and put the right information in a concise and appealing manner. I take you through adding information at each stage so you can update your profile now or down the road (say, when you finish that amazing project or get that spiffy promotion you've been working toward).

At any time, you can go to www.linkedin.com and click the Profile link in the top navigation bar to access your LinkedIn profile to view or make changes.

Determining the Contact Settings for Your Profile

Before you dive right in and start updating your profile, stop and think about what kind of profile you want to construct and show to the world. Specifically, think about how you want to use LinkedIn. For example, some people just want to add to their network, but others are actively looking for a job. You can have many reasons for using LinkedIn, and you can identify yourself through setting up your contact settings on LinkedIn. The settings you choose mainly depend on what you plan to use LinkedIn for. You can always go back and update your contact settings as your situation changes.

You can select from eight main contact settings in your LinkedIn profile. Each describes a type of opportunity that lets other people how to approach you on the site:

- **Career opportunities:** You're looking to augment your skill set so you can advance your career, or you want to network with people who could approach you with a career opportunity now or in the future.

- **Expertise requests:** You're available to provide expertise on your main subject areas to someone with a question or opportunity.

- **Consulting offers:** You're open to receiving offers for consulting work.

- **Business deals:** You're open to doing a business deal, either for your main job or your entrepreneurial venture. Deals here could range from supplier/vendor requests, launching a new line of products, or doing a joint venture.

- **New ventures:** You're interested in participating in a new company as an employee, a co-owner, a financier, or anything else.

- **Personal reference requests:** You're open to providing references for your first-degree connections. (Read what defines a first-degree connection in Chapter 1.)

- **Job inquiries:** You're open to receiving job offers or interests.

- **Requests to reconnect:** You're interested in old friends, colleagues, and classmates and wouldn't mind if such folks sent a request to connect with you on LinkedIn.

After you select your settings, they show up as a bulleted list on your profile. In addition, they help determine (and potentially block) the type of communication that you receive on LinkedIn. For example, if you aren't interested in job inquiries, you shouldn't receive any direct solicitations to apply for a job.

Adding Your Summary and Basic Information to LinkedIn

Your LinkedIn profile Summary section, which appears in the top third of your profile, should give any reader a quick idea of who you are, what you've accomplished, and most importantly, what you're looking for on LinkedIn. Some people think of their summary as their "elevator pitch," or their 30-second introduction of themselves that they tell to any new contact. Other people think of their summary as simply their resume summary, which gives a high-level overview of their experience and job goals. Each summary is as individual as the person writing it, but there are right ways and wrong ways to prepare and update your summary.

The $5,000 profile update

I have a great example of why you should update your profile. Jefre Outlaw's LinkedIn profile says that he's a "portfolio entrepreneur." His profile doesn't mention, however, that he spent more than 20 years as a real estate investor and developer, nor that he recently obtained his own real estate license and joined his cousin Blake's agency, Outlaw Real Estate Group. He realized a golden opportunity was available to him through LinkedIn.

Outlaw was interviewed for the LinkedIntelligence blog (www.linkedintelligence.com/the-5000-profile-update). "At first I completely forgot about updating my LinkedIn profile," he said. "But I got a request to forward an introduction, and it reminded me that I should probably go update my profile to include my new gig as a realtor."

This turned out to be a valuable update for Outlaw.

Several weeks later, someone from his extended network was using LinkedIn to search for realtors and saw Outlaw's profile.

This person contacted Outlaw about listing a home for sale. Well, the potential client signed up with Outlaw's agency, which was able to sell the house quickly for $170,000. When you do the math, $170,000 home × 3% commission = about $5,000 to the brokerage.

As Outlaw relayed his experience to LinkedIntelligence, he wanted his story to be clear. "Let's not overstate what happened," said Outlaw. "Being on LinkedIn didn't get me the business. We [Outlaw's real estate agency] were one of several realtors the client talked to, and I brought in my cousin, who's a great closer and more experienced than I, to meet with the client. But the fact that I was in [LinkedIn], that my profile was up-to-date, that I have over 20 really good Recommendations on my profile — all that put us on the short list."

The moral of the story is simple. Keep your profile up to date on everything you're doing. If your profile isn't up to date, plan to update it right away — you may never know what opportunities you're missing by ignoring your profile.

LinkedIn divides the Summary section into two distinct parts:

- **Your professional experience and goals:** This is typically a one-paragraph summary of your current and past accomplishments and future goals. See the next section for more on how to construct the right paragraph for this part.

- **Your specialties in your industry of expertise:** This is a list of your specific skills and talents. This is separate from your professional experience in that this section allows you to list specific job skills (for example, contract negotiation or writing HTML software code) as opposed to the daily responsibilities or accomplishments from your job that you would list in the professional experience and goals paragraph.

Other core elements of your LinkedIn profile are stored in the Basic Information section. Be sure to polish these elements so they reflect well on you:

- **Your name:** Believe it or not, defining your name properly can positively or negatively affect your LinkedIn activity. Because people will be searching for you in order to connect to you, it's important that LinkedIn knows any sort of variations, nicknames, maiden names, or former names that you may have held, so be sure you correctly fill in your First, Last, and Former/Maiden name fields. Also, LinkedIn allows you to choose a display name of your first name and last initial, in case you want to keep your name private from the larger LinkedIn community outside of your connections.

- **Your professional headline:** Think of this as your job title. This is displayed underneath your name on LinkedIn, in search results, in connections lists, and on your profile. Therefore, you want a headline that grabs people's attention. Some people put their job titles; other people add some colorful adjectives and include two or three different professions. For example, I use "Dummies Book Author; Owner, NewComix. Com," indicating two of my main professions. Your headline changes only when you update the headline field, so if you add a new position to your profile, your headline doesn't update to show that addition. You have to decide what changes are worth being reflected in your headline.

- **Your primary location and industry of experience:** As location becomes a more important element when networking online, LinkedIn wants to know your main location (in other words, where you hang your hat . . . if you wear a hat) so it can help identify connections close to you. Then, LinkedIn provides a list of industries you can choose from to indicate your main industry affiliation.

Writing your summary first

Before you plan to update your summary on LinkedIn, I advise writing it out, using a program like Microsoft Word so that you can easily copy and paste it. This allows you to organize your thoughts, decide the right order of your statements, and pick and choose the most important statements to put in your summary.

Of course, the goals of your summary should be the same as your goals for using LinkedIn. After all, your summary is the starting point for most people when they read your profile. As you write your summary, keep these points in mind:

- ✔ **Be concise.** Remember, this is a summary, not a 300-page memoir of your life. Most summaries are one paragraph long, with a separate paragraph to list your skills and/or specialties. Give the highlights of what you've done and are planning to do. Save the detailed information for when you add your individual employment positions to your profile.

- ✔ **Pick three to five of your most important accomplishments.** Your profile can have lots of detail regarding your jobs, skill sets, education, and honors, but your summary needs to reflect the three to five items throughout your career that you most want people to know. Think of it this way: If someone were introducing you to another person, what would you want this new person to know about you right away?

    Depending on your goals for LinkedIn, the accomplishments you put in your summary might not be your biggest accomplishments overall. For example, if you're trying to use LinkedIn to get a new job, your summary should include accomplishments that matter most to an employer in your desired field.

- ✔ **Organize your summary in a Who, What, Goals format.** Typically, the first sentence of your summary should be a statement of *Who* you are currently, meaning your current profession or status: for example, "Software project manager with extensive experience in Fortune 500 firms." The next few sentences should focus on *What* you've done so far in your career, and the end of your summary should focus on your *Goals.*

- ✔ **Use the right keywords in your summary.** Keywords are especially important if you're looking for a new job or hoping to pick up some consulting work. Although you should use a few keywords in your professional experience paragraph, you should really use all the appropriate keywords for skills you've acquired when you write the Specialties section of your summary. Potential employers will scan that section looking for the right qualifications first, before making any contact.

✔ **Be honest with your specialties, but don't be shy.** Your Specialties section is your opportunity to list any skill or trade that you feel you've learned and demonstrated with some ability. Some people stuff their Summary section with the buzz-worthy skills for their industry (even if the person doesn't know those skills at all) in hopes of catching a potential employer's eye. Typically, a prospective employer will detect this resume skill padding during the interview phase, which wastes everybody's time. Conversely, however, some people don't list a skill here unless they feel they're an expert at it. You should list any skill or specialty where you believe you are above the level of a novice or pure beginner.

If you need help coming up with your various summary sections, click the See Examples link below each section header to see LinkedIn-provided examples, or you can view profiles of other people in similar industries.

Updating your LinkedIn profile's Summary and Basic Information sections

When you have an idea of what you want to put in your profile's Summary and Basic Information sections, it's time to go into LinkedIn and plug that data into the correct fields. When you're ready, follow these steps:

1. **Go to LinkedIn and log in:**

   `www.linkedin.com/secure/login?trk=hb_signin`

2. **Click the Profile link in the top navigation bar.**

   You're taken to the Profile page, as shown in Figure 3-1.

3. **Scroll down to the Summary section and click the Add Summary link below the Summary section header.**

   You see the Professional Summary page, as shown in Figure 3-2.

4. **In the Professional Experience & Goals text box, enter a paragraph or two that sums you up professionally (as discussed in the previous section).**

   You're limited to 2,000 characters, but keep your text concise and focused.

5. **Scroll down to the Specialties text box, also shown in Figure 3-2, and enter your skills and/or specialties.**

   Separate each item with a comma and don't put any punctuation after the last item in your list. You don't need to press Enter/Return between skills.

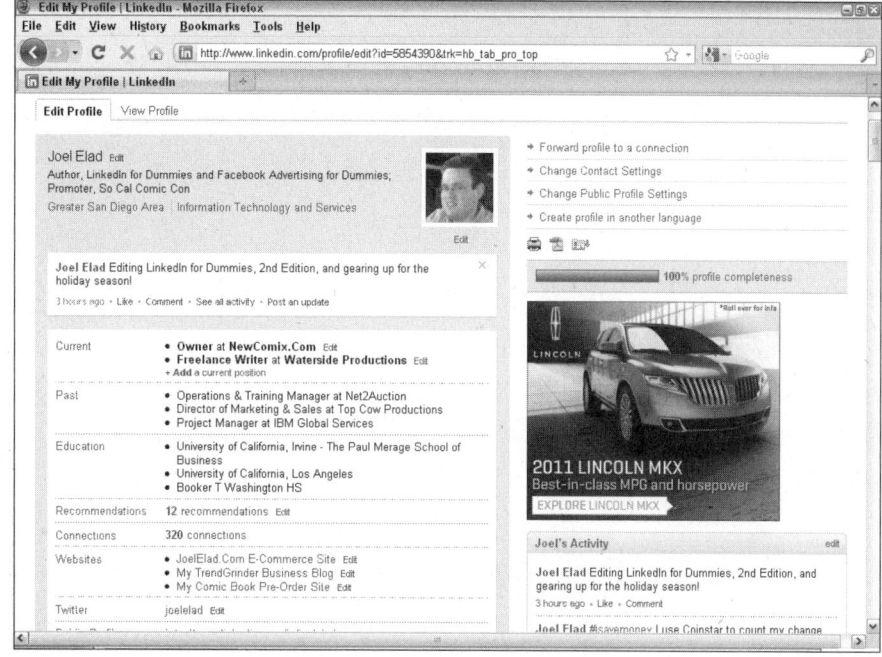

Figure 3-1:
Bring
up your
LinkedIn
profile page.

6. Click the Save Changes button to save your summary.

You're taken back to your Profile page. Next, you need to update the Basic Information section of your LinkedIn profile.

7. Click the Edit link next to your name to update your professional headline and industry.

You now see the Edit Your Profile Name and Location page, as shown in Figure 3-3.

8. At the Edit Your Profile Name and Location page, double-check your name and add any maiden or former name in the text box provided. Next, enter your professional headline (your main job title).

You can put any job title here, but make sure it conveys your main role as you want others to see it. Also, if you want to maintain a higher level of privacy for your profile, you can choose the Display Name option so that only your first name and last initial show up on your public profile. If you select that option, your first-degree connections can see your full name, but the general public can see only your first name and last initial, such as Joel E. for me.

Figure 3-2:
Update your
profile's
Summary
section
here.

Figure 3-3:
Create your
professional
headline on
LinkedIn.

9. **Click the drop-down arrow next to the Industry heading and select the industry you most associate with your career.**

    You can choose from more than 140 designations, so take a few moments to do a quick scan of the list. Note that some of the industries listed are more specific than others. You want to pick the best match possible. For instance, if you create custom graphics for Web sites, you could select Internet as your industry, but an even better choice would be Online Media.

10. **Click the Save Changes button.**

    You're taken back to your Profile page. You've now covered the core of your LinkedIn profile. In the next sections, you find out about the other essential elements to include in your profile, namely your current/past experience and education.

Adding a Position to Your LinkedIn Profile

One of the most important aspects of your LinkedIn profile is the list of positions you've held over the years, including your current job. This list is especially important if you're using LinkedIn to find a new or different career or to reconnect with past colleagues. Hiring managers want to see your complete history to know what skills you can offer, and past colleagues can't find you as easily through LinkedIn if the job they knew you from isn't on your profile. Therefore, it's critical to make sure you have all the positions posted on your profile with the correct information.

For a company in LinkedIn's directory, you need to fill in the following fields:

- Company name (and display name, if your company goes by more than one name)
- Your job title while working for the company
- The time period you worked for the company
- Description of your job duties

If your company is *not* listed in LinkedIn's directory, you need to fill in the industry and Web site for the company when you're adding your position to your LinkedIn profile.

Use your resume when completing this section because most resumes have all or most of the information required.

To add a position to your LinkedIn profile, follow these steps:

1. **Go to LinkedIn and log in. Click the Profile link in the top navigation bar.**

   This step takes you to the Profile page. Scroll down your profile until you see the Experience header, shown in Figure 3-4.

2. **Click the Add a Position link to the right of the Experience header.**

   You're taken to the Add Position page, as shown in Figure 3-5.

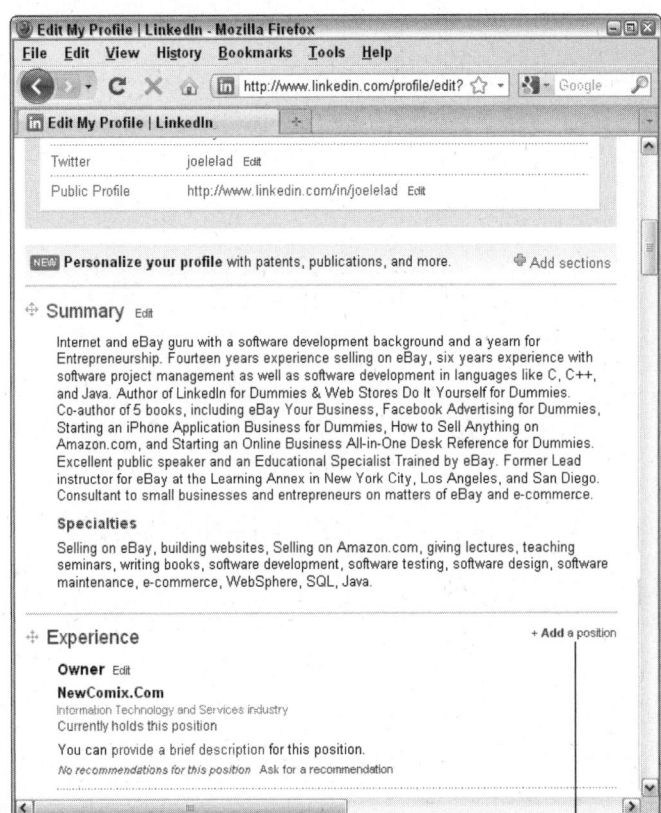

Figure 3-4:
Start at your Experience section within your profile.

The Add a Position link

3. **In the text boxes provided, enter the information about your position, including company, title, time period, and job description.**

When you type in your company name, LinkedIn checks that name against its Company Profiles list of thousands of companies from its records, and you see suggested company names while you type. (An example is shown in Figure 3-6.) If you see your company name in that list, click the name, and LinkedIn automatically fills in all the company detail information for you.

When you're defining the company where you held your position, LinkedIn either finds a match among its Company Pages or asks you for more information about your company (as shown in Figure 3-7) so it can better connect you with any colleagues or business partners. After entering the company name, enter your title, the time period when you worked there, and a description of your position.

4. **Click the Save Changes button.**

This adds the newly entered position into your profile, and you're taken back to your Profile page.

5. **Repeat Steps 2–4 for any additional position you want to enter.**

To edit a position you already listed, simply click the Edit link next to that record in the Experience section instead of clicking the Add a Position link.

Figure 3-5:
Enter your
job informa-
tion here.

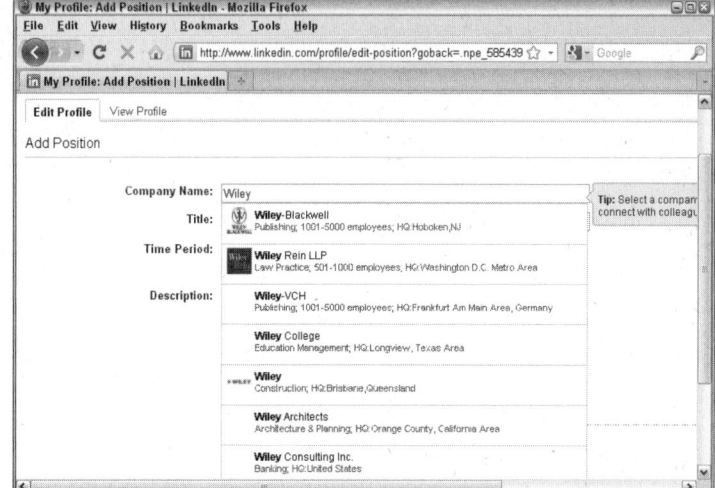

Figure 3-6:
LinkedIn checks its Company Pages for your company listing.

Figure 3-7:
LinkedIn may ask for more information about the company.

The Experience section isn't just for paid full-time employment. You can add position information for any contract work, nonprofit assignments, or other valid work experience that added to your skill set. If you've written a book, maintain a blog, or have a regular magazine column, you might want to list that as a separate position.

If you have most of the information that LinkedIn asks for a given position but you're missing a few details in the description, go ahead and add what you have. (You must provide a job title, company, and time period to save the position in your profile.) You can always come back later and fill in any missing information. In addition, if you make your profile public (as discussed later in this chapter in the section "Setting your profile URL and public view"), make sure any position information you enter is something you don't mind the whole world — including past employers — seeing on your profile.

Reporting Your Education on Your Profile

After you document your past and current jobs, it's time to move on to the next part of your profile: education. After all, besides at your jobs, where else are you going to meet and stay in touch with so many people? At school, of course! Your Education section says a lot about you, especially to potential employers and to former schoolmates who are looking to reconnect with you.

When you signed up with LinkedIn, you might have been asked to provide your basic education information. Maybe you have more than one school to list, or perhaps you didn't create a full listing for the schools you put down upon registration. In either case, whenever you find a moment, you can go back to make sure that your profile is up to date and has all your education listed.

Some people ask how much education to list on their profiles. Although you could theoretically go all the way back to preschool or kindergarten, most people start with high school or undergraduate college. This is up to you, but keep in mind that the more items you list, the greater the opportunity that your past schoolmates can locate and contact you.

This section isn't limited to high school, undergraduate, and post-graduate education. You should also list any vocational education, certification courses, and any other stint at an educational institution that matters to your career or personal direction.

When you're ready to update or add your education information, follow these steps:

1. **Go to LinkedIn and log in. Click the Profile link in the top navigation bar.**

2. **Scroll down your profile until you see the Education header. Click the Add a School link to continue.**

   The Add Education page appears, as shown in Figure 3-8.

3. **From the drop-down lists provided, select the Country and State where your school was located.**

   LinkedIn displays a drop-down list of schools, as shown in Figure 3-9.

4. **Look through the alphabetized list to find your school and select it. If your school name doesn't appear, select Other and then type the school name in the new text box provided.**

5. **Complete the degree information about your education.**

   This includes filling in your degree type, fields of study (if applicable), and the years you attended this institution. For your degree type, you can either provide an abbreviation (BS, BA, and so on) or write the entire degree name (Masters of Science, Doctorate, and so on). The Fields of Study text box is optional, but if you had a specific major or emphasis, this is where to put that information. Finally, for dates attended, if you're still attending this institution, simply fill in your expected graduation date.

6. **Scroll down to the Activities and Societies text box and fill it in.**

   Enter any extracurricular activities you participated in while attending this school. Also list any clubs or organizations you belonged to (including any officer positions you held in those clubs) and any societies you joined or were given membership to, such as honor societies, fraternities, or sororities.

Separate each activity with a comma.

7. **Scroll down to the Additional Notes text box and enter any additional information about your education experience.**

   Enter any awards or honors received from this school, as well as any special events or experiences that didn't fit in the Activities and Societies box, such as studying abroad, events you organized, or committees that you served on at this school. You can separate each item with a period if you want.

   You should also list all your awards and honors under the appropriate field in Additional Information, which I cover in the next section.

8. **When you're done entering information, scroll down and click the Save Changes button.**

   This step adds the newly entered education listing into your profile, and you're taken back to your Profile page.

9. **Repeat Steps 2–8 for any additional education listings you want to enter.**

   To edit an existing education record, click the Edit link next to that record in the Education section, instead of the Add Education button.

Completing the Additional Information for Your Profile

Whenever you meet someone, the most common questions you ask are, "So, what do you do?" and "Where did you go to school?" However, there's more to you than your jobs and education, and LinkedIn has an Additional Information section to reflect that and to tie your LinkedIn profile to your other Internet and real-life identities.

The Additional Information section allows you to provide lots of information in these areas:

- ✔ **Web sites:** LinkedIn allows you to add up to three different Web site links, which will point from your LinkedIn profile to whatever Web site(s) you designate, such as your personal Web site, your company Web site, a blog, an RSS feed, or any other promotional mechanisms you use online.

  Adding a link from your LinkedIn profile to your other Web sites helps boost search engine rankings for those pages. Those rankings are partially determined by the quantity and quality of Web pages that link to them, and LinkedIn is a high-quality site as far as the search engines are concerned. *Note:* You must make your profile public to receive these benefits. You can find out more about your public setting later in the chapter, in the section "Setting your profile URL and public view."

- ✔ **Twitter:** You can now link your Twitter and LinkedIn accounts so that your Twitter updates show up on your LinkedIn profile, and your LinkedIn network activity can be tweeted to your Twitter followers automatically.

- ✔ **Interests:** Highlight your extracurricular activities and what you like to do in your spare time. It allows potential contacts to see what they have in common with you (favorite hobbies or sports) and gives potential employers a glimpse into what else interests you outside a job.

- ✔ **Groups and Associations:** Illustrate what organizations you belong to and what formal activities you do in your spare time. Many people use this section to highlight charity work, networking groups they belong to, or affiliations with religious or political groups.

- ✔ **Honors and Awards:** Announce to the world your distinctions or awards. This could be work-related, like Salesman of the Year; education-related, like Summa Cum Laude or Dean's List; group-related, like Best Fundraiser; or even sports-related, like 1st Place Men's Singles in the City Tennis Tournament.

These items are completely optional for you to complete, but a strong, well-rounded profile usually helps you in your career or networking goals because it gives you more opportunities to connect with someone ("Hey, Joel's a big travel fan. So am I!") or allows people to identify with your situation.

When you're ready to update the rest of the information on your profile, simply follow these steps:

1. **Go to LinkedIn and log in. Click the Profile link in the top navigation bar.**

2. **On the Profile page, scroll down your profile until you see the Additional Information section header. Click the Edit link next to that header.**

    You're taken to the Additional Information page, as shown in Figure 3-10, where you enter the additional information about yourself, from associated Web sites to interests, groups, and awards.

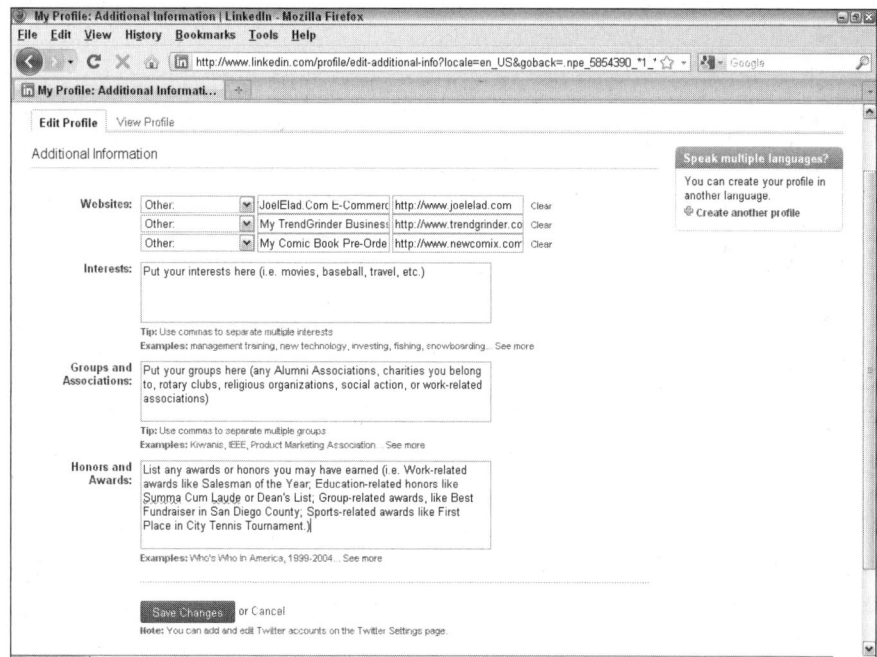

Figure 3-10: Enter your Web sites and interests here.

3. **Under Websites, in the drop-down lists on the left, select short descriptions for the sites you intend to display.**

   You can pick from the predefined list of descriptions (like My Company, My Website, and so on). Or, you can pick Other; in the blank text box that appears, type in a brief custom description for your Web site link (like My Rotary Club page or My eBay page).

   This description appears as a link on your profile — the reader isn't going to see the site's URL.

   Search engines look at the text used in these links when calculating rankings. So if there are certain keywords for which you want your site to rank higher, you may want to include them in the link text. So for example, you might want to say "Springfield Toastmasters" rather than "My Toastmasters Club."

4. **Still in the Websites section, in the text boxes to the right, enter the URLs of the Web sites you want to list on your profile, corresponding to the correct descriptions on the left.**

   You can add up to three URLs to your LinkedIn profile, so use them wisely.

   This might seem obvious, but, well, people are going to be able to click those links and check out your Web sites. Sure, that's the point, but do you remember that hilarious yet embarrassing picture of yourself you added to your personal site, or that tirade you posted in your blog about a co-worker or tough project? Before you link to a site from your LinkedIn profile, scour it and make sure you won't end up scaring off your contacts.

5. **Complete the Interests text box.**

   This is your chance to tell the world a little more about you besides your jobs and education. Make sure to separate each interest with a comma.

   You probably want to omit any interests that a potential employer wouldn't like to see. For instance, if you work in the entertainment industry, talking about how you love to download pirated movies will not make any hiring manager happy. Talk instead about how you love to watch licensed content from approved sources like iTunes or Amazon Unbox!

6. **Fill in the Groups and Associations text box.**

   This is the text box where you can list your groups not listed under any school, such as any charity groups, religious organizations, alumni associations, rotary clubs, and so on.

7. **Fill in the Honors and Awards text box.**

   List your accolades from jobs, school, or any extracurricular activity. Even if you listed an award under your Education section, feel free to repeat it here.

   If you want to update your Twitter setting, click the Twitter Settings Page link at the bottom of this page to bring up the Twitter Settings page, as shown in Figure 3-11.

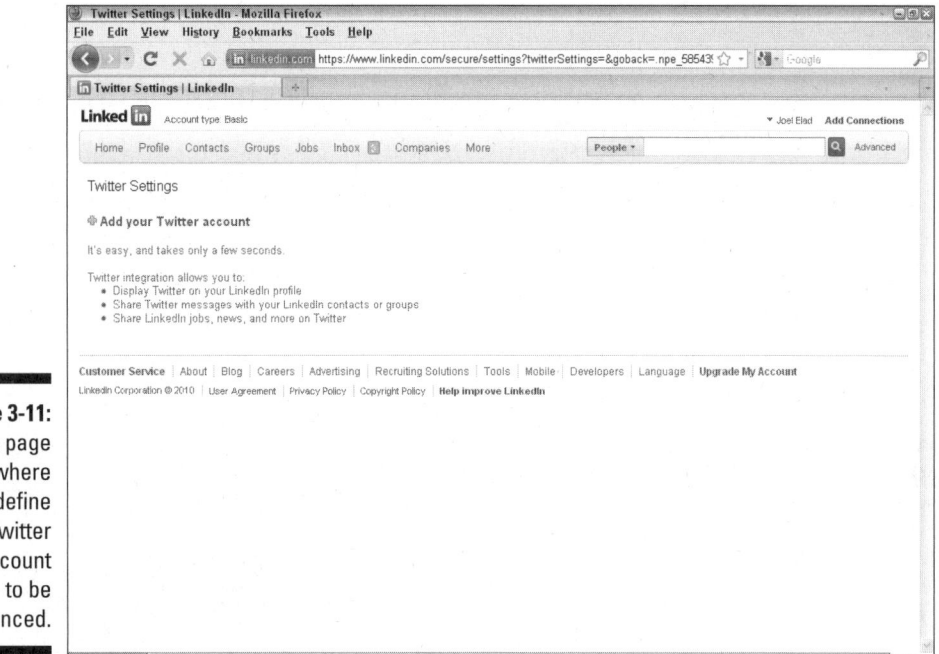

8. **Click the Save Changes button.**

   This step updates your Additional Information section in your profile, and you're taken back to your Profile page.

Reviewing Your LinkedIn Profile

After you go through the various sections of your LinkedIn profile and add the critical information, review your profile to make sure it appears exactly the way you want other people to see it, as well as decide how much information is visible to the public and what others on LinkedIn can contact you about in what regard.

Viewing your profile as others see it

While you're updating your LinkedIn profile, take a minute to view your profile to see how it will be displayed on the computer screen when anyone clicks to view your profile. You have several ways of accomplishing this:

✔ In the top navigation bar, roll your mouse over the Profile link until the View Profile link appears; click the link to see your profile as it would appear. The link whisks you away to the Profile page, and there you can see that the View Profile tab is selected and waiting for your review.

✔ While editing your profile, you can see two tabs under the Profile header in the middle of the screen: Edit Profile, and View Profile, as shown in Figure 3-12. Click the View Profile tab to see your profile.

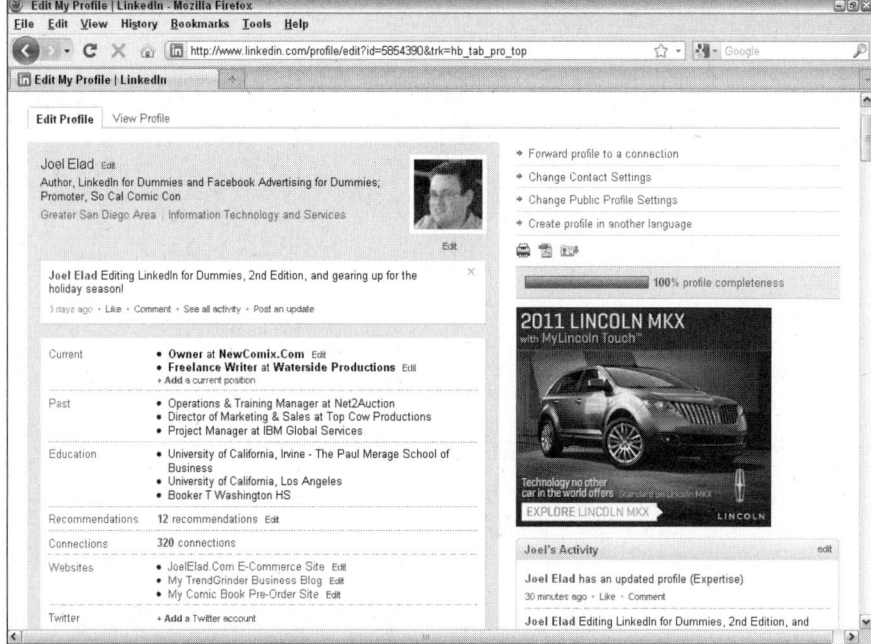

Figure 3-12: You have several options for viewing your LinkedIn profile in action.

Setting your profile URL and public view

After you fully update your LinkedIn profile, your next goal is probably to share it with the entire world, not just your LinkedIn network. The best way to accomplish this is to set up your profile so that your full profile is available for public viewing.

Setting your profile to full public view gives you several advantages:

✔ Anyone looking for you has a better chance of finding you because of the increased information tied to your name.

✔ When you make your profile public, it gets indexed in both the Google and Yahoo! search databases. This makes your online identity accessible and controlled by your access to LinkedIn.

✔ You give increased exposure to any companies, projects, or initiatives that you're working on by having that credit published on your LinkedIn profile.

When you're ready to set your profile to Public, just follow these steps:

1. **Go to LinkedIn and log in. Click the Profile link in the top navigation bar.**

   You arrive at the Profile page. Look to the right of the Edit Profile and View Profile tabs, for a link that says Change Public Profile Settings, like in Figure 3-13.

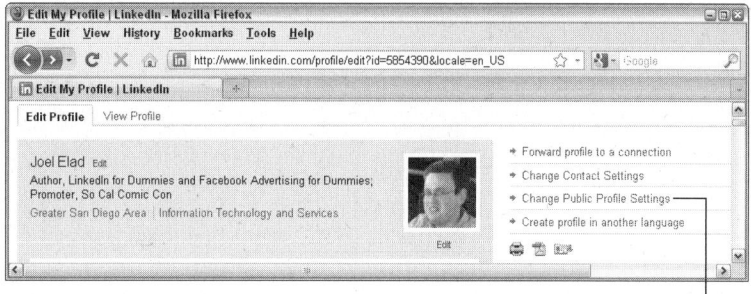

Figure 3-13: Edit your LinkedIn profile settings.

The Change Public Profile Settings link

2. **Click the Change Public Profile Settings link.**

   This step takes you to the Edit My Public Profile settings page, as shown in Figure 3-14.

3. **(Optional) To set a custom URL for your LinkedIn profile, fill in the text box next to the Set Address button.**

   You can enter anywhere between 5 and 30 numbers or letters, but don't put in any spaces, symbols, or special characters. Then click the Set Address button to save your changes.

   Keep in mind that it's much easier to point people to `www.linkedin.com/in/joelelad/` than to `www.linkedin.com/5a6e4b/`.

   Keep your URL changes to a minimum (preferably, just set it once and leave it) so that everyone will know how to get to your profile, especially search engines. (If you change your custom URL later, the previous custom URL is no longer valid.) Otherwise, you'll have different versions of your profile with different URLs in different places on the Internet.

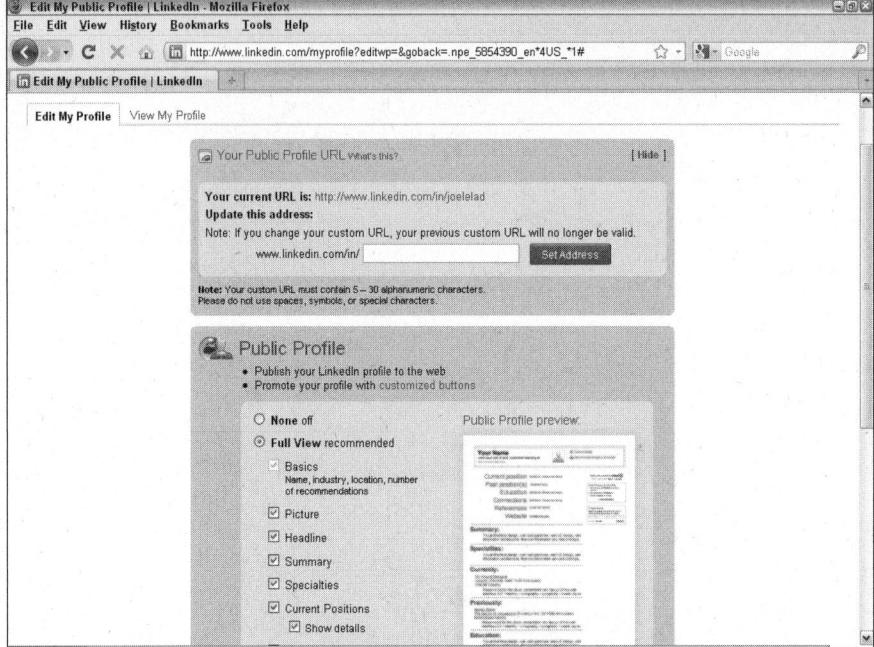

Figure 3-14:
Create a
customized
URL for your
Linked
profile.

4. Scroll down the main Public Profile section on the page and determine what parts of your LinkedIn profile you want available for public viewing.

Pick which sections of your LinkedIn profile are public. To reveal a section on your public profile, simply select the check box next to that given section, as shown in Figure 3-15. Your basic information is already selected for you by default, but you can decide whether to add your education, positions, groups, or any other indicated section. As you add more sections, a preview of your Profile page on the right side of the page gets updated.

5. Click the Save Changes button.

You're taken back to the same Edit My Public Profile settings page, but now you see a confirmation message at the top of the screen.

Whenever you're editing your profile, you can scroll down and click the View My Public Profile as Others See It link to see your public profile. On that page, you can click a button to view your full profile. This way, you can see the difference between your public and full profiles.

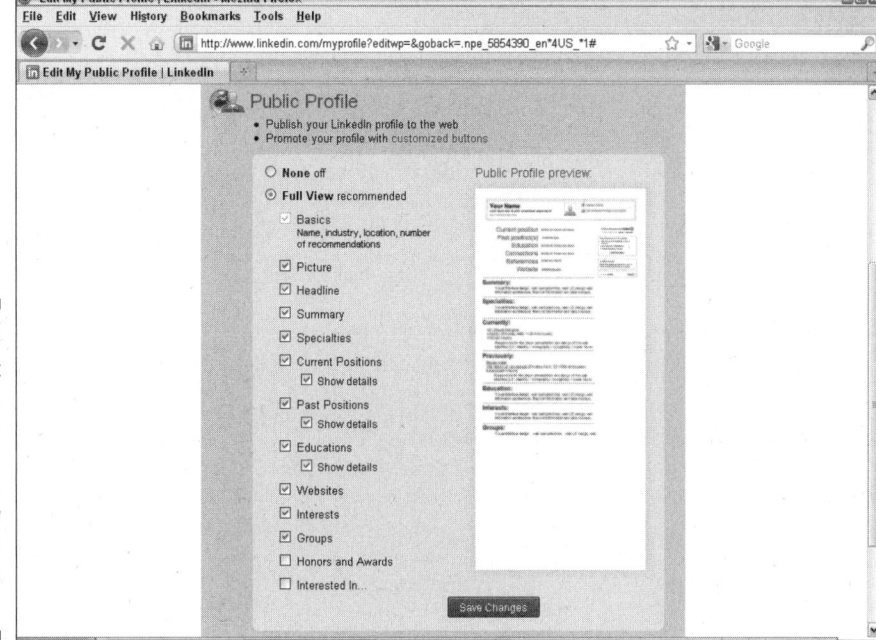

Checking your contact settings

You definitely want to make sure that you select the correct contact settings for your LinkedIn profile. After all, if you're looking for a new job, for example, you want to make sure that the option for Career Opportunities has been checked. (I go into plenty of detail about the eight main contact settings in the earlier section "Determining the Contact Settings for Your Profile.") When you're ready to check your contact settings, just follow these steps:

1. **Go to LinkedIn and log in. Click the Profile link in the top navigation bar.**

   Your browser presents you with the Profile page.

2. **Scroll down the page to the bottom of your profile. Next to the Contact Settings section header, click the Edit link.**

   This brings you to the Contact Settings page, as shown in Figure 3-16.

3. **Select an option under the What Type of Messages Will You Accept? question.**

   If you want to receive InMail e-mails from people who aren't direct connections in your network, make sure the I'll Accept Introductions and InMail option is selected.

   Otherwise, select the I'll Accept Only Introductions option to block anyone sending you InMail. Your first-level (direct) connections will always be able to send you a message through LinkedIn. (This is different from the InMail e-mails you can send any LinkedIn user, which you find out about in Chapter 5.)

4. **Make sure the correct options are selected in the Opportunity Preferences section.**

   The items you have selected here show up as a bulleted list in your profile and will limit (or allow) the ways in which other LinkedIn members can contact you. If you don't want to receive any InMail or Introductions from other LinkedIn users, you can clear those check boxes, and no options to contact you will be displayed on your profile.

5. **(Optional) To give special instructions on how people can contact you, fill in that information in the indicated text box.**

   For example, if you require a few pieces of information from someone before you will add them to your network, you can indicate that in this text box. You can also indicate whether this is a good time to contact you, or what projects or subject areas you're involved in.

6. **Click the Save Changes button.**

   You're taken to your Profile page.

Figure 3-16:
Update your contact settings for your profile.

Part II
Finding Others and Getting Connected

The 5th Wave   By Rich Tennant

@RICHTENNANT

"Here's an idea. Why don't you start a social network for doofuses who think they know how to set a broken leg, but don't."

In this part . . .

There are days when I'm amazed at how small the world is — for instance, when I find out that someone I met randomly while I was 3,000 miles from home is related to a good friend of mine from California. The more you ask around and get involved, the more you realize that all these great connections are out there, just waiting to be discovered. Maybe Kevin Bacon is less than six degrees apart from me. But I digress. . . .

This part covers the essentials of building and growing your network of connections on LinkedIn. I start by talking about how you can search the database far and wide for the person or people you know, and then I tell you how you can send them Invitations or use a friend to send an Introduction to someone new. I go through a lot of tips and advice on how to grow your network, using LinkedIn functionality and your own ingenuity. I end the part by talking about one of the great ways to see others and be seen on the site — the LinkedIn Answers section, where you can share and gather knowledge on all sorts of topics.

Chapter 4

Searching LinkedIn

. . . .

. . . .

After you sign up for LinkedIn and build your profile (see Chapters 2 and 3, respectively, for more on those topics), it's time to go forth and find connections! As you start searching your own immediate network and your first, second, and third degrees of connections' networks as well, you can see just how valuable LinkedIn can be to you. LinkedIn is the embodiment of the Six Degrees of Separation concept because in most cases, you can connect to any other person in the network regardless of whether you already know that person.

In this chapter, I demonstrate the different ways you can search the LinkedIn network. By that, I mean your ever-growing personal network and the greater LinkedIn member network. I talk about viewing your own network, searching within the second and third levels of your network, and performing searches on LinkedIn using different types of criteria or search terms.

Viewing Your Connections

I seem to recall an old saying: "Before you know where you can go, you have to know where you are" or something like that. This holds true even for LinkedIn. Before you start searching throughout the network, it's helpful to understand the reach of your own immediate network and how your first-degree connections' networks add up to keep you connected with a lot of people. The first thing you should do is get familiar with your own LinkedIn network.

To view your LinkedIn network and also some nifty statistics about your network, just follow these steps:

1. **Log in to LinkedIn. From the top navigation bar, roll your mouse over the Contacts link and then click the My Connections link that appears.**

   This brings up a list of your current connections on the My Connections page, as shown in Figure 4-1. You can scroll through the list or roll your mouse over the ABC link and then click the letter of the alphabet (located below the ABC link and above the list) to go straight to that section of your Connections list.

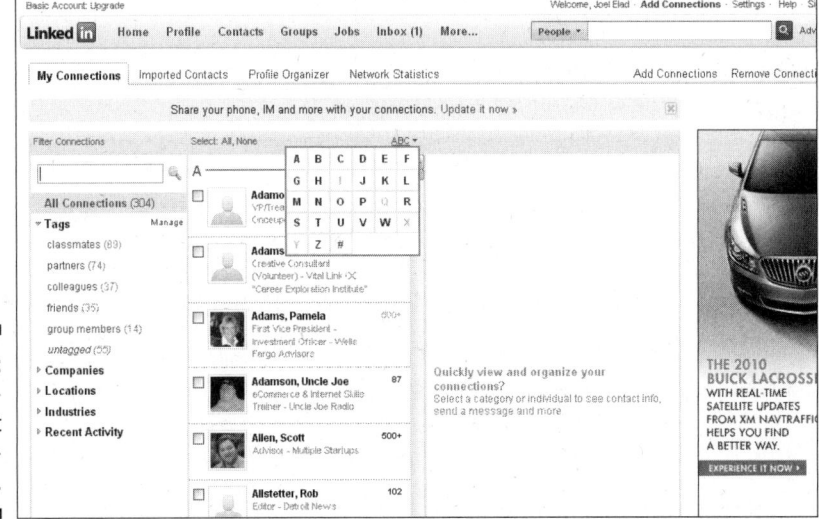

Figure 4-1: An alphabetical list of your connections.

2. **Use the search box and drop-down lists on the left side of the screen to filter your list of connections.**

   Enter any keyword into the search box or use one of the predefined filters (Tags, Companies, Locations, Industries, and Recent Activity) to display connections who, say, live in a greater metropolitan area of a certain city or work in a particular industry.

   The drop-down lists contain options only for your first-degree contacts.

   Suppose you're looking for Internet professionals. You simply expand the Industry filter by clicking the triangle next to Industry (as shown in Figure 4-2) and then clicking Internet. LinkedIn can show you who in your network matches that request! If you're looking for an option in any of these filter lists (like Austin, TX as a location) that don't appear on the filter list, none of your first-level connections have that option defined in their profiles. (In this case, it would mean that none of your first-level connections reside in Austin.)

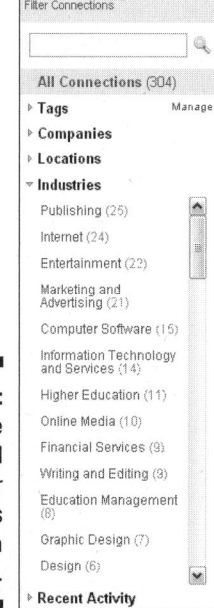

Figure 4-2:
Generate
a targeted
list of your
connections
based on a
filter.

3. **Click the Network Statistics tab to see the overall summary of your network.**

   You see a page like the one in Figure 4-3. Not only do you see the current count of your connections but also how many people are your second-degree connections (a friend of one of your connections) or third-degree connections (a friend of a friend of your friend) who you can search or reach through an Introduction.

4. **Scroll down this page to the Regional Access and the Industry Access sections (as shown in Figure 4-4) to see a breakdown of where the folks in your network are located and what they do.**

   LinkedIn shows you the percentage breakdown of which regions are the most popular in your network and which industries are represented in your extended network.

   Click any of the top five regions or industries on this page, and LinkedIn automatically performs a search of your network with that criteria. So, to see your first-degree contacts who live in the greater New York City area, click the Greater New York City Area link in the Regional Access list.

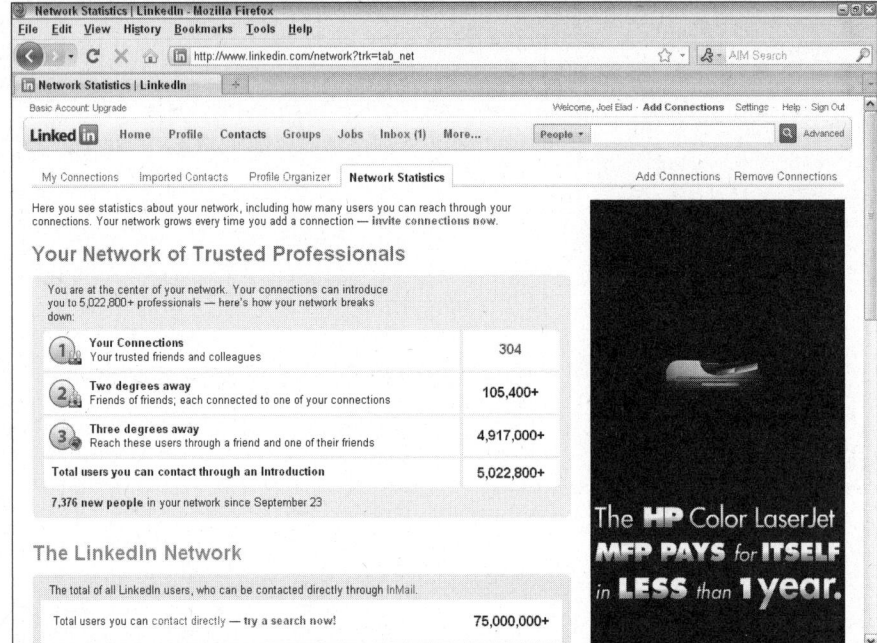

Figure 4-3: Behold the power of your LinkedIn network!

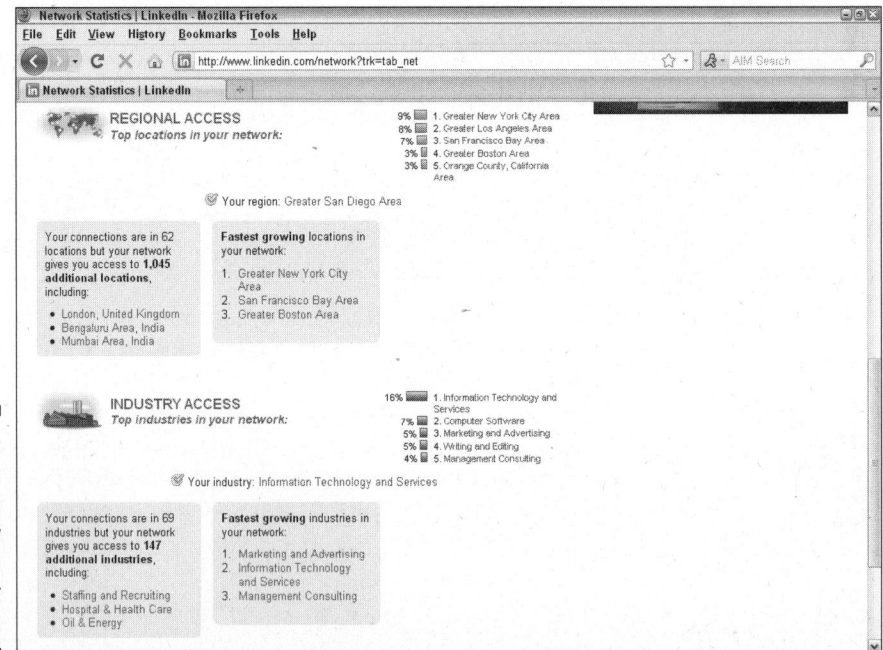

Figure 4-4: See the region and industry breakdown of your network.

Searching the LinkedIn Network

When you're ready to find a specific person, use the LinkedIn search engine, with which you can scan the tens of millions of LinkedIn members, based on keywords. The two main ways to search the network are a basic search and an Advanced Search.

At the top-right corner of every page on LinkedIn is a simple search form, with which you can run a keyword search via the LinkedIn database. This is your go-to tool if you're searching only for a specific name, employees of a particular company, or people with a specific job title. In fact, you'll get a lot of results with the basic search because you're searching each LinkedIn member's entire profile for your keywords, not just one field. For example, if you type **Mike Jones** in the basic search box (as opposed to searching by the name Mike Jones; see the upcoming section, "Searching by name"), you get a larger set of results because you see every profile where the words *Mike* and *Jones* were anywhere in the profile. (When you search by name, LinkedIn searches only everyone's Name field.) Keep this in mind when you do your search, and pick the method you want based on your goals.

In some situations, though, a simple search just doesn't cut it because you want to specify whether you're searching for someone's name, title, employer, industry, skills, location, or some combination thereof. In those cases, use the Advanced Search function:

 ✔ From almost any page on LinkedIn, click the Advanced link, near the top-right corner of the page, to bring up the search page. If you're using LinkedIn Jobs or LinkedIn Answers, clicking this link brings up the Job Search or Advanced Answers search page, respectively.

 ✔ Click the drop-down arrow next to People near the top-right corner of the LinkedIn home page to bring up links to the Advanced searches for People, Jobs, Companies, Answers, Groups, or your messages Inbox, as shown in Figure 4-5.

 ✔ If you download one of the toolbars or companion software (as discussed in Chapter 10), you can perform a search from the search box in that toolbar or software program.

The examples in the rest of this chapter assume that you're clicking the Advanced link. Of course, feel free to pick the method of search you're most comfortable with.

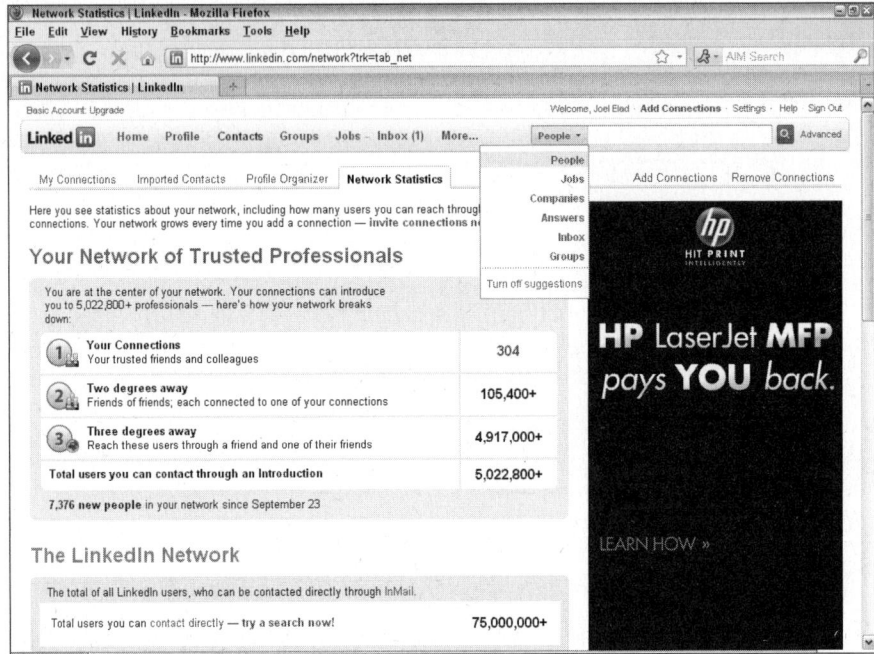

Figure 4-5: Access the LinkedIn search page from one of several links.

Sorting your advanced search results

Whenever you run an advanced search, LinkedIn defaults to sorting your search results by the keywords you provided in your search. However, that's not your only option. When you're setting up your advanced search, note the Sort By option, with a drop-down list containing five options, as shown in Figure 4-6. (If you've already generated search results, you can click the arrow next to Sort By to bring up this option.) Sort your search results by picking from the following methods:

Figure 4-6: Sort your search results by different criteria.

✔ **Relevance:** This sort method is the default when you search on LinkedIn, and it simply returns the people whose profiles have the keywords you inputted in your search. Therefore, this sort result might put people at the top of the list who simply have the keywords in their profile multiple times. It gives some weight to members who are featured on LinkedIn, which means they have premium accounts or an OpenLink membership. Typically, the sort results also give weight to your first-, second-, or third-degree connections on the list. This search is intended for situations where the keyword is more critical than the person.

✔ **Relationship:** This sort method shows you the people who are closely connected to you at the top of the list. This is incredibly helpful if you're searching for someone whom you plan to contact because you have a better chance of connecting with someone who is only two or three degrees away from you, in which case you can be introduced by one of your connections.

✔ **Relationships + Recommendations:** This sort method gives the top spots on the search result to people who are not only closely connected to you but also people who have received Recommendations from other LinkedIn members. This sort result helps you find the most recommended person who is closely connected to you, as opposed to the Relationships sort, which simply shows the closest connected person in terms of degrees of separation.

✔ **Connections**: This sort method gives the top spots on the search result to people who have the most LinkedIn first-degree connections. This sort result helps you find the most connected people to help you in your goals.

✔ **Keyword:** This sort method shows you the people who best match the search terms in your query without cross-referencing the results to the connections in your network. This sort result helps you when your search doesn't involve finding someone in your extended network.

Searching by keyword

Quick. Who do you know that knows how to write software code in PHP? Who do you know that enjoys mountain climbing or hiking? Do you know anybody who gives presentations on a regular basis? Well, with LinkedIn's search capabilities, you can find out when you search by keyword.

When you search by keyword, LinkedIn analyzes everyone else's profiles to find that matching word. You can put any sort of skill, buzzword, interest, or other keyword that would be present in someone's profile to see who in your network is a match. To search by keyword, just follow these steps:

1. **While logged in to LinkedIn, click the Advanced link at the top right of the page.**

   You're taken to the Advanced People Search tab.

2. **Enter the keyword(s) in the Keywords text box.**

   In Figure 4-7, I'm searching for "Six Sigma". If you enter multiple keywords like I did, LinkedIn looks for members who have all the keywords in their profile.

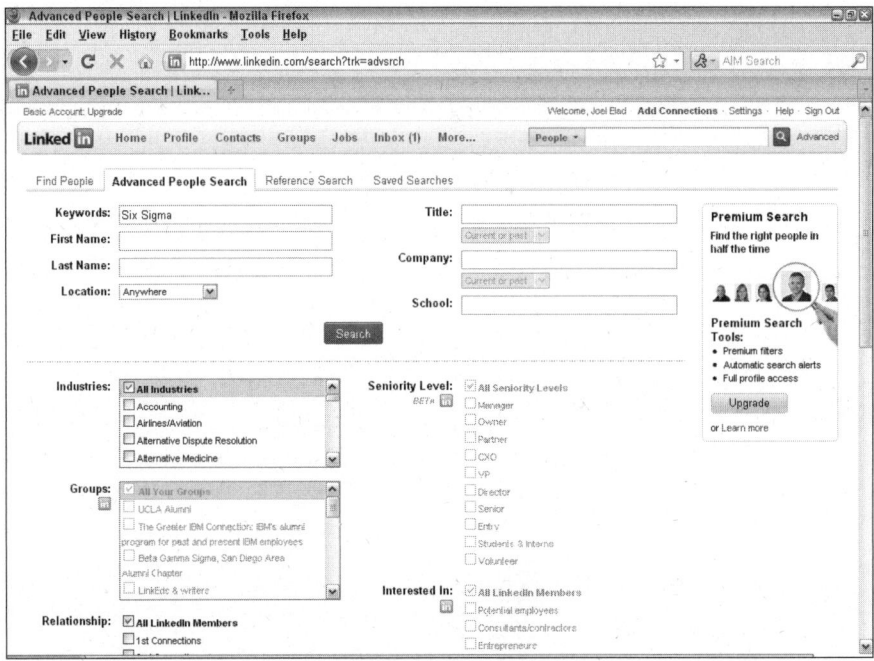

Figure 4-7: Search for people by the keywords in their profile.

I recommend tacking on additional search criteria, such as picking one or more industries, location information (country and ZIP/postal code), or perhaps a job title to get a more meaningful search result. Otherwise, your result list will be long and unhelpful.

If you're searching for a specific keyword phrase, put those words in quotation marks so LinkedIn will search for the exact phrase: for example, "Six Sigma". Otherwise, LinkedIn searches each individual word, and you might get a result like mine in Figure 4-8, where I have the words *six* and *Sigma* in different places in my profile. Because LinkedIn found both words in my profile, even though those words didn't appear together in one phrase, I came up on the search results page.

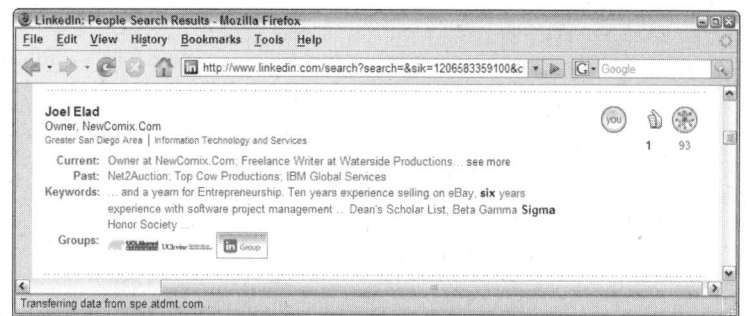

Figure 4-8:
Enclose
keyword
phrases in
quotes.

3. **Click the blue Search button.**

   You see the people in your extended network with those keywords in their profile.

4. **(Optional) Fine-tune your results with the Filter By options.**

   You can expand the various filters along the left side of the Search Results screen and use them to refine your results by entering more information, such as keywords, job titles, user types, and location information by selecting the check boxes provided. (See Figure 4-9.) As you select each filter, LinkedIn automatically updates the search results to give you a more precise search that narrows down the list.

Searching by name

When you want to find a specific person on LinkedIn, you can search by name. LinkedIn has developed special First and Last Name Search fields to help you find that person. When you search by name, you are required to enter the last name; entering the first name is optional.

When you're ready to search by name, just follow these steps:

1. **While logged in to LinkedIn, click the Advanced link at the top right of the page.**

   You're taken to the Advanced People Search page

2. **Enter the last name (and first name, if you know it) into the Last Name and First Name text boxes. (See Figure 4-10.)**

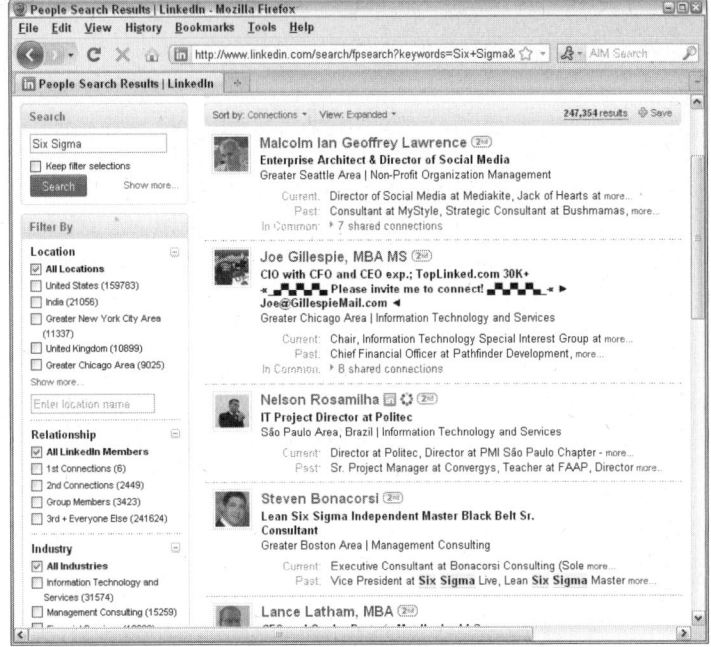

Figure 4-9:
Add more
informa-
tion to get
a more
targeted list
of matching
people.

3. (Optional) Input additional information to help find the person you're looking for.

If you know a company where the person used to work or is currently employed, you can input a company name into the Company text box.

4. (Optional) If you know the approximate location of this person, use the Location drop-down list to select the Located In or Near option. Then use the Country drop-down list and fill in the Postal Code text box.

Only after you select Located In or Near can you pick a country from the Country drop-down list and input a ZIP code in the box indicated, as shown in Figure 4-11.

5. Click the Search button.

You see a results list of people, sorted by the relevance of your name search and then by the degrees of connection in your overall LinkedIn network. (For example, people who are second-level connections appear above people who are third-level connections.)

Figure 4-10:
Search LinkedIn by someone's name.

Figure 4-11:
Give LinkedIn location information to find your person.

6. **(Optional) For better results, use filters in your search.**

   If you haven't done so already, you can add more keywords, a company name, or location information into the boxes provided on the left side of the Search Results screen. Then click the Search button. Also, you can also scroll down and pick specific filters to refine your search results.

Searching by company

Sometimes, you might need to search by company. Maybe you're thinking of applying to a company, and you want to see who you know (or, rather, who is in your extended network) who works for that company so you can approach them to ask some questions or get a referral. Perhaps you're looking for a decision maker at a company who can help you with a deal, or you're curious how active a particular company's employees are on LinkedIn.

Whatever the reason, LinkedIn is an excellent place for searching detailed corporate profiles of specific companies. When you're ready to search by company, just follow these steps:

1. **While logged in to LinkedIn, click the Advanced link at the top right of the page.**

   You're taken to the Advanced People Search page.

2. **Enter the name of the company in the Company text box (as shown in Figure 4-12).**

   If you want to search for only current employees of the company, change the drop-down list choice from the Current or Past option to just Current. If you don't change the default option, your search results will include all the people who ever worked for that company and included that job on their LinkedIn profiles.

3. **Click the Search button.**

   You see as many as 100 results that match your company and exist somewhere in your extended network. (If you've paid for a premium account, you see more results, depending on the level of your account.)

4. **(Optional) For better results, modify your search.**

   You can enter more information, such as job titles, user types, or location information into the boxes provided on the left side of the Search Results screen. Then click the Search button. Also, you can also scroll down and pick specific filters to refine your search results.

Searching by job title

Sometimes you might need to look for someone in a specific position rather than for a specific person. After all, who knows what you go through better than other people with the same job, right? Who better to give advice on a topic like search engine optimization (SEO) than someone whose job relates to SEO, correct?

Therefore, LinkedIn gives you the ability to search by job title instead of person. When you're ready to search by job title, just follow these steps:

1. **While logged in to LinkedIn, click the Advanced link at the top right of the page.**

   You're taken to the Advanced People Search page.

2. **Enter the job title in the Title box provided; Figure 4-13 shows Project Manager entered.**

   To search for only those people who currently have that title, change the drop-down list choice to Current. If you leave the default choice of Current or Past, your search results will include all the people who have ever defined that job title in one of the positions on their LinkedIn profiles.

3. **(Optional, but do it anyway if you can.) Select at least one Industry from the list provided so your search results are relevant to the job title search.**

   I highly recommend doing this step. After all, a Project Manager in Construction is completely different from a Project Manager in Computer Software.

You can actually select multiple industries from the list. Simply scroll through the list and select the check box next to each industry you want to select.

4. **Click the Search button to see your results.**

You see a set of results that match your job title request. You can always use the Filter By options on the left side of the Search Results screen to add more information and get a highly targeted list.

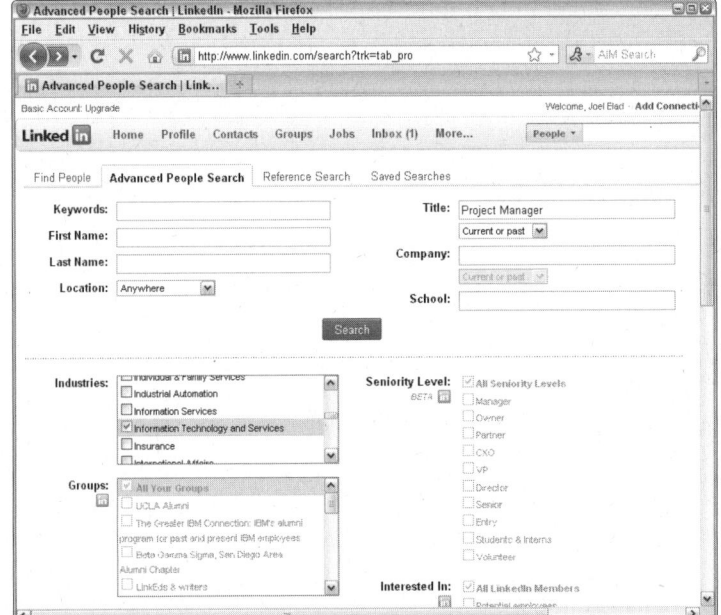

Figure 4-13: Search for people by their current or previous job titles.

Performing a reference search

One of the benefits of LinkedIn is that you can search for someone who might have worked with someone you're researching. Perhaps you're about to hire someone but would like to speak with someone else who knows your potential candidate because they worked together. Say you're deciding to hire a consultant for a project but want to contact someone who has hired this consultant in the past to get a better idea of his work quality. Or maybe you're about to enter a business deal and want some information from someone who knows your potential new partner.

LinkedIn has created the reference search to give you a better window into the person or company. All you need is the company name and the range of years someone has worked there, and LinkedIn searches your network and shows you the people who match that search and how closely they're connected to you.

To perform a reference search, just follow these steps:

1. Click the Advanced link at the top right of the LinkedIn home page.

You're taken to the Advanced People Search page.

2. Click the Reference Search tab along the top of the page.

The Reference Search tab is shown in Figure 4-14.

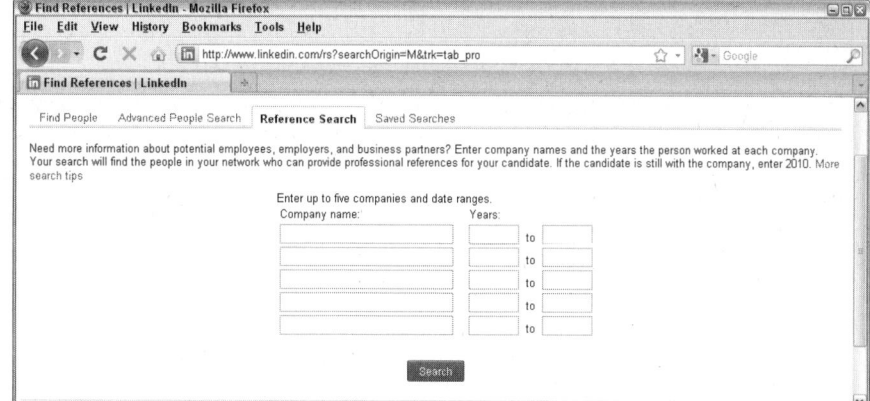

Figure 4-14: Search LinkedIn for potential references for someone.

3. Enter the name of the company and a date range.

For example, suppose you have a job candidate who claims to have worked for Top Cow Productions from 2000 to 2002. You would enter that company name and date range into the text boxes provided.

You can enter more than one company and date range. That will garner you a list of potential references who worked at any of the companies on your search.

4. Click the Search button.

If you have the basic account, you see a Summary page like the one shown in Figure 4-15. This gives you an idea of how many potential connections exist and how many are connected to your immediate network. If you have a Premium account, you would see a list of people (like in a name or job title search) who worked at the designated company in that timeframe, *and* you'd have the ability to contact them. (For more on the different account types, take a gander at Chapter 1.)

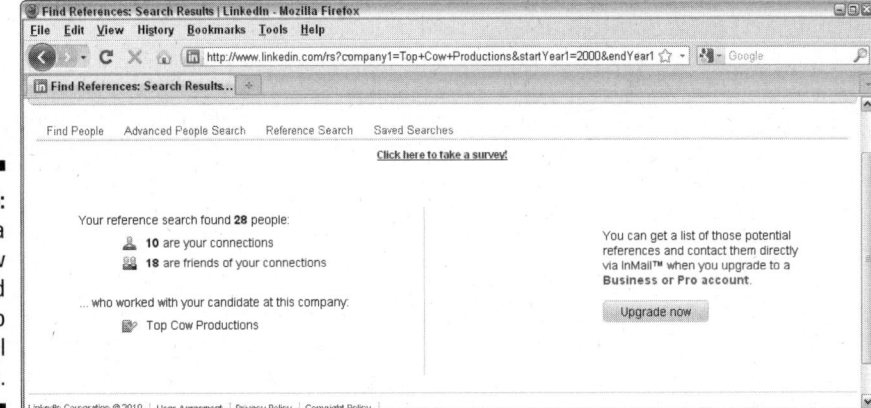

Figure 4-15: Get an idea of how connected you are to potential references.

Chapter 5

Managing Introductions and InMail

*O*ne of the goals of using LinkedIn is to expand your personal network of friends and colleagues by seeing who is connected to you at each degree level. When you can see the second and third degrees of your network, your next goal is to start interacting with these people and see how they might fit into your network, goals, or ambitions. However, the whole system of contacting people requires some order and decorum (otherwise, nobody would feel comfortable signing up for the site in the first place). Therefore, LinkedIn offers two methods for meeting and connecting with people outside your immediate network: Introductions and InMail. Not so coincidentally, I cover Introductions and InMail in this very chapter.

Introductions are simply where you ask to be introduced to a friend of a friend, and your friend can decide whether to pass along your Introduction to the intended target. InMail allows you to directly communicate with anyone in the LinkedIn network through a private LinkedIn message. I also cover what to do when you get a request from a connection on LinkedIn.

InMail Versus Introductions

Your first question is most likely, "What's the difference between Introductions and InMail?" (Figure 5-1 shows an InMail example at the top and an Introduction at the bottom.) The answer depends on how involved your common friend or colleague is in connecting you with this new contact.

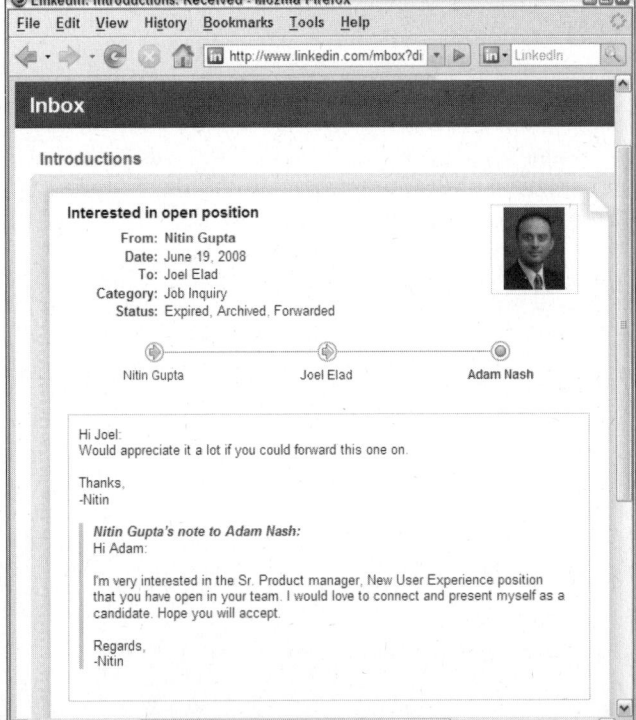

Figure 5-1:
LinkedIn
offers two
ways of
connecting
with people
outside your
network.

Every LinkedIn user decides on his own contact level, and a user can decline to allow any Introduction or InMail to reach him, regardless of sender. If you don't want to receive any Introductions or InMail, simply deselect all the Contact Settings options. (See Chapter 3 for the section on checking your contact settings.)

If you don't mind Introductions but really don't want to have to deal with any InMail, just clear the InMail option in the Contact Settings section and leave the Introductions option alone.

Understanding Introductions

Say you're at a party with your friend Michael, and you say to him, "You know, I'd really like to meet someone who can help me with some software tasks for my company." Michael looks around, sees his friend James, and introduces you to James by saying, "Hello, James. This is my entrepreneur friend from business school, [Your Name Here]. [Your Name Here], this is my old buddy James. He and I studied computer science together in college." After that, Michael might give some more background information about each person to the other.

On LinkedIn, an *Introduction* is very similar to my real-world example. You send a request to someone in your immediate first-degree network (Michael) and ask that person to introduce you to someone in his or her network (James) by forwarding your request to the intended party. In some cases, if you're trying to reach someone in your third-degree network (maybe James has a programming buddy you should talk to), your Introduction request would have to go to two different parties before reaching the intended recipient.

Here are some benefits of using Introductions:

- ✔ **You're represented by someone close.** Instead of sending a random, unexpected e-mail to a stranger, you're introduced by somebody who knows the intended party, even if that introduction is done with an e-mail. That gives your Introduction request a much higher chance of being read and getting a response.

- ✔ **You get your network involved.** When you ask people in your network to get involved, they learn more about you and your intentions, and sometimes you might find what you're looking for is closer than you think. In addition, when you ask them to pass along your Introduction request, you can offer to facilitate an Introduction on their behalf as well, which helps both parties.

- ✔ **You leverage the power of your network.** By using LinkedIn, you not only expand your network by using your first-degree connections to help you meet new people, but you can also decide who would make the Introduction for you. I recommend that you read up on your friend's profile and your intended party's profile to see what they have in common.

- ✔ **You can have multiple Introductions going on at one time.** With a LinkedIn free account, you can have up to five open Introductions going at any one time. When you get introduced to your intended party, that spot opens up, and you can make another Introduction request. InMail, in all cases, costs money, either on a per-mail basis or as part of a premium paid account. (That means even someone with a free basic account can use InMail, but it will cost you.)

You can get more Introductions at one time by upgrading to a Premium account. I discuss the different paid accounts in Chapter 1.

Getting to know InMail

Because everyone on LinkedIn has a profile and a secure message Inbox, communicating with other people online is easy. LinkedIn allows you to send InMail directly to an intended party, regardless of whether he is directly or indirectly connected with you. The e-mail gets immediately delivered to the recipient's Web-based Inbox on the LinkedIn site (and, if the recipient has configured their settings to get e-mails of all their InMail, in the Inbox at their e-mail address); the sender never learns the recipient's address, so each party has some privacy. The recipient can then read your profile and decide whether to respond.

The cost of using InMail depends on whether you subscribe to a premium account. You can purchase InMail credits (one credit allows you to send one message) at a cost of $10 per InMail message. Premium accounts, such as the Business account for $24.99/month, come with a set number of InMail credits per month that roll over to the next month if unused. The Business account gets 3 credits per month, the Business Plus account gets 10 credits per month, and the Executive account gets 25 credits per month.

Here are some benefits of using InMail:

- ✔ **Delivery is instant.** With InMail, you simply write your message or request and send it directly to the intended party. There's no delay as a request gets passed from person to person and waits for approval or forwarding.

✔ **You owe no favors.** Sometimes, you just want to reach somebody without asking your friends to vouch for you. InMail allows you to send a request to someone new without involving anyone else.

✔ **It's sure to be delivered.** With Introductions, the party(ies) involved in the middle could choose to deny your request and not pass along the message. With InMail, you know that the intended party will get a copy of your message in his or her e-mail account and LinkedIn Inbox.

Setting Up an Introduction

When you want to bring two (or more) parties together, you usually need to apply some thought to the process, whether it's figuring out what both parties have in common, thinking up the words you'll use to introduce party A to party B, or coming up with the timing of exactly when and where you plan to make the Introduction. On LinkedIn, you should do your best to make sure the Introduction process goes smoothly — but don't worry, there's not nearly as much social pressure. The following sections give you tips and pointers for setting up an Introduction.

Planning your approach to each party in the Introduction

When you want to send an Introduction request, spend some time planning your request before you log on to LinkedIn to generate and send it. Preparing a quality and proper Introduction goes a long way toward keeping your network in a helpful and enthusiastic mood, and it increases your chances of making a new and valuable connection.

You need to prepare two messages: one for your intended recipient and one for your connection/friend. Each message needs to perform a specific objective. Start with the message to your friend and keep the following tips in mind when you're writing it:

✔ **Be honest and upfront.** Say exactly what you hope to achieve so there are no surprises. If you tell your friend that you're hoping her contact will be a new bowling buddy for you, but when you reach that contact, you ask for funding for your new business plan, you're in trouble. Your friend will probably never forward another request again, and the contact, who expected one type of interaction and got another, will see you as untrustworthy and be unlikely and/or unwilling to help on this request or any in the future.

✔ **Be polite and courteous.** Remember, you're asking your friend to vouch for you or back you up when your request goes to the intended party. So be polite when making your request and show your gratitude regardless of the outcome.

✔ **Be ready to give in order to get.** One of the best ways to go far with your network is to offer some sort of reciprocal favor when you want someone to do a favor for you. Perhaps you can introduce your friend to one of your other contacts in exchange for your friend accepting your Introduction request.

✔ **Be patient.** Although you might be eager and under a deadline, your friends probably operate on different schedules driven by different levels of urgency. Some people are online all the time, other people log in to LinkedIn infrequently, and most people are completely disconnected at times, like when they're on vacation or behind on a project. Asking your friend every 20 minutes whether she forwarded your request is an almost sure-fire way of getting that request bounced back to you.

When writing your message to your intended recipient, keep these tips in mind:

✔ **Be honest and upfront.** Just like with your friend, when you have a specific goal or request in mind, make it known in the message. The recipient is most likely busy and doesn't know you, so if he spends the time to talk to you and finds out that you have an ulterior motive, he feels like his time was wasted and that he was deceived, which are *not* good feelings to create when trying to get help from someone.

✔ **Be succinct.** You're asking someone for his time, resources, or advice, so don't beat around the bush too much. You should introduce yourself in your first sentence or two. Then you should explain why you're contacting the recipient and how you hope he can help you.

✔ **Be original.** If you stick to the sample text that LinkedIn gives you, your message has an air of "Hey, I want to talk to you, but I don't have a few seconds to really tell you what I'm after." When you customize your message, you have a greater chance of capturing the other person's attention. If your intended recipient gets a lot of requests, you'll stand out if you show some effort to rise above the daily noise this person encounters.

✔ **Be ready to give in order to get.** You're asking for help of some sort, so be ready to give something, whether it's gratitude, a reciprocal favor, or something more tangible. Most people are eager to help, especially when they understand the situation, but having something to offer in exchange rarely hurts. Explain how you might provide something useful in return.

Sending an Introduction

When you've prepared your messages (one to your contact and one to the recipient) and you're all ready to send an Introduction request, just follow these steps:

1. **While logged in to LinkedIn, search for the person you'd like to meet.**

   You can use the Search box in the top-right corner of any LinkedIn page, or you can click your Connections and search your friend's networks. (See Chapter 4 for the lowdown on searching LinkedIn.)

2. **From the list of search results, click the name of the person you want to contact. (If you didn't find the person you're looking for, try another search.)**

   This step takes you to the recipient's profile page, where you should see two things: a chart along the right side of the page showing how you're connected to this person and a link entitled Get Introduced through a Connection. (If you don't have anyone in your network yet, you won't see the chart or the link.)

   Suppose I'm hoping to be introduced to Patrick Crane, VP of Marketing & Advertising over at LinkedIn. When I get to Patrick's profile page, I see that I have a connection to him (see Figure 5-2) in the form of an old high school buddy who now works with Patrick at LinkedIn.

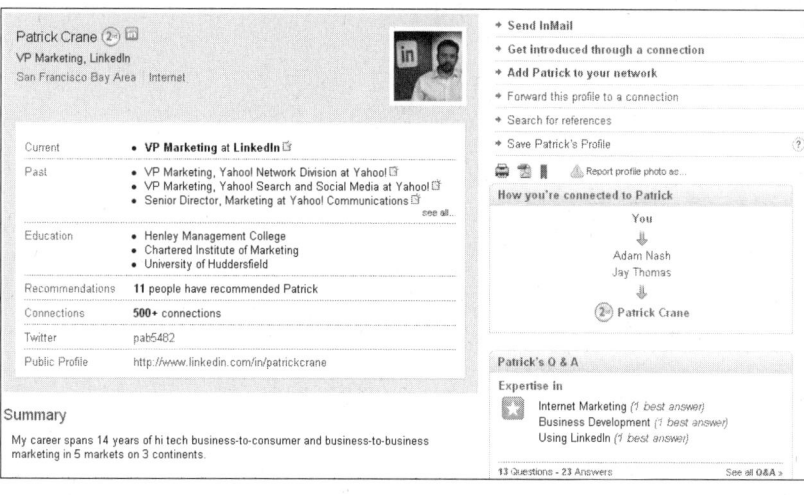

Figure 5-2:
See how you're connected to your intended recipient via LinkedIn.

3. On the person's profile page, click the Get Introduced through a Connection link to start the Introduction process.

You're taken to the Request an Introduction page, as shown in Figure 5-3. Fill out the contact information section that you would like to share with this individual. Then pick a category and subject for this request. Write a short but informative message as to why you want to meet this person. (See the preceding section, "Planning your approach to each party in the Introduction," for more about writing this message.)

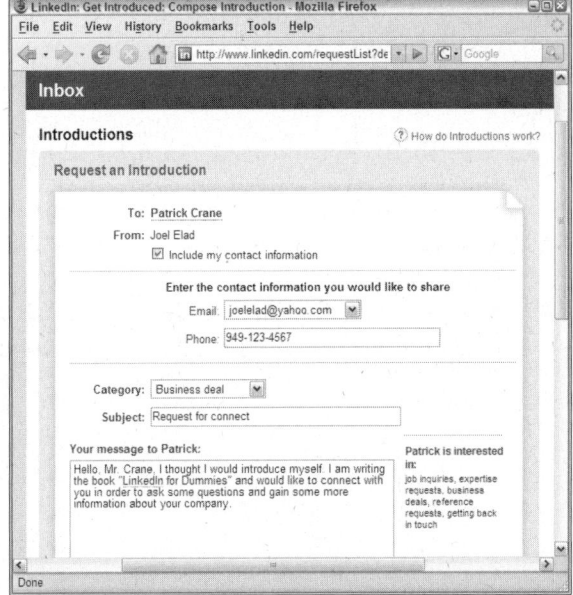

Figure 5-3:
Fill out the Request for an Introduction form.

4. Scroll down and add a message for the person who will be passing on your Introduction.

Adding a note here is required (see Figure 5-4) so the *facilitator* (the person who receives this Introduction request from you) knows why you want to reach the other party. After all, this facilitator is going to vouch for you when he sends this request to the intended party, so the more information you give, the better. (See the preceding section, "Planning your approach to each party in the Introduction," for more about writing this message.)

5. Click the Send button.

You see a green confirmation message as you're taken back to your main LinkedIn page, and your first-degree connection will receive this Introduction request in his LinkedIn Inbox.

After that, your facilitator friend will accept or decline your request, and you'll get a notification about the facilitator's decision.

You might want to send an e-mail to your facilitator friend first before starting the Request for Introduction, especially if you think he might not want to forward your request or the intended recipient might be too busy to receive an Introduction request.

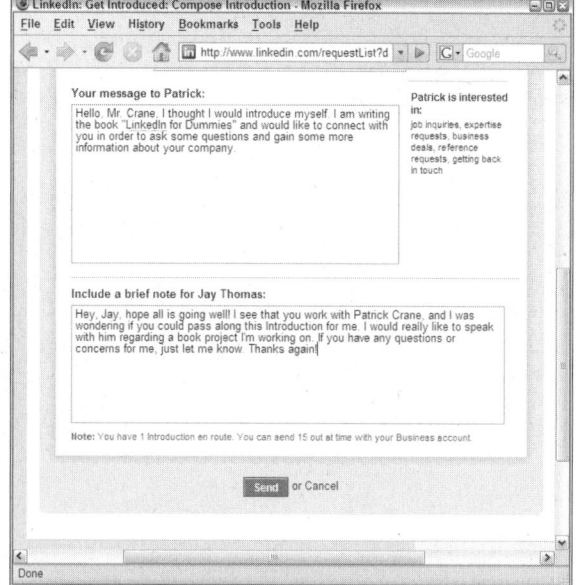

Figure 5-4:
Tell your friend why you're requesting an Introduction.

Sending InMail

If you're looking to connect with someone right away and you don't have an immediate or secondary connection with someone, you can use the InMail feature to send a message directly to another LinkedIn member without anyone else getting involved.

This feature is currently available to paid members of LinkedIn with available InMail credits. If you're using a free account, you have to pay for individual InMail credits to reach other members through InMail. Consult the LinkedIn Help section for more information (http://linkedin.custhelp.com).

InMail is basically a private e-mail message that enables you to reach other members, but it protects those members' privacy and e-mail address information. If your message is accepted, you'll receive a message in your LinkedIn inbox with the other party's name and e-mail address, and you can communicate further. In some cases, you see only the other person's professional headline first, and then you see the person's name after he accepts the InMail message.

When you're ready to send someone an InMail, just follow these steps:

1. **While logged in to LinkedIn, search for the person you'd like to meet.**

   You can use the Search box in the top-right corner of any LinkedIn page, or you can click on your Connections and search your friend's networks. (Chapter 4 has all sorts of details for you about searching LinkedIn.)

2. **From the list of search results, click the name of the person you want to contact. (If you didn't find the person you're looking for, try another search.)**

   You're taken to the person's profile page.

3. **Click the Send InMail link.**

   For example, suppose that I want to connect with Lynn Dralle, the Queen of Auctions, who can not only teach you how to sell on eBay, but who sells more $100,000 per year in antiques and collectibles herself. When I look at her profile (see Figure 5-5), I see the Send InMail link, which means she is open to receiving InMail. I would click the Send InMail link to send her a message.

   Now you can start filling out the Compose Your Message form.

The Send InMail link

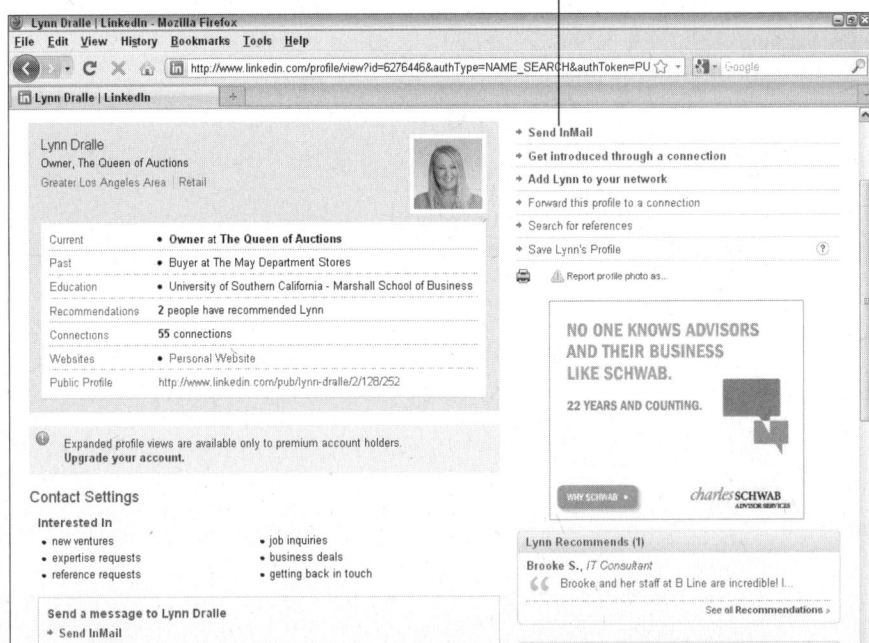

Figure 5-5:
See
whether
who you
want to
contact
receives
InMail.

4. In the Compose Your Message form, select or deselect the Include My Contact Information check box, depending on your preference.

You're asked whether to provide contact information that your recipient can use to contact you, in the form of e-mail and/or a phone number. Simply select the Include My Contact Information check box (as shown in Figure 5-6) if you want to send contact information.

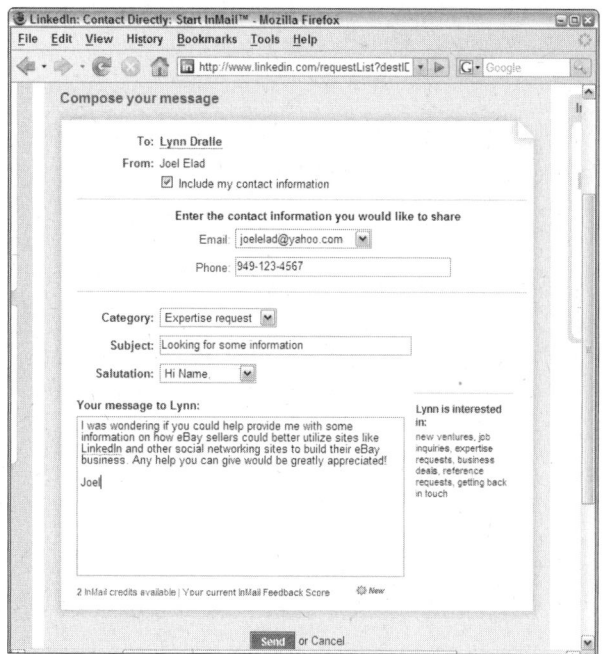

Figure 5-6:
Compose your InMail message.

5. Complete the Category, Subject, and Salutation fields, and then enter a message in its text box.

Your Salutation options are Dear Name, Hi Name, Name, or no salutation. As with an Introduction, keep your message focused on why you would like to talk with this person, and/or what information you were hoping to exchange. (The earlier section, "Planning your approach to each party in the Introduction," contains advice about writing to an intended recipient that applies to InMail messages as well.) At the bottom of Figure 5-6, you can see how many InMail credits you have; remember that you need at least one credit to send this message.

6. Click the Send button to send off your InMail.

Your recipient receives this InMail in his LinkedIn Inbox and can decide whether to accept it. (If they have configured LinkedIn to get immediate e-mails of their InMail messages, they will receive the InMail in their e-mail account Inbox as well.) If your message is accepted, it's up to the recipient to contact you in return. Be patient. While you're waiting, I recommend a game of Connect Four or Internet Chess.

Managing Introduction Requests

What if someone in your network is looking for your help to meet someone in your network? You can facilitate the introduction between your LinkedIn first-degree connections. Now that your reputation is on the line, too, you should spend some time thinking about and processing any and all Introduction requests that come your way.

You really have only two options for handling an Introduction request:

- ✔ Accept it and forward it on to the party it's intended for.
- ✔ Decline it (politely!).

I cover these two options in more detail in the following sections.

However you decide to handle the request, keep these tips in mind:

- ✔ **Act or reply quickly.** The reason why LinkedIn works so well is that people are active with their networks and build upon their profile by answering questions, meeting new people, or joining groups. When you get an Introduction request, you should either act on it or respond to the person with the reason why you won't act on it. Ignoring it isn't a productive use of the LinkedIn system and makes you look very unprofessional.

- ✔ **Don't be afraid to ask for clarification.** Sometimes you might need someone to remind you exactly how you're connected with her. Hopefully, in the note you get from this person, she includes some reminder or thought that helps you place her. If not, don't be afraid to shoot back a message and ask for clarification or a gentle reminder.

- ✔ **Read your friend's request before forwarding.** Chances are good that the person to whom you forward this request might come back to you and ask, "Hey, why did I get this?" or "What do you really think about this person?" If you don't know the details of your friend's request, the intended party might think you're a quick rubber-stamper who sends off stuff without offering to screen anything, and that lowers this person's impression of you.

Accepting requests and forwarding the Introduction

When you're ready to accept your friend's request and forward her Introduction, follow these steps:

1. **Click the Inbox link in the top navigation bar.**

   This will bring up your Inbox of messages, as shown in Figure 5-7 below. When you're looking at all your messages, look for a drop-down arrow next to the words `All Messages`.

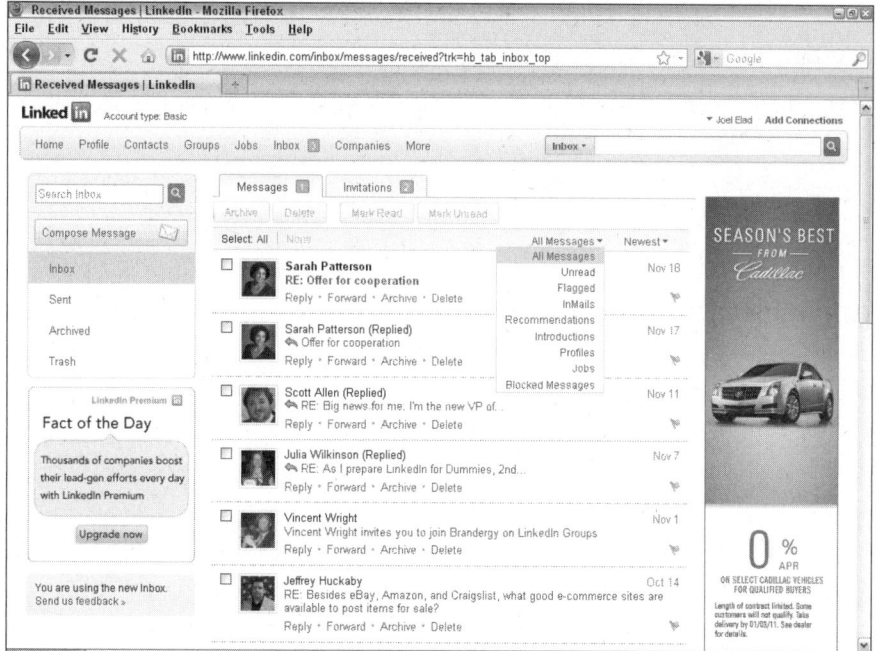

Figure 5-7: Go to your LinkedIn Inbox to find any Introduction requests.

2. **Click the drop-down arrow and select Introductions from the list provided to see your requests.**

   This brings up your Introductions page, as shown in Figure 5-8. Here you can see Introduction requests from fellow members, as well as the results from Introductions you have requested yourself.

3. **Click the subject line of the request you're evaluating.**

In this example, I clicked Real Estate questions from Jared Elad, my brother. Doing so brings up the Introduction request, as shown in Figure 5-9.

Read the full text before acting on the request. Don't just skim it — you might miss an important detail.

4. **If you accept the request, click the Forward button.**

A new window opens where you can compose your message to the recipient, as shown in Figure 5-10. The text box in the middle contains the note from your friend to you, which you can supplement with a note to the intended recipient. Be sure to add your own comments, in the place I indicated in Figure 5-10, to help connect the two people properly. You can also delete the first person's note to you, especially if that personal note was for your eyes only, not the intended recipient.

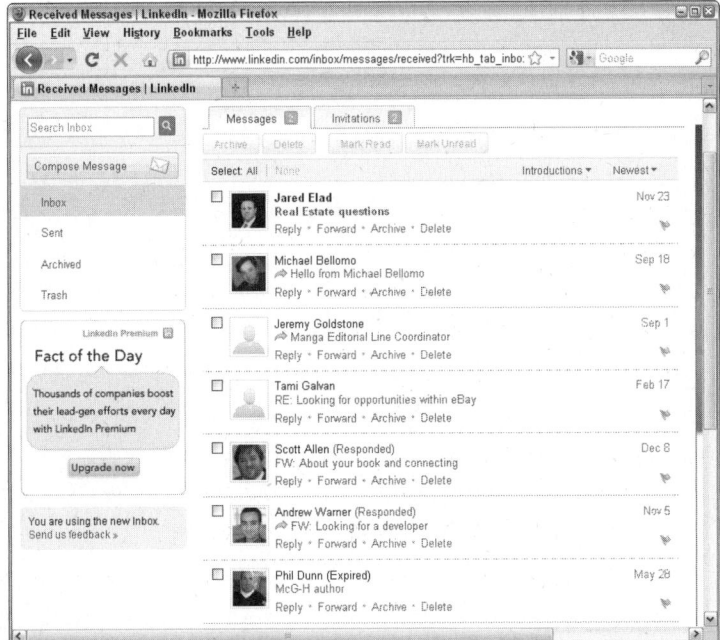

Figure 5-8: See your Introduction requests in one place.

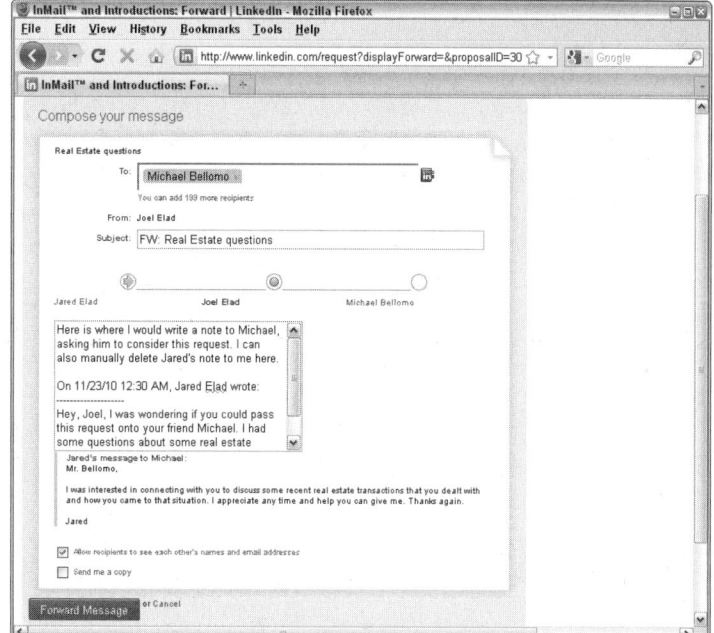

5. **Click the Forward Message button to send the request.**

   In this case, Michael Bellomo will get the Introduction request from me on behalf of Jared Elad. Jared will never see Michael's direct e-mail address, and Michael can decide whether to reach out to Jared and form a connection.

Gracefully declining requests

You might receive an Introduction request that you just don't feel comfortable sending to the recipient. Perhaps you don't know enough about your contact who made the request, or you're unclear about that person's true motivations. Or maybe your connection with the recipient isn't at the stage where you feel you can introduce other people to this person.

Whatever the reason, the best response is simply to gracefully decline the request. Here are some tips on how to respond:

- ✔ **It's not you, it's me.** The most common way to decline is to simply inform the initial contact that you're not that deeply connected with the intended recipient, and you really don't feel comfortable passing on a request to someone who isn't a strong contact. Often, you might have first-degree connections in your network who are "weak links" or people who you're acquainted with but aren't particularly close to or tight with.

- ✔ **The recipient doesn't respond well to this approach.** You can respond that you know the intended recipient, and you know what she's going to say, either from past requests or other experiences with that person. Because you know or feel that the intended recipient wouldn't be interested, you would rather not waste anyone's time in sending the request.

- ✔ **I just don't feel comfortable passing along the request.** Be honest and simply state that you don't feel right passing on the request you've received. After all, if the original contact doesn't understand your hesitation, he'll probably keep asking, and LinkedIn will want you to follow up on any unresolved Introduction. Just as in life, honesty is usually the best policy.

- ✔ **I think your request needs work.** Because you're vouching for this person, you don't want to pass along a shoddy or questionable request that could reflect badly on you. In this case, simply respond that you think the request needs to be reworded or clarified, and offer concrete suggestions on what should be said as well as what requests you feel comfortable forwarding.

When you're ready to decline the request, follow these steps:

1. **Click the Inbox link in the top navigation bar, then click the drop-down arrow next to All Messages and select Introductions from the list provided.**

   This should bring up the list of Introductions within your Inbox. If you receive copies of Introductions in your e-mail and then click the link from the e-mail message, you will have completed Step 2 already.

2. **Click the subject line of the Introduction request.**

   You see the Introduction request. (Refer to Figure 5-9.)

3. **Click the Decline button.**

   The Not Interested in Forwarding page appears, as shown in Figure 5-11.

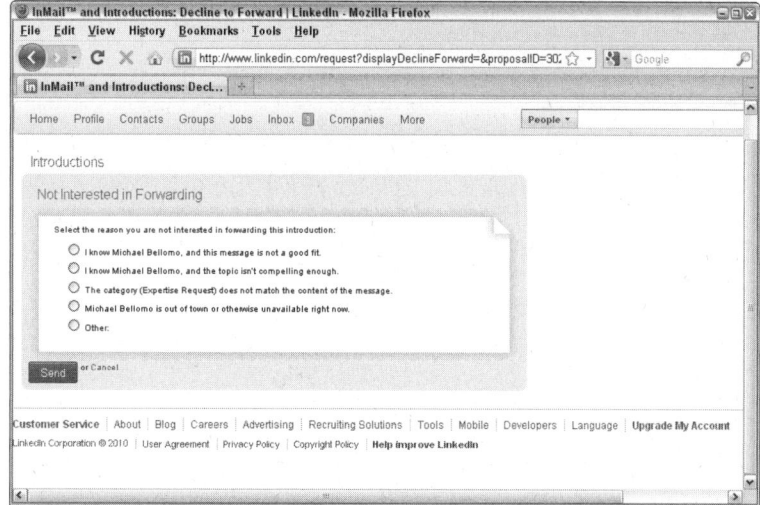

Figure 5-11:
Describe why you're declining to forward the request.

4. **Pick a reason for not forwarding the request, or select the Other option and write a message why you're declining to forward.**

   If you pick any of the main options, like "I know X, and this message is not a good fit," you don't have to provide any additional message. Unless one of these options really states your case, you should probably select Other and write a custom message (or send a separate e-mail message giving more information).

5. **Click the Send button to decline the request.**

   The original contact receives an e-mail as well as a message in his LinkedIn inbox.

Chapter 6

Growing Your Network

Maybe by now, you've signed on to LinkedIn, created your profile, searched through the network, and started inviting people to connect to you — and you're wondering, what's next? You certainly shouldn't be sitting around on your hands, waiting for responses to your Invitations. LinkedIn is designed to open doors to opportunities using the professional relationships you already have (and, with luck, by creating new ones). The best use of it, therefore, is to capture as much of your professional network as possible in the form of first-degree connections to your LinkedIn network so that you can discover those inside leads as well as those friends of friends who can help you.

In this chapter, I discuss how you can grow your LinkedIn network. You find out some guidelines to keep in mind when growing your network. I also cover various search tools for you to use to stay on top of LinkedIn's growing membership and how others may relate to you.

Of course, to expand your network, you need to know how to send Invitations as well as how to attract LinkedIn members and your contacts who haven't yet taken the plunge into LinkedIn membership. I cover all that here, too. And finally, this chapter helps you deal with the etiquette of accepting or declining Invitations that you receive, and shows you how to remove connections that you no longer want to keep in your network.

An *Invitation* is when you invite a colleague or friend of yours to join LinkedIn and stay connected to you as part of your network. An *Introduction* is when you ask a first-degree connection to introduce you to one of her connections so you can get to know them better. I cover Introductions in more depth in Chapter 5, while Invitations are covered right here.

Building a Meaningful Network

When you build a house, you start with some blueprints. When you start an organization, you usually have some sort of mission statement or guiding principles. Likewise, when you start to grow your LinkedIn network, you should keep in mind some of the keys to having and growing your own professional network. These guiding principles will help you make decisions regarding whom to invite to your network, whom to search for and introduce yourself to, and how much time to spend on LinkedIn.

Undoubtedly, you've heard of the highly popular social networking sites Facebook and MySpace. LinkedIn is different from these sites because it focuses on business networking in a professional manner rather than encouraging users to post pictures of their latest beach party. The best use of LinkedIn involves maintaining a professional network of connections, not sending someone a Super Hug.

That said, you'll find variety in the types of networks that people maintain on LinkedIn, and much of that has to do with each person's definition of a meaningful network:

- **Quality versus quantity:** As I mention in Chapter 1, some people use LinkedIn with the goal of gaining the highest number of connections possible, thereby emphasizing quantity over the quality of their LinkedIn connections. Those people are typically referred to as LinkedIn open networkers (LIONs). At the other end of the spectrum are people who use LinkedIn only to keep their closest, most tightly knit connections together without striving to enlarge their network. Most people fall somewhere in between these two aims, and the question of whether you're after quality or quantity is something to keep in mind every time you look to invite someone. LinkedIn strongly recommends connecting only with people you know, so its advice is to stick to quality connections. Here are some questions to ask yourself to help you figure out your purpose: Are you looking to

  • Manage a network of *only* people you personally know?

  • Manage a network of people you know or who might help you find new opportunities in a specific industry?

  • Maximize your chances of being able to reach someone with a new opportunity or job offering, regardless of personal interaction?

✓ **Depth versus breadth:** Some people want to focus on building a network of only the most relevant or new connections — people from their
current job or industry who could play a role in one's professional
development in that particular industry. Other people like to include a
wide diversity of connections that include anyone they have ever professionally interacted with, whether through work, education, or any kind
of group or association, in hopes that anyone who knows them at all
can potentially lead to future opportunities. For these LinkedIn users,
it doesn't matter that most of the people in their network don't know
99 percent of their other connections. Most people fall somewhere in
between these two poles but lean toward including more people in their
network. Here are some questions to keep in mind regarding this question: Do you want to

- Build or maintain a specific in-depth network of thought leaders
  regarding one topic, job, or industry?

- Build a broad network of connections that can help you with different aspects of your career or professional life?

- Add only people to your network who may offer an immediate benefit to some aspect of your professional life?

- Add a professional contact now and figure out later how that
  person might fit with your long-term goals?

✓ **Strong versus weak link:** I'm not referring to the game show "The
Weakest Link" but rather to the strength of your connection with someone. Beyond the issue of quality versus quantity, you'll want to keep
differing levels of quality in mind. Some people invite someone after
meeting him once at a cocktail party, hoping to strengthen the link as
time goes on. Others work to create strong links first and then invite
those people to connect on LinkedIn afterward. This issue comes down
to how much you want LinkedIn itself to play a role in your business
network's development: meaning, do you see your LinkedIn network as a
work in progress or as a virtual room in which to gather only your closest allies? Here are some questions to keep in mind:

- What level of interaction needs to have occurred for you to feel
  comfortable asking someone to connect to you on LinkedIn? A
  face-to-face meeting? Phone conversations only? A stream of
  e-mails?

- What length of time do you need to know someone before you feel
  that you can connect to him or her? Or, does time matter less if
  you have had a high-quality interaction just once?

- Does membership in a specific group or association count as a
  good enough reference for you to add someone to your network?
  (For example, say you met someone only briefly once, but he is a
  school alum: Does that tie serve as a sufficient reference?)

✓ **Specific versus general goals:** Some people like to maintain a strong network of people mainly to talk about work and job-related issues. Other people like to discuss all matters relating to their network, whether it's professional, personal, or social. Most people fall somewhere in between, and herein lies what I mean by the "purpose" of your network. Do you want to simply catalog your entire network, regardless of industry, because LinkedIn will act as your complete contact management system and because you can use LinkedIn to reach different parts of your network at varying times? Or do you want to focus your LinkedIn network on a specific goal, using your profile to attract and retain the "right kind" of contact that furthers that goal? Here are some more questions to ask yourself:

- Do you have any requirements in mind for someone before you add him to your network? That is, are you looking to invite only people with certain qualities or experience?

- Does the way you know or met someone influence your decision to connect to that person on LinkedIn?

- What information do you need to know about someone before you want to add him to your network?

By the way, this has not been a quiz — there is no one right answer to any of these questions. You decide what you want to accomplish through your LinkedIn network, and how you want to go from there. Also keep in mind that although you might start LinkedIn with one goal in mind, as with most other things in life, your usage and experience might shift you to a different way of using the site. If that happens, just go with it, as long as it fits with your current goals.

After you establish why you want to link to other people, you can start looking for and reaching out to those people. In the next section, I point you to a number of linking strategies that can help you reach your goals for your network. When you start on LinkedIn, completing your profile (see Chapter 3) helps you get your first round of connections, and you're prompted to enter whatever names you could remember to offer an Invitation for them to connect with you. Now you're ready to generate your next round of connections, and to get into the habit of making this a continual process as you use the site.

Checking for LinkedIn Members

When you fill out your LinkedIn profile, you create an opportunity to check for colleagues and classmates as well as import any potential contact and invite that person to connect with you and stay in touch using LinkedIn. However, that search happens only after you define your profile (and when you update or add to your profile). After that, it's up to you to routinely check the LinkedIn network to look for new members on the site who might want to connect with you or with whom you might want to connect. Fortunately, LinkedIn provides a few tools that help you quickly scan the system to see whether a recently joined member is a past colleague or classmate of yours. In addition, it never hurts to use your friends to check for new members, as I discuss in a little bit.

Every time you send an Invitation to someone, one of the following functions might pop up automatically. Feel free to click the link and take advantage of the reminder to keep your network current.

Finding newly added colleagues

If you've worked at least one job in a medium-size or large company, you're probably familiar with the concept of the farewell lunch. The staff goes out to lunch, reminiscences about the good old days, and wishes the departing employee well as that person gives out her e-mail address and phone number, and pledges to keep in touch. But as time goes on, jobs change, people move around, and it's easy to lose touch with that co-worker. Thankfully, LinkedIn allows you to stay connected regardless of moves.

Sometimes people you've fallen out of contact with have joined LinkedIn since the last time you checked, so do an occasional search to see whether you know any newly added colleagues.

When you want to search for colleagues (and add them to your network, if you choose), just follow these steps:

1. **While logged in to your LinkedIn account, click the Add Connections link at the top right of the screen.**

2. **In the Add Connections window that opens, click the Colleagues tab next to the Add Connections tab below the top navigation bar.**

   The Colleagues window, shown in Figure 6-1, appears.

3. **Pick an employer (current or past) from the list.**

   If you've never searched this employer, you see one button entitled "View All <Company Name> Colleagues, as Figure 6-1 shows under Net2Auction. If you've already searched this employer, not only do you see the last time you checked for colleagues (to the right of the employer name), but you see two buttons: Find New and View All. To check for just the latest additions, click the yellow Find New button. Clicking the Find New button under Waterside Productions, for example, brings up the new colleagues list shown in Figure 6-2.

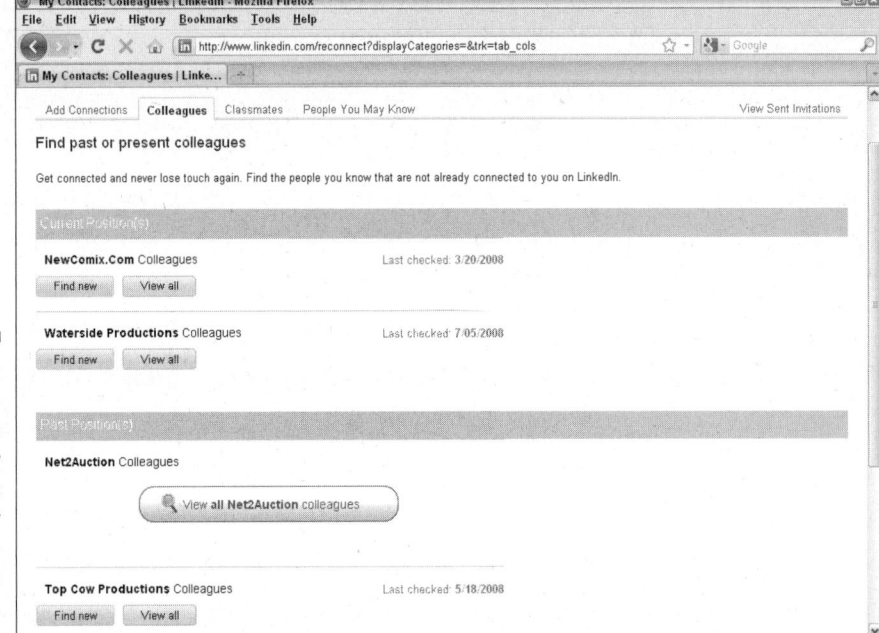

Figure 6-1:
The
Colleagues
window
shows
whether
former col-
leagues are
on LinkedIn.

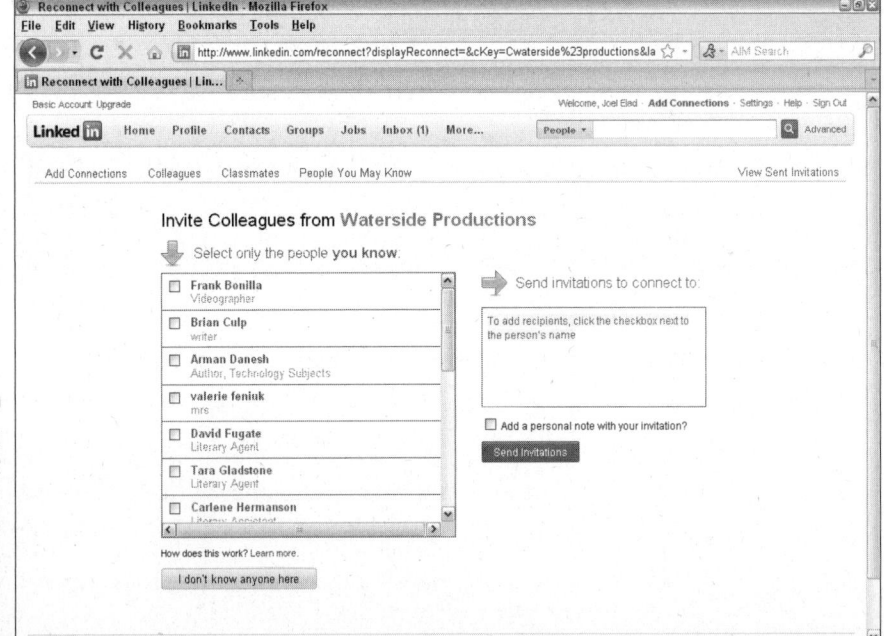

Figure 6-2:
A list
of former
colleagues
who are
now on
LinkedIn.

4. **Go through the list of names to see names you recognize or wish to connect with via LinkedIn.**

   Click a name to see the person's profile for more information. If you want to invite someone to your network, select the check box next to the person's name, and it appears in the Send Invitations to Connect To field, as shown in Figure 6-3.

   I encourage you to select the Add a Personal Note with Your Invitation? check box and add some text to help the contact remember who you are.

5. **Click the blue Send Invitations button.**

   Each person on your list receives an Invitation to join your network. If you don't know or want to invite anyone on the list, click the gray I Don't Know Anyone Here button to cancel the entire process. You'll see up to 50 names; if you don't see any company names on this page, you didn't add any companies to your profile.

Finding newly added classmates

No matter how much time goes by since I graduated from college, I still remember my school years well. I met a lot of cool and interesting people, folks I wanted to stay in contact with because of common goals, interests, or experiences. As time progressed and people moved on to new lives after graduation, it was all too easy to lose touch and not be able to reconnect.

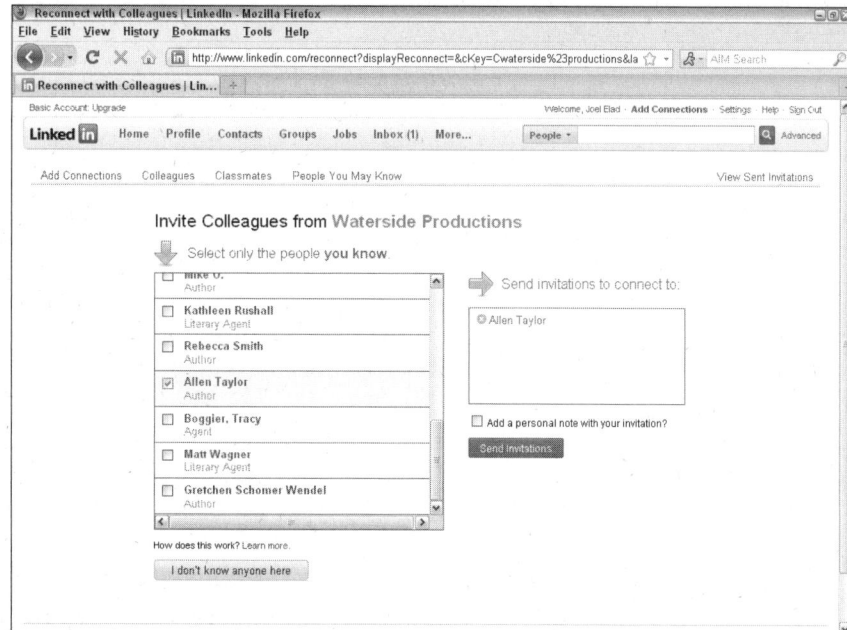

Figure 6-3:
Invite one or more colleagues to your network.

Through LinkedIn, though, you can reconnect with them and maintain that tie through your network, no matter where anyone moves on to. For you to find them to begin with, of course, your former classmates have to properly list their dates of receiving education. And, just as with the search for former colleagues, it's important to do an occasional search to see what classmates recently joined LinkedIn.

To search for classmates — and to add them to your network, if you want — just follow these steps:

1. **While logged in to your LinkedIn account, click the Add Connections link at the top right of your screen.**

2. **In the Add Connections window that opens, click the Classmates tab.**

   The Classmates window appears, as shown in Figure 6-4. If it's blank, you haven't yet added any education entries to your profile. (I discuss how to add education information to your profile in Chapter 3.)

3. **Look over the list of schools and click the name you want.**

   A list of potential classmates comes up, as shown in Figure 6-5.

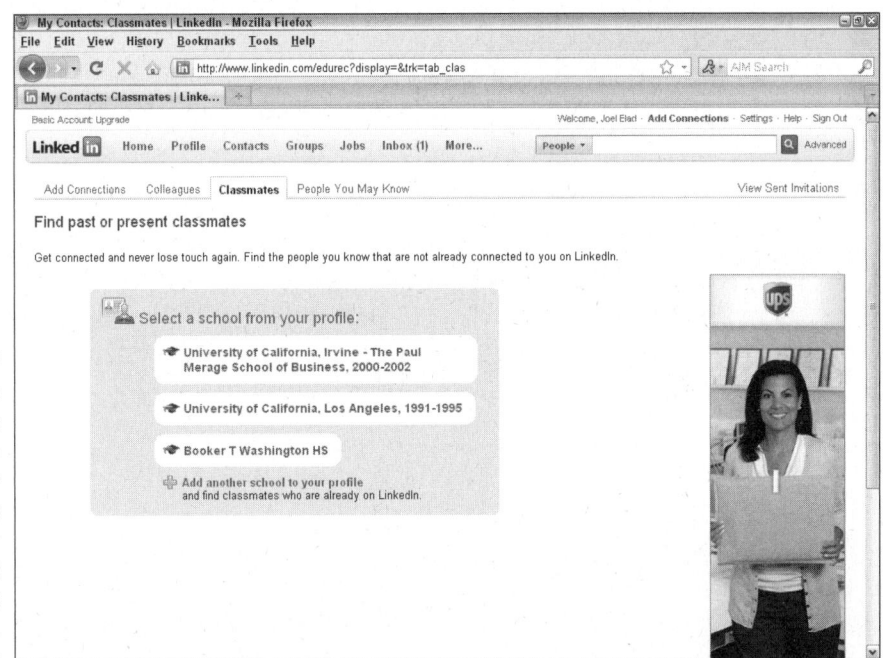

Figure 6-4:
The schools you identified in your profile appear in the Classmates window.

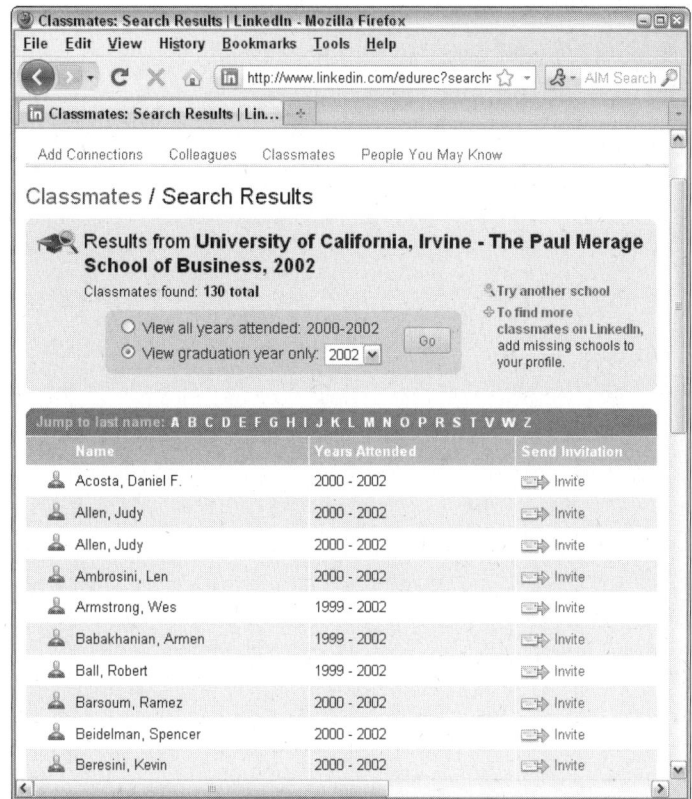

Figure 6-5:
Find former
classmates
on LinkedIn.

4. Go through the list of names.

You can view this list by graduation year only (which means you see only people who graduated the same year as you), or you can switch the view to all the years you attended the school by selecting that radio button. When you find someone to reach out to, click the Invite link you see on the same line as the person's name (it's there in the Send Invitation column) in order to bring up an Invitation for that person, as shown in Figure 6-6.

Before you invite people, click their name to read their profiles and see what they've been doing. Why ask them what they've been doing when you can read it for yourself? By doing your homework first, your Invitation will sound more natural and be more likely to be accepted.

5. Write a personal Invitation (using the one in Figure 6-6 as an example, if you need some ideas) and click the blue Send Invitation button.

Your Invitation is sent, and a page appears like the one shown in Figure 6-7. To invite more classmates, simply click the yellow Find Classmates button and repeat Steps 3 and 4.

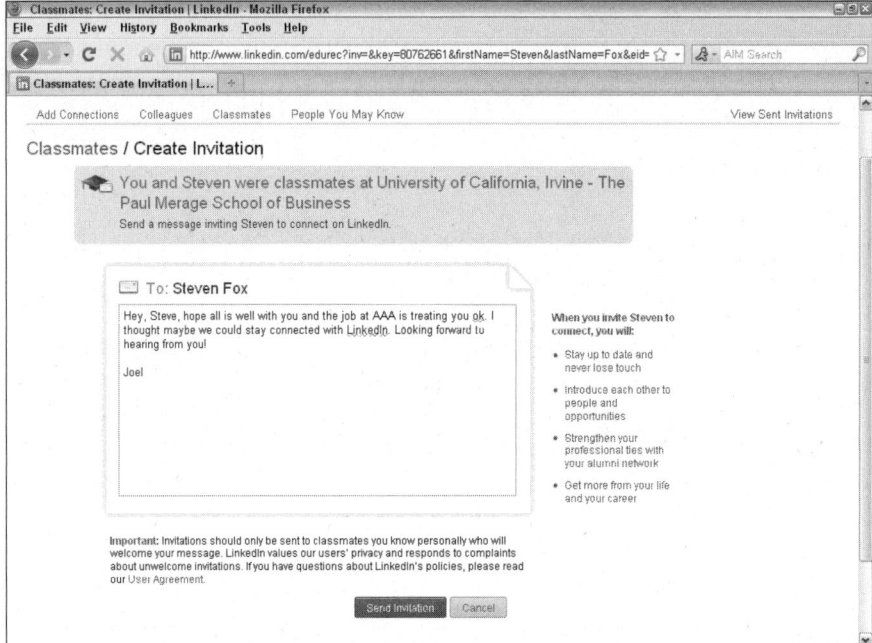

Figure 6-6:
Invite an old
classmate
to network
with you!

I cover more about sending Invitations later in this chapter, in the "Sending Connection Requests" section.

Here's another way to keep on top of newly added colleagues and classmates. Go to your LinkedIn home page and scroll to the very bottom of the page to find Just Joined LinkedIn section. Here, you can find links that take you to see how many new colleagues and classmates joined LinkedIn since the last time you logged on to the site. You can click each link (of past jobs or schools) to view the names of these people.

Browsing your connections' networks

Although it's helpful for LinkedIn to help you search the network, sometimes nothing gives as good results as some good old-fashioned investigation. From time to time, I like to browse the network of one of my first-degree connections to see whether he has a contact that should be a part of my network. I don't recommend spending a lot of your time this way, but a "spot check" by picking a few friends at random can yield some nice results.

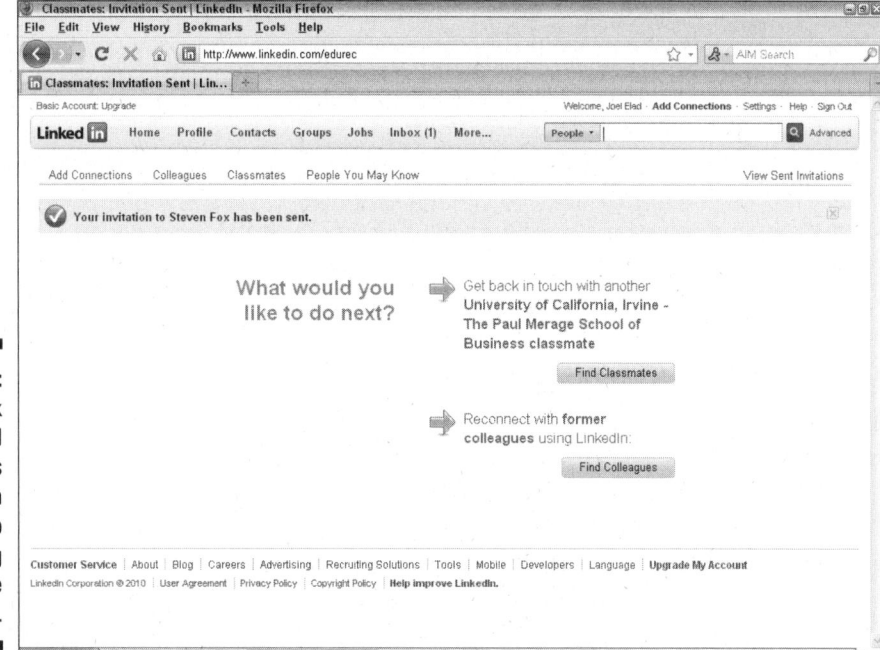

Figure 6-7:
Click
the Find
Classmates
button
to keep
searching
for more
people.

Why is this type of research effective? Lots of reasons, including these:

- ✔ **You travel in the same circles.** If someone is a part of your network, you know that person from a past experience, whether you worked together, learned together, spoke at a conference together, or lived next door to each other. Whatever that experience was, you and this contact spent time with other people, so chances are you will have shared connections — or, better yet, you will find people in that person's network who need to be a part of your network.

- ✔ **You might find someone newly connected.** Say that you've already spent some time searching all your undergraduate alumni contacts and adding as many people as you could find. As time passes, someone new may connect to one of your friends.

One effective way to keep updated about who your connections have recently added is to review your Network Activity (which I discuss in Chapter 1).

- ✔ **You might recognize someone whose name you didn't fully remember.** Many of us have that contact whom we feel we know well, have fun talking to, and consider more than just an acquaintance, but for some reason, you can't remember that person's last name. Then, for some reason, when you search a common contact's network and see the temporarily forgotten name and job title, you suddenly remember. Now you can invite that person to join your network. Another common experience is seeing the name and job title of a contact whose last name changed after marriage.

✔ **You might see someone you've wanted to get to know better.** Have you ever watched a friend talking to someone whom you wanted to add to your network? Maybe your friend already introduced you, so the other person knows your name, but you consider this person a casual acquaintance at best. When you see that person's name listed in your friend's LinkedIn network, you can take the opportunity to deepen that connection. Having a friend in common who can recommend you can help smooth the way.

To browse the network of one of your connections, follow these steps:

1. **Click the Contacts link from the top navigation bar, and then choose My Connections from the menu that appears to bring up your network.**

2. **Click the name of a first-degree connection.**

   Alternatively, search for the name via the search box on the home page. Then, on the search results page, click the name you want.

   When perusing the person's profile, look for a link next to the word `Connections` below the name and professional headline: something like `58 connections`. If you see the number of connections but those words aren't hyperlinked, you can't proceed with this process because that person has chosen to make their connection list private. If that's the case, you need to select a different first-degree connection.

3. **Click the Connections link of the first-degree connection.**

   For the example in these steps, I picked a friend and associate, Michael Wellman, of the Comic Bug in Redondo Beach, California, and his connection list is shown in Figure 6-8.

4. **Look through the list to see whether you'd like to send an Invitation to anyone. If so, click the person's name to pull up his profile.**

   When I scan through Mike's list, I notice that his wife, Carol Mendolsohn, is in his network. I spoke with her once about some questions she had regarding search engine optimization (SEO), so I clicked her name to bring up her profile, which is shown in Figure 6-9.

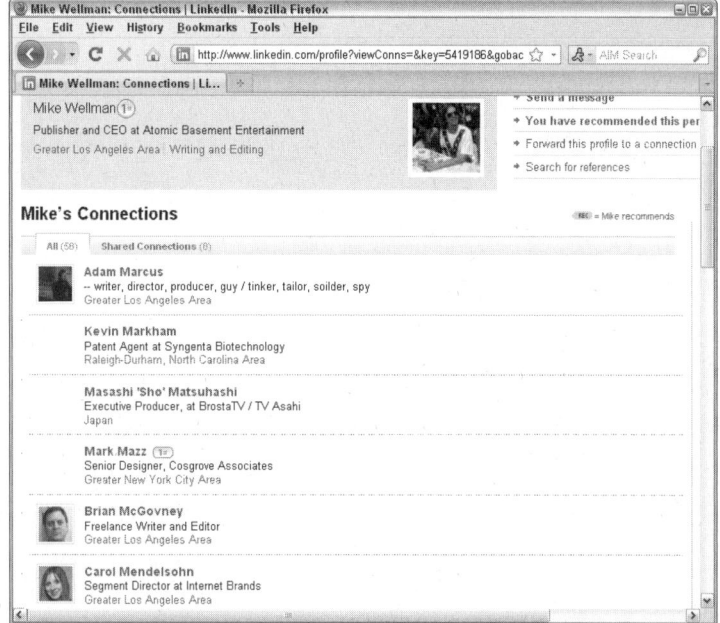

5. **Click the Add *Person's Name* to Your Network link, which appears at the top right of the page.**

   The Invitation page appears, as shown in Figure 6-10.

6. **Select the option that best describes your connection to this person or provide the person's e-mail address.**

   In some cases, you might have to input the person's e-mail address to help prove that you actually know the person. In other cases, like in Figure 6-10, you simply have to indicate whether you're a colleague, classmate, business partner, or friend, or have another association with this person. It's a good idea to enter some text in the Include a Personal Note field. This text customizes your Invitation, and you can use it to remind the person of you and why you'd like to connect.

7. **Click the blue Send button.**

   Presto! You're all done.

The Add Carol to Your Network link

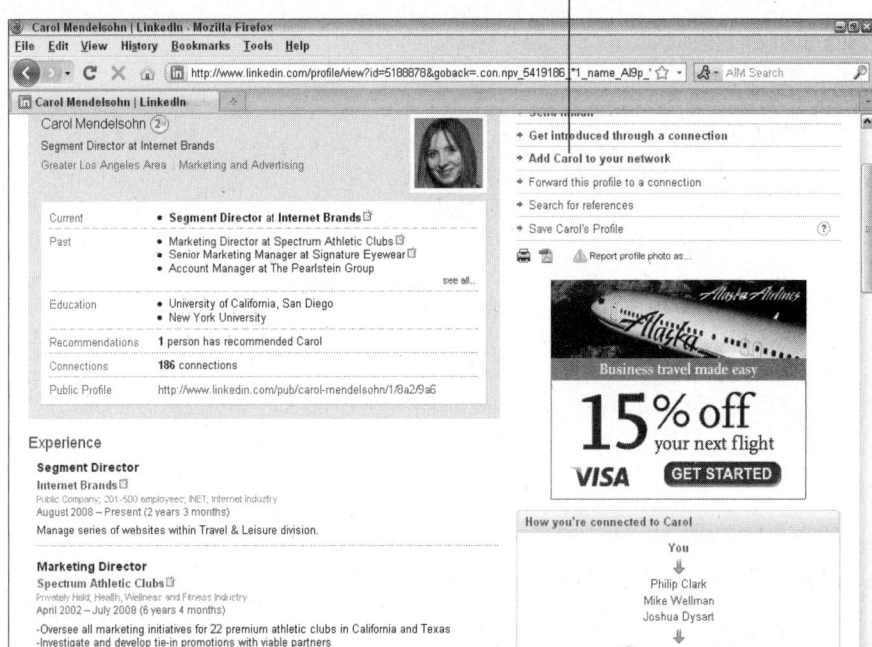

Figure 6-9:
Pull up the
person's
profile to
add her
to your
network.

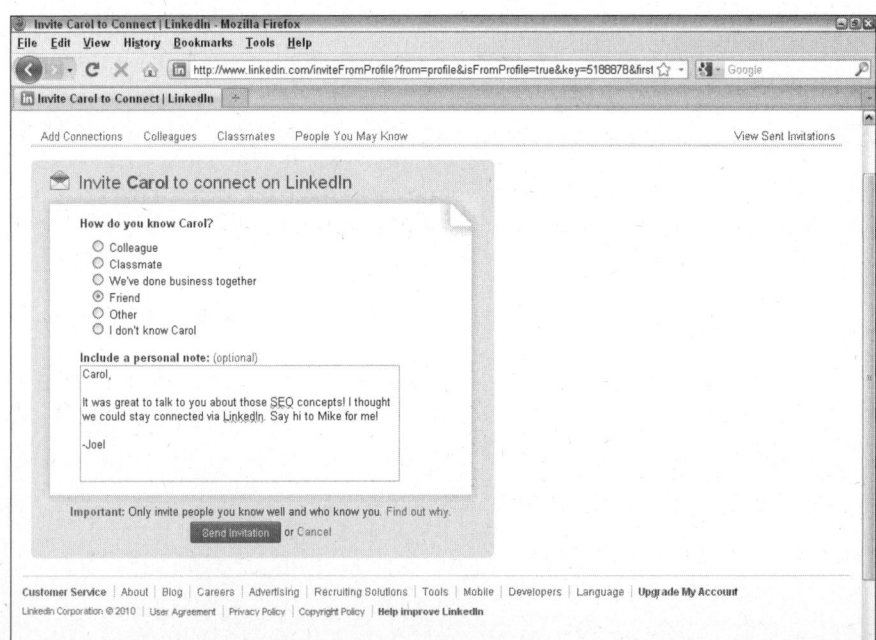

Figure 6-10:
Send a
custom
Invitation to
your new
contact.

Sending Connection Requests

You can check out previous sections of this chapter to find out how to use LinkedIn to search the entire user network and find people you want to invite to join your personal network. In the following sections, I focus on sending out the Invitation, including how to go about inviting people who haven't yet decided to join LinkedIn.

Sending requests to existing members

When you're on a LinkedIn page and spot the name of a member whom you want to invite to your network, you can follow these steps to send that person a Connection Request to add him to your network:

1. **Click the person's name to go to his profile page.**

   You might find people to invite using one of the methods described in the "Checking for LinkedIn Members" section earlier this chapter. You might also find them while browsing LinkedIn Answers (which I cover in more detail in Chapter 7) or the advanced people search, which I cover in Chapter 4. Figure 6-11 shows the profile page of a LinkedIn member.

Click here to add a person to your network.

Figure 6-11: Adding a person to your network from that person's profile page.

2. **Click the Add *Person's Name* to your Network link (where *Person's Name* is, of course, the real name of the person you're adding).**

   The Invitation page appears, as shown in Figure 6-12.

3. **From the list of connection reasons, choose the option that best describes your relationship to this person.**

   You might have to input the person's e-mail address to help prove that you actually know the person. If you select the I Don't Know *Person's Name* option, LinkedIn will deny the request, so keep that in mind. If you pick a category such as Colleague or Classmate, LinkedIn displays a drop-down list of options based on your profile. For example, if you pick Colleague, LinkedIn displays a drop-down list of your positions. You need to pick the position you held when you knew this person.

4. **Enter your Invitation text in the Include a Personal Note field.**

   I highly recommend that you compose a custom Invitation rather than use the standard text, "I'd like to add you to my professional network on LinkedIn." In my example in Figure 6-12, I remind the person how we recently met, acknowledge one of his achievements, and ask him to connect.

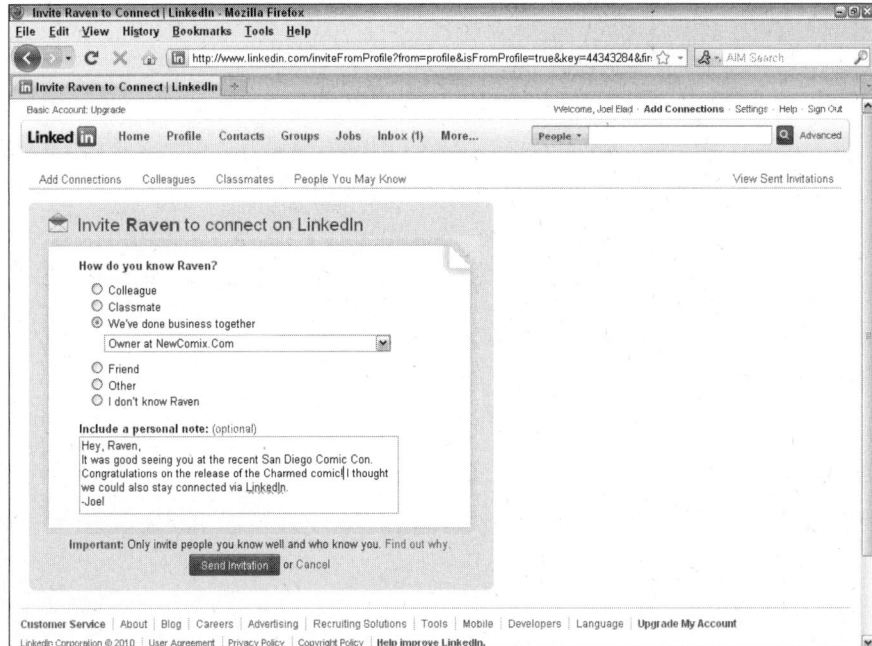

Figure 6-12: Here is where you can invite someone to connect with you.

5. **Click the blue Send Invitation button.**

   You'll be notified by e-mail when the other party accepts your connection request.

Why you shouldn't use canned Invitations

You might be very tempted to look at the "canned" Invitation that LinkedIn displays when you go to the Invitation Request page, especially if you're having a rough or busy day, and just send off the Invitation without adding to or replacing the canned Invitation with some custom text. We all have things to do and goals to accomplish, so stopping to write a note for each Invitation can grow tedious. However, it's becoming increasingly important, for the following reasons, to replace that text with something that speaks to the recipient:

✔ **The other person might not remember you.** Quite simply, your recipient can take one look at your name, see no additional information in the note that accompanied it, and think, "Who is that guy (or gal)?" A few might click your name to read your profile and try to figure it out, but most people are busy and won't take the time to investigate. They are likely to ignore your request. Not good.

✔ **The other person could report you as someone he doesn't know.** Having someone ignore your request isn't the worst possibility, though. Nope, the worst is being declined as unknown. Recipients of your Invitation see an I Don't Know This Person button. If several people click this button from an Invitation you sent, LinkedIn will consider you a spammer and will suspend you — and possibly even remove your profile and account from the site!

✔ **You offer no motivation for a mutually beneficial relationship.** When people get an Invitation request, they understand pretty clearly that you want something from them, whether it's access to them or to their network. If you've sent a canned Invitation, what they can't answer is the question, "What is in it for me?" A canned Invitation gives no motivation for or potential benefit of being connected to you. A custom note explaining that you'd love to swap resources or introduce them to others is usually enough to encourage an acceptance.

✔ **A canned Invite implies you don't care.** Some people will look at your Invitation request with a canned Invitation and think, "This person doesn't have 30 to 60 seconds to write a quick note introducing herself? She must not think much of me." That impression will quickly kill your chances of getting more connections.

Sending requests to nonmembers

Only members of LinkedIn can be part of anyone's network. Therefore, if you want to send a Connection Request to someone who hasn't yet joined LinkedIn, you must invite that person to create a LinkedIn account first. To do so, you can either send your invitee an e-mail directly, asking him to join, or you can use a LinkedIn function that generates the e-mail Invitation that includes a link to join LinkedIn.

Either way, you need to have the nonmember's e-mail address, and you'll probably have to provide your invitee with some incentive by offering reasons to take advantage of LinkedIn and create an account. (I give you some tips for doing that in the next section of this chapter.)

When you're ready to send your request using LinkedIn, just follow these steps:

1. **Click the Add Connections link at the top right of the LinkedIn home page.**

   The Add Connections window appears.

2. **Fill in the e-mail addresses of the people you want to invite to LinkedIn, as shown in Figure 6-13.**

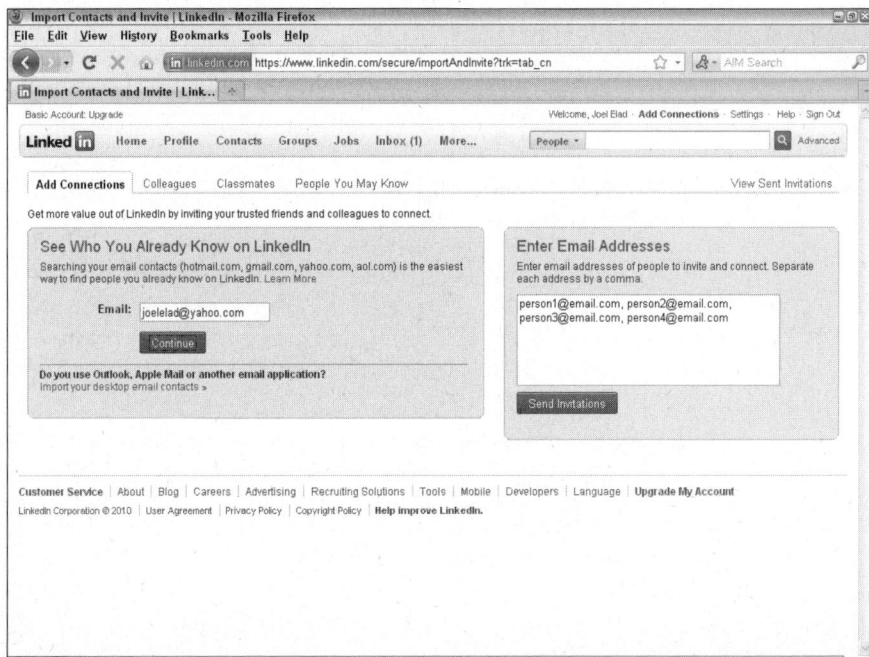

Figure 6-13: Fill in the e-mail addresses of anyone you want to invite to LinkedIn.

3. Click the blue Send Invitations button.

You're returned to the Add Connections page, where you see a green confirmation message. From here, you can invite additional people to your network.

Communicating the value of joining LinkedIn

So you want to add some people to your LinkedIn network, but they haven't yet taken the plunge of signing up for the site. If you want them to accept your request by setting up their account, you might need to tout the value of LinkedIn to your contact. After all, recommendations are one of the most powerful sales tools, which is why all types of businesses — from e-commerce stores and retail businesses to service directories and social networking Web sites — use recommendations so often.

Because LinkedIn (as of this writing) does not allow you to personalize your invitation to nonmembers (as I cover in the previous section), you will need to make this pitch either via e-mail or directly with the person you are recruiting.

So, how do you make the "sale"? (I use that term figuratively, of course. And as you know, a basic LinkedIn account is free — a feature that you should definitely not neglect to mention to your invitees!) If you send a super-long thesis on the merits of LinkedIn, it'll most likely be ignored. If you send a simple "C'mon! You know you wanna. . . ." request, that might or might not work. (You know your friends better than me.) You could buy them a copy of this book, but that could get expensive. (But I would be thrilled! C'mon! You know you wanna. . . .) The simplest way is to mention some of the benefits they could enjoy from joining the site, such as

- ✔ **LinkedIn members always stay in touch with their connections.** If people you know move, change their e-mail addresses, or change jobs, you still have a live link to them via LinkedIn. You'll always be able to see their new e-mail addresses if you're connected (assuming that they provide it, of course).

- ✔ **LinkedIn members can tap in to their friends' networks for jobs or opportunities, now or later.** Although someone might not need a job now, she will eventually need help, so why not access thousands or millions of potential leads? LinkedIn has tens of millions of members in all sorts of industries, and people have obtained consulting leads, contract jobs, new careers, and even startup venture capital or funding for a new film! After all, it's all about "who you know."

✔ **LinkedIn can help you build your own brand.** LinkedIn members get a free profile page to build their online presence, and can to link to up to three of their own Web sites, such as a blog, personal Web site, or e-commerce store. The search engines love LinkedIn pages, which have high page rankings — and this can only be a boost to your online identity.

✔ **LinkedIn can help you do all sorts of research.** You might need to know more about a company before an interview, or you're looking for a certain person to help your business, or you're curious what people's opinions would be regarding an idea you have. LinkedIn is a great resource in all these situations. You can use LinkedIn to get free advice and information, all from the comfort of your own computer.

✔ **A basic LinkedIn account is free, and joining LinkedIn is easy.** There are a lot of misconceptions that users have to pay a monthly fee or spend a lot of time updating their LinkedIn profiles. Simply remind people that joining is free, and after they set up their profiles, LinkedIn is designed to take up very little of their time to keep an active profile and get some usefulness from having an account there.

Removing people from your network

The day might come when you feel you need to remove someone from your network. Perhaps you added the person in haste, or he repeatedly asks you for favors or Introduction requests, or sends messages that you don't want to respond to. Not to worry — you're not doomed to suffer forever; simply remove the connection. When you do so, that person can no longer view your network or send you messages, unless he pays to send you an InMail message.

To remove a connection from your network, just follow these steps:

1. **While logged in to your LinkedIn account, click the Contacts link from the top navigation bar and then choose My Connections from the menu that appears to bring up your list of connections.**

2. **Click the Remove Connections link that appears on the right side of the page, as shown in Figure 6-14.**

Figure 6-14:
Removing
connec-
tions.

3. **On the Remove Connections page that appears, select the check box next to the name of anyone in your connections list whom you want to remove, as shown in Figure 6-15.**

   Any names you select appear on the right side of the page under Remove These Connections, as shown in Figure 6-16.

4. **Click the Remove Connections button to remove them from your network.**

   Your removed connections won't be notified of the removal.

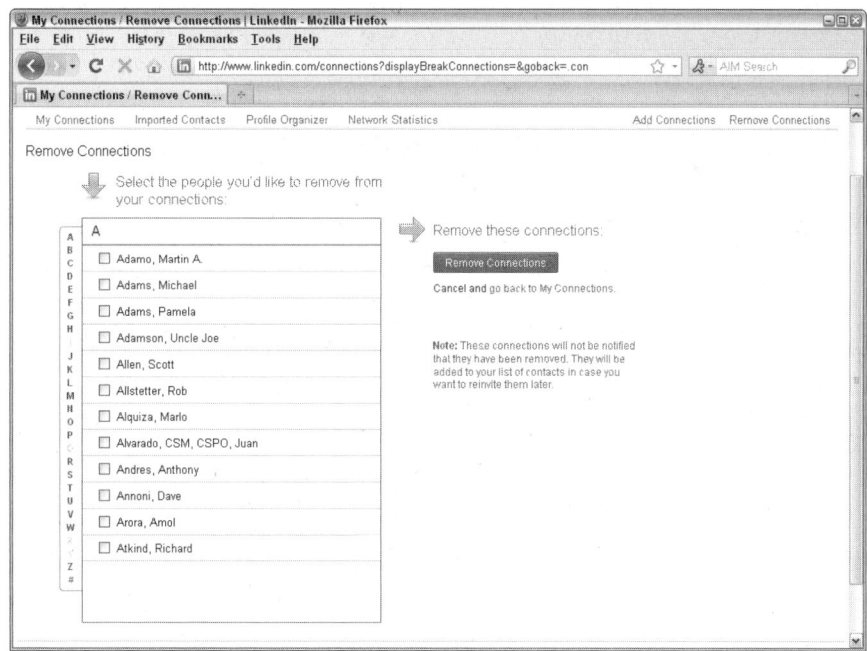

Figure 6-15:
Select the
contacts
you want to
remove.

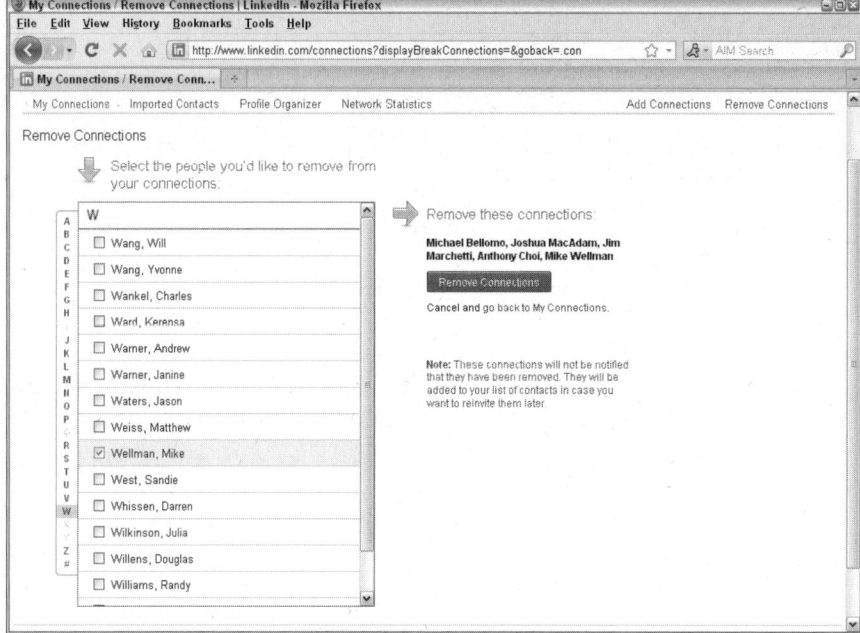

Figure 6-16:
Make sure
to select all
the names
you want to
remove.

Accepting Invitations (Or Gracefully Declining)

In this chapter, I talk a lot about how and why you might send Invitations and add people to your network, and even cover what to do when you need to remove someone from your network. But what about the flip side of that coin — that is, being the invitee? In this section, I offer some guidance on what to do when you're faced with an Invitation, and you have to decide whether to happily accept or gracefully decline it.

When you receive an Invitation to join someone's network of connections and you're not whether to accept or decline the Invitation, ask yourself these questions:

✔ **How well do you know this person?** With any luck, the inviter has included a custom message clueing you in to who she is, in case you don't remember. You can, of course, click the name to read that person's profile, which usually helps trigger your memory. If you don't know or remember this person, you probably don't want to add him to your network just yet. If you do know him, you need to consider whether he's worth adding to your network.

✔ **Does this person fit with the goals of your network?** As I mention early in this chapter, it's easier to put together a network when you've established a sense of the purpose you want it to serve. When you're looking at this Invitation, simply ask yourself, "Does accepting this Invitation help further my goals?"

✔ **Is this someone with whom you want to communicate and include in your network?** If you don't like someone or don't want to do business with him, you should certainly not feel obligated to accept the Invitation. Keep in mind that these people will have access to your network and can hit you up with Introduction and Recommendation requests (see Chapters 5 and 8, respectively).

If you're thinking of declining an Invitation, here are some tips to help you do so gracefully:

✔ **Respond quickly.** If you wait to respond to the Invitation and then decide to go ahead and decline the invite, the other person might be even more offended and confused. Respond quickly so that this issue isn't hanging over anyone's head.

✔ **If necessary, ask for more information.** If you feel uncomfortable because you don't know the person well but want to consider the invitation before you decline, respond with a request for more information, such as, "I appreciate your interest, but I am having trouble placing our previous meetings. What is your specific interest in connecting with me on LinkedIn? Please let me know how we know each other and what your goals are for LinkedIn. Thanks again."

✔ **Respond politely but with a firm no.** You can simply write something along the lines of, "Thank you for your interest; I appreciate your eagerness. Unfortunately, because I'm not familiar with you, I'm not interested in connecting with you on LinkedIn just yet." Then, if you want, you can spell out the terms on which you might be interested in connecting, such as if the opportunity ever arises to get to know the person better or if he is referred to you by a friend.

Chapter 7

Using LinkedIn Answers

*I*f you believe the phrase, "Knowledge is power," you'll find the LinkedIn Answers feature to be a very powerful tool. Imagine being able to ask your network or the entire LinkedIn network a question and draw on the expertise and experiences of a potential pool of tens of millions of users. This is exactly what LinkedIn Answers was designed for, and it's a free service available to any LinkedIn user!

In this chapter, I discuss how to use LinkedIn Answers properly. I start by helping you find questions you can answer, and then I walk you through how to put together an answer and post it on the LinkedIn Answers site. Then, I shift gears and focus on the ability to ask questions. You find out how to phrase your question, determine what kind of information is the best to request, and then post your question.

How LinkedIn Helps You Find Answers to Your Questions

The goal of LinkedIn Answers is to allow professionals to exchange expertise. Now, upon hearing that, your first question might be: "Well, what kind of question can I ask on LinkedIn Answers?" LinkedIn members have a lot of personal and professional experiences to share, so there's no end to the questions you can pose. Plus, the network makes it easy to organize and gather information.

You should *not* use LinkedIn Answers to simply forge connections, create a personal advertisement, or run a group poll. Users can flag inappropriate questions, which moderators can then review and possibly remove from the site. If your questions keep getting flagged, you won't be able to use this feature anymore. Inappropriate questions include asking for direct contact, posting just an advertisement for your business, or posting inappropriate content not suitable for public viewing.

Therefore, to encourage an orderly and productive exchange, LinkedIn organizes questions into the following categories:

- **Administration:** Do you have questions about rules and regulations? Are you putting together your small business benefits package? Or are you planning to move your business to a bigger building and need some ideas on how to pick the right facility? With topics that run from business insurance to purchasing and facilities management, you can post a question on LinkedIn and draw on expertise from company administrators, commercial real estate agents, and even customer service professionals.

- **Business Operations:** From supply chain and inventory issues to manufacturing, packaging, and quality management concerns, this category is your area to ask operations-related questions and read questions from other like-minded professionals, whether it's project management issues or something on your shop floor.

- **Business Travel:** Because many professionals still have to travel for their jobs or personal enjoyment, this category is dedicated to letting you ask all those questions about air travel, hotels, car rentals, and the different travel tools out there. Ask a question about the best place to host a business dinner in a certain city, or how people save money while booking travel on the Internet.

- **Career and Education:** Because lifelong learning and the eternal job search are two important benefits of using LinkedIn, this category is dedicated to questions for everything from resume writing, professional networks, and job searches to getting certifications and licenses, coaching, freelancing, and contracting.

- **Conferences and Event Planning:** Before you rack your brain figuring out how to plan the perfect conference or event for your company, you can use LinkedIn to ask others about this topic. This category is dedicated to questions regarding conference planning, conference venues, and event marketing and promotions. So, if you need help picking the right facility to accommodate your staff, or how to get the word out about your software development seminars, this is the place.

✔ **Finance and Accounting:** From Accounting 101 to Risk Management, anything you were afraid to ask your microeconomics professor is fair game here. Find subsections devoted to corporate debt and taxes, budgeting, and mergers and acquisitions, and your questions could be answered by an entrepreneur or a CFO from a Fortune 500 company.

✔ **Financial Markets:** This isn't the place to hope to find that next hot stock tip, but it is a great place to ask questions about different markets like the bond markets, commodity markets, currency, derivatives, and, of course, equity markets. If futures and options make your head spin, you might find some guidance here.

Just like any other category, the answers posted in the Financial Markets category are the opinions of the poster only and should not be assumed as fact. Check with your financial expert or attorney before acting on any advice you receive here.

✔ **Government and Non-Profit:** When you deal with government entities, each country has its own guidelines. Makes sense, therefore, to bounce some questions off folks who work in those arenas and benefit from their experience and guidance. Unclear about government policy? Ask a question and see whether a fellow LinkedIn member has dealt with it or can point you to the person, document, or Web site that can help.

✔ **Health:** Open wide and say, "Ahhhh." This area is more for questions regarding health administration, health care issues, public health and safety concerns, and even the work-life balance. You can even raise questions regarding environmental health issues and appeal to professionals in that area for an informed answer.

✔ **Hiring and Human Resources:** Although Donald Trump can make HR look easy with two famous words, the world of human resources is full of staffing, recruiting, policies, and benefits rules and regulations that are always changing and sometimes complex. Use the Answers section to find someone who knows his way around a 401(k) plan so you can focus on your main job.

✔ **International:** Thinking of doing business outside your country? Reach out with LinkedIn to ask questions of people who live in your target areas. Or ask questions of fellow countrymen (and women) who have entered those new areas, and find out what works and what doesn't. From customs to exporting to outsourcing, if you need to understand the ins and outs of international law you can get all the answers you need in this category.

✔ **Law and Legal:** No matter what you do in the business world (not to mention the real world), you're bound to have a legal question sooner rather than later. Whether it concerns corporate, tax, or employment/labor laws, see what fellow business owners or legal experts have to say about your legal question.

Because we're talking about the law here, we should note that any answers or advice you get here should not be construed as pure fact. In legal matters pertaining to you or your company, I recommend you consult with a licensed attorney. (There's no harm in doing your own research before hand, as long as you understand any final decisions or actions should involve a licensed attorney.)

- **Management:** When you're the boss or running your own division, tap the expertise of fellow managers when you're stuck with a question or curious about some of the newest trends or practices. This category has subsections devoted to labor relations, business analytics, and organizational development. When you have a planning or governance question, why not poll the community and see what other leaders have to say.

- **Marketing and Sales:** Still trying to sell that refrigerator to someone in the Arctic Circle? From advertising to business development to writing and sales, you can pose your question to a potential pool of millions of eager networkers and gain insight, anecdotes, and some valuable advice from marketers, salespeople, and management who might not share the same product line, but probably have faced the same issues.

- **Non-Profit:** When you deal with non-profit entities, there are plenty of rules about what the organization can and cannot do with their funds. This category is dedicated to answering your questions about topics like fundraising, managing a non-profit organization, and philanthropy as well as the growing area of social entrepreneurship. If you have a question about innovative ways to have a fundraiser event, filing for your 501(c)(3) government status with the IRS, or how you can encourage overseas entrepreneurs with small microloans, you can post something in this section.

- **Personal Finance:** If you have a question about your bank account, your investments, or your retirement goals, you can pose a question here on anything from wealth management to debt management. Odds are good that regardless of your current status, LinkedIn members can relate and share some advice or stories.

- **Product Management:** This is probably one of the most exciting categories. This category is presented to a worldwide audience, and you can now benefit from the ideas, opinions, and perspectives of potential customers and business partners. I profile one company who used this category for market research (see the sidebar "How LinkedIn made Mahalo a better search engine"), but you can also get advice on everything from positioning to pricing.

- **Professional Development:** As you grow in your career, your success will partially be determined by the amount of lifetime learning and skills development you undergo as you do your job. You have to grow your skills to keep up with new technology and new processes, and this category is dedicated to help you with topics like career management, ethics, professional books, communications and public speaking, and professional organizations.

✔ **Startups and Small Businesses:** The life of an entrepreneur can feel lonely sometimes, but now with millions of entrepreneurs all looking for the next step, you have an audience to pose questions on a wide range of issues from your business plan and incorporation steps to everyday small business concerns.

✔ **Sustainability:** A key concern for almost every business is how that business deals with their energy usage and how the company affects the environment. This category is dedicated to handling questions regarding energy and development, green business, and green eco-friendly products. If you are wondering about such concepts as carbon footprints, offset credits, or alternative energy, this is the category to post your question.

✔ **Technology:** With the ever-changing world of technology, you need to be able to get information fast without scratching your head over how to use the newest gee-whiz device in your business. You can post a question or share your knowledge about the newest, latest, and greatest software development techniques, Internet and e-commerce tips, blogging advice. You can even gain insight into ever-changing areas like biotechnology and wireless communications.

✔ **Using LinkedIn:** As LinkedIn develops and adds new functionality (and users), it's great to have a place where new members can ask questions. Questions posted here are typically answered by established members who have clicked and connected their way around LinkedIn and can offer friendly guidance to those just starting out.

Finding Questions to Answer

When you're ready to contribute some knowledge, you can start by checking out the LinkedIn Answers home page. Click the More link from the top navigation bar on any LinkedIn page, and then the Answers link from the expanded menu to get to the Answers home page. (See Figure 7-1.) This is the hub for LinkedIn Answers.

When you go to find a question to answer, you have several ways to search for one that's right for you:

✔ **Browse the Open Questions section.** Click the Answer Questions tab and browse through all open questions (see upcoming Figure 7-3), with the default sort being questions from people in your LinkedIn network.

✔ **Browse by category.** You can browse through the categories listed on the Answers home page and go through subcategories until you find a question that's right up your alley.

Answer Questions tab

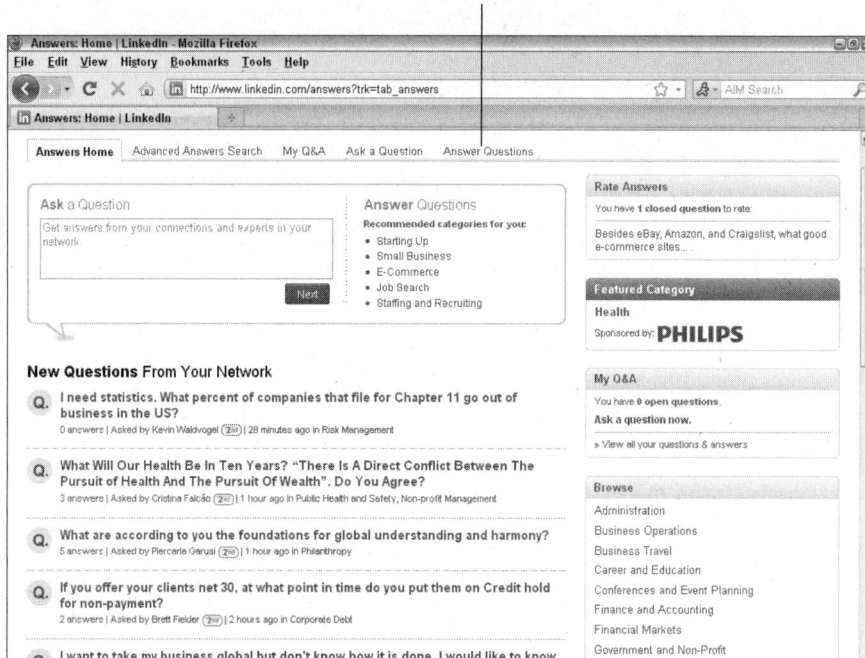

Figure 7-1:
Get all your
questions
answered
with
LinkedIn
Answers!

TIP

Each category has its own RSS feed, which you can use to monitor categories in your RSS reader or personalized home page such as My Yahoo! or iGoogle. You can find out more about RSS by searching online, or you can get more in-depth information about how to subscribe to RSS feeds (a popular activity when reading blogs) in *Blogging For Dummies,* 3rd Edition by Susannah Gardner and Shane Birley, or *Syndicating Web Sites with RSS Feeds For Dummies* by Ellen Finkelstein.

✔ **Browse questions in other languages**. LinkedIn gives you the option to answer questions in other languages besides English. If you want to answer someone in your native language of Spanish, French, German, Italian, or Portuguese, simply scroll down the screen. On the right side, below the list of categories, is the More Questions in Other Languages header. Click the appropriate language link to see the Answers page appear in that language. Follow the same instructions to answer a question using a foreign language.

✔ **Use Advanced Answers Search.** You can click the Advanced Answers Search tab and search through the Answers database (see Figure 7-2). Based on the criteria you enter on the search page, you can limit yourself to a specific category, or you can go after completely unanswered questions.

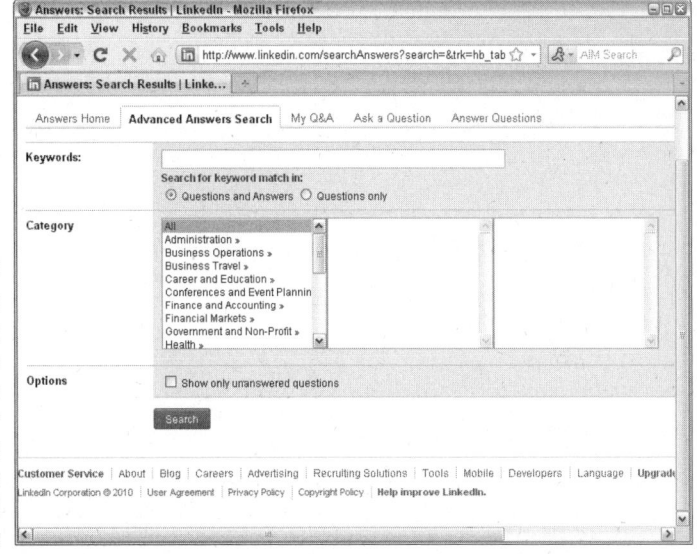

Figure 7-2:
Search
through the
Answers
database for
a question
only you can
answer!

To get a better idea of what questions are being asked and how people are answering them, spend some time looking through the list of questions. When you're ready to contribute, post your answer.

Answering a Question

As you go through LinkedIn Answers, you might see a question you'd love to contribute an answer to, whether it's to help someone avoid the same mistake you made about something, or a topic you enjoy discussing. Perhaps you want to share your knowledge, hoping the person who posed the question will want to work with you further on their problem. Whatever the reason, when you're ready to answer a question, just follow these steps:

1. **Locate a question you can answer. Click the More link from the top navigation bar on any LinkedIn page, and then the Answers link from the expanded menu to get to the Answers home page (refer to Figure 7-1).**

2. **Click the Answer Questions tab to browse the categories of open questions.**

   You see an Open Questions list, as shown in Figure 7-3.

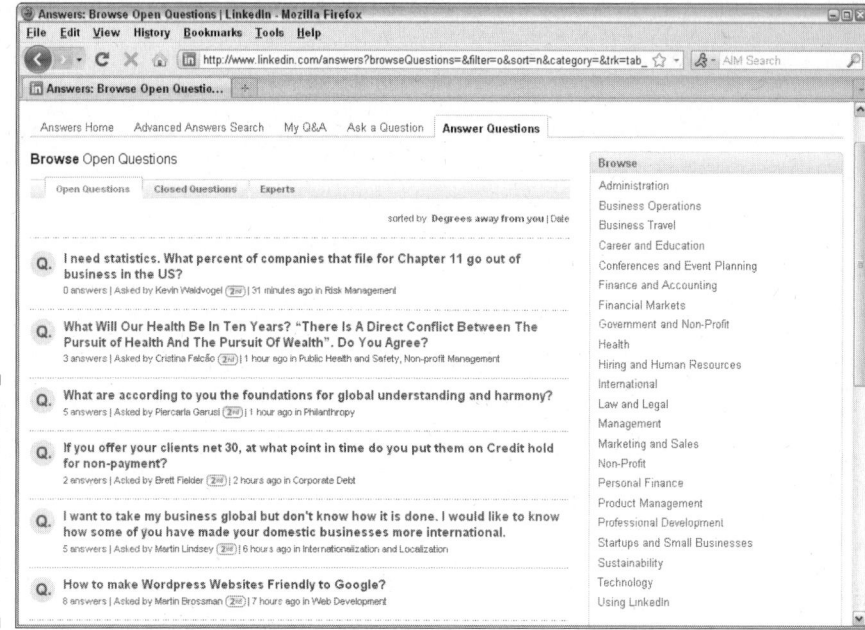

Figure 7-3:
See the
list of open
questions
waiting
for your
answer.

3. **Click a category name in the pane on the right.**

   This step narrows down the Open Questions list. Suppose you choose the Startups and Small Businesses category. You see the Open Questions list for that category, as shown in Figure 7-4. You also see a new pane of subcategories on the right.

4. **(Optional) If you need to, click a subcategory on the right to narrow down your search even further.**

5. **When you find a question you want to answer, click the link for that question.**

   This brings up the Question page, as shown in Figure 7-5. Read through the specifics of what the person is asking.

   Scroll down to see what answers, if any, have already been given. This way, you can incorporate their information into your answer so you're not repeating the same thing and you are providing new, helpful information.

6. **Click the Answer button to start preparing your response.**

   The Your Answer form smoothly pops open right in the middle of the page you're looking at, like in Figure 7-6. How's that for sleek?

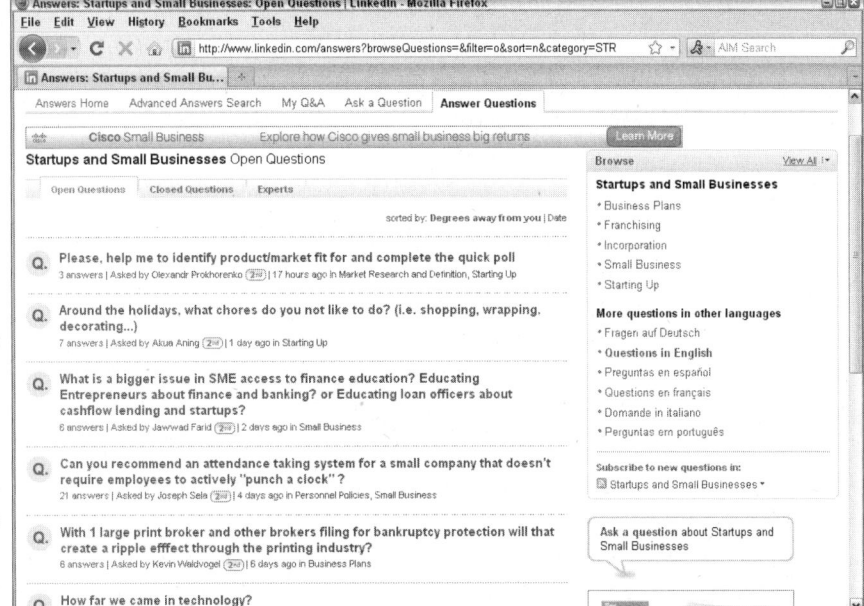

Figure 7-4:
There has
to be a
question I
can answer
somewhere
around
here.

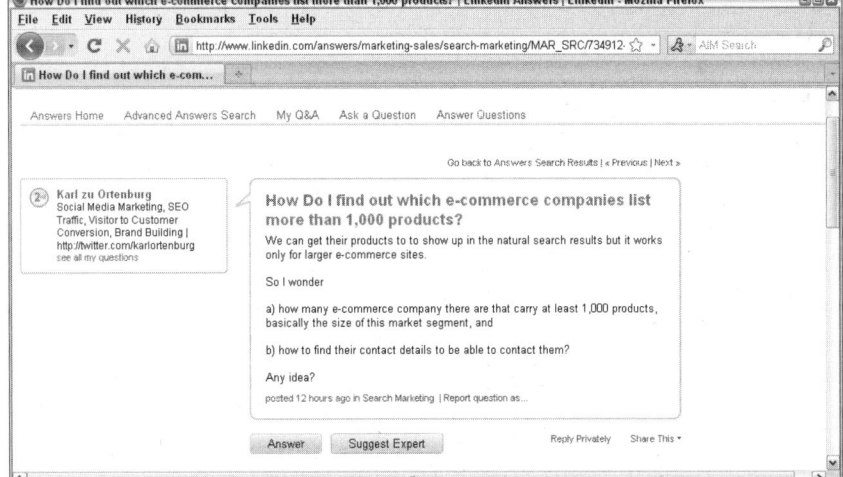

Figure 7-5:
Read
through
the entire
question
and speci-
fications
before you
provide your
answer.

If you don't see the Answer button, perhaps this question has been closed by the person who posted the question, meaning that person isn't looking for any more answers to this question. It could also be that the question automatically closed after seven days of being on LinkedIn. You can contribute to open questions only.

7. Type your response in the Your Answer text box.

Additionally, you can enter Web sites that are part of your answer. You can also suggest up to three experts who could further expand on your answer. (See the Tip right after these steps for more info on this.)

8. Click the Submit button.

You're taken back to the Question posting page, and your answer is posted along with any other answers. The person who posted the question will be notified that a new answer has been posted.

If you feel like you can't provide a quality answer but you know someone who should be able to give an expert answer, click the Select Experts button in the Your Answer form. This opens up a window (Figure 7-7 shows an example) where you can pick up to three people from your network. You can also select the check box (as shown in Figure 7-6, earlier) to write a private note to the person who posted the question.

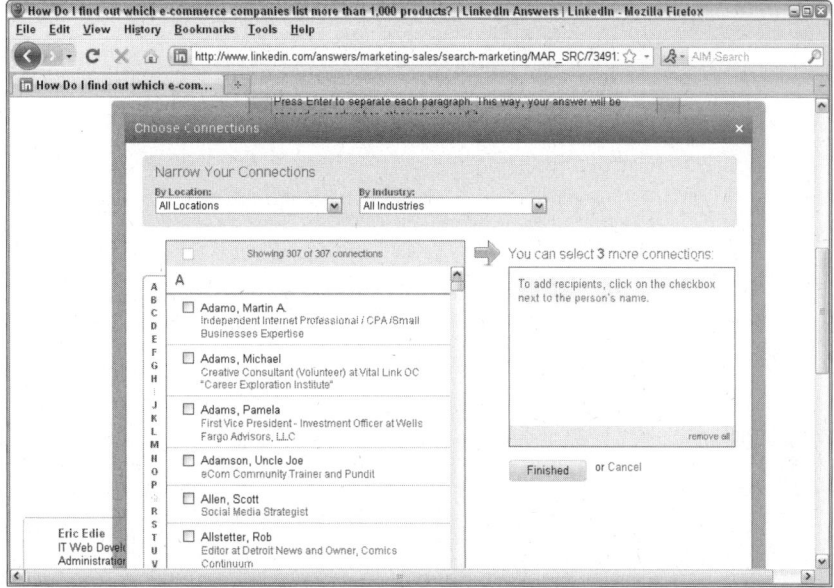

Figure 7-7:
Suggest an
Expert to
answer the
question.

Asking a Question

Technology can be overwhelming. For example, has your boss ever asked you to figure out how to set up something for the business like an RSS feed? (And your first question was something like, "What the heck is an RSS feed?") Imagine that you can put the question to your connections and the rest of the LinkedIn network, drawing from the knowledge of a potential pool of up to tens of millions of professionals. Whether it's a question pertaining to what you do, what you're planning to start, or something that you need some fresh insight on, LinkedIn allows you to post your question to be answered by the community.

Your LinkedIn question is available for up to seven days from the time you post your question on the site. You can always reopen your question later for more answers, but typically one week is enough for members of the community to start responding. Sometimes, a question gets anywhere from one to five responses. You might get anywhere from 10 to 20 answers for a popular question, while others might elicit 30, 50, 70, or more answers if lots of people have something to say.

How LinkedIn made Mahalo a better search engine

Imagine you're the head of a new human-edited search company called Mahalo. This was the case for Jason Calacanis, who started this company and built it up. He got to the point where he was looking for people's opinions about where the company should proceed and focus. Therefore, he turned to LinkedIn and posted the following question:

What would you do next if you were the CEO of Mahalo.com?

Background:

1. We've got a great team: tech, admin, research, and editorial.

2. We've got an amazing server setup and can handle massive traffic.

3. We've got 4,000 (Web) pages done and can do 500 per week.

4. The public hs suggested links already (if you do a search for apple, iPhone, a car, or a TV show, you'll fine some suggested links).

5. Folks are not chatting on the message board yet.

6. We have a very stable and robust technology platform (MediaWiki).

So, given what we've got . . . what would you do next?!?!?

What he got was 88 responses, ranging from thoughtful insight, in-depth advice, balanced critique, to even a few requests to work at Mahalo! Not only did Jason make his network aware of Mahalo, but he got a lot of valuable insight and some in-depth "consulting" work just by posting a question!

The kinds of questions to ask

You don't have to ask a giant question (like Jason Calacanis did in the sidebar "How LinkedIn made Mahalo a better search engine," but LinkedIn Answers are more useful to you if you think about the kind of question you want to ask and make sure it's something appropriate that can be answered by the community you're posting the question to.

Here are some questions to ask yourself before you, well, ask a question on LinkedIn Answers:

- **Is your question really a comment or an opinion?** It can be tempting to post an opinion, a comment, or something designed to get a response, but that's not the intent of this function. Try to pose a question that can be answered by an expert.

- **Is your question nontrivial or useful?** Remember, the goal of LinkedIn Answers is to exchange useful information that matters to other people using the site. Try to keep the question focused on something business or professionally related.

✔ **Is your question worded clearly?** If you're hoping for some helpful replies, people need to clearly understand what it is you want to know. You can provide additional details about your question, but make sure the actual question is clear, concise, and simply put.

✔ **Is your question an appropriate question?** Some people try to post spam or generic advertising messages, or simply make negative, philosophical, bizarre, or highly personal statements. Make sure that this question is something you would feel comfortable asking of a person in a networking group or a fellow colleague.

LinkedIn prohibits using the Answers page for posting jobs, announcing your job search, or openly requesting people to connect with you. If you post such things, the questions will be deleted, and your account may be subject to suspension or closure.

Getting the most and best responses

After you come up with your question, take a moment to consider the best way to present your question, so as many people as possible provide useful responses for you.

✔ **Provide as much detail as you can.** After you pose your question, you can (and should) fill out a details section that lets people know exactly what kind of answer you're hoping to receive. Add whatever detail is necessary for someone to properly answer your question. Include links to relevant Web sites that could help answer the question. If you already know a part of the solution, state that in the detail section so people don't waste their time answering something you've already figured out. Also be sure to provide clarification if people ask for it. If you need to know more about how to clarify your question, see the upcoming section, "Adding clarification to a posted question."

✔ **Use the right keywords in your question.** As LinkedIn Answers continues to grow and expand, more people are using the search engine to find questions to answer instead of browsing open questions or categories. Therefore, if you need an expert in a certain subject matter, make sure the right keywords of that subject are in the question so it shows up in search results.

✔ **Use the right category(ies) for your question.** Because many people search LinkedIn Answers by category, picking the right category for your question is important. Go through the different categories, see what previous questions match your question the best, and keep in mind that you can assign up to two categories per question in case you need information that doesn't fit neatly into one specific category.

✔ **Keep your question as simple as possible.** It can be tempting to get on a roll and start asking multiple questions that seem related in one posting.

If people see a massive or highly complex question being asked, they typically are more reluctant to answer it, or they might answer a minor question and ignore the major one you really wanted an answer for.

- **Engage your audience.** Sometimes, the point of your question is to make your audience members think about a topic and share their opinions or advice in that situation. Therefore, provide some focus to your question but leave it open-ended (meaning a question that cannot be answered in a few words) to generate different perspectives when people answer your question. (For example, "How would you do X in this situation?")

- **Keep your question clean and readable.** Nothing can distract your audience quite like an obvious spelling or grammatical error. Before you post your question, take a minute or two to make sure the question and detail sections flow and are visually clean. Reword your question if necessary to make that first sentence as logical as possible to anyone who would read it.

The 20-year-old question — and 12 LinkedIn Answers

Tom Clifford is an award-winning corporate filmmaker who goes by the moniker "Director Tom." For more than 20 years, Director Tom has helped companies large and small tell their stories through documentary videos. These videos relate the purpose of their companies, and Tom makes sure the videos are "energetic, engaging, compelling, meaningful and authentic."

On a guest blog entry, Clifford relates one aspect of his career: "No one has ever successfully answered a question I've been seeking in over 20 years. So, I asked the folks on LinkedIn for their thoughts." Clifford posted the following question on LinkedIn Answers:

ROI Using Corporate Videos?

Is there a way to measure or express the return on investment with corporate videos... financial or otherwise?

My experience has taught me that the ROI on a video is easier to calculate after it is produced vs. before production begins ... especially for non-commercial productions like raising awareness of issues or corporate culture and values.

Perhaps, in a way, this is an unanswerable question. But, clearly, the corporate video market is a huge industry and one that continues to expand yearly.

So, how does this industry continue to expand without a clear model for ROI?

By posting his question to a wide audience, Clifford gained some fresh insights from the LinkedIn community. Twelve answers came in, each taking a different perspective. Today, Clifford credits his LinkedIn colleagues with providing him "a goldmine of information" that he uses in presentations about his business. Sometimes, all it takes is the right audience!

Posting your question on LinkedIn Answers

Okay, you thought about the right question and prepared enough detail to help someone prepare a good answer for your question, and now you want to put your question on LinkedIn. To post your question, just follow these steps:

1. **On the LinkedIn home page, click the More link in the top navigation bar, and then click the Answers link from the expanded menu.**

   You're taken to the LinkedIn Answers home page (refer to Figure 7-1).

2. **Start by clicking the Ask a Question tab to prepare your full question.**

   You end up at the Ask a Question page, as shown in Figure 7-8.

   Alternatively, on the Answers home page, you can also fill in the text box under Ask a Question and then click Next. That would also take you to the Ask a Question page, and your question would already be filled in.

Figure 7-8:
Post your question for LinkedIn Answers here.

3. **Type your question in the Ask a Question field.**

4. **(Optional) If you want your question to go only to designated contacts, select the Only Share This Question with Connections I Select check box.**

   Selecting this option makes your question completely private and only available to your designated first-degree connections. No other LinkedIn user will be able to access or answer this question.

   The Only Share This Question with Connections I Select box is intended to relay the main question you're asking. Don't try to squeeze in every detail — you have a detail section for that information.

5. **Type any additional details for your question in the Add Details field.**

   Filling in the Add Details box is optional, but I recommend doing so to give readers a more complete idea of what kind of response you're seeking, and any additional information they may need to answer your question.

6. **Under Categorize Your Question, pick a category for your question and then a subcategory.**

   You're presented with a list of categories, where you can assign one to your question. When you click the category that most represents your category, the box to its right may appear with subcategory options. Continue to select subcategories that best represent the topic of your question. (You might even be able to pick a sub-subcategory in the right-most box.) After you select a valid category, you see the full category name represented below the boxes, as shown in Figure 7-9.

   Sometimes a question overlaps categories, such as when an entrepreneur asks about funding strategies from mergers as well as venture capital. If your question applies to more than one category, you can add a second category to expand the readership of your question and get different answers.

7. **Select any check boxes relating to your question (regarding location and/or question content).**

   LinkedIn asks you to identify whether your question relates to a specific geographic location. If so, select that check box. In addition, if your question relates to recruiting, specific promotions, or a job search, select the appropriate check box so LinkedIn can flag the question and display it appropriately.

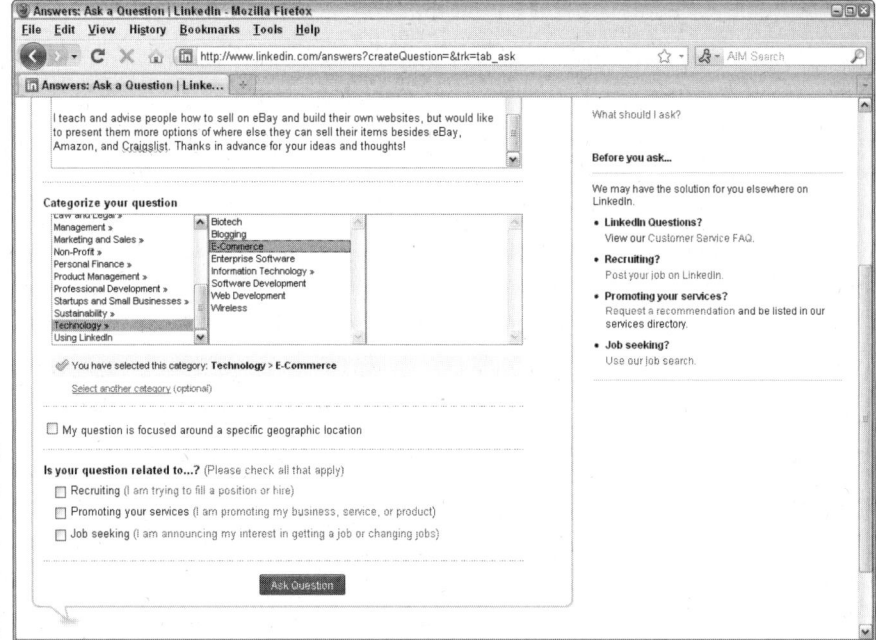

Figure 7-9:
Finish pre-
paring your
question
posting.

8. **Click the Ask Question button to post your question to LinkedIn Answers.**

   You see a confirmation bar (see Figure 7-10) telling you that your question has been posted and will remain open for seven days to gather answers. You also see a new screen that gives you the option to send your question to your LinkedIn network.

9. **Fill out the form to send your question to connections and then click the Send button, or just click the Skip link.**

   Click the blue In button (next to the To field) to pick people from your network to receive a copy of your question sent to their Inbox. When you're ready, click the Send button to distribute your question to your network.

You can customize the subject line and details of your message before you send your question. After you click the Send button or the Skip button, your question is posted to the community.

Confirmation bar

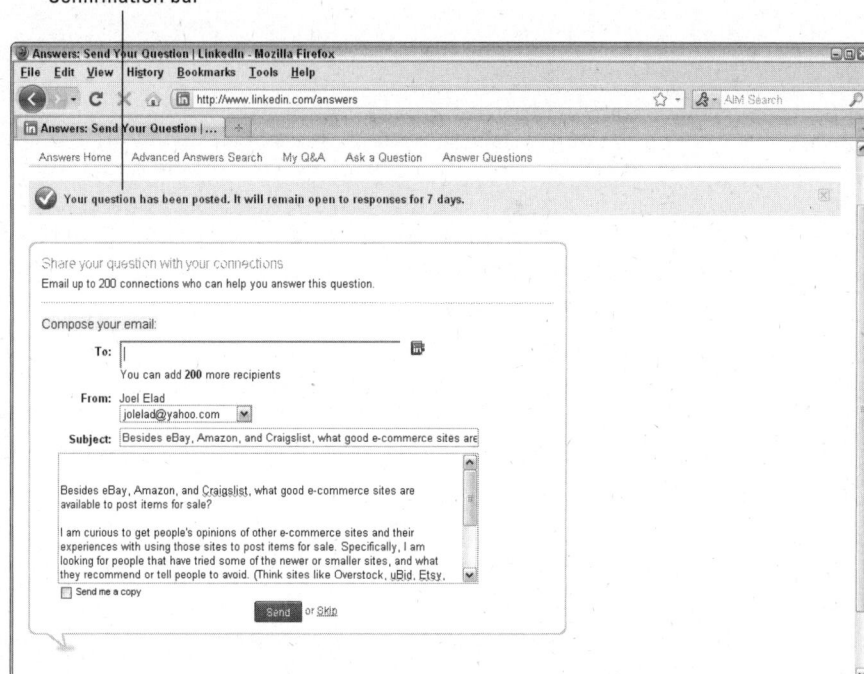

The more people you send this to, the more interest and response you should get in your question. Balance that, though, with some consideration of the people in your network and send it to the people you feel it would be most relevant to and who would likely provide a thoughtful answer. Remember, though, that these will be the only people who receive this question and can answer it, so choose your connections wisely.

Adding clarification to a posted question

After you post your question and people start to respond, you might notice that

✔ You remember additional information you forgot to put in your post.

✔ The answers being posted aren't targeting the correct area for your question.

✔ The people posting answers are asking for follow-up information.

In any of these cases, or for whatever reason, you can post a clarification to your original question. If that's the case, just follow these steps:

1. **On the LinkedIn home page, click More from the top navigation bar, and then click Answers from the menu that appears.**

2. **Click the My Q&A tab to bring up your list of questions.**

3. **Select the question you need to update to bring up the question details.**

4. **From the question detail page, click the link Clarify My Question to add any extra detail to your original question (see Figure 7-11).**

   You can't edit your original question, so the only way to change your question is to add information through clarifying your question. If you decide you want to close or delete your question before the seven-day period elapses, simply click the yellow Close Question Now button, as shown in Figure 7-11.

5. **On the Clarify Your Question page, add your clarification into the text box provided and then click the Clarify Question button to add your message to your original question.**

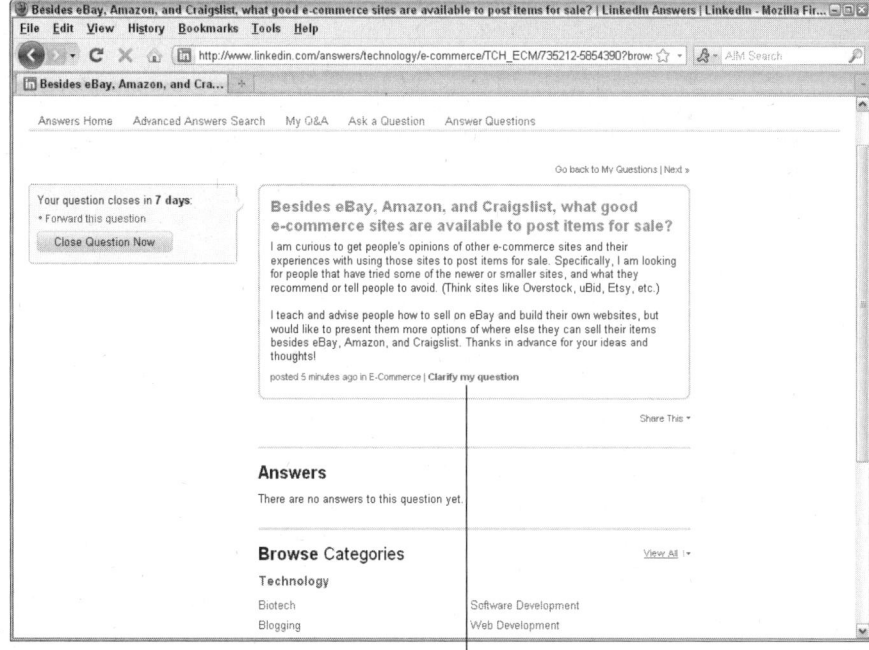

Figure 7-11:
Add more information or clarify the question.

Click the Clarify My Question link

Selecting a Best Answer for your question

After your question has been on LinkedIn and you start receiving responses from the community, you should go back into your question and review the answers you've received. At this stage, LinkedIn gives you the option to identify the Best Answer to your question so that anyone else reading your question can understand what you felt to be the most appropriate answer.

As you scroll through the answers that people have submitted, pick the answer that best defines your question and assign it as a Best Answer. Doing this helps LinkedIn recognize experts in these different categories — and this can be your way of rewarding the person who spent time answering your question most effectively.

I recommend waiting until either the question automatically closes in seven days or waiting until you have several great answers and you feel ready to close the question on your end.

I also recommend that you select at least one Good Answer in addition to the Best Answer. This way, you reward members who took the time to rate your question because this designation will show up on their profile: Best Answer or Good Answer.

Part III
Growing and Managing Your Network

The 5th Wave   By Rich Tennant

"I know it's a short profile, but I thought
'King of the Jungle' sort of said it all."

In this part . . .

The ball is rolling, you feel some traction, and you're raring for more. Many people get to a certain level, look around, and go, "Okay, great, but what's the next step?" Well, I'm here to say that there are a lot of next steps and ways that you can save time while using LinkedIn even more.

This part talks about the steps you can take to really raise your LinkedIn identity to the next level. I cover the ins and outs of LinkedIn's Recommendations feature, which can help you earn trust and maybe even a new job. I also talk about the LinkedIn Web site in more detail and look at how you can access some of the functions, like the Inbox, so you can be more efficient as you handle more activity. Finally, I talk about some cool little add-ons you can plug into your Internet experience that give you lots of data on other people, courtesy of LinkedIn, as well as some ways to tie your e-mail system and LinkedIn together.

Chapter 8

Exploring the Power of Recommendations

*E*ndorsements and testimonials have long been a mainstay of traditional marketing. But really, how much value is there in reading testimonials on someone's own Web site, like the following:

> *Maria is a great divorce attorney — I'd definitely use her again.*

Elizabeth T. London

or

> *Jack is a fine lobbyist — a man of impeccable character.*

Emanuel R. Seattle

Without knowing who these people are, anyone reading the testimonials tends to be highly skeptical about them. At the very least, the reader wants to know that they're real people who have some degree of accountability for those endorsements.

The reader is looking for something called *social validation.* Basically, that's just a fancy-shmancy term meaning that a person feels better about his decision to conduct business with someone if other people in his extended network are pleased with that person's work. The reader knows that people are putting their own reputations at stake, even if just to a small degree, by making a public Recommendation of another person.

As this chapter shows you, the LinkedIn Recommendations feature offers you a powerful tool for finding out more about the people you're considering doing business with, as well as a means to build your own reputation in a way that's publicly visible. I walk you through all the steps needed to create a Recommendation for someone else, request a Recommendation for your profile, and manage your existing Recommendations.

Understanding Recommendations

The LinkedIn Recommendation process starts in one of three ways:

- ✓ **Unsolicited:** When viewing the profile of any of your first-degree connections, a Recommend This Person link is clearly displayed at the top of the profile, as shown in Figure 8-1. (For more information on connections, see Chapter 5.) By clicking that link, you can give an unsolicited Recommendation.

- ✓ **Requested:** You can request Recommendations from your first-degree connections. You might send such a request at the end of a successful project, for example, or maybe ask for a Recommendation from your boss before you plan to transition to a new job.

The Recommend This Person link

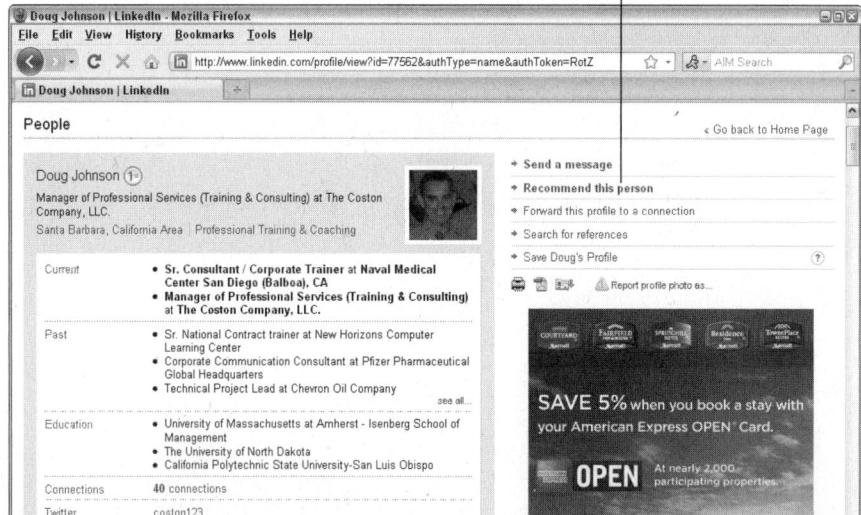

Figure 8-1:
You can start a Recommendation with any first-degree connection.

✔ **Reciprocated:** Whenever you accept a Recommendation from someone, LinkedIn presents you with the option of recommending that person in return. Some people do this as a thank you for receiving the Recommendation, other people reciprocate only because they didn't realize they could leave a Recommendation until someone left them one, and some people don't feel comfortable reciprocating unless they truly believe the person deserves one. You decide in each circumstance whether to reciprocate.

After the Recommendation is written, it's not posted immediately. It goes to the recipient for review, and he has the option to accept it, reject it, or request a revision. So even though the majority of Recommendations you see on LinkedIn are genuine, they're also almost entirely positive because they have to be accepted by the recipient.

With LinkedIn, you can use Recommendations in several ways:

✔ **On your profile page:** LinkedIn shows all Recommendations you've received as well as links to the profiles of the people who recommended you. (See Figure 8-2.) This provides that social validation you want by allowing people to see exactly who is endorsing you.

✔ **In Advanced Search:** One of the options for sorting the results of a LinkedIn search is Relationship + Recommendations. (You can even sort your results before they are generated by taking advantage of the Sort By options — they're there at the bottom of the Advanced Search page.) This option sorts first by the number of degrees or levels a connection is away from you in ascending order (for example, your first-degree connections first), and then by the number of Recommendations someone has received in descending order (for example, those with the most Recommendations first). (We discuss this option in more detail in Chapter 4.)

✔ **In the Companies section:** From the Companies section, you can click the Service Providers link (near the top-right corner of the screen) to get the Service Providers main page to display a list of recent Recommendations within your network. Within each category, you can choose to view either the most recent Recommendations or the most highly recommended service providers within the category. Every service provider listed must have at least one Recommendation to be included. (See Chapter 13 for a more detailed discussion on service providers.)

Because the number of Recommendations is used as both a sort option for searching and a display option in the service provider directory, having a large number of Recommendations — besides just being impressive — has a very real impact on your profile's searchability. More is definitely better.

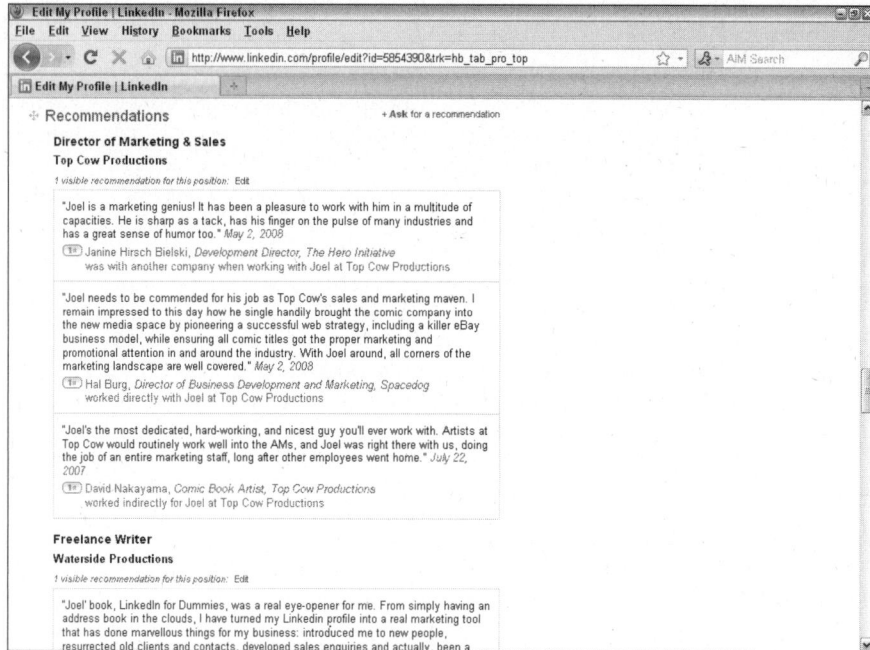

Figure 8-2:
Recommendations shown on a profile page.

That said, the quality of the Recommendations matters as well as who they're from. Five very specific Recommendations from actual clients talking about how you helped them solve a problem is probably worth more than 50 Recommendations from business acquaintances saying, "I like Sally — she's cool," or, "Hector is a great networker." And any Recommendations that heartily endorse the number of cocktails you had at the last formal event probably need revision. Check out the later section, "Gracefully Declining a Recommendation (Or a Request for One)," if you're receiving those kinds of statements.

Writing Recommendations

I suggest you practice making some Recommendations before you start requesting them. Here's the method to my madness: When you know how to write a good Recommendation yourself, you're in a better position to help others write good Recommendations for you. And the easiest way to get Recommendations is to give them. Every time you make a Recommendation and the recipient accepts it, she is prompted to give you a Recommendation. Thanks to the basic desire that most people want to be fair when dealing with their network, many people will go ahead and endorse you in return.

Choose wisely, grasshopper: Deciding who to recommend

Go through your contacts and make a list of the people you want to recommend. As you build your list, consider recommending the following types of contacts:

- ✔ **People you've worked with:** I'm not going to say that personal references are completely worthless, but standing next to specific Recommendations from colleagues and clients, they tend to ring pretty hollow. Business Recommendations are much stronger in the LinkedIn context. Your Recommendation is rooted in actual side-by-side experience with the other party, you can be specific on the behavior and accomplishments of the other party, and the examples you give are most likely to be appreciated by the professional LinkedIn community at large.

- ✔ **People you know well:** You may choose to connect with casual acquaintances or even strangers, but reserve your personal Recommendations for people you have an established relationship with (and by that, I mean friends and family). Remember, you're putting your own reputation on the line with that Recommendation. Are you comfortable risking your rep on them?

Recommend only those people whose performance you're actually happy with. I can't say it enough: Your reputation is on the line. Recommending a real doofus just to get one Recommendation in return isn't worth it! Here's a great question to ask yourself when deciding whether to recommend someone: Would you feel comfortable recommending this person to a best friend or family member? If you say no, well, then, you have your answer.

When you complete your To Be Recommended list, you're probably not going to do them all at once, so I suggest copying and pasting the names into a word processing document or spreadsheet so that you can keep track as you complete them.

Look right here: Making your Recommendation stand out

Here are a few things to keep in mind when trying to make your Recommendation stand out from the rest of the crowd:

✔ **Be specific.** Don't just say the person whom you're recommending is great: Talk about her specific strengths and skills.

✔ **Talk about results.** Adjectives and descriptions are fluff. Clichés are also pretty useless. Tell what the person actually did and the effect it had on you and your business. It's one thing to say, "She has a great eye," and another to say, "The logo she designed for us has been instrumental in building our brand and received numerous positive comments from customers."

✔ **Tell how you know the person.** LinkedIn offers only the very basic categories of colleague, service provider, student, and business partner. If you've known this person for 10 years, say so. If she's your cousin, say so. If you've never met her in person, say so. Save it for the end, though. Open with the positive results this person provided, or the positive qualities the person exhibited in your interaction; then qualify the type of interaction.

✔ **Reinforce the requestor's major skills or goals.** Look at her profile. How is she trying to position herself now? What can you say in your Recommendation that will support that? That will be far more appreciated by the recipient. For example, if you read her profile and see that she's really focusing on her project management skills as opposed to her earlier software development skills, your Recommendation should reinforce *that* message because that's what she's trying to convey on her profile.

✔ **Don't gush.** By all means, if you think someone is fantastic, exceptional, extraordinary, or the best at what she does, say so. Just don't go on and on about it.

✔ **Be concise.** Although LinkedIn has a 3,000-character limit on the length of Recommendations, you shouldn't reach that limit. That should be more than enough to get your point across. Make it as long as it needs to be to say what you have to say, and no longer.

Creating a Recommendation

Now you're ready to write your first Recommendation. To create a Recommendation, first you need to pull up the person's profile:

1. **Click the My Connections link (part of the Contacts set of links) from the top navigation bar of any page.**

2. **Select the person you're recommending from the connections list that appears.**

Your Recommendation goes directly to that person, not prospective employers. Any prospective employer who wants a specific reference can request it through doing a Reference search on LinkedIn, which I cover in greater detail in Chapter 11.

3. Visit the profile of the person you want to recommend.

Before you write up your recommendation, review the person's experience, summary, professional headline, and other elements of his profile. This will help you get a sense of what skills, attributes, or results should be reflected in your recommendation of that person. After all, if the person you want to recommend is trying to build a career as a finance executive, your recommendation will serve this person better if you focus on finance instead of his event planning or writing skills, for example.

After you inform yourself a bit more about the person you're going to recommend and have thought about what you are going to say, you can get your recommending groove on. Follow these steps:

1. Click the Recommend This Person link to the right of her name and photo.

2. Select a category for that person.

As soon as you click the Recommend This Person link, you're immediately prompted to choose an option describing how you know this person, as shown in Figure 8-3.

Your four choices are

- *Colleague:* You worked together at the same company.

- *Service Provider:* You hired the person to provide a service to you or your company.

- *Business Partner:* You worked with the person but not as a client or colleague. (Of course, common usage of "business partner" traditionally means that you're partners in a business together, but that isn't what this means. If you work in the same company as the other party, choose Colleague, even if you're both owners and not manager or employee.)

- *Student:* You went to school with the person, either as a fellow student or as a teacher.

As of this writing, there is no option for a personal relationship nor for you being a service provider to the person. In these cases, I recommend that you select Business Partner.

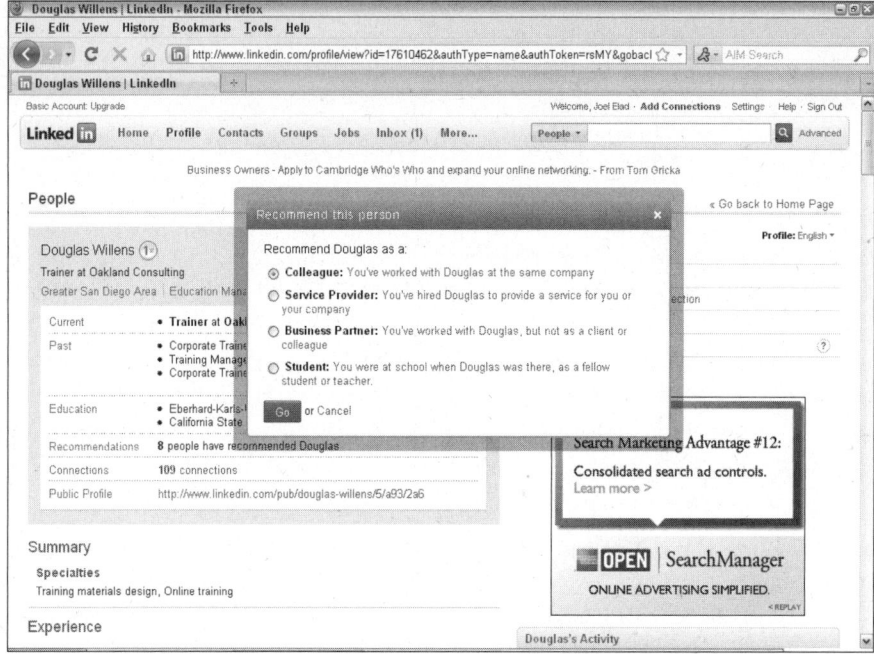

Figure 8-3:
Tell LinkedIn
how you
worked with
the person
you are rec-
ommending.

3. **Click the Go button.**

   The Create Your Recommendation page appears, as shown in Figure 8-4.

   In the case of a Service Provider, the page will look different, but I cover that Recommendation in detail in Chapter 13.

4. **Define your relationship with the person you're recommending by answering a few questions.**

   Each of the three drop-down boxes asks you to pick an answer from a predefined list. Specifically, you will be asked to

   a. *Define the basis of the recommendation.*

   If you're a colleague of the person, LinkedIn wants to know whether you managed or worked side by side with the other party, or whether that person was the manager or senior official. If you're a business partner, LinkedIn wants to know whether you worked at a different company from the other person or whether the person was a client of yours.

   b. *Define your title at the time.*

   Identify which position you held when you observed the behavior in the other person you're recommending. This list is generated from the positions you defined in your LinkedIn profile. If your experience overlaps multiple positions, pick the position that best defines your relationship with the other party.

c. Define the other person's title at the time.

You have to select at least one position that the other party held to associate the Recommendation. You can enter only one Recommendation per position, but you can recommend the other party on multiple positions.

By answering these questions, this informs anyone reading the Recommendation about how you know the person you're recommending. Perhaps you were the person's manager at one time.

5. Write the Recommendation in the Written Recommendation field.

In earlier chapters, I stress staying specific, concise, and professional while focusing on results and skills. Keep in mind that Recommendations you write that end up getting accepted by the other party also appear in your own profile in a tab marked Recommendations. Believe it or not, people judge you by the comments you leave about others, not just what they say about you. So, look over your Recommendation before you post it, and watch for obvious spelling or grammatical errors. (You may want to prepare your recommendation in a word processing program like Microsoft Word, use its Spelling & Grammar check, and then cut and paste your newly pristine prose into the Written Recommendation field.)

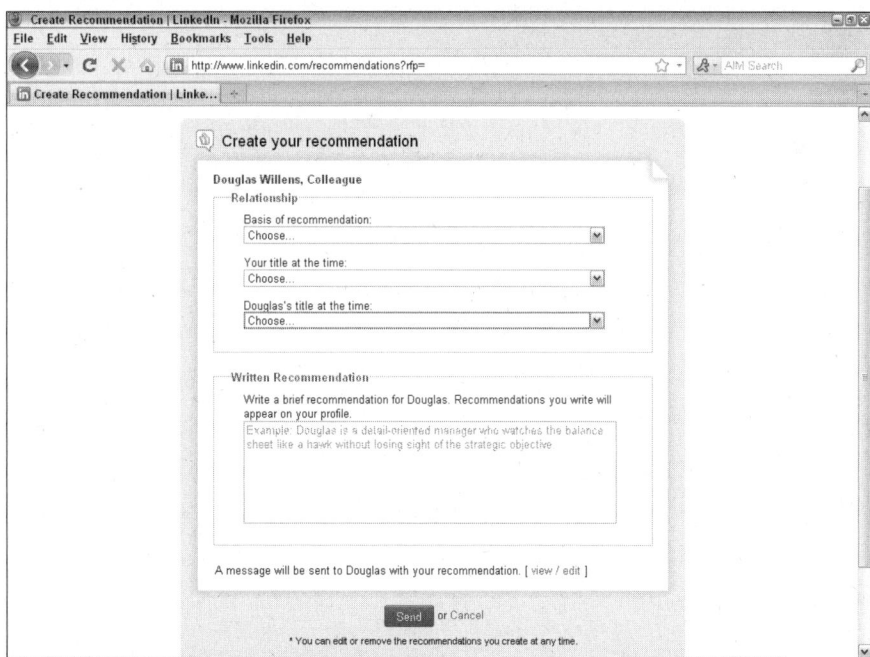

Figure 8-4:
Create your Recommendation here.

6. (Optional) Include a note in the Personalize This Message text box.

When you send your Recommendation, you have the option to also attach a personal note. Simply click the View/Edit link next to the line `A message will be sent to X with your Recommendation`. If it's someone you're in recent contact with, the note is probably unnecessary — the endorsement should speak for itself. But if it's someone you haven't spoken to in a while, take advantage of the opportunity to reconnect with a brief note. (See Figure 8-5.) You can keep the boilerplate text, "I've written this Recommendation of your work to share with other LinkedIn users," or you can write your own note, like I did in Figure 8-5.

7. Click Send.

The Recommendation is sent to the recipient.

After you send your Recommendation, the other person has to accept it before it's posted. Don't take it personally if she doesn't post it, or at least not right away. After all, it's a gift, freely given. The primary value to *you* is in the gesture to the recipient, not the public visibility of your Recommendation. And if she comes back with requested changes to the Recommendation, by all means accommodate her as long as it's all true and you feel comfortable with it. It's a service to her, not you.

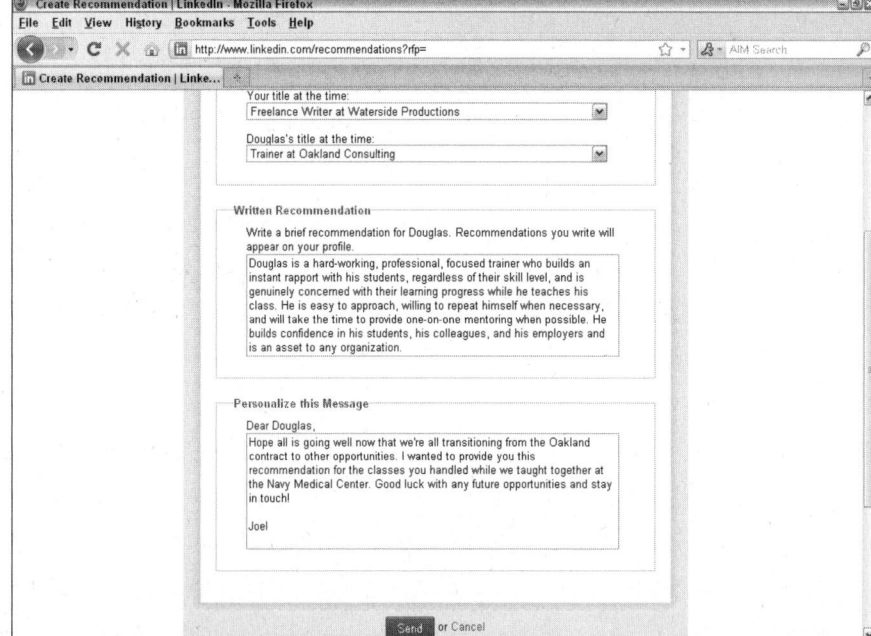

Figure 8-5:
Sending a personal note with a Recommendation is a good idea.

Requesting Recommendations

In an ideal world, you'd never request a Recommendation. Everyone who's had a positive experience working with you would just automatically post a raving Recommendation on LinkedIn. But the reality is that most likely only your raving fans and very heavy LinkedIn users are going to make unsolicited Recommendations. Your mildly happy customers, former bosses whose jokes you laughed at consistently, and co-workers who you haven't seen in five years could all stand a little prompting.

Be prepared, though: Some people feel that Recommendations should only be given freely, and they may be taken aback by receiving a Recommendation request. So it's imperative that you frame your request with a personal message, not just a generic message from LinkedIn.

Choosing who to request Recommendations from

Request Recommendations from the same people whom you might write them for: colleagues, business partners, and service providers. The only difference is that you're looking at it from his point of view.

Relationships aren't all symmetrical. For example, if someone hears me speak at a conference and buys this book, that person is a customer of mine. My customers know my skills and expertise fairly well — perhaps not on the same level as a consulting client, but still enough to make a Recommendation. I, on the other hand, might not know a customer at all. I'm open to getting to know him, and I'm willing to connect, but I can't write a Recommendation for him yet.

Creating a polite Recommendation request

When you identify the person (or people) you want to write you Recommendations, you're ready to create a Recommendation request. To get started on authoring your request, follow these steps:

 1. **Roll your mouse over the Profile link from the top navigation bar and then choose Recommendations from the menu that appears.**

2. **Click the Request Recommendations tab, then click the drop-down box arrow (right there next to Step 1— see Figure 8-6) to choose what you want to be recommended for from the list provided.**

   LinkedIn will tie this recommendation to a particular position or school attended from your profile, so you need to select the position (or school you were attending) where the recommender observed you and is providing their recommendation.

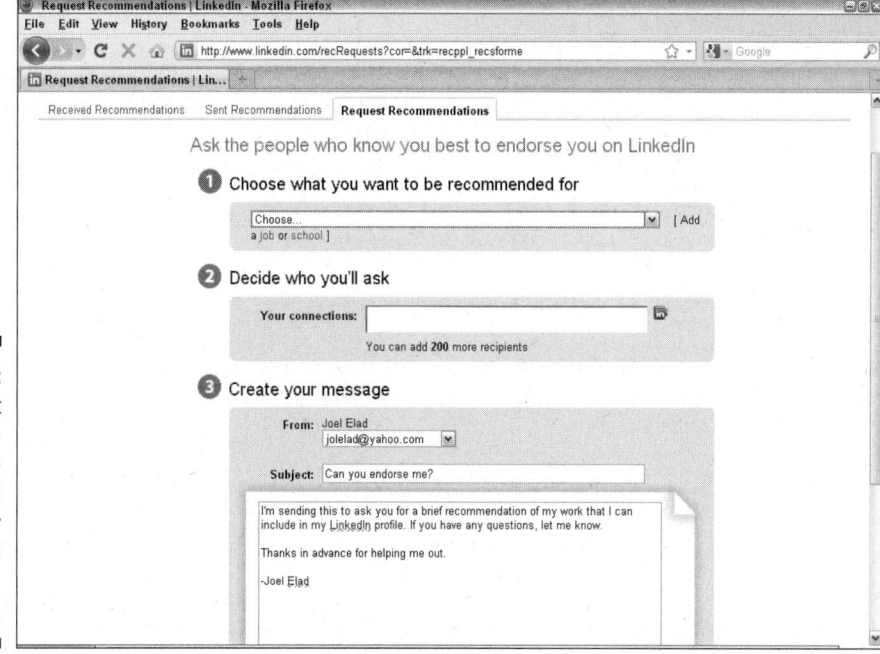

Figure 8-6:
Select the position to be associated with your requested Recommendation.

3. **Under the Decide Who You'll Ask header, type the name of the person you want to request a Recommendation from into the Your Connections text field.**

   You can add the names of up to 200 people in this text field, and all will get a Recommendation request.

   If you click the little blue In icon to the right of the text box, LinkedIn will open up a new window containing the list of your connections, which you can select by checking the checkbox next to someone's name in the window.

   As you start typing the name of the person, you should see that name pop up like what you see in Figure 8-7. Clicking the name adds it to the list of names visible in the Your Connections field. You can now type in another name if you would like to send this Recommendation request to more than one person.

4. Type your message in the field provided, as shown in Figure 8-8.

The same etiquette is recommended here as in other requests: Don't just accept the boilerplate text that LinkedIn fills in, but rather customize it to create a personal note, like I did in Figure 8-8. You can customize not only the body of your message but the subject line as well.

5. Check your spelling and grammar.

You can write your message first using a program like Microsoft Word, run the Spelling & Grammar check, then cut and paste your message into the space provided, if you like.

6. Click Send.

The Recommendation request is sent to the intended recipient.

Giving people some context as to why you're making the request helps motivate them more effectively. Also, even though you should be asking only people that would be comfortable recommending you (you are, aren't you?), you still want to give them a gracious way to decline. After all, you're asking a favor. The person you're contacting is in no way obligated, so don't expect anything, and you won't be disappointed.

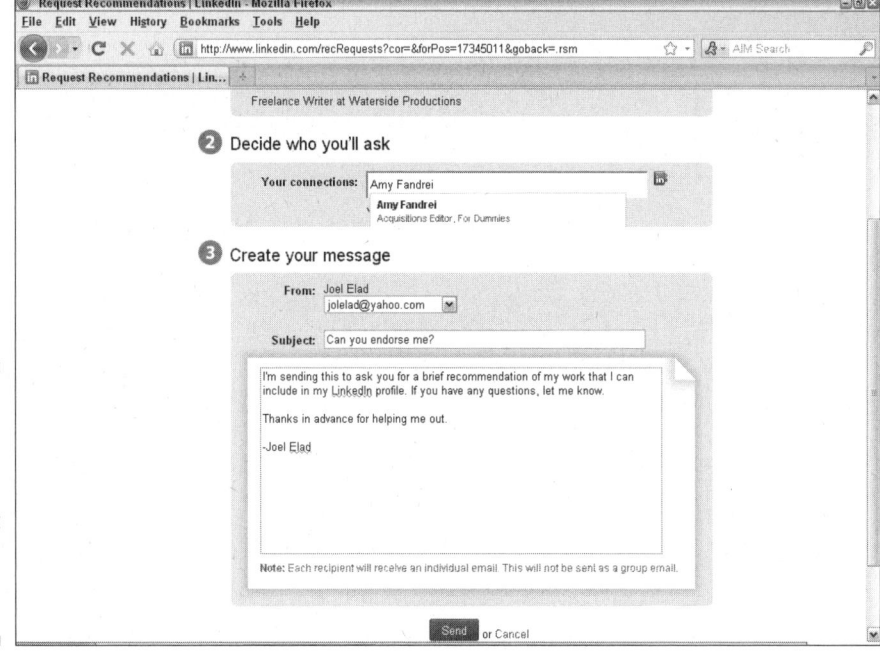

Figure 8-7:
Confirm the person (or people) to request Recommendations from.

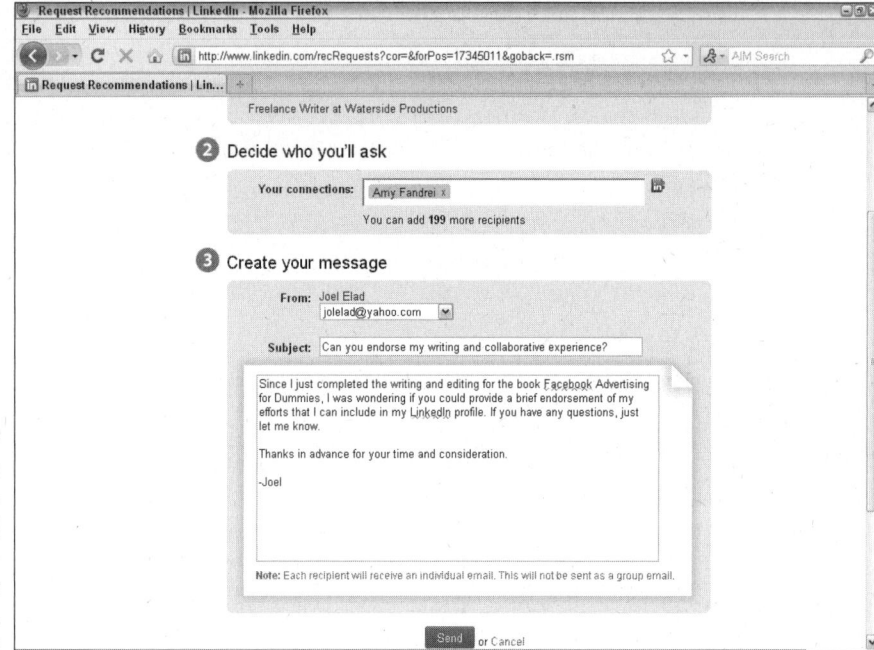

Figure 8-8:
A cus-
tomized
Recom-
mendation
request.

There's really no such thing as too many Recommendations as long as the quality is good. Once you start accepting mediocre recommendations, though, on the assumption that "something is better than nothing", people will start to think that a lot of them are fluff. LinkedIn doesn't give you control over the display order, either, so you have all the more reason to make sure that the ones displayed are good quality.

Gracefully Declining a Recommendation (Or a Request for One)

Unfortunately, not everyone naturally writes good Recommendations, and all your LinkedIn connections haven't read this book, so it's bound to happen eventually: Someone will write a Recommendation that you don't want to show on your profile.

No problem. Just politely request a replacement when you receive it. Thank him for thinking of you, and give him the context of what you're trying to accomplish:

Wei:

Thank you so much for your gracious Recommendation. I'd like to ask a small favor, though. I'm really trying to position myself more as a public speaker in the widget industry, rather than as a gadget trainer. Since you've heard me speak on the topic, if you could gear your Recommendation more towards that, I'd greatly appreciate it.

Thanks,

Alexa

If he's sincerely trying to be of service to you, he should have no problem changing it. Just make sure you ask him for something based on your actual experience with him.

You also may receive a request for a Recommendation from someone you don't feel comfortable recommending. If it's because she gave you poor service or was less than competent, you have to consider whether you should even be connected to her at all because, after all, LinkedIn is a business referral system. I discuss how to remove a connection in Chapter 6.

Perhaps, though, maybe you don't have sufficient experience with her services to provide her a Recommendation. If that's the case, just reply to her request with an explanation:

Alicia:

I received your request for a Recommendation. While I'm happy to be connected to you on LinkedIn, and look forward to getting to know you better, or even work together in the future, at this point in time I just don't feel like I have enough basis to give you a really substantive Recommendation.

Once we've actually worked together on something successfully, I'll be more than happy to provide a Recommendation.

Thanks,

Wei

Managing Recommendations

Relationships change over time. Sometimes they get better, occasionally they get worse, and sometimes they just change. Also, as you get more Recommendations, you might decide that you don't want to display them all, or that you would like some of them updated to support your current branding or initiatives.

Fortunately, neither the Recommendation you give nor those you receive are etched in stone (or computer chips, as the case may be). You can edit or remove the Recommendations you've written at any time, and you can hide or request revisions to those you receive.

Editing or removing Recommendations you've made

To edit or remove a Recommendation you've made, follow these steps:

1. **Roll your mouse over the Profile link from the top navigation bar.**

2. **Choose Recommendations from the Profile drop-down menu that appears.**

   Doing so brings up the Recommendations page.

3. **Click the page's Sent Recommendations tab.**

   All the Recommendations you've made are listed in reverse chronological order, as shown in Figure 8-9. You can narrow the list down by clicking the link for Colleagues, Service Providers, Business Partners, or Students below the Manage Recommendations You've Sent header.

4. **To edit or remove the Recommendation, start by clicking the Edit link next to the Recommendation you want to change or remove.**

   You're taken to the Edit Recommendation screen, as shown in Figure 8-10.

   • *Edit:* You can update some of the Relationship choices, such as Basis of Recommendation, or update your Written Recommendation text. Then click Send at the bottom of the screen.

   • *Remove:* Simply click the Withdraw This Recommendation link to ditch the recommendation completely. This link can be found at the top of the page, between the person's name and the Relationship header.

An edited Recommendation is submitted to the recipient again for approval. If you remove it, it comes off immediately, and the recipient (or is that the *un*recipient?) doesn't receive any notification.

Withdraw This Recommendation link

You can change the Basis of the Recommendation field, which describes the exact relationship, such as whether you worked in the same department, or one of you was subordinate to the other. However, you can't change the type of Recommendation: for example, Colleague versus Service Provider versus Business Partner. If you need to do so, you have to remove the current Recommendation and write a new one, choosing the appropriate option.

Handling new Recommendations you've received

Every time you receive a Recommendation from someone else, you see a message show up in your LinkedIn Inbox, as shown in Figure 8-11.

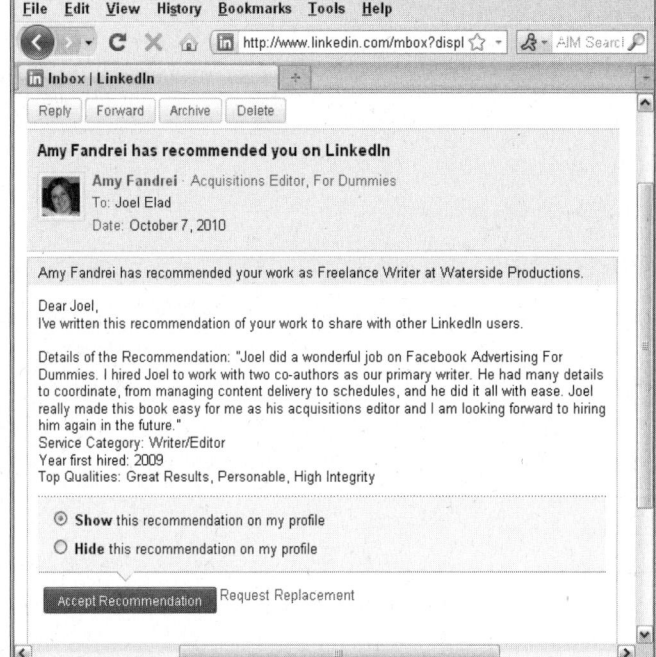

Figure 8-11:
Here is where you can accept an incoming Recommendation.

When you receive a Recommendation, you have these options:

- ✔ **Accept and show it on your profile.** Click the Accept Recommendation button but also make sure the Show This Recommendation on My Profile option is selected.

- ✔ **Accept and hide it.** You might choose this option if you don't want to decline the person's Recommendation, but for some reason you don't want to display it (see the following section).

- ✔ **Request replacement.** If you aren't completely happy with his Recommendation, click the Request Replacement link to be given the opportunity to send him a brief note explaining what you would like changed.

- ✔ **Archive it.** This removes the Recommendation message from your LinkedIn Inbox. It is available for later retrieval, just not as easily as if you choose the Hide option. You simply have to click the Show Archived Messages link when looking at your LinkedIn Inbox for Recommendations; I cover the Inbox in further detail in Chapter 10.

Removing a Recommendation or requesting a revision

To remove a Recommendation you've received or to request a revision, here's what you do:

1. **Roll your mouse over the Profile link from the top navigation bar, and then choose Recommendations from the menu that appears.**

2. **Scroll down to the position the Recommendation is for and click the Manage link.**

   Doing so takes you to the Manage Received Recommendations page, as shown in Figure 8-12.

3. **To remove a Recommendation, deselect the Show check box. Then scroll down and click the Save Changes button to hide your Recommendation.**

4. **To request a new or revised Recommendation, click the Request a New or Revised Recommendation From *Name* link.**

   This takes you back to the Request Recommendation screen (which I cover in the earlier section, "Creating a polite Recommendation request"), where you should write a brief note explaining why you're requesting a change.

5. **Click Send.**

Negotiating the social graces around Recommendations might feel a little awkward at first, but you'll quickly become comfortable with a little practice. By both giving and receiving good Recommendations, you'll build your public reputation, increase your social capital with your connections, and have a good excuse for renewing some of your relationships with people you haven't contacted recently.

Figure 8-12:
Remove a Recommendation or request a revision here.

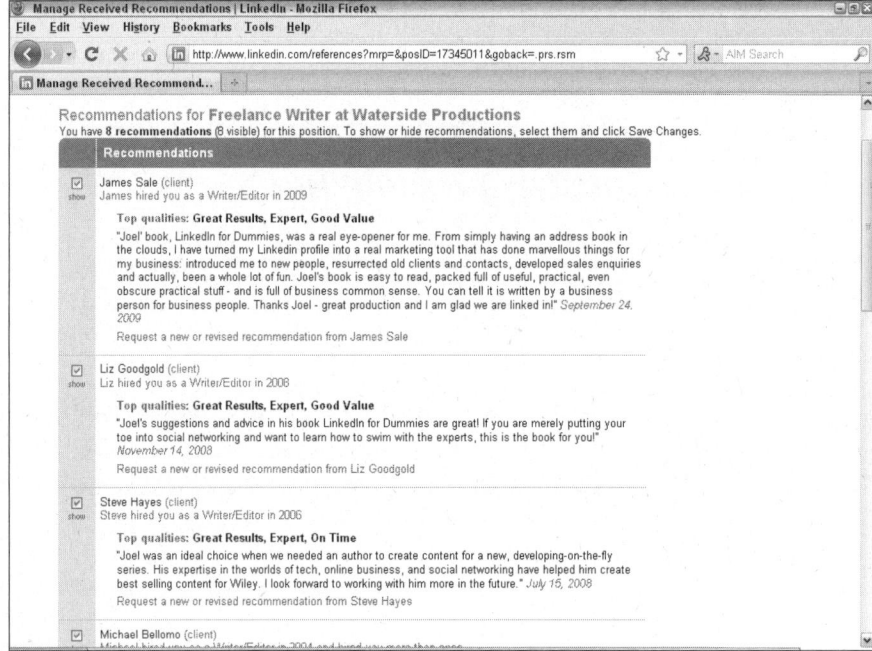

Chapter 9

Keeping Track of Your LinkedIn Activities

1 talk a lot about the different functions available on LinkedIn for you to use, and hopefully you started to set aside some time on a regular basis to keep track of various tasks as you build up your profile and network. Because of the growing amount of functions available on LinkedIn, you should take a look around the site to see how you can manage this new set of tasks most effectively.

In this chapter, I detail the different ways you can access the LinkedIn functions as well as how you can keep track of incoming mail, Invitations, and other messages that require your input or approval. I discuss the functions that you can access from the top navigation bar on the LinkedIn home page. I also discuss the LinkedIn Inbox, where all your messages, Invitations, answers, and communication are received. Then, I go over some ways you can set up LinkedIn to communicate with you through e-mail and keep you informed of communication from other LinkedIn users, whether Invitations, Introductions, Recommendations, Answers, or other LinkedIn functions.

Using the LinkedIn Home Page as Your Command Console

The LinkedIn home page is, by default, full of information about how you use the site. Think of the home page as your command console for working with LinkedIn. You can get to the home page at any time by clicking the LinkedIn logo in the top-left corner of every LinkedIn Web page. The home page holds a variety of information. Of course, your home page is unique to your LinkedIn identity, so it will look different from mine (shown in Figure 9-1) or any other user on LinkedIn. And remember that your home page is based on the first-degree connections in your network, your pending messages in your Inbox, and the level of participation with functions, such as LinkedIn Answers or Recommendations, or applications like SlideShare or the Amazon Reading List.

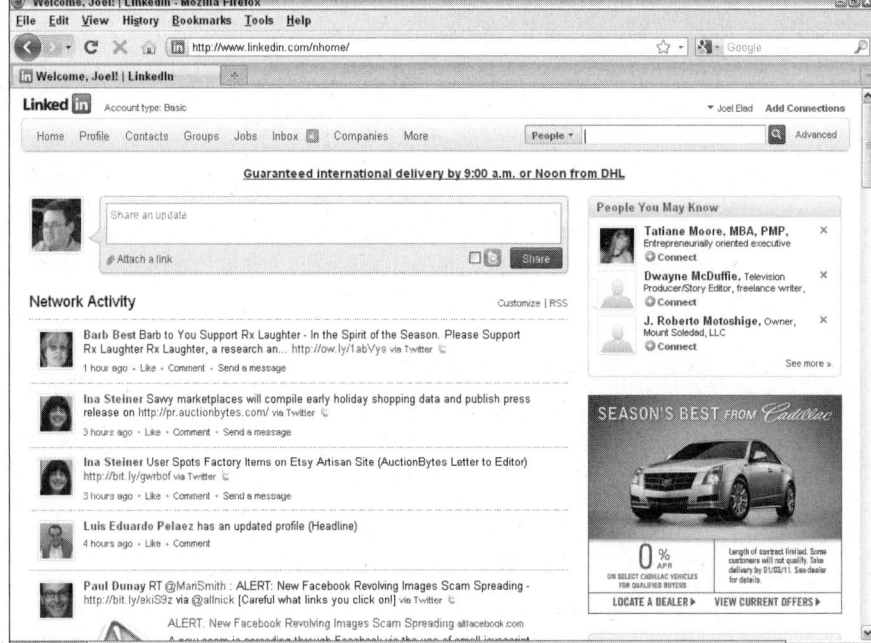

Figure 9-1: Coordinate all your LinkedIn activities through the home page.

First off, check out the menu along the top of the site. As I mention earlier in the book, I refer to this menu as the top navigation bar. This bar has all the major categories for checking your activities on LinkedIn. Just roll your mouse over each function to expand the menu item to see more options. Figure 9-2 shows an expanded More menu.

The number of unanswered messages or invitations in your Inbox is shown (in an orange box) next to the Inbox menu option. Just roll your mouse over the Inbox link and click a category to go straight to the Inbox.

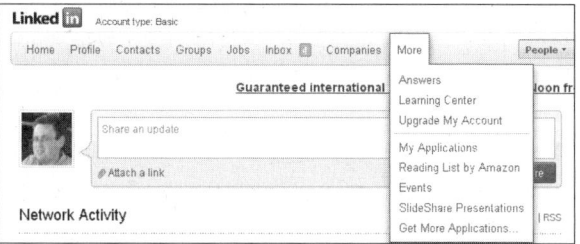

Figure 9-2:
Expand
your menu
options.

Scroll down your LinkedIn home page to see modules of other aspects of LinkedIn, such as Answers, Jobs, and Network Activity. Based on your profile, positions, and whether you participate in functions like LinkedIn Answers, the site provides a default configuration for your home page and includes the modules it thinks are most useful to you. When you want to change any of the Settings of your account, simply roll your mouse over your name (in the top-right corner of the screen) and click the Settings link to bring up your Account and Settings page, as shown in Figure 9-3. Later on this chapter, I will discuss the different categories on this page.

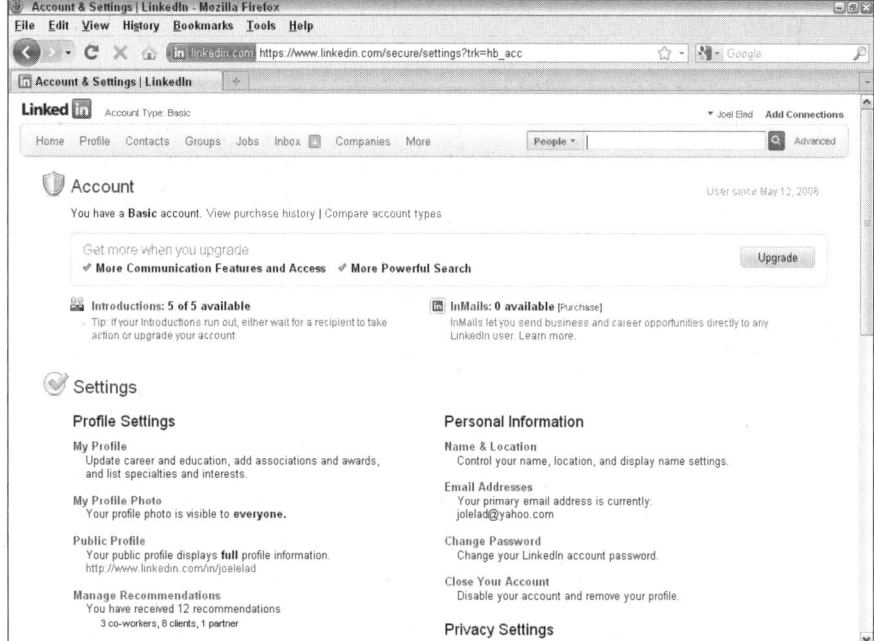

Figure 9-3:
See
LinkedIn
modules on
your home
page.

Reading your network activity

One of the ways to stay involved with your LinkedIn network is to stay up to date on how your first-degree connections are using LinkedIn. (For more on connection degrees, see Chapter 1.) To that end, the Network Activity section gives you a summary of all the activity within your immediate LinkedIn network.

Figure 9-3 gives you an idea of what this Network Activity section can contain. (Typically, it contains the most recent 25 Network Activity items. I will discuss how to change the number of items in a few paragraphs.) If you're looking at the Network Activity section of your LinkedIn home page, click the header Network Activity (these words are a link) to get a full listing of your Network Activity items, as shown in Figure 9-4.

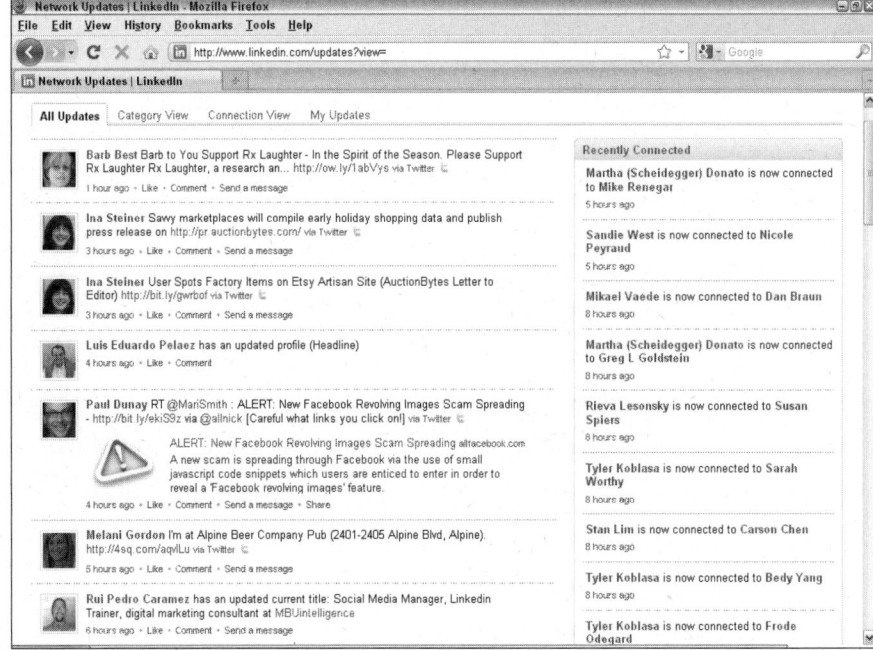

Figure 9-4:
Get the
full story
on your
LinkedIn
Network
Updates.

Because you can customize the network updates you see in your section, you need to decide which of the following events are worth keeping track of:

- ✔ Posts (status updates) from your first-degree connections

- ✔ Photo updates to your connections' profiles

- ✔ Profile updates your connections make to their profiles

- ✔ Recommendations given by a first-degree connection

✔ New connections in your extended network (meaning any new connections your first-degree contacts made)

✔ Events that your first-degree connections are attending

✔ Questions posed by a first-degree connection

✔ Answers given by a first-degree connection

✔ Groups that a first-degree contact of yours has joined

✔ Discussions from any of your LinkedIn groups

As a default, each of these categories is set up to show in your Network Activity section, and 15 updates show up on your home page. To set the criteria of your Network Activity section, just follow these steps:

1. **Roll your mouse over your name in the top-right corner of any LinkedIn page, then click the Settings link.**

   You arrive at the Account & Settings page.

2. **Scroll down to the Settings header, look for the Home Page Settings section, and click the Network Updates link. Then click the Manage Updates by Type tab.**

   You see the Show or Hide Updates page, as shown in Figure 9-5. By default, all the criteria shown on this page should be set to Show.

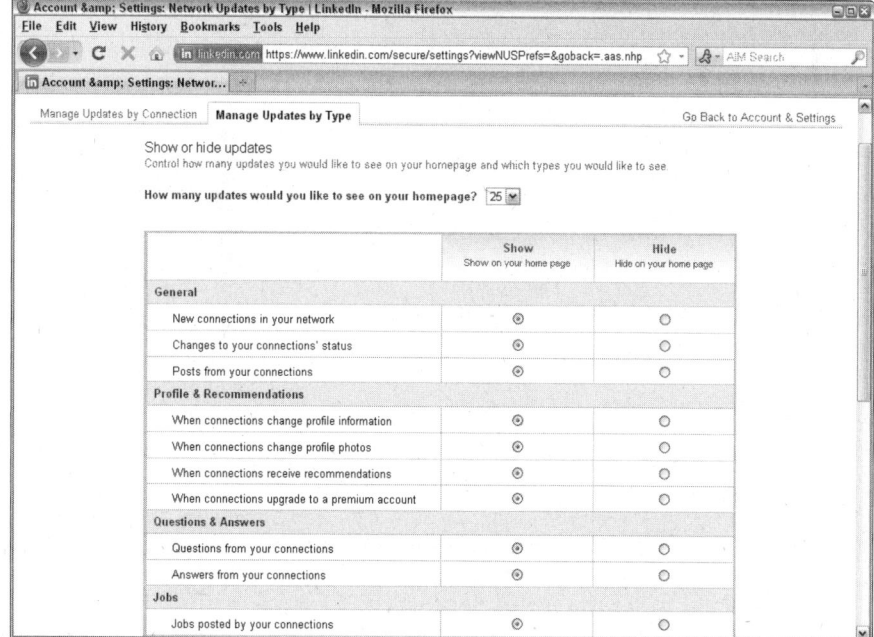

Figure 9-5: Decide what network updates you want to see.

3. **To remove any criteria from the list, simply select the Hide radio button for that feature.**

Additionally, you can change the number of network updates displayed on your home page by picking a number from the drop-down list near the bottom. (The default is 15; you can choose between 10 and 25.)

4. **Click the Save Changes button.**

You're taken back to the Account & Settings page.

Having LinkedIn automatically contact you

Sure, you can do all the footwork by going to the LinkedIn home page and looking around to see what messages or changes have occurred. The true power of staying connected, however, is having LinkedIn automatically contact you with the information you need to stay informed.

As I mention in the preceding section, clicking the Settings link (after rolling your mouse over your name from the home page) takes you to the Account & Settings page, which contains information about your account and your LinkedIn settings. Scroll down to the Settings section, as shown in Figure 9-6. This is your hub for controlling how you interact with LinkedIn and how the site will communicate with you.

Start by setting preferences in the Email Notifications section by deciding when LinkedIn should send you an e-mail to your e-mail account on file with LinkedIn:

1. **On the Account & Settings page, click the Receiving Messages link in the Email Notifications section.**

You're taken to the Receiving Messages page, as shown in Figure 9-7.

2. **Review the list of options and decide how you want to receive your e-mails. Select the radio button in one of the columns:**

   • *Individual Email:* As soon as something occurs in a given category, like Introductions, Invitations, or Job Notifications, LinkedIn sends you an e-mail with that one item in the e-mail.

   • *Daily Digest Email or Weekly Digest Email:* Instead of individual e-mails, LinkedIn groups all the activities in a given category and sends you one e-mail in a digest format, with a summary at the top of the e-mail and the detailed activities below the summary. Note that Daily Digests are for Group updates, while Weekly Digests are available for General and Group updates.

   • *No Email:* Turn off e-mail notification. You can read the message, though, when logged in to the LinkedIn site.

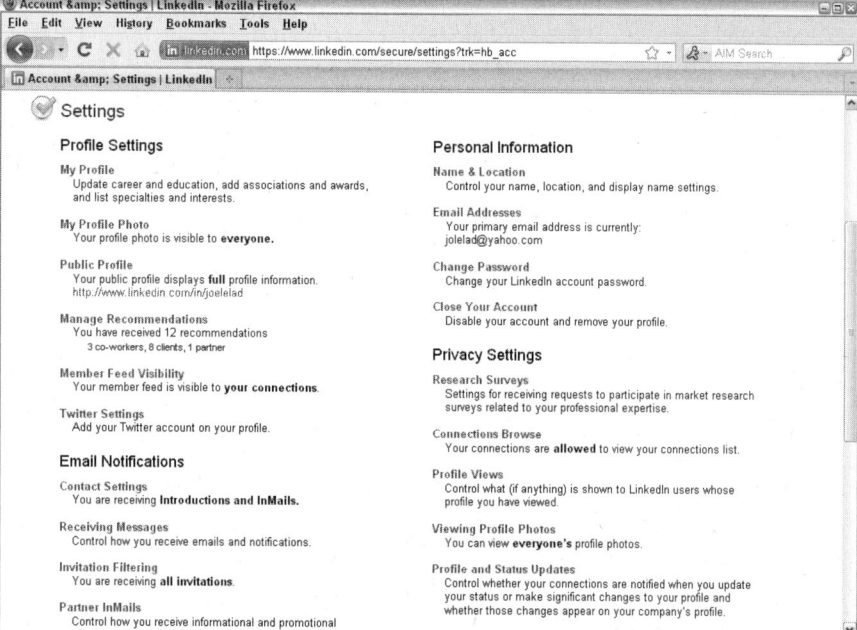

Figure 9-6:
Control your
LinkedIn
settings
from the
Account
& Settings
page.

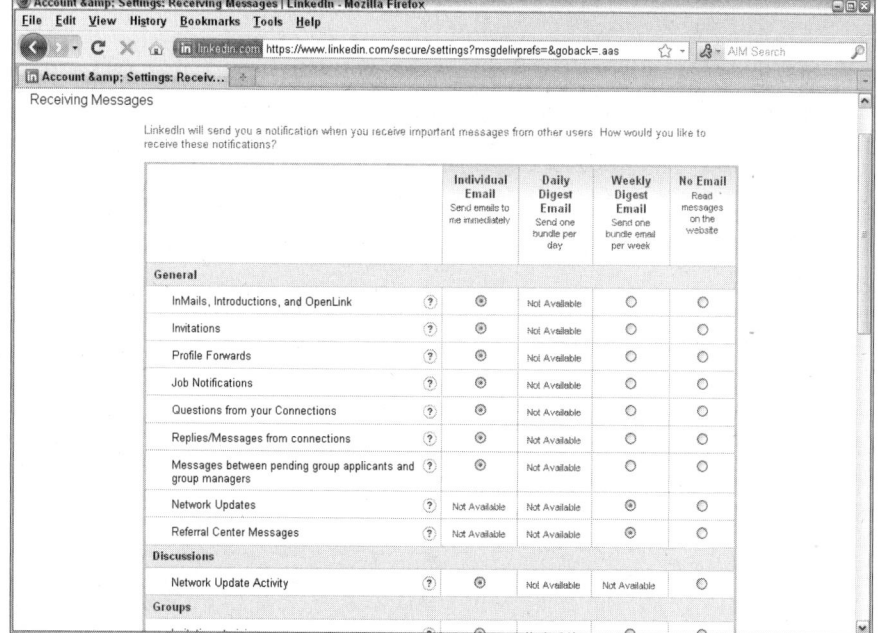

Figure 9-7:
Decide what
e-mails
you want
to get from
LinkedIn
and how
often.

3. **(Optional) Select the LinkedIn May Send Me Marketing Messages about New Products, Features and Tips check box to sign up for a monthly newsletter from LinkedIn.**

4. **Scroll down to the bottom of the page and click the Save Changes button.**

   You return to the Account & Settings page.

Understanding your Inbox

The best hub for your communications is the LinkedIn Inbox, which you can access by clicking the Inbox link in the top navigation bar. In most cases, you go to the action items (or new messages that require your attention) in your Inbox, as shown in Figure 9-8. If you have no pending items, you see a link to display all your archived (old) messages.

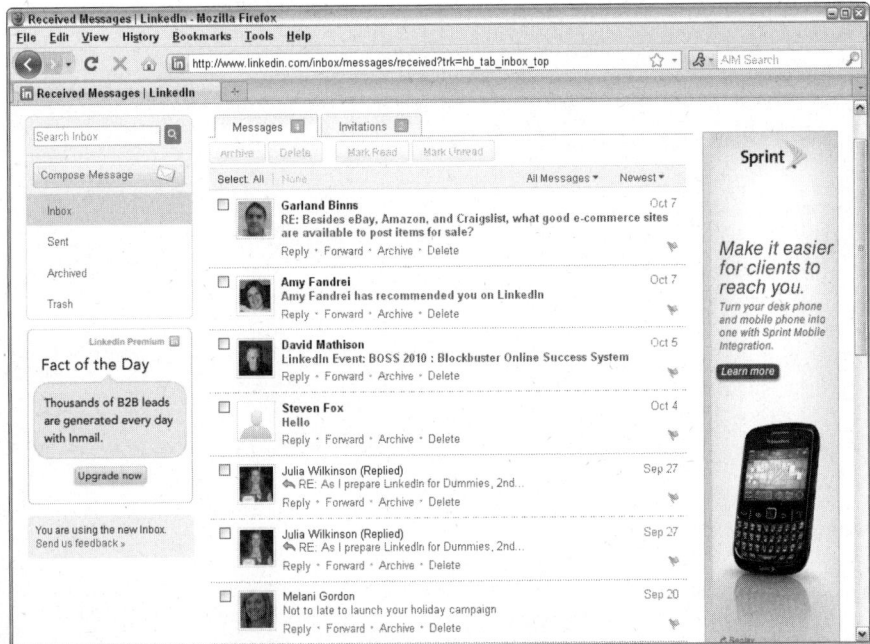

Figure 9-8:
Review the
action items
in your
Inbox.

Here are some things to keep in mind when navigating your Inbox:

✔ **Using the links on the left:** You can click any of the links along the left side to see your Inbox, Sent items, Archived items, or your Trash.

✓ **Using the filters:** By default, when you're looking at your Inbox, you see all messages. If you click the drop-down arrow next to the All Messages heading (above your first item), you can pick a specific category (such as InMail, Introductions, Jobs, Unread Messages, Forwarded Profiles, or Recommendations).

✓ **Archiving:** After you read your message, you can archive the message for later viewing. However, unlike other e-mail systems, you can't (as of this writing) create your own folders within your LinkedIn Inbox. Instead, you simply archive a message into a general archive. From within the message, or in the list of messages in your Inbox, just click the Archive link to move the item from your Inbox to your Archived folder.

✓ **Deleting:** If you don't want to keep a message, click the Delete link.

✓ **Viewing the archive:** To view your archived messages, click the Archived link from the left side of your screen when looking at your Inbox. Your archived messages appear in the same place where your Inbox messages appeared. You can also filter your Archived messages the same way you filter your Inbox messages.

Tracking Your InMail and Your Introductions

Although many of your communications with immediate first-degree LinkedIn connections take place through your own e-mail system, communications with people *outside* your network of first-degree connections need to be tracked and responded to via LinkedIn. So take a look at how you can track InMail and Introductions through your LinkedIn Inbox.

To go directly to your list of InMail messages or Introductions, click the InMail link or the Introductions link from the All Messages filter in your Inbox. For example, when I click the InMail link, I go to the InMails page shown in Figure 9-9. In addition, if you want to switch between received and sent InMails, click the Sent folder link and then filter all the Sent messages by using the All Messages filter to select only InMail.

And your Introductions message list uses a similar setup, like the one shown in Figure 9-10. The top Introduction in this example, Michael Bellomo, has been accepted. The second Introduction, from Jeremy Goldstone, has also been acted upon. You can tell because both items have the green arrow next to the subject line.

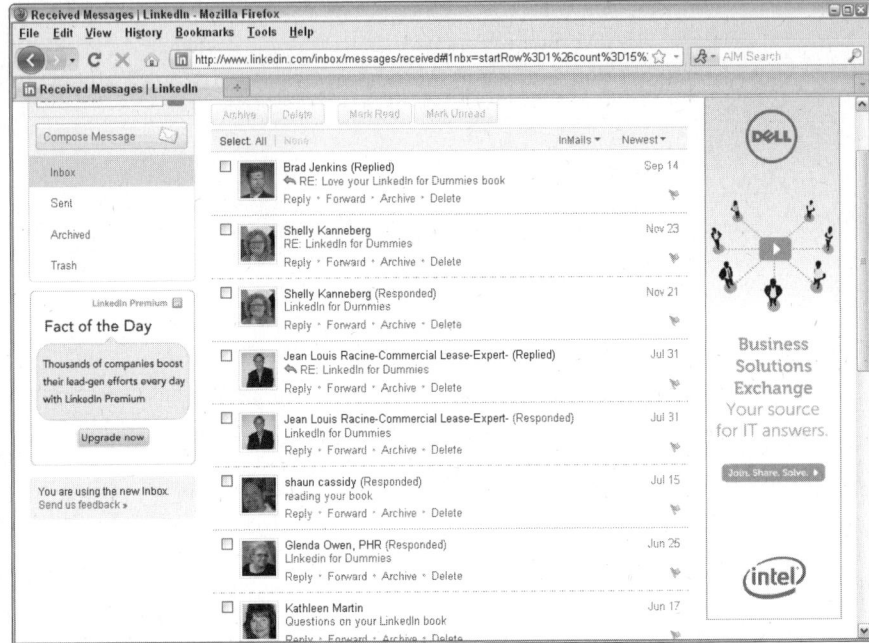

Figure 9-9:
Take a look
at the InMail
you've
received.

Note green arrows.

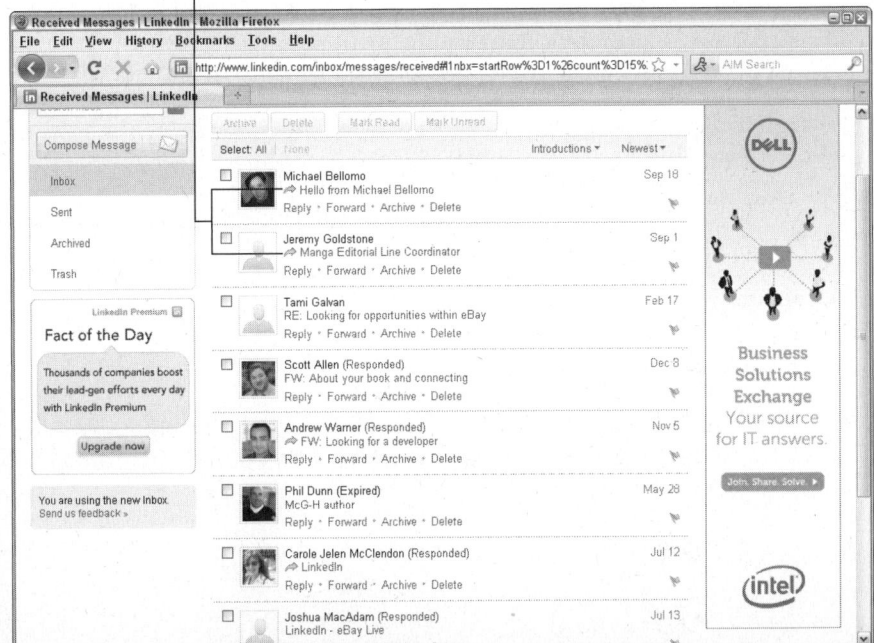

Figure 9-10:
Take a
look at the
Introduction
messages
you've
received.

The process is similar for tracking your answers for any questions you've posed on LinkedIn Answers and for any Recommendations you've received. Turn to Chapter 7 to find out about how to respond to Answers, and see Chapter 8 for more info on Recommendations.

Tracking Invitations

As you grow your network, you need to keep track of the Invitations you sent to your connections and any incoming Invitations. I cover Invitations in Chapter 2, and I talk about setting up your notifications for receiving e-mail about Invitations (in the section "Having LinkedIn automatically contact you," earlier this chapter), but the following sections tell you about monitoring your Invitations on the LinkedIn Web site.

Tracking sent Invitations

The last thing you want to do is send repeat Invitations to the same person because you didn't monitor your Sent Invitations list. Also, you might want to review your Sent Invitations list to see whether someone has responded; if not, you can send that person a follow-up e-mail either through LinkedIn or via your own e-mail account. To help you, LinkedIn keeps a running list of all the Invitations you sent, with the current status (Accepted, Doesn't Know, Expired, or Sent) of each Invitation on that page as well.

Here's how to track your sent Invitations:

1. **Click the Add Connections link from the top-right corner of any LinkedIn page.**

   You can also roll your mouse over the Contacts link in the top navigation bar, and then select Add Connections from the menu that appears.

   This opens the screen for adding connections to your network, as shown in Figure 9-11.

2. **Click the View Sent Invitations link to pull up a list of all your sent Invitations.**

   You see the Sent Invitations page, as shown in Figure 9-12. The status of each Invitation depends on whether (Accepted) appears next to each name. If so, that Invitation was accepted. If not, the Invitation has merely been sent.

View Sent Invitations link

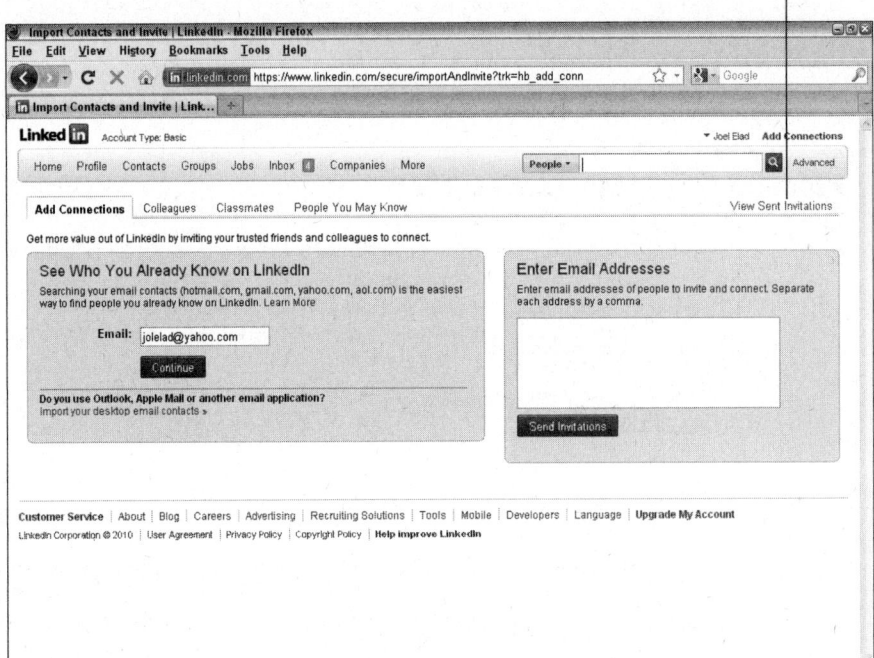

Figure 9-11:
Time to add connec-
tions.

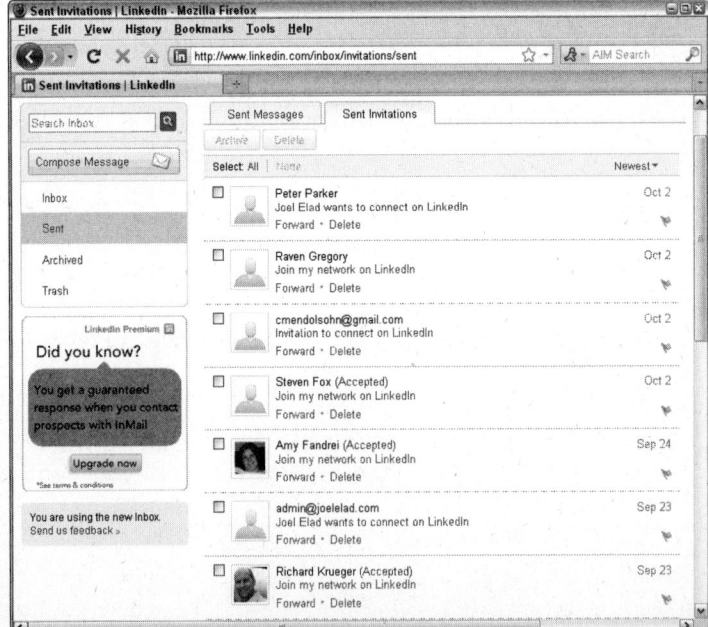

Figure 9-12:
See a list of
your sent
Invitations
and their
statuses.

3. To view an Invitation, click its Subject line.

You see a copy of your Invitation, like the one shown in Figure 9-13. In this particular case, Resend and Withdraw buttons appear because the recipient hasn't yet acted on the Invitation.

- *Resend:* Send a reminder to this person.

- *Withdraw:* Delete your Invitation request.

  When you withdraw the request, no message is sent to the other person.

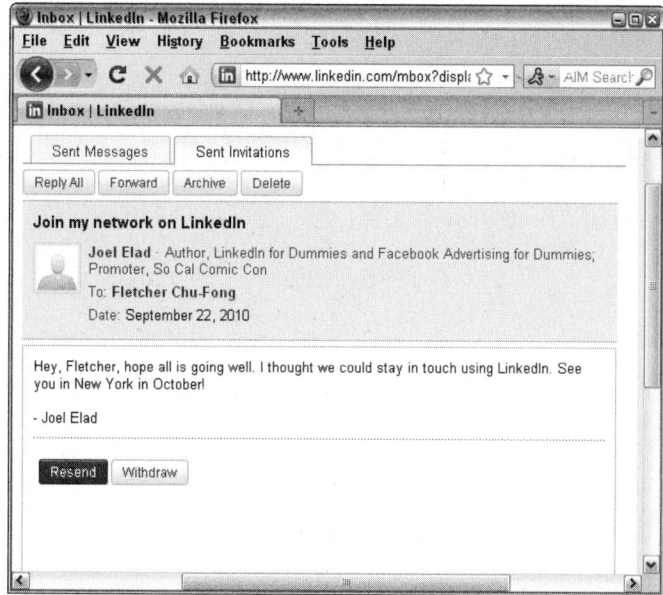

Figure 9-13:
Review an
Invitation
you've sent.

Tracking received Invitations

When growing your LinkedIn network, you should be responsive to others who want to add you to their LinkedIn connections lists. To review your received Invitations, follow these steps:

1. Click the Inbox link from the top navigation bar and then click the Invitations tab (next to the Messages tab) in the middle of the screen.

You're taken to a list of your received Invitations, as shown in Figure 9-14.

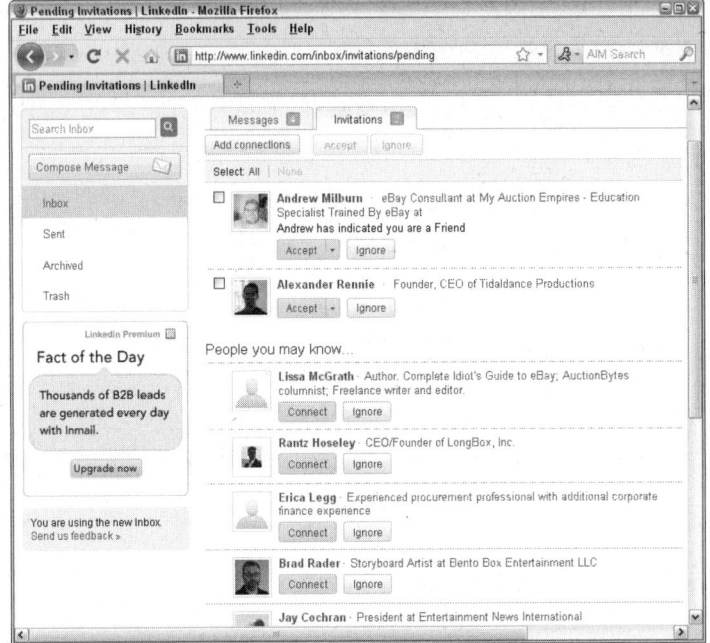

Figure 9-14:
Review your
received
Invitations
here.

2. **To accept a pending Invitation, click the Accept button.**

   If you want to reply to the person without immediately accepting that invitation (say, to get further clarification in case you don't recognize the person), click the drop-down arrow next to the Accept button and then select Reply (don't accept yet) to open a new message to that person. You can also click the Ignore button to remove this Invitation from your Inbox. (See Chapter 6 for tips on growing your network.)

   After you click Accept, Reply, or Ignore, that invitation disappears from your view.

3. **Continue to act on each Invitation in your list until there are no more new Introductions.**

Chapter 10

Using LinkedIn with Your E-Mail and Browser

. . . .

In This Chapter

▶ Importing contacts from Microsoft Outlook

▶ Importing contacts from a Web-based e-mail program

▶ Exporting your LinkedIn contacts to Outlook and other programs

▶ Enhancing your e-mail programs with LinkedIn toolbars

▶ Switching easily between the Web and LinkedIn with a browser toolbar

▶ Creating e-mail signatures

. . . .

*T*his chapter delves in to how you can use LinkedIn as a part of your overall presence on the Internet, especially when it comes to communication. Specifically, I focus on two aspects of your Internet experience: your e-mail account and Internet Web browser.

LinkedIn makes it convenient for you to exchange information between your e-mail program and your LinkedIn profile and to enhance your World Wide Web browsing experience with specialized LinkedIn functions. One feature that LinkedIn offers is the capability to import your contact list from programs such as Microsoft Outlook into LinkedIn. You can also do the reverse: Export your LinkedIn contact list to a variety of e-mail programs, including the Mail program that's part of Mac OS X. Other neat features in LinkedIn include toolbars you can easily install to work with your e-mail program and Web browser. For example, from the Outlook toolbar, you can access certain LinkedIn information while writing e-mails in Outlook. I cover all these cool features in this chapter.

I also tell you about a nifty tool that LinkedIn offers to create an e-mail signature block for you that helps you promote your LinkedIn profile.

Importing Contacts into LinkedIn

One of the most popular (and necessary) activities people use the Internet for is e-mail. Your e-mail account contains a record of e-mail addresses of everyone you regularly communicate with via e-mail. And from your established base of communications, LinkedIn offers a way for you to ramp up your network by importing a list of contacts from your e-mail program. Importing your e-mail contacts into LinkedIn eliminates the drudge of going through your address book and copying addresses into LinkedIn. The next sections show you how to generate a list of contacts and import that list into LinkedIn to update your connections.

Importing a Contacts list from Outlook

Microsoft Outlook is one of the most popular e-mail programs out there. This section shows you how to import your Microsoft Outlook Contacts list into LinkedIn. To do so, follow these steps:

1. **On the main Outlook screen, click Contacts to bring up your Contact List (similar to that shown in Figure 10-1).**

Figure 10-1: Pull up your Outlook Contacts list.

2. **Choose File⇨Import and Export.**

   The Import and Export window appears.

3. **Select the Export to a File option, click the Next button, and then select a file type in the Export to a File window.**

   You see a list of options, including Comma Separated Values (DOS), Comma Separated Values (Windows), Microsoft Access, and so on.

4. **Select the Comma Separated Values (Windows) option and then click Next.**

   The Export to a File window appears. Here, you're asked to pick a folder that you want to export, as shown in Figure 10-2. You need to look for the Contacts folder, which contains your list of contacts through Microsoft Outlook.

Figure 10-2:
Select your
Contacts
folder to
export.

5. **Select the Contacts folder to export and then click Next.**

   If you created categories within your Outlook Contacts list, you can select one of those subcategories under the main Contacts folder and export just those contacts.

6. **In the next Export to a File window that appears, enter a suitable file-name, click the Browse button to locate a folder for storing the new (exported) file, and then click Next.**

   In the Export to a File window, Outlook displays the action it's about to take, as shown in Figure 10-3.

Figure 10-3:
Outlook
verifies
the export
action.

Note the filename and location of your exported Contacts file because you need this information in a few steps. Pick a memorable name and save the file to a commonly used folder on your computer.

7. **Click Finish to start the export of your Outlook Contacts file.**

   Depending on the size of your Contacts list, the export process might take a few minutes. When the export is complete, the status indicator disappears, and you're ready to go to the next step.

8. **Using your Web browser, go to LinkedIn and log in to your account; then, on the top right of the page, click the Add Connections link to bring up that screen.**

9. **On the new page that appears, click the Import Your Desktop Email Contacts link.**

   The Import Your Desktop Email Contacts box appears onscreen, as shown in Figure 10-4.

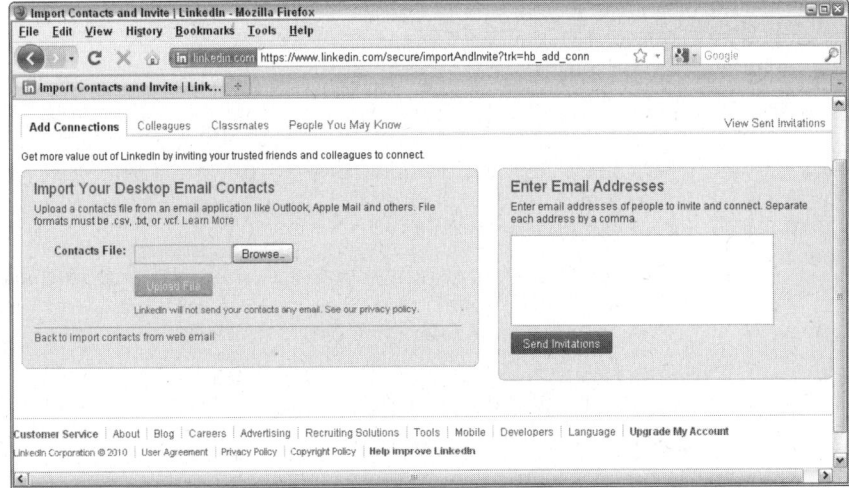

Figure 10-4: LinkedIn is ready to accept your Outlook Contacts list.

10. **Click the Browse button to locate the Contacts file you just exported from Microsoft Outlook. When you locate that file, click the Upload File button to start the process.**

    After LinkedIn reads your entire contacts list, it displays the names of contacts from your list already on LinkedIn first, as shown in Figure 10-5; and then, underneath those names, the remaining contacts from your list.

    When LinkedIn imports the list, it usually drops the middle name from each person's full name when creating the imported contacts. You might need to edit your contacts to add the appropriate information.

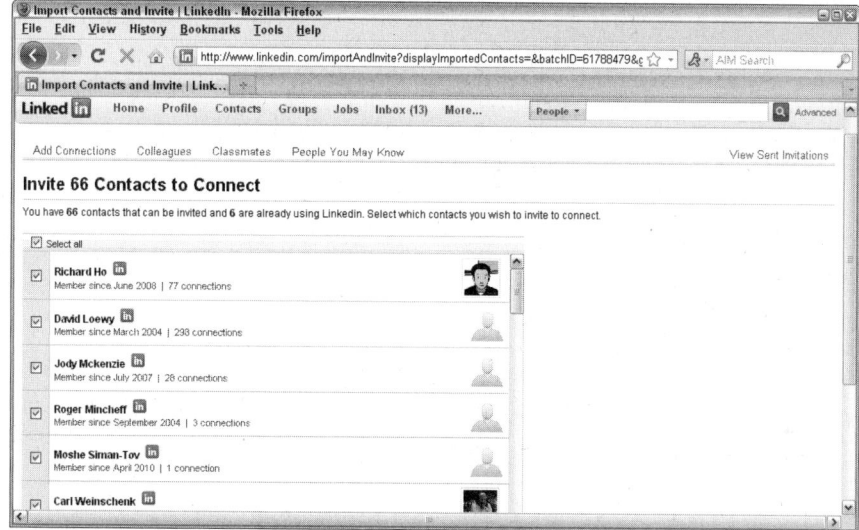

Figure 10-5:
LinkedIn
asks you
which
names
from your
Contacts list
should get
an invita-
tion.

11. **Review the names, clear any check box for someone you don't wish to invite, and then click the Send Invitations button to complete the process.**

If the names you see on the screen aren't correct (perhaps LinkedIn did not read the file properly and everyone's first and last names are reversed, for instance), you can click Cancel to abandon the process.

Importing contacts from a Web-based e-mail program

Many people use a Web-based program *(Webmail)* to send and receive e-mail. Gmail (from Google), Yahoo! Mail, and Hotmail are among the most popular of these programs. Just like Outlook, you can import your Webmail program contact list and feed it into LinkedIn to expand your network. For the example in this section, I use Yahoo! Mail, but the other systems work similarly for importing contacts.

To import a Webmail contact list, just follow these steps:

1. **Using your Web browser, go to LinkedIn and log in to your account.**

2. **Click the Add Connections link at the top right of any LinkedIn page to bring up the Add Connections window.**

The See Who You Already Know on LinkedIn page appears, as shown in Figure 10-6.

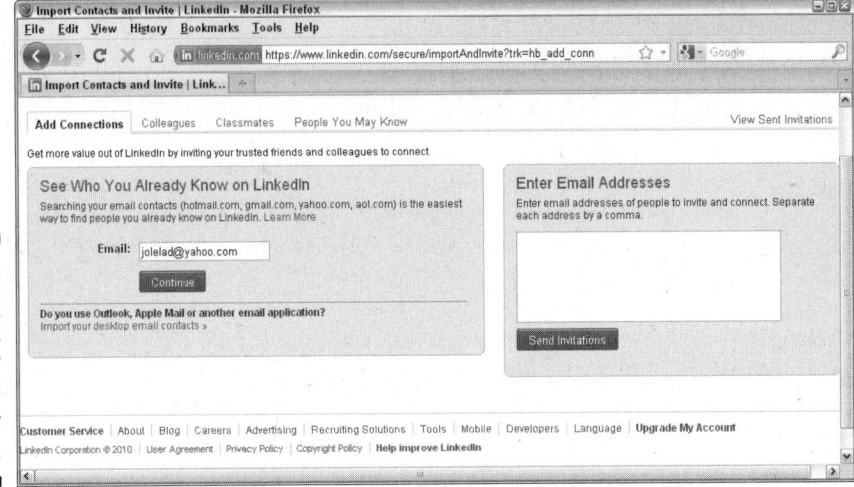

Figure 10-6:
LinkedIn
can check
your
Webmail
program for
contacts.

3. **Enter your Webmail e-mail address into the Email text box and then click the Continue button.**

   LinkedIn opens a new window in which you can connect with your Webmail program. (You may be asked for your e-mail password, so LinkedIn can log in to your account for you.)

4. **Follow the instructions to access your Webmail account.**

   For this example, I used my Yahoo! account, which took me to the Yahoo! login screen. After I logged in to my account, Yahoo! requested my permission to let LinkedIn access my Yahoo! Address Book, as shown in Figure 10-7. You must click the I Agree button if you want LinkedIn to import your contacts. After you do, LinkedIn automatically goes into the account and starts importing contacts, and you're returned to the LinkedIn Web site.

5. **Review the imported contacts and whom you want to invite to your LinkedIn network.**

   LinkedIn may select all your contacts who aren't yet connected to you via LinkedIn and offer to send them an invitation, as shown in Figure 10-8. If that is the case, uncheck the check box next to each person you don't want to invite. For some e-mail systems, you will see your imported contacts and have to manually select which contacts you want to invite by selecting the check box next to each person you want to invite. When you are ready, click the Invite Selected Contacts button to send Invitations to the contacts you wish to add to your network.

6. **When you're done, close the newly opened window that was created back in Step 3 when you started the import process.**

Figure 10-7:
You need
to allow
LinkedIn to
read your
Webmail
address
book.

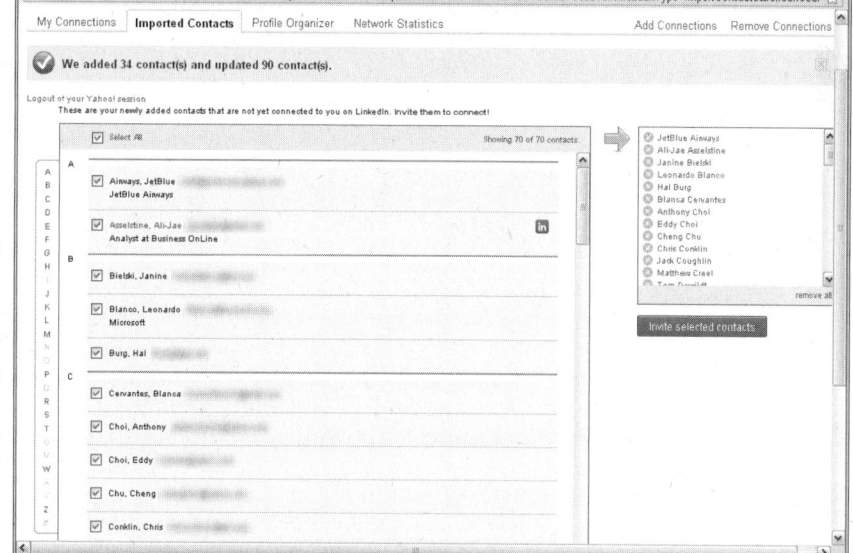

Figure 10-8:
From your
imported
address
book,
decide who
gets invited
to your
network.

Exporting Contacts from LinkedIn to Your E-Mail Application

As you use LinkedIn and build up your contact network, you might end up with more contacts "on file" in your LinkedIn network than stored away in your e-mail program. However, you may want to use your own e-mail system to communicate with all your LinkedIn first-degree connections instead of relying on LinkedIn's message system. Adding these people one by one to your e-mail address book could take a while. Thankfully, LinkedIn has a function to make this easier.

In essence, your list of LinkedIn connections is similar to a list of names in any e-mail program's address book. And just like you can import contacts from an e-mail program into LinkedIn, you can export your LinkedIn contacts to your e-mail program. Exporting is a simple process that amounts to the following:

1. You export your LinkedIn connections into a contacts file.

2. You import the contacts file into your main e-mail program.

You can always pick and choose which contacts to export, and your e-mail program should be able to detect any duplicates — meaning that if you try to import any names that already exist, you should get a warning message. I walk you through the process of exporting your LinkedIn contacts in the next few sections.

Creating your Contacts export file in LinkedIn

First, you need to generate your exported file of contacts from LinkedIn. To do so, follow these steps:

1. **On any LinkedIn page, roll your mouse over the Contacts link in the top navigation bar, choose My Connections from the menu that appears, and then scroll to the bottom of the new page.**

2. **Click the Export Connections link.**

   You'll be taken to the Export LinkedIn Connections page, as shown in Figure 10-9. From the drop-down list provided, pick the e-mail program to which you want to export your contacts. Then enter the security image text into the box provided.

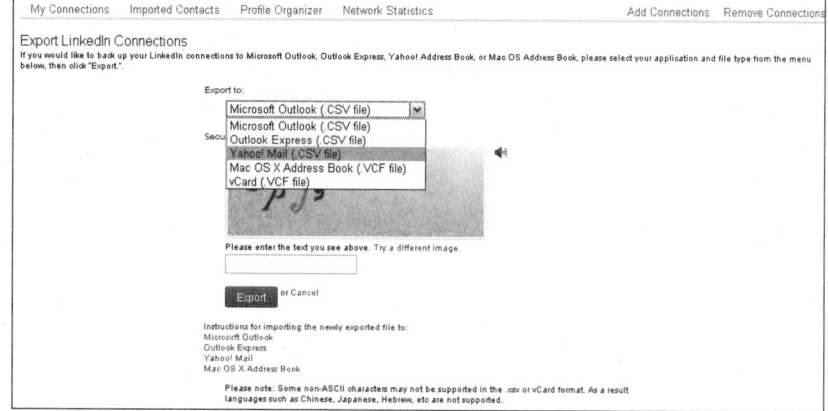

Figure 10-9:
Pick your
e-mail pro-
gram and
create an
exported file
of contacts.

3. Click the Export button to generate your Contacts file.

The File dialog box appears, asking whether you want to open or save the file. Click Save to save the file to your computer. Give it a custom name, if you like, but remember the filename and location because you need that information when you load this file into your e-mail program, which I discuss in the next sections.

Exporting contacts to Outlook

Now that you've created your Contacts file, it's time to import it into your e-mail program. For my first example, I'm going to use Microsoft Outlook, but the procedure will be similar with other e-mail clients. The next few sections will give you an idea of how to handle other e-mail clients.

After you create your LinkedIn export file and are ready to export your LinkedIn contacts to Microsoft Outlook, just follow these steps:

1. On the main Outlook screen, choose File⇨Import and Export.

The Import and Export window appears.

2. Select the Import from Another Program or File option and then click Next.

3. When Outlooks asks you to select a file type to import from, select the Comma Separated Values (Windows) option and then click Next.

4. When Outlook asks you for the file to import, enter the path and file-name of your exported file, or click the Browse button to find the file on your computer. Be sure to select the Do Not Import Duplicate Items option and then click Next.

If you don't select the Do Not Import Duplicate Items option, you risk flooding your Outlook account with multiple e-mail addresses and names for the same people, which will make your life more difficult and flood your connections with unnecessary e-mail messages.

5. **When Outlook asks you to select a destination folder, click the Contacts folder and then click Next.**

6. **Verify that you're importing your contacts file into Outlook and then click Finish to start the process.**

Exporting contacts to Outlook Express

Fortunately, even if you prefer Outlook Express to the full Outlook program, you're in luck: Your LinkedIn contacts can go live there just as easily as they can elsewhere. After you create your export file (as described earlier, in the "Creating your Contacts export file in LinkedIn" section), you can export your connections to Outlook Express by following these steps:

1. **On your main Outlook Express screen, choose File⇨Import.**

2. **In the Import window that opens, select the Other Address Book option and then click Next.**

3. **When Outlook Express asks you to select a file type to import from, select the Text File (Comma Separated Values) option and then click the Import button.**

4. **When Outlook Express asks you for the file to import, enter the path and filename of your exported file, or click the Browse button to find the file on your computer. Click Next.**

5. **Verify the fields that you're importing into Outlook Express (click the Change Mapping button if you want to change how the information is being imported) and then Click Finish to start the process.**

Exporting contacts to Yahoo! Mail

If you're using a Web-based mail program, like Yahoo! Mail, you can follow this basic procedure to export your LinkedIn contacts into your Webmail program. After you create your export file (as described earlier, in the "Creating your Contacts export file in LinkedIn" section), you can export your connections to Yahoo! Mail by following these steps:

1. **Using your Web browser, go to Yahoo! Mail and log in. Click the Contacts tab or the Address Book link to go to the Yahoo! Address Book.**

You'll see a page similar to that shown in Figure 10-10.

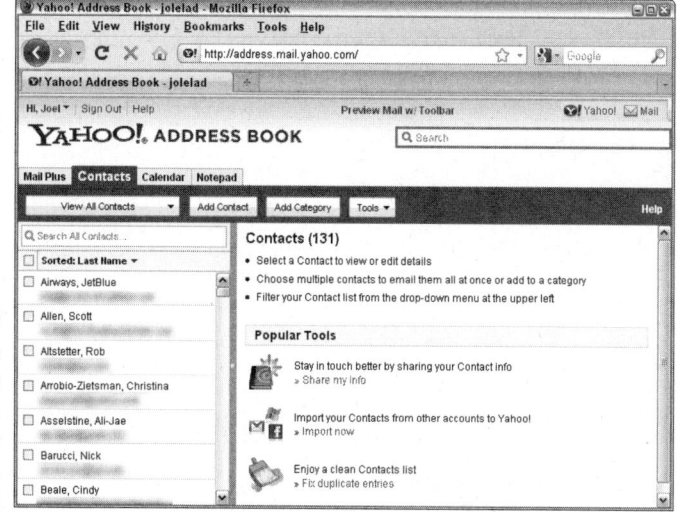

Figure 10-10:
Start at
your Yahoo!
Address
Book.

2. Click the Import Now link under the Popular Tools header.

The Import Contacts screen appears, as shown in Figure 10-11.

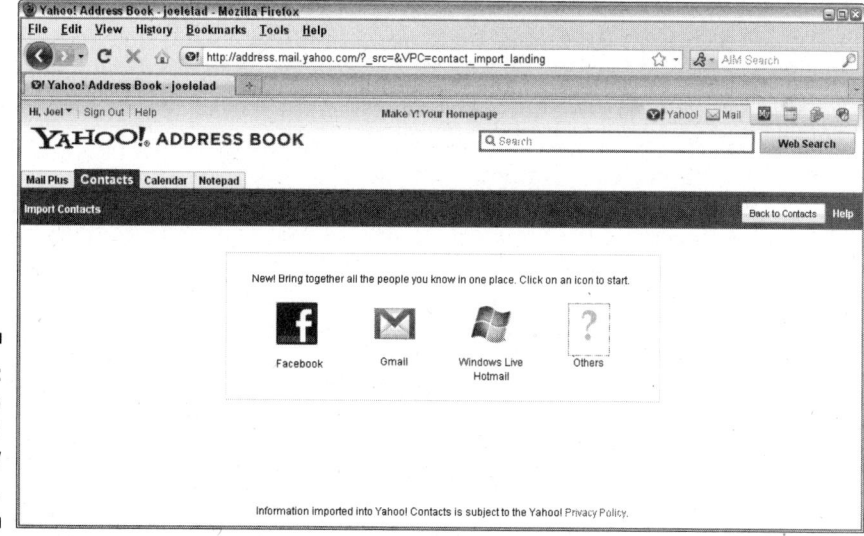

Figure 10-11:
Using the
Yahoo!
Import/
Export tool.

3. Click the Others link.

The Transfer Contacts tab or window appears.

4. **From the Select Source list, first clear the Another Yahoo! Account check box and then select the A Desktop E-mail Program option, as shown in Figure 10-12.**

Figure 10-12:
Select a
desktop
e-mail
program to
import your
contacts.

5. **In the Select a File text box, enter the path and filename of your exported file, or click the Browse button to find the file on your computer.**

6. **Select the Yahoo! permission check box to obtain contacts for you; then click Continue.**

On the next screen, you can review the list of contacts from the file. Make sure that the names you wish to export to Yahoo! (or any Web-based) mail are selected, and then click the Import button. Yahoo! will ask whether you want to send any notifications to the contacts you're importing. You can select the people you wish to get notified and click Finish, or click the Skip Notification and Just Import link to finish the process without any e-mails.

Exporting contacts to Mac OS X Address Book

After you create your export file (as described earlier, in the "Creating your Contacts export file in LinkedIn" section), you can export your connections to Mac OS X Address Book by following these steps:

1. **Locate your Mac OS X Address Book icon in either the Dock or the Applications folder.**

2. **Look for the contacts file you created in the previous section.**

3. **Drag this file onto the Address Book icon.**

   This should start the importing of contacts from your LinkedIn contacts file.

Using the LinkedIn Outlook Toolbar

If you use Microsoft Outlook for your e-mail and you find yourself constantly switching between Outlook and the LinkedIn Web site to retrieve information, send e-mail to your connections via Outlook and then screen incoming e-mail by jumping to LinkedIn to read those profiles, you're in luck! LinkedIn has developed a special toolbar that you can install in your system that automatically ties into its Web site. This toolbar appears as part of your Microsoft Outlook screen and gives you several functions to make the connection between Outlook and LinkedIn smoother.

Understanding the toolbar's requirements and features

To use the LinkedIn Outlook toolbar, you need to have certain levels of software on your computer for the toolbar to work correctly.

- ✔ Your operating system needs to be either Microsoft Windows XP or Vista.

- ✔ Your Microsoft Outlook program should be the XP (or 2002), 2003, or 2007 version.

- ✔ You should have at least 5–10MB of free space on your hard drive before installing this program.

Here are the main benefits you can enjoy after installing this toolbar function:

- ✔ **This toolbar will suggest sending an Invitation to someone to join your network based on the number of times you e-mail that person.** The higher the "e-mail frequency," the more likely you should add him to your LinkedIn network.

- ✔ **This toolbar allows you to send Invitations with one click, instead of your having to find the person's profile on LinkedIn and clicking through the Invite process.** You can also pull up the LinkedIn Web site with one click using the toolbar.

✔ **This toolbar automatically displays a LinkedIn "mini-profile" of some-one when you read an e-mail from that person using Outlook.** This way, you can get more information about the sender, in the form of a pop-up instantly, rather than manually going to LinkedIn to research the person.

✔ **Your Outlook contact information for a LinkedIn connection is auto-matically updated with that connection's profile information.**

✔ **You can receive e-mail notifications when someone in your LinkedIn network updates his or her profile information.**

✔ **You can access a LinkedIn "dashboard" to get a snapshot of your LinkedIn network and the status of your connections.**

Installing the Outlook toolbar

To install the Outlook toolbar, just follow these steps:

1. **Go to the LinkedIn home page, scroll to the bottom of the page, and click the Tools link.**

2. **From the Tools screen that appears, click the Outlook Toolbar tab.**

   The Outlook Toolbar screen, shown in Figure 10-13, appears.

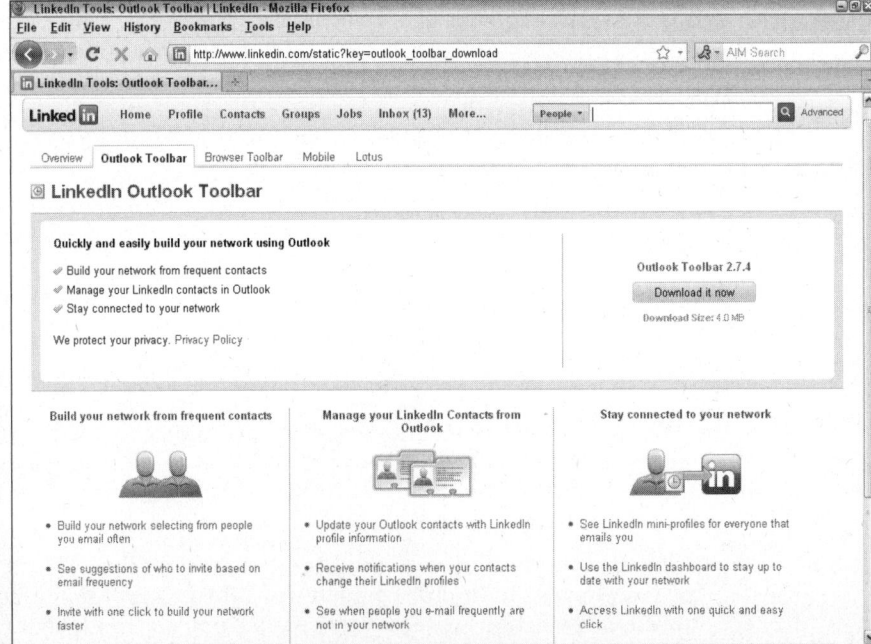

Figure 10-13:
Install the
Microsoft
Outlook
LinkedIn
Toolbar
here.

3. **Click the Download It Now button. When the LinkedIn Outlook Toolbar Setup Wizard opens, click Next.**

4. **On the page with the License Agreement that appears, review the License Agreement, select the I Accept check box, and then click Next.**

5. **In the Choose Install Location screen that appears, accept the default location (recommended) or pick a new directory to install the toolbar program; then click Install to start the process.**

   LinkedIn installs all the necessary files for the toolbar onto your computer. Allow at least a few minutes for this process to be completed. When the toolbar is installed, a Build Network Wizard window appears.

6. **Click the Start button and follow the steps to have the toolbar scan your Outlook program for contacts.**

   You can send an Invitation to these contacts to join your LinkedIn network.

If you already imported your Microsoft Outlook Address Book into LinkedIn, going through the Build Network Wizard might not result in a lot of new contacts, but this process can find contacts you might not have saved to your Outlook Address Book.

Using the LinkedIn Browser Toolbar

Do you find yourself going back and forth between LinkedIn and other Web sites? Whether you do further research on someone from a general Web search by looking up his LinkedIn profile, or you're actively looking for a job and frequently switch between LinkedIn and other career job sites, LinkedIn has the tool for you.

Regardless of whether you use Microsoft Internet Explorer or Mozilla's Firefox Web browser, LinkedIn offers you a toolbar you can install that shows up as part of your Web browser and provides you with instant access to the LinkedIn Web site. The toolbar also offers integrated functions that give you access to items such as profile information with the click of a mouse.

Get to the main LinkedIn Browser toolbar page (shown in Figure 10-14) by clicking the Browser Toolbar link from the Tools menu along the bottom of the LinkedIn home page. The following sections tell you how to install the toolbar, depending on your browser.

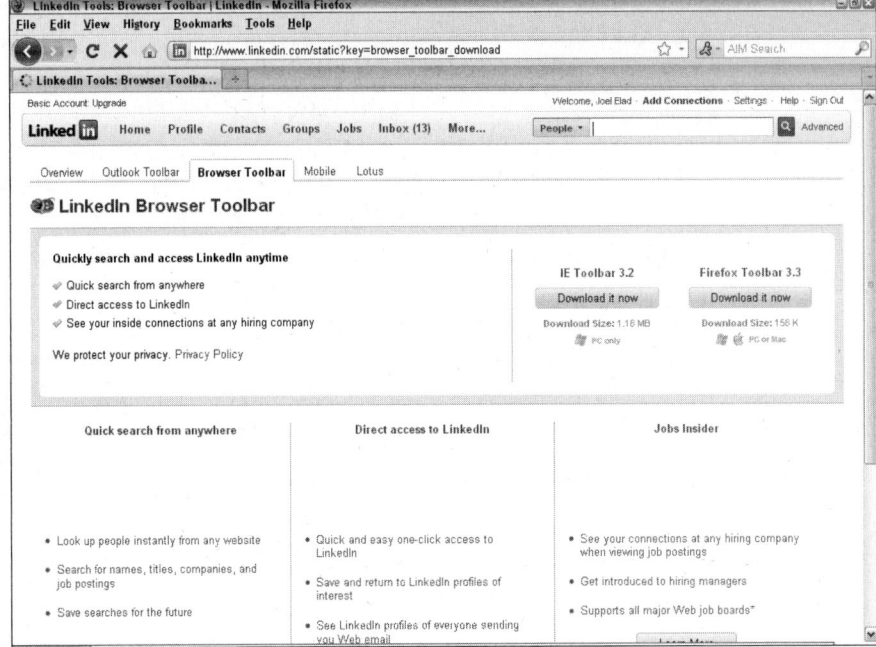

Figure 10-14:
LinkedIn
offers
two Web
browser
toolbars.

How to install the Internet Explorer toolbar

When you're ready to install the Internet Explorer toolbar, just follow these steps:

1. **Log in to LinkedIn, scroll to the bottom of the page, and click the Tools menu bar item. Then, from the Tools window, click the Browser Toolbar tab.**

2. **Click the Download It Now button under the IE Toolbar header.**

   A window like the one shown in Figure 10-15 opens, asking whether you want to run this installation file directly from the Internet or to save the installation file to your computer, where you can run it locally. Pick the option best for you and click the appropriate button.

   If you have a fast Internet connection, you can click Run to have the toolbar installed over your Internet connection. Otherwise, I recommend saving the file to your computer and then running the file from your hard drive.

3. **When the LinkedIn Internet Explorer Toolbar Setup Wizard appears, click Next.**

   Accept the License Agreement and then click Next.

4. **On the Choose Install Location screen that appears, click the Install button to accept the default and start the installation of the toolbar.**

   You can also click the Browse button to pick another directory for the toolbar, but the default location should be fine.

   When the toolbar starts installing, you need to close all Internet Explorer windows. When you see the warning message from LinkedIn, click Yes, and the installation program will close all active windows for you.

5. **When a screen appears confirming that LinkedIn has installed the IE Toolbar successfully, select the Launch Internet Explorer with LinkedIn Toolbar check box and then click Finish.**

   A new Internet Explorer window opens containing the LinkedIn toolbar, as shown in Figure 10-16.

Installing the Firefox Companion toolbar

To install the Firefox Companion toolbar, just follow these steps:

1. **Log in to LinkedIn, scroll to the bottom of the page, click the menu bar item labeled Tools. From the Tools window, click the Browser Toolbar tab.**

2. **Click the Download It Now button under the Firefox Toolbar header.**

   A window like the one in Figure 10-17 appears, asking whether it should install this software.

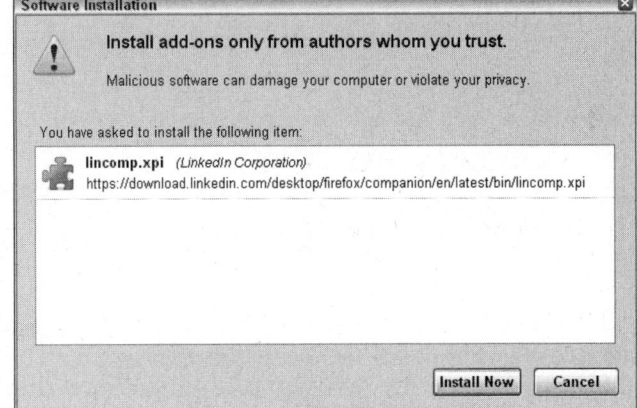

Figure 10-17:
Firefox
needs your
permission
to install the
toolbar.

3. **Click the Install Now button.**

   LinkedIn installs the toolbar onto your computer, and you should see a confirmation message that the toolbar was installed successfully.

4. **Click the Restart Firefox button to close and restart your Web browser session.**

   The LinkedIn button is installed in the top-right area of your browser window, as shown in Figure 10-18. Anytime you need a LinkedIn function, just click the LinkedIn logo in the toolbar to bring up the special menu.

Figure 10-18:
Your
LinkedIn
companion
is ready
for use in
Firefox.

Creating E-Mail Signatures

One of the best ways to communicate your presence on LinkedIn is to add your LinkedIn profile to your e-mail signature, if you've created one. Every time you send an e-mail, you can have text appear automatically at the end of your message similar to a written signature you would put at the end of a letter. Some people just sign their name; others use this space as an opportunity to put their name and some contact information, such as phone numbers, e-mail addresses, physical addresses, and, more recently, Web site addresses. Some LinkedIn members include their profile URL, so anyone getting an e-mail from them can take a look at their person profile and learn more about them.

LinkedIn developed a cool tool with which you can build your own advanced e-mail signature using the LinkedIn Web site. You can decide what information you want to include in your signature, and LinkedIn helps you with formatting, graphics — the entire "look and feel" of your signature.

Access the e-mail signature tool by clicking the Tools link at the bottom of the LinkedIn home page. When you get to the Tools page, skip down below the toolbar sections and look for the Email Signature section (shown in Figure 10-19).

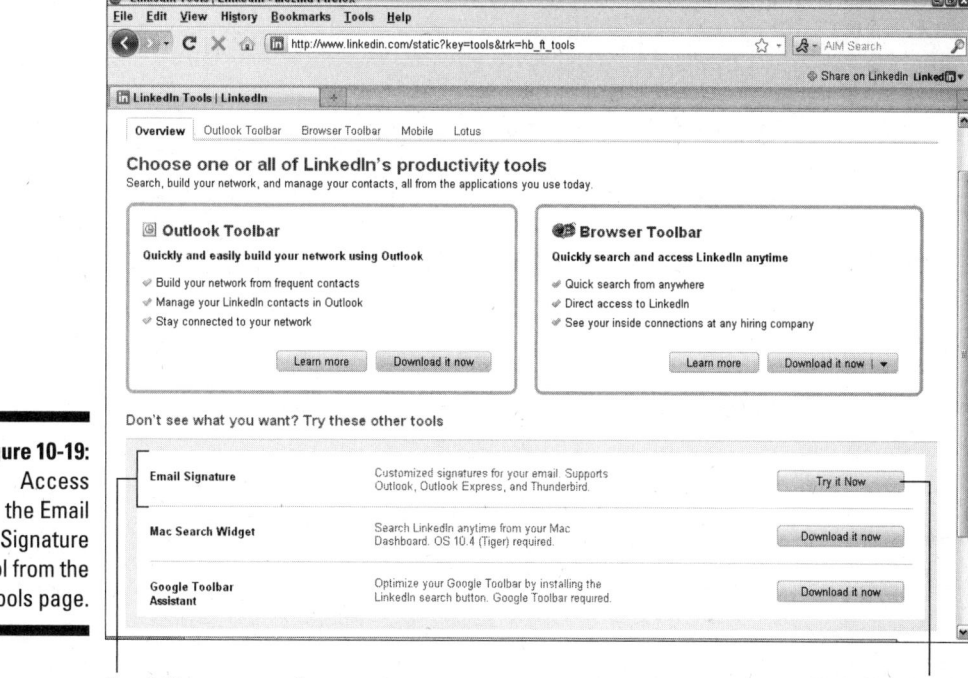

Figure 10-19: Access the Email Signature tool from the Tools page.

Email Signature section   Try It Now button

When you're ready to create your e-mail signature, just follow these steps:

1. **Log in to LinkedIn, scroll to the bottom of the page, and click the Tools menu bar item.**

2. **On the Tools Overview page, scroll down to the Email Signature section and click the gray Try It Now button.**

   LinkedIn takes you to a special Profile page: Create Email Signature.

3. **On your Profile page, click the drop-down arrow next to Select Layout to pick which Layout option you want.**

   You have multiple options to select from. Some (such as Ingot or Plastic Curve) add a graphical look; the Simple option lists your information as text; and the Executive layout presents your information in a more professional manner.

   Click around and pick a few layouts to see the automatic preview of that layout on your screen. This gives you an idea of which layout and color scheme you want. You may want to revisit this step after you enter all your information so that you know how your finished signature will appear.

4. **After you pick your layout style, enter the contact information you want to appear in your signature.**

   You can input as much or as little as you'd like (see Figure 10-20), and that information will be reflected in your signature file (see Figure 10-21).

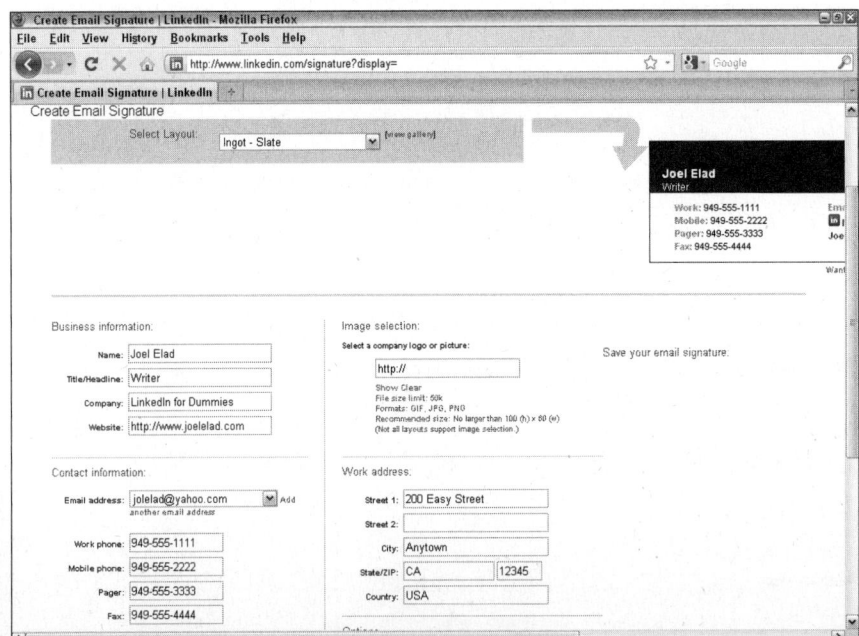

Figure 10-20: Enter your contact information.

5. (Optional) Add a picture to your signature by entering the URL of that picture's location in the Image Selection field.

If you already uploaded a picture of yourself for your LinkedIn profile, you can include it here as well.

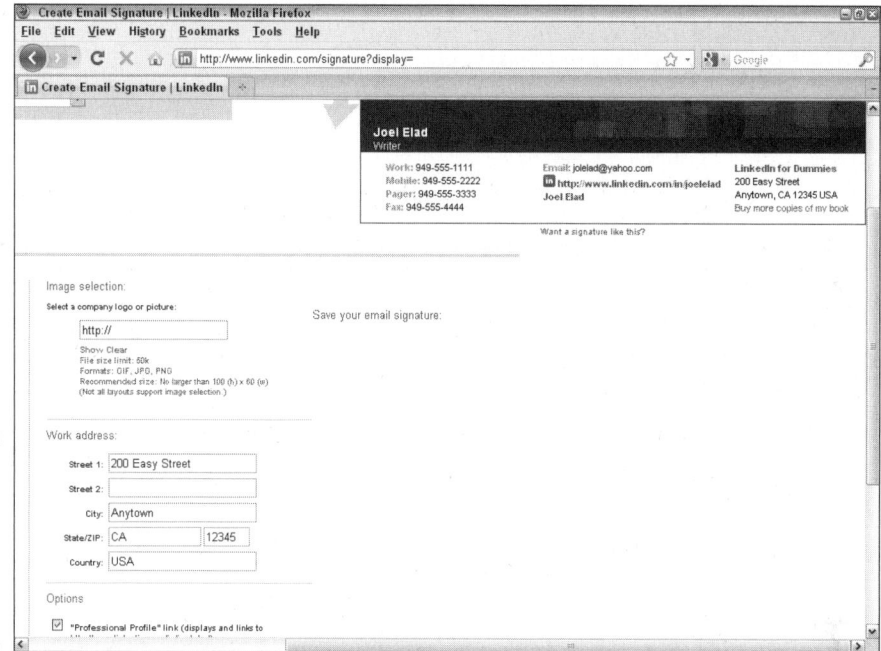

Figure 10-21: Preview how your info looks in your e-mail signature!

6. Scroll down to the Options section (below Work Address) and decide which of three links can appear as part of your signature by selecting the appropriate check box(es):

- *Professional Profile:* Create a URL link to your LinkedIn Profile page.

- *See Who We Know in Common:* Create a link to LinkedIn that, when a LinkedIn member clicks the link, shows other LinkedIn members who are connected to you and that person.

- *We're Hiring:* Creates a link that takes someone back to LinkedIn and starts a Job Search query for job openings in the company you've listed in your LinkedIn profile.

I highly recommend enabling the Professional Profile option. The other two links are fine to enable as well, especially if you want to promote job listings at your own company.

7. Near the bottom of the page, click the Click Here for Instructions link under the Save Your Email Signature header to create and save your e-mail signature (see Figure 10-22).

A pop-up window appears with your e-mail signature information. If you have a pop-up blocker on your Web browser, you may want to deactivate it temporarily before performing this step, or be ready to temporarily allow pop-ups from LinkedIn.com.

Figure 10-22: Click this link to generate your e-mail signature.

8. When the page with the pop-up window containing the "code" of your e-mail signature appears, as shown in Figure 10-22, simply select all that text and then paste it into your favorite e-mail program, or you can scroll down and follow the instructions.

LinkedIn provides instructions for the most popular e-mail programs, such as Outlook and Yahoo! Mail. Click the drop-down arrow to bring up your e-mail program and instructions will appear at the bottom of the window, as do the instructions for Outlook Express in Figure 10-23.

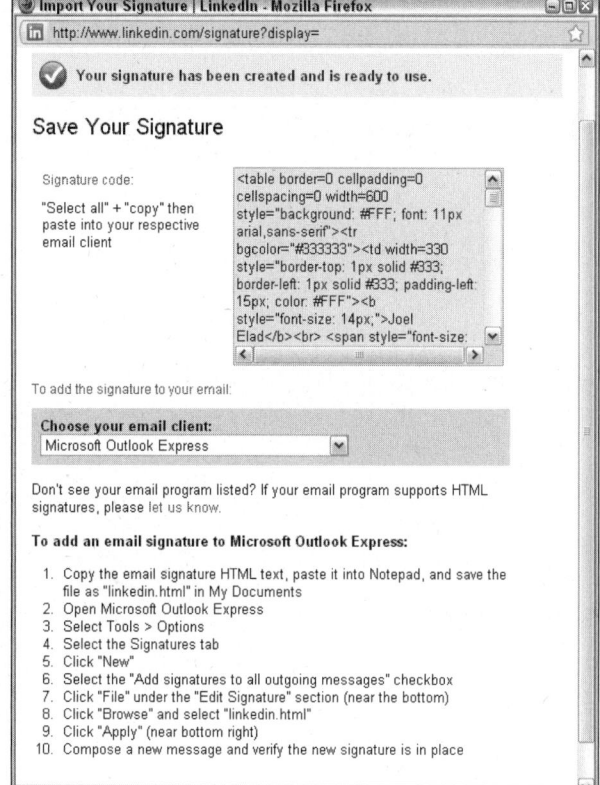

Figure 10-23:
Your e-mail
signature
is created.
Copy and
paste it into
your e-mail
program.

Part IV
Finding Employees, Jobs, and Services

The 5th Wave   By Rich Tennant

"Still trying to create a flock on LinkedIn?"

In this part . . .

1'm a firm believer in the phrase, "Good help is hard to find." I'm not sure why that's the case, but it seems to be tougher and tougher to find someone you can trust who can help you out. I could get all philosophical and wax poetic about the good ol' days, when everything cost a nickel and you had to hike up the mountain, covered in two feet of snow, *both ways,* to get a jug of milk.

This part of the book talks specifically about how LinkedIn can help you do one of three things: Find a good employee, find a job, or find a qualified service professional, like a graphic designer, an accountant, or even a gardener. I provide detailed instructions on how to access the Jobs portion of LinkedIn, whether you're a job seeker or an employer, and tailor my discussion of the myriad functions that LinkedIn offers with specific advice on how you accomplish these three tasks.

Chapter 11

Finding Employees

*W*hen you have a handle on the key elements of improving your LinkedIn profile and experience, it's time to look outward toward the LinkedIn network and talk about some of the benefits you can reap from a professional network of tens of millions of people.

Whether you're an entrepreneur looking for your first employee, a growing start-up needing to add a knowledgeable staffer, or a part of a Fortune 500 company filling a recent opening, LinkedIn can provide a very rich and powerful pool of potential applicants and job candidates, including the perfectly skilled person who isn't even looking for a job! One of the benefits of LinkedIn, when it comes to looking for an employee, is that you aren't limited to an applicant's one- or two-page resume and cover letter. Instead, you get the full picture of the applicant's professional history, coupled with recommendations and his knowledge and/or willingness to share information. Even if you find your candidate outside LinkedIn, you can use the site to perform reference checks and get more information about your candidate.

In this chapter, I cover the basics of using LinkedIn to find an employee for your company or startup. I start with the basics of how you can post your job listing on LinkedIn and review your applicants. I then move on to the Reference Check function, where you can use LinkedIn to screen potential candidates, and I finish the chapter with search strategies you should employ to find the right person.

Posting a Job Listing

LinkedIn offers a Hiring Solutions page for companies to manage their job listings. Roll your mouse over the Jobs link on the top navigation bar on the home page, and choose Hiring Solutions from the drop-down menu that appears to see the Hiring Solutions home page, as shown in Figure 11-1. This is where you start the process of creating a job listing, reviewing the applicants you get, and paying LinkedIn to post the listing.

As of this writing, it costs $195 for one standard, 30-day job listing on LinkedIn. LinkedIn also offers packs of five or ten Job Credits (one Job Credit allows you to post one job listing) that reduce the per-listing cost by up to 35 percent or so. You can pay for your job listing with a major credit card such as Visa, MasterCard, American Express, or Discover.

If you know that you're going to need multiple or ongoing job postings on LinkedIn, you might want to consider LinkedIn Corporate Recruiting Solutions to get discounts on multiple credits for job postings and InMail. You can get more information by completing a request at `http://talent.linkedin.com`.

You can choose to renew your listing at the end of the 30-day window. Your *date posted* (the date you set up the job listing) will be updated with the renewal date instead of the original posting date, so the listing will appear at the top of search results. The cost for renewing a job listing is the same as the initial job posting cost.

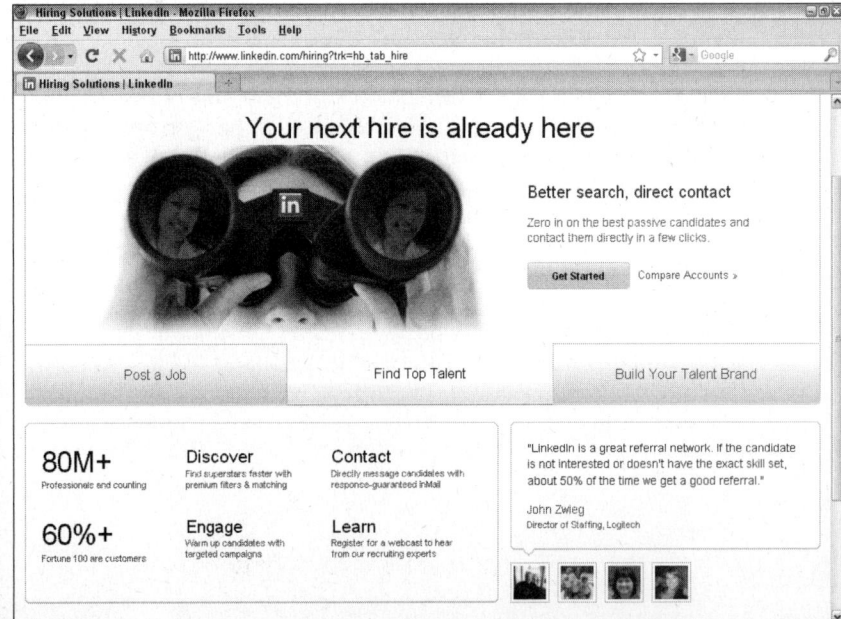

Figure 11-1: LinkedIn offers a Hiring Solutions page to manage your job listings.

You can advertise only one open position per job listing. If you solicit applications for more than one position within a single job listing, LinkedIn will remove your listing or require you to purchase multiple job credits.

Posting a job listing

To post your job opening, follow these steps:

1. **Roll your mouse over the Jobs link in the top navigation bar, and choose Post a Job from the drop-down menu that appears.**

   You see the Compose Job screen, as shown in Figure 11-2.

2. **Using the text boxes and lists provided, enter the required information about your company and the job you're offering.**

   When it comes to your company, LinkedIn asks for your company name, its location, and the company URL (optional). As for the job posting itself, you'll need to specify the job title, job type, experience level, function, industry, compensation (pay), and a referral bonus, if any. When you're done with that, you can scroll down and compose your job description in the text box provided (see Figure 11-3) or copy the description from another source and paste it into the box. Just make sure any formatting (like spacing, bullet points, font size, and so on) is correct after you paste the text.

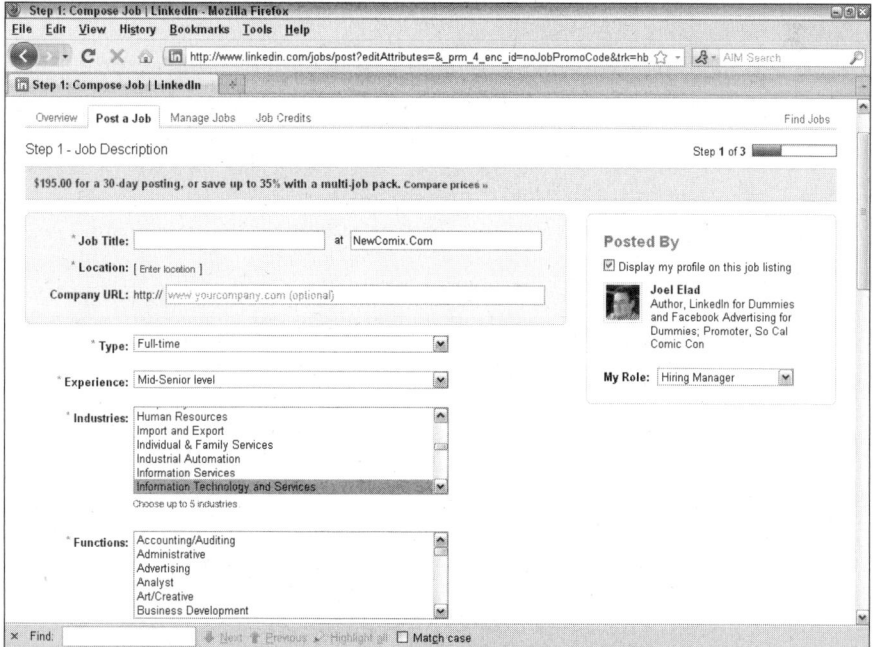

Figure 11-2: Start composing your job posting here.

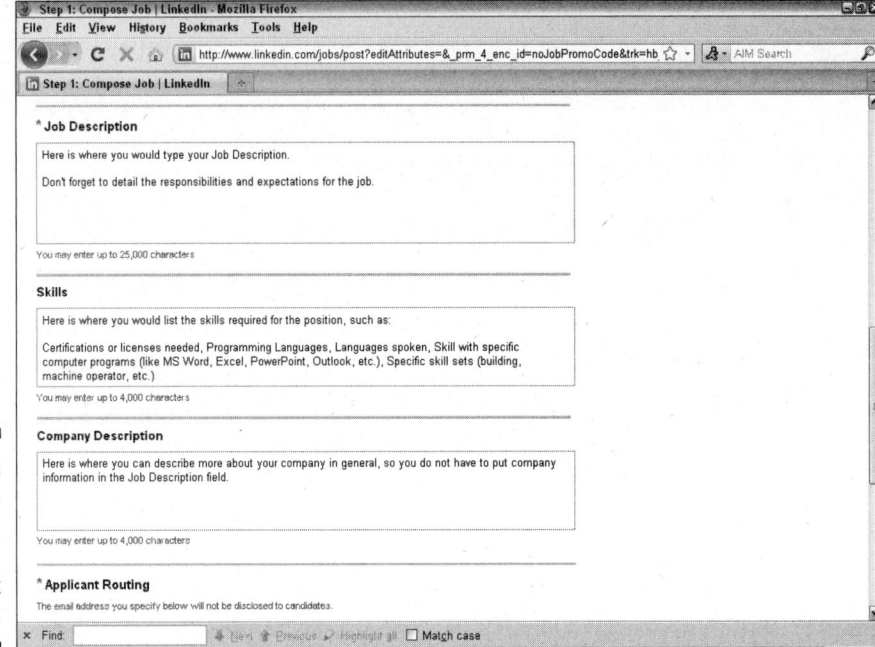

Figure 11-3:
Enter the job description in the text box provided.

If your company isn't that well known, you should include some details about the company in the Company Description field. If the job title seems a bit ambiguous, you can elaborate a bit by filling out the skills required for the job title in the Skills field.

3. Scroll down and fill in the Applicant Routing and Additional Information sections, as shown in Figure 11-4.

LinkedIn automatically offers you the ability to receive applications at one of your existing e-mail addresses, but you can decide which e-mail address should receive applications, or whether applicants should use a direct URL to apply to your job position.

Don't overlook the Additional Information section (again, see Figure 11-4), which you can use to add more requirements to the job.

4. Click the Continue button to proceed to the next step, Billing Verification, as shown in Figure 11-5.

LinkedIn will analyze your job listing and look for matches, but first, it will need your billing information. Even if you are using a pre-paid Job Credit, you'll still need to have a credit card on file for verification purposes. Complete all the fields required and click the Buy Now button.

That's it! You have completed the all-important first step: You posted your job listing, as shown in Figure 11-6. This listing will be available through LinkedIn's Jobs Home page, which you can get to by rolling your mouse over the Jobs link (in the top navigation bar) and clicking Find Jobs.

After your job listing is posted, LinkedIn will pop up a window over the screen (as shown in Figure 11-6), encouraging you to use your LinkedIn network members to spread the word about your job listing and see who they recommend. You can pick from among these sources: Your LinkedIn News Feed, Twitter, any LinkedIn groups you belong to, or e-mail forwarding.

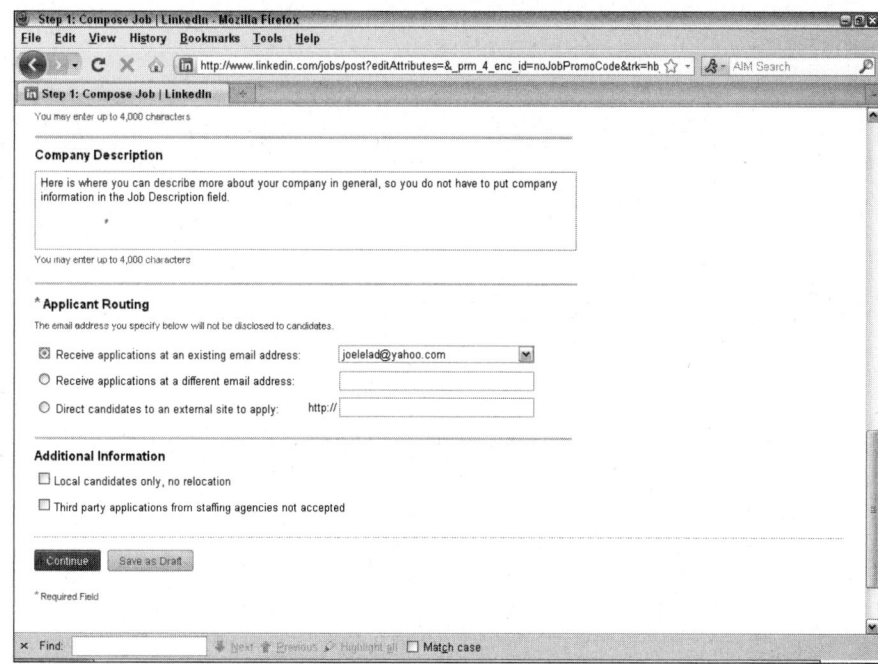

Figure 11-4:
Set your applicant routing and additional requirements.

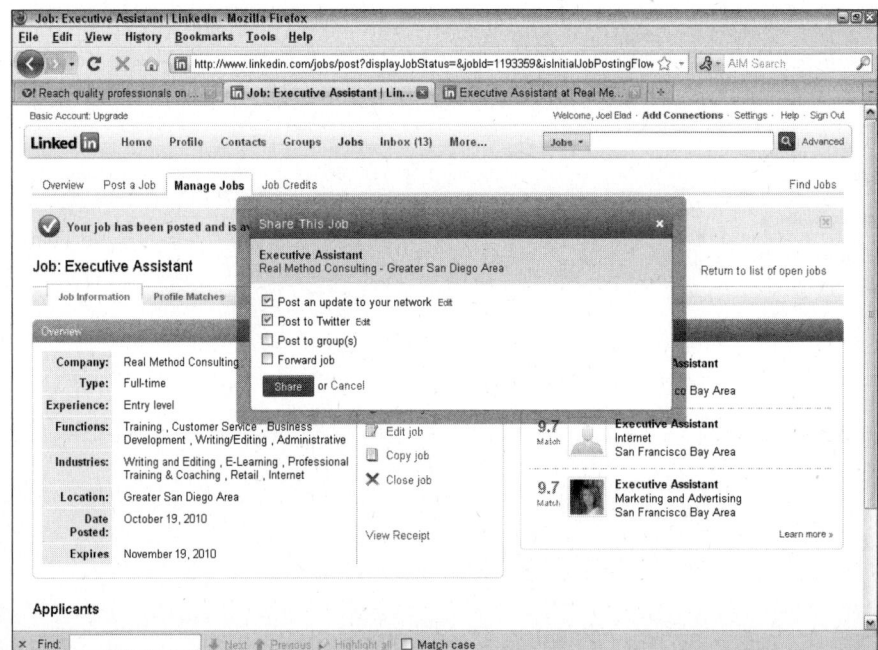

Figure 11-5:
Fill out
the billing
information
for your job
listing.

Figure 11-6:
After your
job listing is
posted, start
announcing
it!

Advertising your job listing to your network

Traditionally, when someone posted a job opening on the Internet using one of those ubiquitous job search sites, that person would hope that the extensive pool of job seekers would find the posting and that the appropriate parties would submit their resumes and cover letters. When you use LinkedIn to fill a job, however, you will still benefit from the pool of job seekers who search LinkedIn's Jobs page, but you have a distinct advantage: *your own network*. You're connected to people who you know and trust, people who you have worked with before so you know their capabilities, and most importantly, people who know you and (hopefully) have a better idea than the average person as to what kind of person you would hire.

Besides the Share a Job window I describe in the previous section, LinkedIn allows you to send all or some of the people in your network a message, letting them know about your job opening and asking them if they, or anyone they know, might be interested in this job. When you're ready to advertise your job listing, follow these steps:

1. **Roll your mouse over the Jobs link (on the top navigation bar) and then select Manage Jobs from the drop-down menu that appears.**

   After you've posted your job, you should see the position listed in the Manage Jobs window under Open Jobs. Click that job title to bring up the Job Status window for that job listing, as shown in Figure 11-7.

2. **Click the Share Job link to generate a LinkedIn message.**

   LinkedIn automatically generates a Share This Job box, as shown in Figure 11-8, that you can send to your network in a variety of ways. You can generate an automatic network update by clicking the check box next to "Post an update to your network." If you have an active Twitter following and your Twitter account is defined in your LinkedIn profile, you can send out a Twitter message by clicking the checkbox "Post to Twitter." If you belong to a LinkedIn group that might be right for this job, you can click the checkbox "Post to group(s)" and then specify the LinkedIn group(s) to be notified. You should definitely click the check box next to 'Forward job.' Feel free to edit the text in the message box to make it sound like it's coming from you, or just leave the default message in place.

3. **If you opt for the Forward Job option, start typing names in the To: box to decide who will get this message from you.**

   As you start typing in a name of a first-degree connection, LinkedIn automatically displays its best guesses as to the correct name and headline right there below the To box. When you see the name you want, click on her name, and it will appear in the To box. Continue to type in additional names, up to a maximum of ten people.

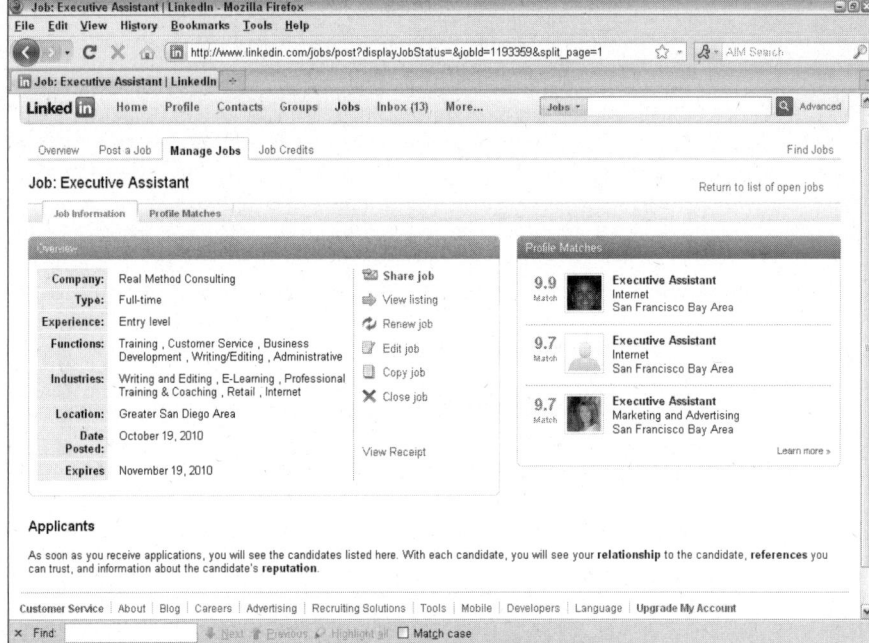

Figure 11-7:
Tell your network about your new job listing.

Figure 11-8:
LinkedIn lets you ask your network for help.

4. **Look over the subject line and text in the window again, make sure you have the right people selected, and when you're ready, click the Share button as shown in Figure 11-9.**

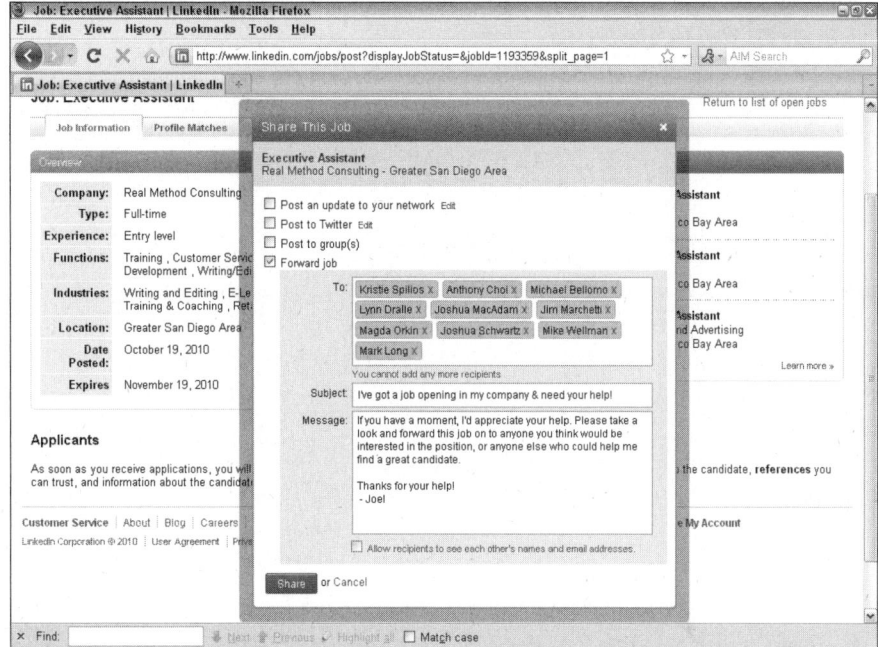

Figure 11-9:
Proofread
your
message
and send it!

Your LinkedIn connections will receive a message in their LinkedIn inboxes and, depending on their notification settings, an e-mail with this message as well. They can click a link from the message to see the job listing and either apply themselves or forward it to their contacts for consideration.

Reviewing applicants

Once you've posted your job listing on LinkedIn, you should expect to get some applicants for the position. Every time someone applies for that job, you'll receive an e-mail from LinkedIn notifying you of their application. In addition, LinkedIn records their application in the Applicants section of the Job Status window. (Refer to Figure 11-7.)

When you're ready to review the applicants for your job, follow these steps:

1. **Roll your mouse over the Jobs link (on the top navigation bar) and then choose Manage Jobs from the drop-down menu that appears.**

   You should be taken to the Manage Jobs: Open Jobs window as shown in Figure 11-10.

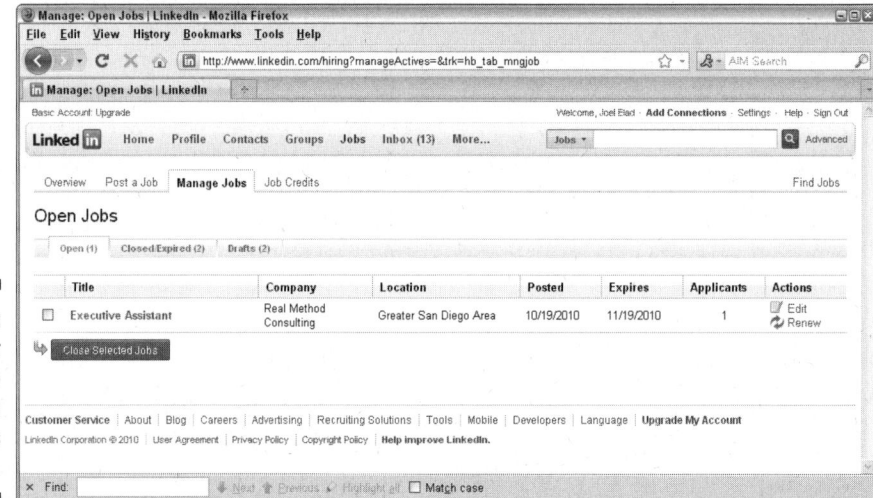

Figure 11-10: Review your open job listings to see who has applied.

2. **Click the Job Title of the job listing you want to review.**

   This brings up the Job Status page for the job listing, as shown in Figure 11-11. You should see the Applicants listed under the Overview statistics for the job listing.

3. **Roll your mouse over an applicant's line item to access the links for the applicant's LinkedIn profile, resume, and cover letter; click the link associated with whatever you'd like to review.**

   If you scroll down the page, you can see all the applicants for the job listing, as shown in Figure 11-12.

4. **Click the Find references link in an applicant's summary line to do a reference check on that applicant.**

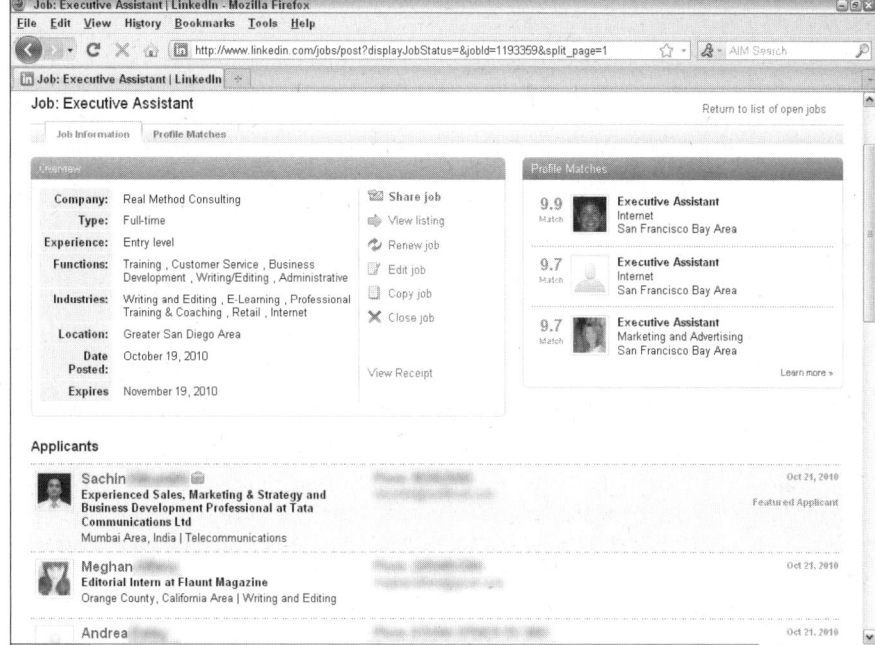

Figure 11-11:
Go through
each
applicant's
resume and
cover letter.

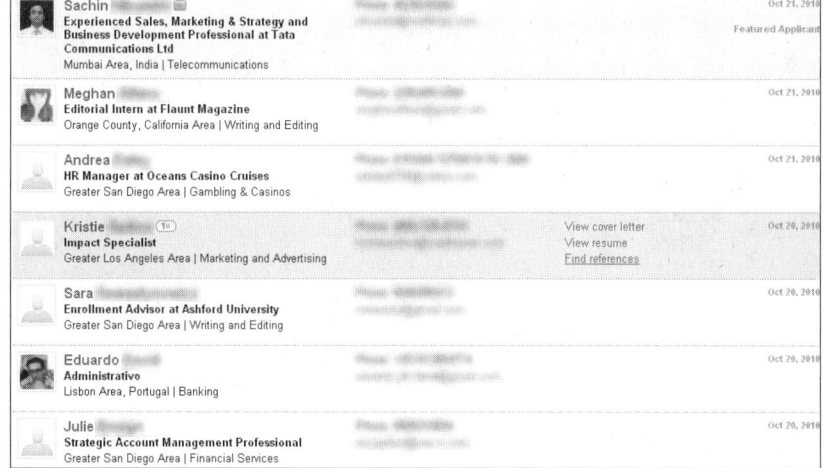

Figure 11-12:
Review
all your
applicants'
information.

In this example, I am going to attempt a reference check for Kristie S., one of the applicants. When I click the Find References link, I am taken to a Reference Search Results page, as shown in Figure 11-13. LinkedIn displays all the positions in Kristie's profile and highlights the common position between each result and Kristie in the search results. This will help you determine whether the person in the search result worked alongside the applicant.

At this point, you should go through the search results and look for someone you'd want to approach to request a reference for your applicant. Preferably, you want someone who is only two or three degrees away from you because then you can use a first-degree connection to introduce yourself to this person and that might encourage the other person (who is two or three degrees away) to respond.

5. **Click the name of a potential reference check and ask her for a recommendation of your applicant.**

   When you click the name in the search results, you'll bring up the person's profile. For example, if I clicked Rob Evans, I would see his profile as shown in Figure 11-14 below. You can use InMail or an Introduction to send a message to this person (which I cover in Chapter 5) and you can ask if she has worked with your applicant and whether she's willing to offer her own assessment of the person.

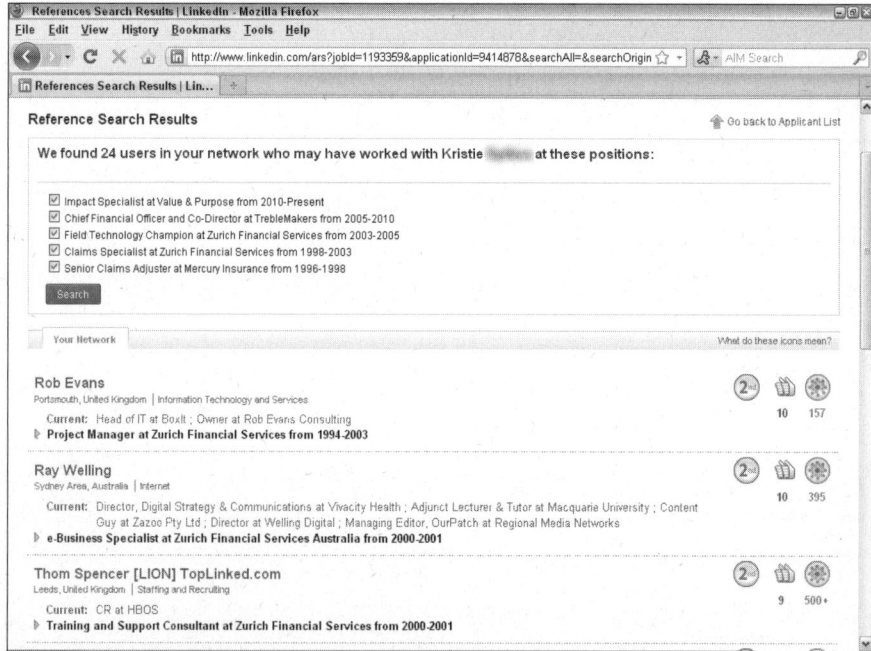

Figure 11-13: See who in the LinkedIn network might have worked with your applicant.

Get introduced through a Connection link

Send an InMail link

Figure 11-14:
Send a
message
to this
potential
reference
through his
profile.

6. **You can ask for additional recommendations by repeating Steps 4 and 5 and identifying other individuals who might be able to help.**

   Because the first person you ask may not respond, you may want to contact additional people in the Search Results screen, in the hope that one person will respond in the necessary timeframe. See the next section of this book for some specific reference search and screening techniques.

Performing Reference Checks and Screening Candidates with LinkedIn

When you use LinkedIn to post a job request, the screening part of your hiring process clearly benefits from using LinkedIn. Rather than asking for references from the applicant and ordering a background check from a services company, you can use LinkedIn to verify a lot of the information in your applicant's resume and application at any stage of the process, without paying a dime!

Here are some reference search strategies to keep in mind:

- ✔ **Start by checking for the applicant's LinkedIn profile.** If the applicant has a common name, use additional information from her resume or application (such as past jobs, location, or education) to narrow down your search. When you find her profile, compare it with her resume or application. Is she consistent in how she presents her experience?

- ✔ **Read through the applicant's recommendations and follow up.** If your candidate has received recommendations, go through them and see whether it's applicable toward your open position. Pay attention to recommendations from former bosses or co-workers. If necessary, ask your candidate whether you can contact the recommender through InMail and use that person as a reference.

- ✔ **See whether you're connected to your candidate.** When you pull up your candidate's profile, you'll see whether she is a second- or third-degree network member, which would mean there are one or two people who connect you with the candidate. If so, contact that person (or ask for an Introduction to reach the correct party) and ask for more information about the candidate. Chances are good that you might get a more honest assessment from someone you know rather than the recommendations provided by the candidate.

- ✔ **Evaluate the candidate's total picture.** If your candidate mentions any Web sites, blogs, or other Web presences on her LinkedIn profile, click the links and see how they're involved. Take a look at the listed interests and group affiliations and see whether they add to (or detract from) your picture of the job candidate.

Because most LinkedIn users have already defined each company where they worked and the years of employment, LinkedIn offers an interesting and helpful application called Reference Search. It works like this: Say you're evaluating a candidate who says he worked at Microsoft from 2000 to 2005. You'd like to find out whether you know anyone in your immediate or extended network who might have worked with your candidate. LinkedIn scans everyone's profile and looks for matches in the company name and years employed, and it shows you who is a possible match. You can then follow up and hopefully will get a much more honest, unbiased opinion of the candidate than someone the candidate has pre-selected to deliver a glowing recommendation. Beware, though, in case you get the ex-employee with an axe to grind.

There is one catch: You have to have a paid account in order to use Reference Search. (I discuss the benefits of paid accounts in Chapter 1.)

Performing a reference check using Reference Search is easy; just follow these steps:

1. **Log in to LinkedIn and click on the Advanced link next to the search box at the top right of the screen. When you get to the Advanced**

Search screen, click the Reference Search tab to bring up the window shown in Figure 11-15.

Figure 11-15:
Use
Reference
Search
to see
whether
you can find
someone
who
knows the
candidate.

2. **Enter the company name and years of employment in the text boxes provided.**

   If the candidate is currently working at the company, enter the current year in the second year box. You can enter more than one company in the boxes provided, and your result list will contain anyone who matches at least one of the companies provided.

3. **Click the Search button to start the reference search.**

   You see a results screen, as shown in Figure 11-16, where you get to see a summary of the number of first degree connections as well as the number of their friends who match your reference search.

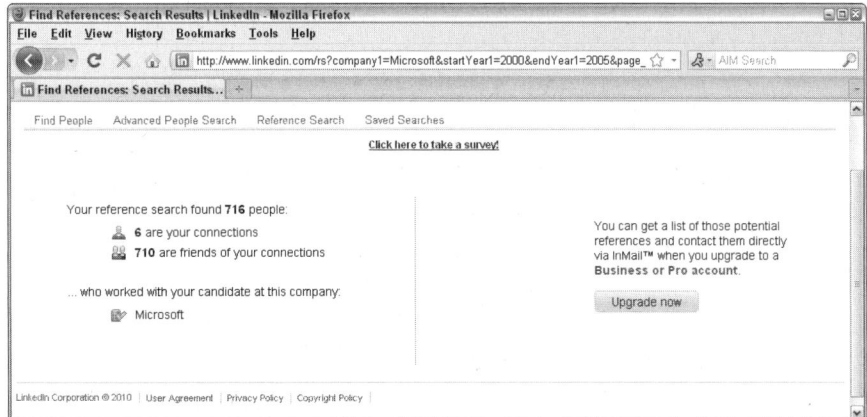

Figure 11-16:
See who
you know
might've
worked
with your
candidate.

4. **If you have a premium account — or decide to take the plunge to upgrade — you can evaluate each profile in your results list to see whether the applicant worked in the same division, and if so, contact the person in your Results list for a reference.**

   Obviously, for a big company, like Microsoft in my example, you may have to search multiple people to find the right division.

If you add a division name right after the company name (for example, you put Microsoft Excel instead of Microsoft), you're severely limiting your search to people who have defined their positions in that exact word order.

Search Strategies for Finding Active or Passive Job Seekers

One of the powers of LinkedIn is the ability not just to find the active job seeker, but the passive job seeker or someone who didn't even realize she wanted a new job! You can tap an extensive network of professionals who have already identified their past experiences, skill set, interests, educational backgrounds, and group affiliations. Also, through LinkedIn Answers, you can even find out what they're thinking about or how knowledgeable they truly are.

The best piece of advice, in my opinion, for this type of search comes from Harvey Mackay and the book he wrote back in 1999, whose title is:

> *"Dig your well before you're thirsty."*

You should be building a healthy network and keeping your eyes on potential candidates before you have a job opening to fill. The earlier you start, and the more consistent you are with the time you spend on a weekly or monthly basis expanding your network, the easier it is to identify and then recruit a potential candidate to fill your opening.

There are specific steps you should take to make your strategy a reality. Whether you start this process in advance or just need to fill a position as soon as possible, here are some tactics to consider:

✔ **Perform detailed advanced searches.** If you want the perfect candidate, search for that candidate. Put multiple keywords in the Advanced Search form, look for a big skill set, narrow your search to a specific industry, and maybe even limit your range to people who already live close to you. If you come up with zero results, remove the least necessary keyword and repeat the search, and keep doing that until you come up with some potential candidates.

✔ **Focus on your industry.** If you know that you're probably going to need software developers, start getting to know potential candidates on the LinkedIn site and stay in touch with them. Look for people to connect with, whether they share a group affiliation with you or respond to LinkedIn Answers, and actively network with these people. Even if they say no to a future job opportunity, chances are good that someone in their networks will be more responsive than the average connection. While Software Developer A may say no, that person probably has several software developers in his network who could respond favorably.

✔ **Read the LinkedIn Answers section.** If you're looking for outgoing people who love sharing their knowledge and want to see a sample of how they approach a problem, take a look at the LinkedIn Answers section. Search for questions that involve something in your industry and read all the answers to find potential candidates who impress you.

✔ **Ask your own questions in the LinkedIn Answers section.** After you've read through the questions, ask one yourself! Pose a question that you would ask in an interview to potential candidates, and see who responds. Better yet, you'll see *how* the people respond, and you'll be able to decide from their answers who to focus on for a follow-up. You'll be able to see the public profiles of the people who provide answers and send those people who respond messages.

Chapter 12

Finding a Job

....

....

*O*ne of the most important ways that LinkedIn has benefitted people is how it helps improve their job search experience. Before LinkedIn, everyone remembers what was involved when you had a job search — making lots of phone calls and visits (and some e-mails) to people you knew, asking them whether they knew anybody who was hiring, asking whether they knew somebody at Company X who might talk to you, or asking something else related to your search. It was a tedious and inefficient process, and LinkedIn has improved it. Understand, however, that LinkedIn hasn't replaced the entire process. You still need to do some face-to-face meetings and phone calls, but LinkedIn can help you find the right person before you pick up the phone.

In this chapter, I discuss some of the ways that you can use LinkedIn to help find a job, whether you're an active job seeker (I need a job right now!) or a passive job seeker (I don't mind where I'm at, but if the right opportunity comes along, I'm listening) on the market. I start by talking about LinkedIn's job board and how you can search for openings. Then I move into more strategic options like improving your profile, devising specific strategies, searching your network for specific people, and incorporating functions like LinkedIn's JobsInsider tool when surfing the Internet.

Searching for a Job by Using LinkedIn

LinkedIn offers lots of tools that can help you look for a job. The most direct way is to search for open positions on the LinkedIn job board, which I cover in the following section. There are other things to keep in mind when looking for a job, which I cover in the later sections, like improving your visibility and optimizing your profile. Part of the success of finding a job is to have an appealing LinkedIn identity so hiring managers can find you and want to contact you with an opening. After all, the best search is when someone comes to you with an opportunity without you sweating the details.

Searching for an open position

The most obvious way to look for a job is to look through LinkedIn's advertised job openings. After all, someone is getting hired when a company runs a job listing, so why can't that candidate be you? When you search for a job on LinkedIn, you can see what skills seem attractive to companies these days, which you can keep in mind as you refine your job search and LinkedIn profile.

When you're ready to search for a job opening, just follow these steps:

1. **Roll your mouse over the Jobs link from the top navigation bar, and choose Find Jobs from the drop-down menu that appears.**

   The Jobs home page appears, as shown in Figure 12-1.

2. **Enter keywords describing the job you want in the Search For Jobs text box.**

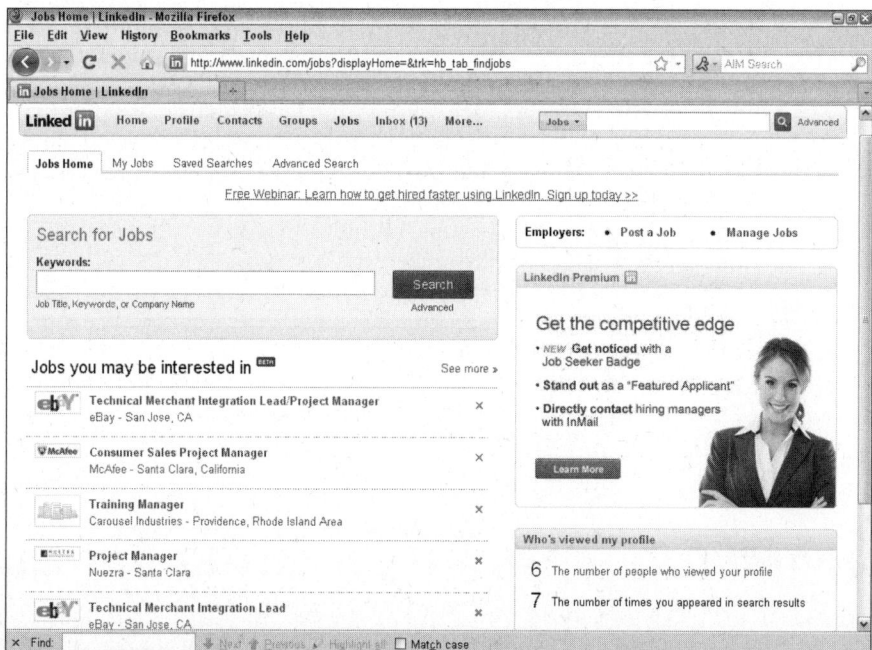

Figure 12-1:
Look for a job on LinkedIn.

To be more precise in your search, you can click the Advanced link underneath the Search button to bring up the Advanced Search tab and enter additional criteria, such as location, specific job title or company, or job function or industry.

3. **Click the Search button.**

   You're taken to a LinkedIn Jobs results screen like the one shown in Figure 12-2, where you see the basic components of the job listings, like Title, Company, and Location.

   To refine your job results, enter additional keywords or use the additional filters on the left-hand side of the screen. You can scroll down the page to see additional filters like the name of the company, how old the job posting has been online, and the location of the job.

4. **Click an individual job title to see the details of that job posting.**

   You see the detailed write-up on the next screen, as shown in Figure 12-3, where you can find out more about the job and the job poster. If the person who posted the job is in your network and has opted to show her name, you will see who in your LinkedIn network can refer you to that person. In the example in Figure 12-3, you can see that Rachel M., one of my first-degree connections, can Introduce me to the job poster, who is a second-degree connection.

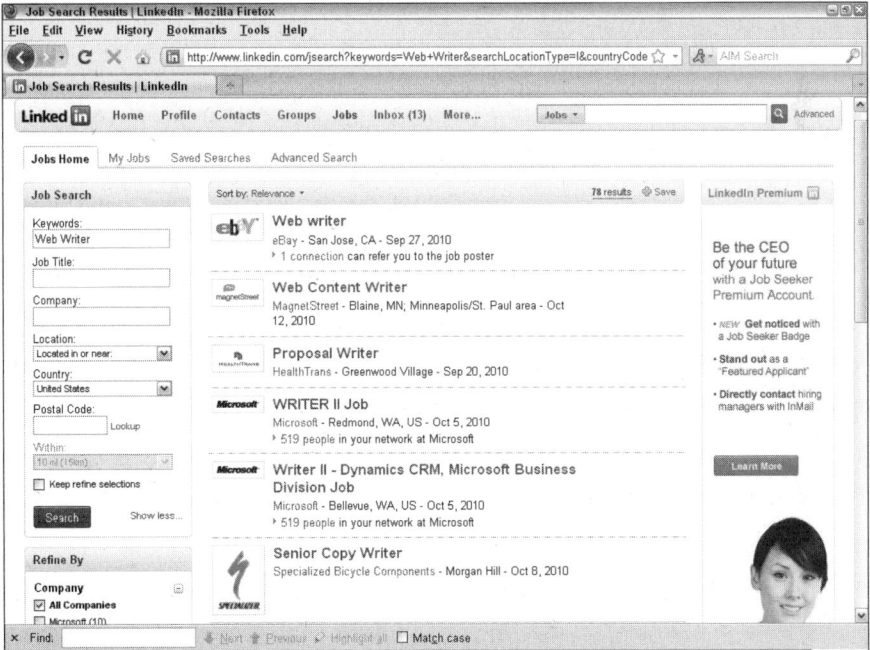

Figure 12-2:
See your job search results.

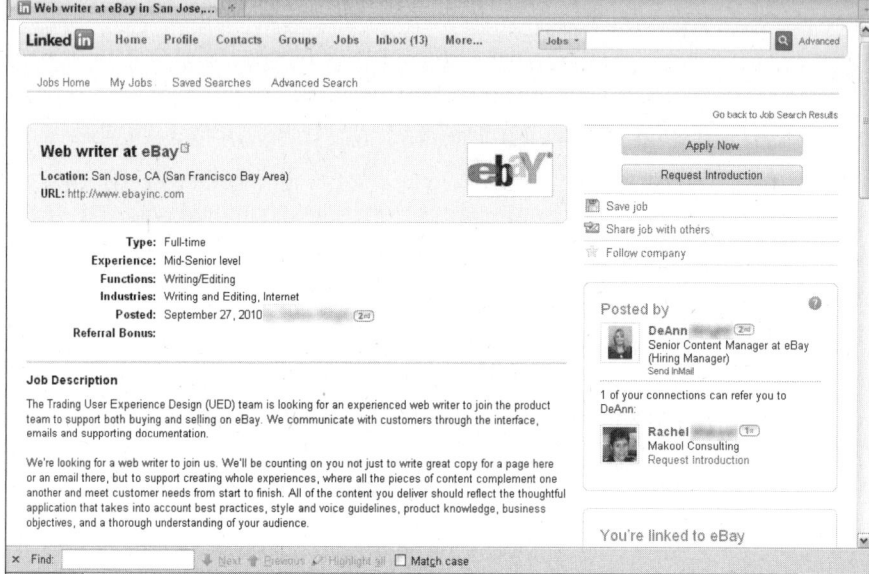

Figure 12-3:
Find out
more about
a specific
job listing.

5. **When you see a job you want to apply for, click the Apply Now button.**

   In most cases, LinkedIn takes you to the job application form, as shown in Figure 12-4. (In some cases, you're taken to the company's specific applicant tracking system — for instance, any job from Google does this. In those cases, simply follow the instructions displayed to apply for that job.)

6. **Enter your contact information, then write a cover letter (or cut and paste one from your word processing program) in the Cover Letter and Resume text box.**

   You should write a brief summary of why you feel you are qualified for the job in the text box provided. If you like, you can update and reuse an older cover letter you've used to apply to a similar job: Simply open a word processing program (such as Microsoft Word), find the letter, copy the contents, and paste it into the text box here on LinkedIn. (Be sure to use your program's spellchecker.)

   If the job poster is in your extended network, I recommend that you read her profile first, see what common interests you have, and incorporate that information into your cover letter. If you have the time, approach that person first with an Introduction or InMail to get some more information about the job posting before you apply. (I discuss Introductions and InMail in length in Chapter 5.)

7. **Click the Browse button to find a copy of your resume on your computer to be uploaded into the job application, as shown in Figure 12-5.**

8. **Scroll down and click Continue to review your application.**

    The Review and Confirm Application page appears, as shown in Figure 12-6. Put this page to good use: Make sure the details of your application are all correct before you submit the application.

9. **Click the Apply Now button.**

    Off your application goes.

Congratulations! You applied for a job! Repeat Steps 2–9 to keep looking and applying for jobs.

Figure 12-4:
Start
applying
for a
job on
LinkedIn.

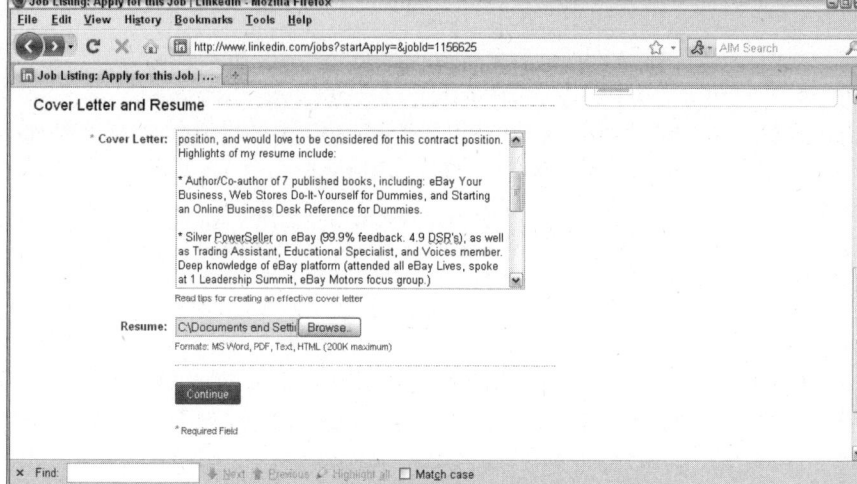

Figure 12-5:
Provide
your resume
for this job
application.

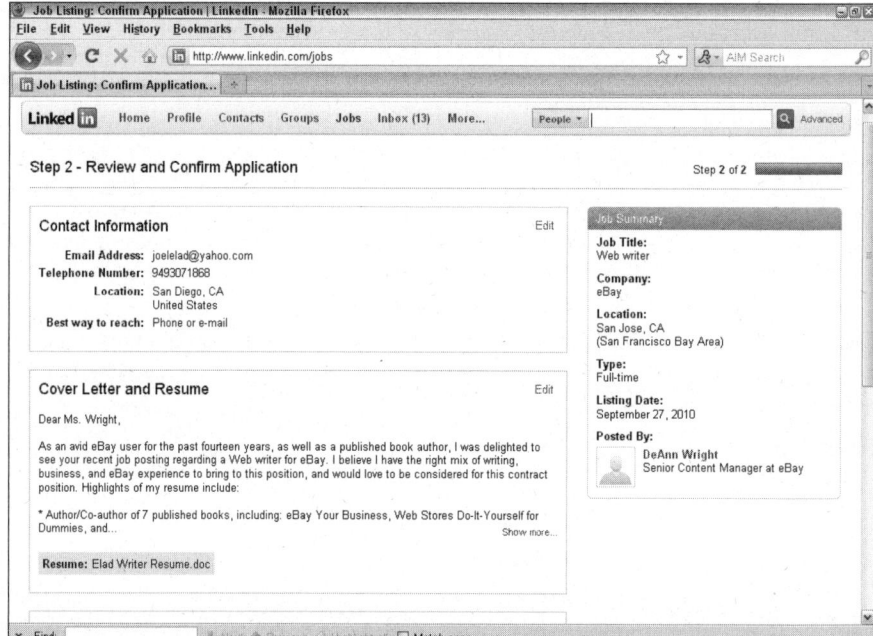

Figure 12-6:
Verify
your job
application
details.

Improving your visibility and attractiveness

When you're looking for a job, manually scanning job listings and sending in resumes are only part of the process. You also have to prepare your job-seeking strategies. The most obvious examples of these are your resume (or CV) and your cover letter. When you include LinkedIn in your job search, you need to prepare your total LinkedIn profile and network in order to get the optimal job search experience.

Although no strategy can 100-percent positively guarantee the job of your dreams, these strategies can improve your odds of getting that right contact person, interview, or extra consideration for your job application that's in a stack of potential candidates.

Here are some strategies to keep in mind:

- ✔ **Connect with former managers, co-workers, and partners.** This might seem like an obvious strategy, but let me elaborate. Part of getting the job is communicating (to your future employer) your ability to do the job. Nobody knows your skills, potential, work attitude, and capability better than people who have worked with you and observed you in action.

  Therefore, make sure that you have connected with your former managers, co-workers, and so on. When these people are part of your network, the Introductions they can facilitate will carry extra weight because they can share their experience with the person you want to meet. You can encourage them to provide recommendations for you to express to the entire community your capability and work ethic.

- ✔ **Look at colleague's LinkedIn profiles.** Using the search functions or your first-degree connections in your network, try to find people with goals and work experience similar to yours. When you see how they describe their work experience on their profiles, you might get some good ideas on how to augment your profile.

- ✔ **Get referrals from past bosses and co-workers.** After you add your past bosses and co-workers to your network, keep in contact with them, let them know your current job search goals, and ask for an appropriate referral or Introduction. They can use their knowledge of your work history and their expanded networks to make more powerful Introductions or requests than just a friend asking another friend, "Hey, can you hire my friend, Joel?"

Don't be afraid to provide extra information to your past bosses or co-workers to help them make an effective referral. Before the Internet, when job seekers asked a past boss or co-worker to write a letter of recommendation, it was acceptable to include some bullet points of stories or points you hoped they would cover in their letters. The same is true in the LinkedIn world. Guide your contact to emphasize a work quality or anecdote that would be effective in the referral or Introduction.

✔ **Collect your Recommendations.** Nothing communicates a vote of confidence from your network quite like a Recommendation. When anyone reads your LinkedIn profile, he can see exactly what other people have said about you. Because he knows that you can't alter a Recommendation, he's more likely to trust the content and believe you're the right person for the job. (See Chapter 8 for more information on how to get more Recommendations.)

✔ **Use LinkedIn Answers to demonstrate your experience and knowledge.** Your network of connections has an idea of your knowledge and capabilities, but what about everybody else out there? If someone is evaluating you for a job, she'll probably access your LinkedIn profile to learn more about you, so the more your profile can say about you at any given point in time, the better. One way you can improve your overall presence is to participate in LinkedIn Answers. You can share knowledge you've gained by answering other LinkedIn member's questions and providing advice. All your replies to questions posted on LinkedIn Answers are available from your profile. (See Chapter 7 for more information on how to use LinkedIn Answers.)

Auditioning with Answers

There are several benefits to actively using LinkedIn Answers. Not only can people see examples of your knowledge or experience by reading your answers, but they can also get an idea of how helpful or enthusiastic you are in a professional environment. After all, most employers want to know that you will be a healthy addition to a team and that you'll communicate well with co-workers and think about the big picture. Your active involvement in LinkedIn Answers shows an employer that you're willing to help others to achieve their goals. They also get a glimpse into your communication and written skills, which are important in many jobs today. When you give with LinkedIn Answers, you receive as well.

Optimizing your LinkedIn profile

The core of your LinkedIn presence is your profile, which is included with every job application you make on LinkedIn. Odds are good that prospective employers are going to check your LinkedIn profile when evaluating you for a job, so you want to make sure your profile is optimized to make you as appealing as possible to your prospective employer. Here are some things to keep in mind when bulking up your profile for a job search:

- ✔ **Complete all the sections in your profile with as much accurate information as possible.** It's easy to put up a skeleton of your employment history and never get around to fully completing your profile. Unlike a resume (where you could feel confined in terms of page length), you can be as expansive as you want with your LinkedIn profile. You never know what part of your profile will get you included in someone's search result, but the more information you provide, the better chance someone will find you.

- ✔ **Focus on accomplishments rather than duties.** I've seen a lot of people prepare their LinkedIn profiles in the same way they do their resumes, focusing solely on the duties they performed at each job. Although you want to give people an idea of what you did, hiring managers want to know the *results* of what you did, and the more concrete the example, the better. Saying you "organized procurement processes in your division" may demonstrate a skill, but saying that you "cut procurement costs by 16% in your first year" carries a bigger impact. Go back and talk to past co-workers or bosses, if necessary, to get whatever specifics they can provide on your performance.

- ✔ **Add all relevant job search keywords, skill sets, and buzzwords to your profile.** When prospective employers are searching for someone to hire, they may simply search for a core set of skills to see who can fill the position. Therefore, just stating your job titles is not enough. If your profile says "Software Developer," prospective hiring managers could assume that you're qualified, but the only way you'd be considered is if these managers ran a search on those keywords. Say that a hiring manager does a search for the programming languages C++, Java, Perl, and Python. If all those keywords are not somewhere in your profile, you won't show up in the list to be considered at all.

✔ **See how other people position themselves.** Imagine if you could get a book of thousands of resumes from current employees that you could then use as models to position yourself. Do a search for people with a job, education, or skill set similar to yours and see how they've worded their profiles or how they put their experiences in context. Use that insight to adapt your profile to make it clearer to others.

✔ **List all your job experiences on your profile, not just full-time positions.** Did you do any short-term or contract jobs? Were you an advisor to another company? Perhaps you're a board member for a local non-profit group or religious organization. Your LinkedIn profile is designed to reflect all of your job experiences, which is *not* limited to a full-time job that provided a W-2 slip. Document any work experience that adds to your overall profile, whether you were paid for that job/experience or not.

Make sure that every experience you list on your profiles helps contribute to your overall career goals. After all, employers might not care that you were a pastry chef one summer — and will question why you thought it was so important that you listed it on your profile.

Job Search Strategies Using LinkedIn

When you're looking for a job, there are a lot of potential ways you can include LinkedIn as part of your overall job search, beyond the direct task of searching their jobs database listings and e-mailing a job request to your immediate network. In this section, I discuss various job search strategies you can implement that involve LinkedIn to some degree and can help add information, contacts, interviews, and hopefully some offers to your job search. Use one or use them all, but pick the methods you feel most comfortable with implementing.

A job search should be treated as a full-time job. Some of these strategies involve a long-term commitment and might not instantly result in multiple offers.

Leveraging your connections

One of the biggest benefits of LinkedIn is being able to answer the question, "Who do my contacts know?" It's important to think of LinkedIn as not only the sum of your first-degree immediate connections, but also as your extended network of second- and third-degree network members that your colleagues can help connect you with for information, referrals, and hopefully, a new career.

Therefore, keep these second- and third-degree network members in mind so you can best leverage your connections to achieve progress. Keep these points in mind when you're working on your job search using LinkedIn:

✓ **Change the Sorted By option to Degrees Away from You, or Degrees and Recommendations.** When searching for the right contacts (such as recruiters, headhunters, or company or job specialists), be sure to change the Sorted By option from Keyword Relevance to another option based on Degrees. This allows you to see which members of your extended network should be at the top of your list.

✓ **Ask for referrals whenever possible.** Exchange information first and then work your way up to request a referral.

✓ **Get your friends involved.** Let your immediate network know about your goals so they can recommend the right people for you to talk to, and hopefully, they'll generate the right Introductions for you as well.

Same title, different place

If you're looking for a specific job, one way to approach your job search is to ask this question: Who out there could possibly know more about the job you're interested in than those folks doing that job right now? The answer to that question is no one. This means one source of help should be people with the same (or very similar) job title or responsibilities. Although these people might not have hiring authority, they can help give you the right perspective, share the right insider tips about what the job truly entails, and let you know what skills or background the hiring manager considered when they were hired.

Because these people are already employed and not your direct competition, they're more likely to offer help and advice. They have practical knowledge of what it takes to do that job and what qualities will best help someone succeed in that position. When you're ready to implement this strategy, just keep these points in mind:

✓ Perform an advanced search for people with a similar job title as the one you're applying for. Put the job title in either the keywords section or the title section.

✓ Narrow and clarify your search by industry. For example, Project Manager of Software Development is much different than Project Manager for the Construction industry. Pick multiple industries if they are similar enough.

✓ When you find someone who has the job title you'd like to have, see whether she's interested in meeting for an informational interview. Asking outright for a job lead will most likely not result in anything positive.

All about the alma mater

Typically, people who share a school in common have an ongoing affinity, whether the school is an undergraduate or graduate college, or even a high school. You can rapidly increase the chance of someone considering your request if you and that person attended the same school. Therefore, take advantage of your alumni status and try to connect and work with people who went to one of the same schools as you. Here are some tips to help further this type of search by using LinkedIn:

- ✓ **Search for alumni association groups of any school you attended. Click Groups, and then Groups Directory from the top navigation bar — and then go ahead and join those groups.** This gives you access to the member list of that group, so you can see other alumni, regardless of graduation year, and communicate with them.

- ✓ **Connect as a former classmate and ask for information first, referral second.** Your shared alumni status will help open the door, but don't expect a golden handout right away. Be ready to offer one of your contacts in exchange for the former classmate's help or consideration.

- ✓ **Use the Find Classmates function available in Add Connections (that link at the top right corner of any LinkedIn page) to look for classmates from the schools in your profile.** (I discuss how to use this function in Chapter 6.) You should expand your range of graduation years to include some years before and after your graduation date. This allows you to find classmates you might have met who were in different grades or levels in their study but might have shared classes or study time with you.

- ✓ **Check the connection list of any of your contacts who attended school with you.** This is a good safety check to look for any classmates on your contacts' lists who you might not have initially considered. (I discuss connection lists in "Browsing your connections' network" in Chapter 6.)

- ✓ **Try doing an Advanced People search with the school name as a keyword, and if necessary, try different variations of the school name.** For example, try the school name with and without acronyms. When I look for classmates from the University of California, Irvine, I search for the term *UCI* as well as *University California Irvine*. (I talk more about doing advanced searches in Chapter 4.)

- ✓ **If your school has changed or updated its name, do an Advanced People search for both the old and new names as keywords in your search.** For example, because my department name at UCI has changed from the Graduate School of Management, or GSM, to the Paul Merage School of Business, I search for the old and new search terms because my classmates may have defined their educational listings differently.

Finding target company referrals

Sometimes your job search involves a specific company and not necessarily a job title. Suppose you know you want to work at one of the top computer database software companies. Now you can use LinkedIn to help you find the right people at those companies that can help you. Here are some points to consider:

- ✔ **Make a list of the ten companies you'd like to work for and do an individual Advanced People search for each company to find potential contacts at these companies.** Put the company name in the search box at the top right of the LinkedIn home page and then click the Search button. You should see a list of people on the Search results page that have the Company name in their titles who are in your extended network. For larger companies, you need to search for a specific department or industry area to find the right contact. Ask these people you've identified for referrals to someone in your target organization like a hiring manager.

- ✔ **Follow the companies themselves.** LinkedIn allows you to "follow" companies through their Companies page, so be sure to "Follow this company" after you're looking at the right company page within LinkedIn Companies. When you know what companies you want to follow, simply roll your mouse over the Companies link in the top navigation bar, and select Find Companies. Then, type in the name of each company into the search box provided, click Search Companies, and when you find the company in the Search results list, click the Follow Company link. Once you are following all your target companies, spend some time each week to review each Company page for news, information, job openings, and useful contacts.

- ✔ **If you can't find someone who currently works at your target company, look for people who used to work there and see what advice they can give you.** You do this through an Advanced People search where you make sure the option under Company is set to Past. Many times, past employees still maintain contacts at their old company, and they can definitely attest to the work environment and corporate culture.

- ✔ **Get some information from the person you're replacing.** Find the person at the company whose job you're taking and ask her opinion of it, information about the hiring manager, company, and so on. (Understand, of course, that this person might not have left under the best of circumstances, so you may not always get a good or useful response.) If you can't find the person you're replacing, try looking for people with a past position like the one you're interviewing for. I got this tip from Garage.com founder Guy Kawasaki in his blog post entitled "How to Change the World: Ten Ways to use LinkedIn," which resides on http://blog.guykawasaki.com.

Using the LinkedIn JobsInsider

As more and more people were using LinkedIn to get the inside track on their job searches, LinkedIn saw the value in providing a tool that gave searchers easy access to the right information that would aid the job search. So the folks at LinkedIn developed the JobsInsider tool that works with the major job search engines by scanning a job listing for the employer's name and then providing a summary of statistics of employees who work at that company and how they're connected to a given LinkedIn user.

And LinkedIn has incorporated the JobsInsider tool into its browser tool-bars, making it an automatic benefit. After all, you can't search a job site like Monster.com without a Web browser, right? The toolbars are designed to augment a Web search with LinkedIn information, and so is JobsInsider, which makes it a logical addition to the toolbar.

JobsInsider benefits

Your job search is a job unto itself, so any tool that can help you do your "job" is definitely an asset. JobsInsider helps expand your regular job search by giving you the insight of your LinkedIn network and job database to make you a better and more effective job applicant.

Some of the benefits of the JobsInsider tool are

- **It's automatic.** After you install the browser toolbar, the JobsInsider tool activates itself automatically anytime you use your Web browser to navigate to any major job site, like Monster.com, CareerBuilder.com, HotJobs, craigslist, SimplyHired, Dice, or Vault.

- **It's informative.** You get several pieces of valuable information that update automatically depending on the job listing you're seeing. You see how many people work at the target company who are in your extended network, how many people are friends of your connections (which means they're second-degree connections), and how many people live in your region, (like the San Francisco Bay area or the Greater San Diego area). Clicking any of those links opens a window to LinkedIn with a search result showing you their profile summaries.

- **It's free.** No monthly cost, no registration cost, no setup fee. Regardless of the status of your LinkedIn account, this tool is free to install and use.

- **It's timesaving.** As you search for a job, instead of stopping your search from a job site to go to LinkedIn to find a contact or more information, you can access that information concurrently through new panes or windows opening.

Using JobsInsider

If you're interested in using JobsInsider, you need to download one of the LinkedIn Browser toolbars and install it on your computer because JobsInsider is available only as part of a Browser toolbar. I cover installing the Internet Explorer and Firefox Companion toolbars in Chapter 10.

After you install the toolbar, whenever you go to one of the main job search sites (like Monster.com, CareerBuilder.com, or Dice) a side pane or new window opens, where you can basically start a LinkedIn job search.

For example, suppose that you're on Monster.com looking for a project manager position. After you start a search and come up with a results screen (as shown Figure 12-7), you see the JobsInsider function come up.

More importantly, however, when you click an individual job posting, you see the JobsInsider pane fill in with information on who you know at the hiring company and how many people you're connected to who can help.

If you can't easily identify the employer from the job listing, or if the company's name is withheld or confidential, no information shows up in the JobsInsider pane.

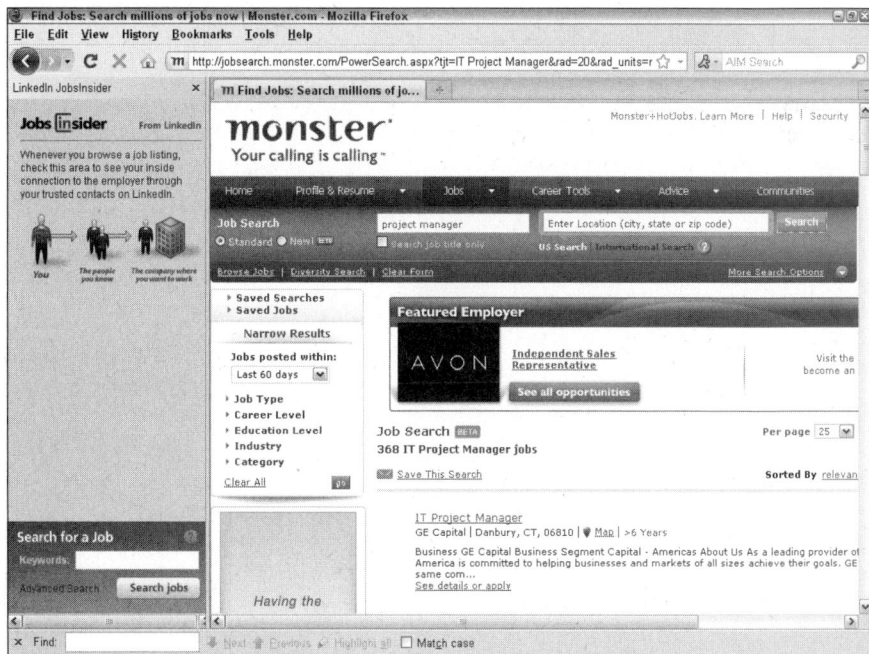

Figure 12-7:
Do a job search online to bring up JobsInsider.

Suppose I click a Web developer position at eBay. My JobsInsider pane shows me precise connection information, as shown in Figure 12-8. I can click any of the numbers to bring up a People search of hiring managers who can help me apply for this job.

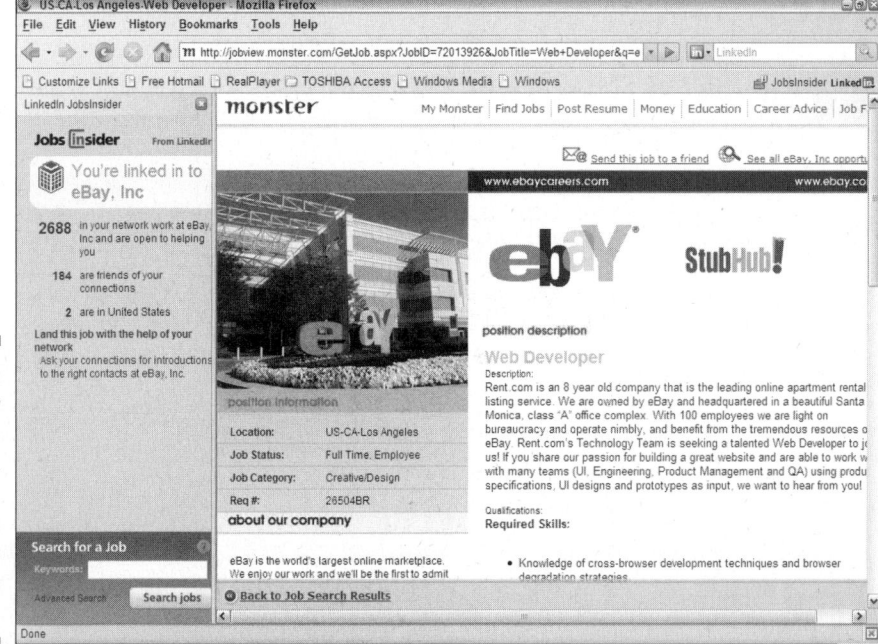

Figure 12-8: For every open position, see which LinkedIn connections can help you apply.

Chapter 13

Finding Professional Services

· ·

· ·

Two of the main reasons why people search the LinkedIn network are to find a job or to find a new employee. And millions of self-employed people who use LinkedIn to promote not only themselves, but also their services, can now take advantage of a new LinkedIn tool.

LinkedIn includes a Service Provider section, where LinkedIn members can write recommendations for service providers they have used who are also members of the LinkedIn network. Because recommendations are one of the top reasons why someone picks one service provider over another, and because many of these service providers are on LinkedIn already to increase their contact base and professional network, it makes sense to allow members to recommend each other based on services, not just shared employment.

In this chapter, I cover how to use LinkedIn to search for a recommended service provider. I also cover how you can file a recommendation for a service provider and get him or her listed in the directory.

Searching for a Service Provider

When you need to hire someone to do a job, you probably open up a big phone directory and search for a provider. Sometimes, you call family members or friends and ask them to refer you to somebody qualified. But LinkedIn has a way for you to search your network of first-, second-, and third-degree contacts, or the greater LinkedIn network, to find qualified professionals referred by other LinkedIn members.

To search for a service provider, just follow these steps:

1. **Roll your mouse over the Companies link from the top navigation bar and select Find Companies from the menu that appears.**

2. **On the Companies page, click the Service Providers link (on the right side of the screen).**

   The Service Provider Recommendations home page appears, as shown in Figure 13-1.

   LinkedIn automatically picks providers based on recent recommendations. If you scroll down the page, you see some of the Top people in different categories, like Top Real Estate Agents and Top Child Care Providers. ("Top" is defined as providers that have received the most recommendations from other LinkedIn users so far.)

3. **In the Categories pane, click the category that matches the type of service provider for your search.**

   I'm searching for a Writer/Editor. Figure 13-2 shows the recommendations for that category.

After you reach a page loaded with recommended service providers, use the following tricks to find the one that's just right for you:

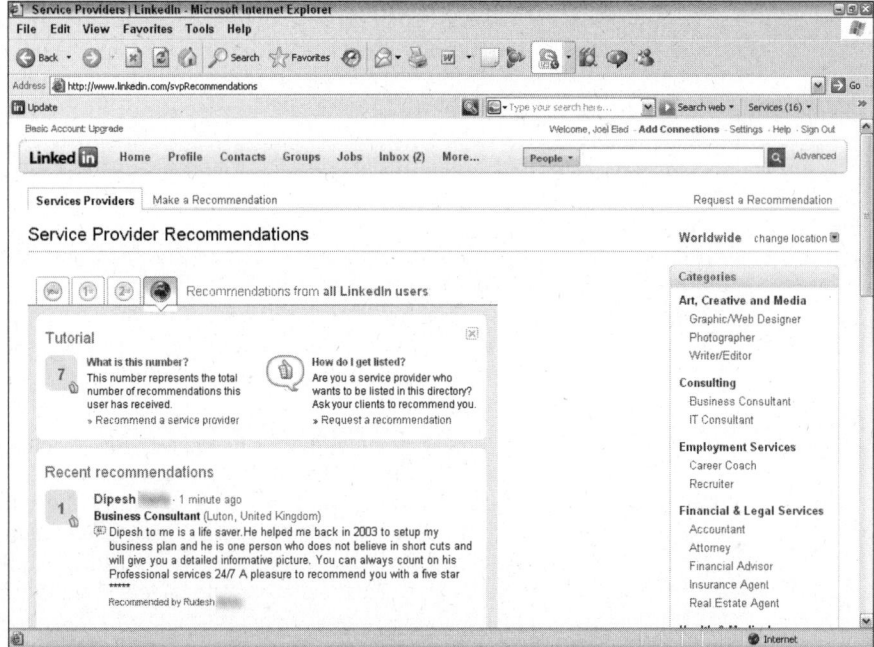

Figure 13-1:
Start your service provider search here.

Figure 13-2:
See recommended service providers based on date.

✓ **Sort based on date or top results.** By default, the list that's returned is sorted based on the date of the most recent recommendation. You can change the sort by clicking the Top Results link. Figure 13-3 shows a list of Writers/Editors with the most recommendations.

✓ **Sort by recommendations from your network.** Click the icon marked 1st or 2nd to get a list of service provider recommendations based on the first- or second-degree connections in your network.

You see something like Figure 13-4. The list of results shows who made the most recent recommendation.

✓ **Sort based on location.** Click the Change Location link to get a targeted search list close to where you live.

When you click the Change Location link, you're asked to input your country and postal code. After you do so, you return to the search results page, but with a target list now sorted by the proximity to your new location setting. After all, if you're looking for a dentist or gardener, you probably want one close to home.

✓ **Read all of a provider's recommendations.** Click any provider's name to read recommendations for that provider.

First-degree connections

Second-degree connections

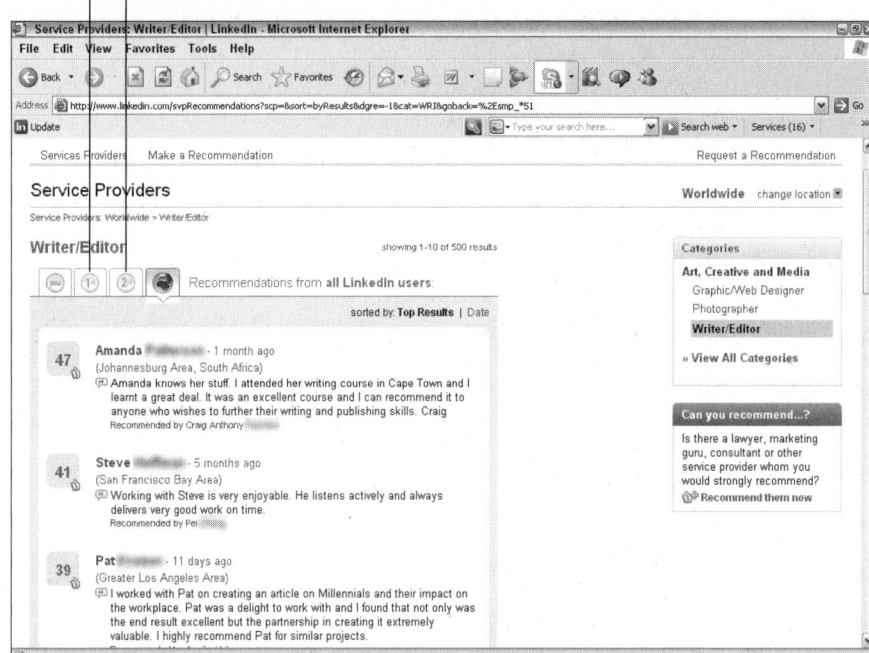

Figure 13-3:
See recommended service providers sorted by the number of recommendations.

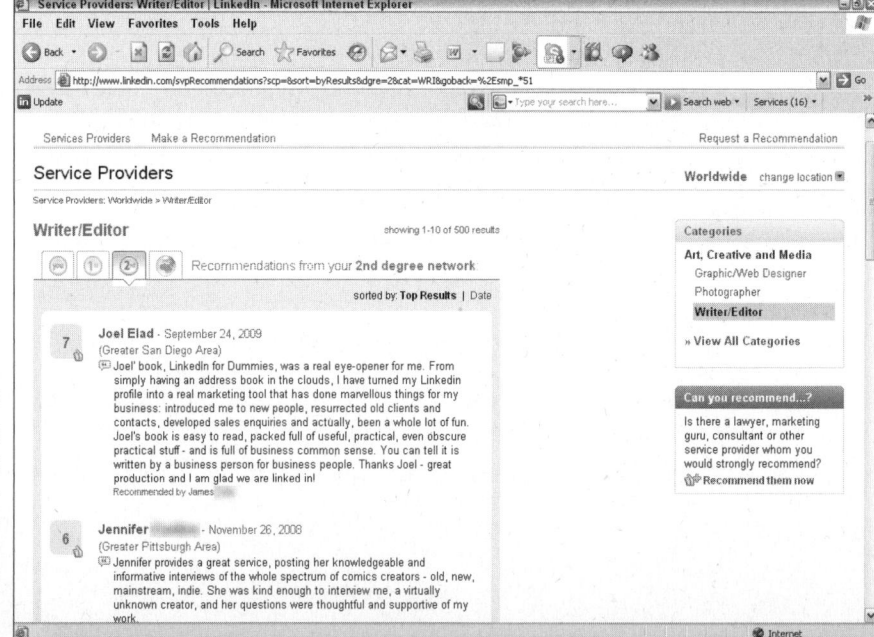

Figure 13-4:
See a list of recommendations from your personal network.

Recommending a Service Provider

The flip side of looking for a good service provider is sharing your experiences and recommending somebody you've hired or worked with. The success of the LinkedIn database depends on sharing this expertise, which simply makes a better network for you to enjoy and benefit from. Before you enter that recommendation, however, you need to keep a few things in mind to make that write-up stand out.

Planning a good recommendation

When you receive excellent service, consider how you can recommend that provider. For your recommendation to have some weight and give prospective customers a good idea of what this provider can accomplish, think about the type of recommendation you plan to leave and make sure that you cover or emphasize the appropriate things. You are a little constrained by a 3,000-character count limit, but you also don't want to provide a thesis of why provider X is the best on Earth.

Instead, provide a concise, factual testimonial that conveys your recommendation that will make sense to the reader and validate the provider's abilities. Here are some things to keep in mind:

- ✔ **Stick to the basics.** Although you might want to gush and go on and on about why this provider is the best, anybody reading this will lose interest and stop reading, which hurts the provider's chance of getting new business and makes you, the recommender, look unprofessional. Provide summaries of your experience, highlighting the most important aspects.

- ✔ **Lead with the most important info.** Most people don't read beyond the first sentence. Therefore, craft your introductory sentence to give a complete picture of the person you're recommending. This way, you hook your reader into finding out why this person is so qualified and deserves his business.

- ✔ **Give examples/accomplishments.** Saying someone is a hard worker or very intelligent is nice, but if that's all you say, someone reading your recommendation might wonder whether this is just your opinion. When you give specific examples of the provider's accomplishments, you provide a measurable aspect that readers can relate to and help prove the quality of that provider. Who would you hire: someone whose recommendation says, "Great accountant," or someone whose recommendation says, "Paul balanced my business receipts and records in 3–4 hours and found me $4,000 in extra deductions for last year's tax returns"?

✔ **Be a little personal.** In the end, no matter how qualified somebody is, people typically hire someone they enjoy working with on a project. Therefore, after you mention a person's great capabilities and accomplishments, be sure to include some personal experiences on what working with this person was like. "I have been Alex's client for the past 5 years, and I am consistently pleased and amazed at the service he has provided."

Posting a recommendation

When you have your recommendation planned, it's time to show it to the world. To leave a recommendation, just follow these steps:

1. **Roll your mouse over the Companies link from the top navigation bar and then click the Find Companies link from the menu that appears. On the Companies page, click the Service Providers link (on the right side of the screen).**

2. **On the Service Providers page that appears, click the Make a Recommendation tab.**

   You're taken to the first step in the process (see Figure 13-5), where you decide to recommend.

3. **Enter the first name, last name, and e-mail address of who you are recommending, or click the Select from Your Connections List link to find someone in your network.**

   Make sure the e-mail address you are providing matches the e-mail address that person has listed on his LinkedIn account. The easiest way to check this is to do an Advanced People Search with the e-mail address as the keyword to see if the correct profile comes back as a result.

Figure 13-5:
Decide who to recommend.

4. **Click the Continue button.**

   You're taken to the Create Your Recommendation page (see Figure 13-6).

5. **From the first drop-down list, select the position this service provider had when you hired him.**

6. **Select an option from the Service Category drop-down list; then, from the Year First Hired drop-down list, select the year you first hired or worked with him.**

7. **If you worked with this person more than once, select the check box next to the Year First Hired drop-down list.**

8. **Scroll down and pick the top attributes that best describe this service provider.**

   You can select up to three check boxes from the list provided. You have a chance to add more detail in a written recommendation in the next step.

9. **Scroll down and write your recommendation (see Figure 13-7).**

   Talk about your provider's accomplishments, qualities, and your experience working with him. (See the previous section for what to focus on in your written recommendation.)

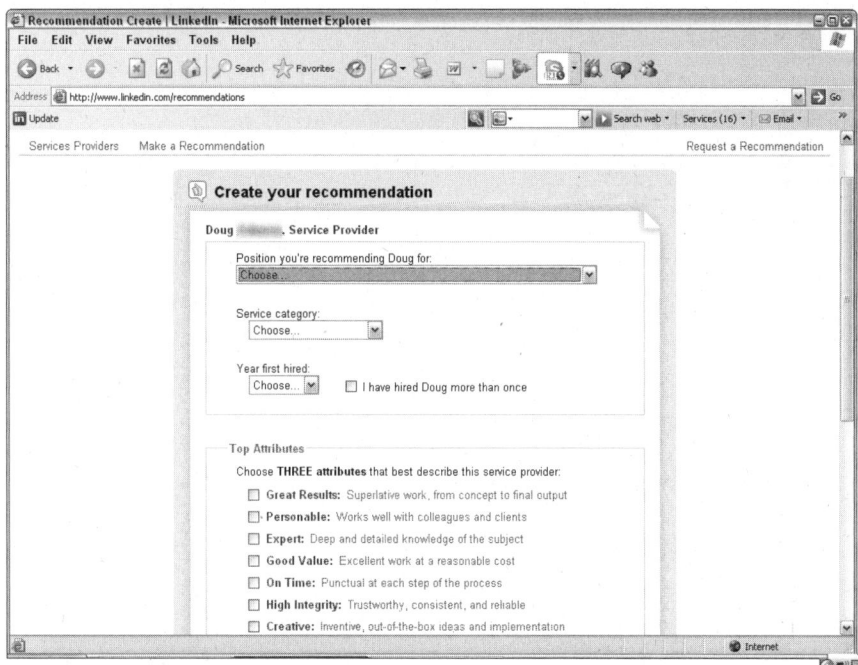

Figure 13-6:
Create your service provider recommendation.

Figure 13-7:
Provide
a more
detailed
recommen-
dation.

10. **Click Send.**

You see a confirmation message that your service provider recommendation has been created. Also, the person you recommended gets notified that there is a recommendation for him to approve.

If you already left a personal recommendation for this person, you now have
two recommendations on this person's profile, with the only visible difference being the Top Qualities line in the Service Provider recommendation.
You might want to delete your old personal recommendation if it overlaps
with your new one. *Service* Recommendations really are best served for service professionals who could benefit from new clients discovering them on
LinkedIn and contacting them. *Personal* recommendations are best served
by working professionals who aren't in a service industry and are looking for
regular employment with a company.

Part V
Using LinkedIn for Everyday Business

The 5th Wave   By Rich Tennant

"Your mail program looks fine. I don't know why you're not receiving any personal e-mails. Have you explored the possibility that you may not have any friends?"

In this part . . .

Have you ever tried to pound the square peg into the round hole, thinking that there might be a purpose for the square peg that no one thought of? Some see that as stubborn, but others see that as curious. It's good to wonder how to use something beyond its stated or obvious purpose, because you might create something new or beneficial for the world.

This part covers some of the specific applications of the LinkedIn Web site that may not be the obvious, but are definitely useful. I apply the LinkedIn Web site to situations that matter to some of you, and I try to tell you all about how LinkedIn can help you increase your sales, how you can use LinkedIn to market yourself, how LinkedIn can help you close a big deal, and why that square peg won't fit. Okay, I can't help you with that last problem, but the rest are good to go. I mix advice with some examples, so find the parts that apply to you and enjoy!

Chapter 14

Getting Connected with LinkedIn Groups

. . . .

. . . .

*W*hen it comes to the reasons why people get to know each other, there's more to a professional's life than colleagues and classmates. People have always been drawn to groups based on common interests, backgrounds, or goals, and this natural tendency to join together can be seen from sports teams to Boy/Girl Scouts, from social action organizations to nonprofit charity groups. Naturally, LinkedIn also offers a way for people to connect with each other as a group — LinkedIn Groups.

In this chapter, I discuss the overall idea and structure of LinkedIn Groups and what you can expect to find. I then talk about how to search for existing groups on LinkedIn, and I walk you through the steps necessary to join that group. Finally, if you see that there should be a group for something on LinkedIn but it doesn't already exist, I discuss how to start your own LinkedIn group and how to invite others to join it.

LinkedIn Groups — What They Are and What They Aren't

When people who are familiar with other social networking tools are first exposed to LinkedIn Groups, they will see some similarities. The group interaction in LinkedIn Groups — members list, discussion threads, and so on — feels just like Yahoo! Groups or groups on most other social networking sites.

And yet, being a member of a LinkedIn group has extra benefits over other networking sites:

- ✔ **Connections:** Group members are a special sort of connection. Although you don't have access to their extended networks for Introductions, you're considered directly connected to them, such that you can see their full profiles, and they can appear in your search results even if you aren't within three degrees of everyone in the group. If you sort search results by degrees of separation from you, fellow group members appear between your first- and second-degree contacts.

- ✔ **Visibility:** By joining several groups — particularly large, open ones — you can increase your visibility in the LinkedIn network without having to add thousands of contacts.

- ✔ **Group logos:** The logos of the groups you're in are displayed on your profile. This is a sort of visual branding, reinforcing your association with those groups without a lot of words. For example, Figure 14-1 shows how the profile for a LinkedIn member who belongs to several groups might appear.

Some LinkedIn Groups are extensions of existing organizations, and others are created on LinkedIn by an individual as a way to identify and network with people who share a common interest. In either case, they're useful tools for growing your network and leveraging your existing affiliations.

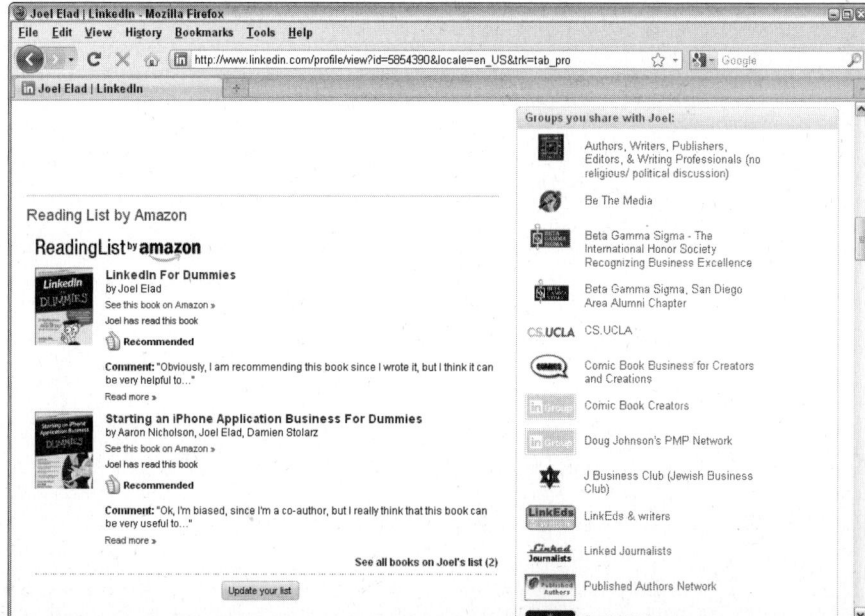

Figure 14-1:
Group logos displayed on a profile.

Types of LinkedIn Groups

Because there are lots of reasons to create a group, LinkedIn has established the following six primary categories of groups:

- ✔ **Alumni:** These groups are alumni associations created by schools or teaching institutions as a means to keep in touch with past graduates. Graduates can also keep in touch with each other through an alumni group. As you develop your career, you can tap in to the alumni network of like-minded, qualified individuals. Loyalty to your alma mater makes you, and everyone else in the group, more likely to help a schoolmate than a complete stranger.

- ✔ **Corporate:** Because every company has its own unique culture, who better to understand that culture than current and past employees? Corporate groups allow employees from a single employer to stay in touch.

- ✔ **Conference:** As conference attendees plan to attend a particular conference, using a conference group to network with attendees before, during, and after the conference can be advantageous.

  Before the conference, you can relay important information, such as subject matter and agenda, and any events, lectures, seminars, parties, or other info that matters to the attendees. Perhaps there are last-minute changes or announcements that need to get disseminated quickly. During the event, you can quickly relay announcements, as well as news being generated at the conference and any on-site changes. After the conference, these conference groups allow attendees to stay in contact and help the conference organizers and presenters see how the subject matter and industries have changed or progressed.

  Also, as the conference becomes a yearly event, the conference group becomes a constant area of discussion and planning.

- ✔ **Networking:** A common interest is all that's needed to come together and meet similarly minded people. Networking groups are organized around concepts like women's networks, angel investors in new companies, or even Rotary Clubs. These LinkedIn groups allow you to stay involved in your interests and meet people with similar or complementary goals to your own.

- ✔ **Nonprofit:** After talking business all day, it's comforting to have a group where you can talk and plan any upcoming events that benefit your favorite nonprofit organization. These LinkedIn groups allow far-flung volunteers to organize, plan, and execute projects and events relating to their charity without being in the same room — which is especially convenient if everybody has a busy schedule. These groups also allow any nonprofit organizers to bring new members up to speed and answer their questions quickly so more people become involved.

✔ **Professional:** Finally, who knows your career issues better than others in your industry and/or job title? Professional groups allow you to network with people in the same type of work who are probably experiencing the same issues, problems, and potential solutions as you. Whether it's an organization of CFOs, workers in the wireless industry, or SAP Certified Consultants, these groups can be invaluable when it comes to furthering your career and giving you an avenue to evaluate job tips and industry news.

Joining a Group

When you look at the LinkedIn groups out there, one of the most important things to keep in mind is that you should join only groups that are relevant to you. Although you might think it fun to join another alumni association group besides your alma mater, it won't really help you in the long run.

As you use LinkedIn more and decide that you want to get involved by joining a LinkedIn group, you have a couple of options for getting started:

✔ Click the Group logo found on the profile of one of your first-degree connections to join the group yourself.

✔ Search the LinkedIn Groups directory to find a group that interests you; then click the logo to join the group.

The first option may come about when you're browsing your first-degree connections list, and you see a group that you're interested in joining. After you click the logo, you simply have to click a Join This Group button on the next page that you see, and you've completed the process.

When you're more proactive and plan to seek out a group to join, just follow these steps:

1. **From the top navigation bar, roll your mouse over the Groups link and then click the Groups Directory link in the drop-down menu that appears.**

   You're taken to the Groups Directory page on LinkedIn, as shown in Figure 14-2.

2. **Enter keywords in the text box underneath the Search Groups heading.**

   Use keywords to describe the group that interests you. Say, for example, that you're looking to join a group that promotes or encourages public speaking. Just enter **public speaking** into the text box.

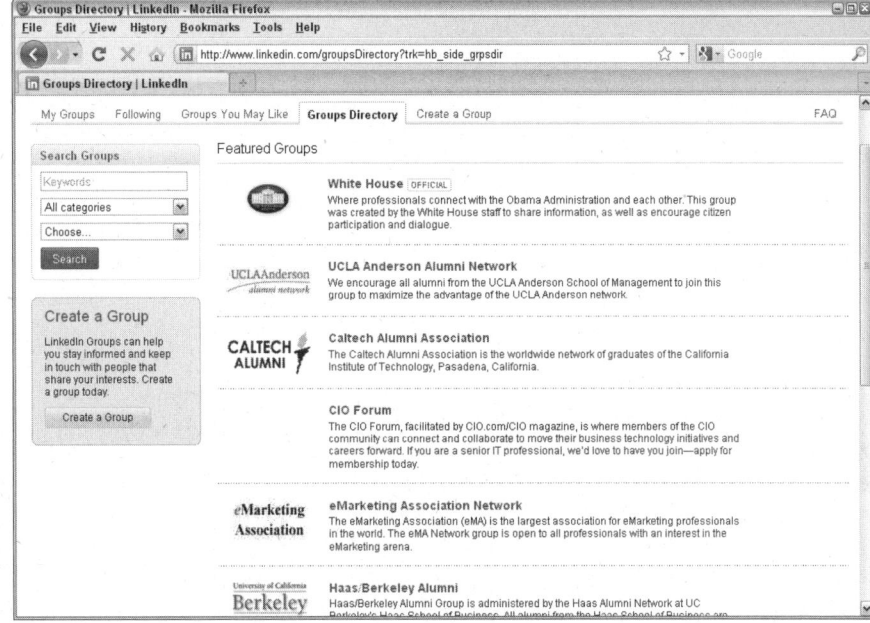

Figure 14-2:
You can
look for
specific
LinkedIn
Groups.

3. **Click the Search button to see a list of groups that match your keywords.**

   Go through the results list, as shown in Figure 14-3, and read the descriptions of each group on the list. If you need more information about the group, click the Owner's name to see his profile and send him a message requesting a few details about the group.

4. **When you see a Group that you want to join, click the Join Group button you see to the right of the group description.**

   You're taken to the Group summary page, as shown in Figure 14-4. You see the details regarding the group's contact e-mail as well as how often (and what types of) messages get relayed to you. You can also choose whether you want the Group logo displayed on your profile after joining.

5. **Click the Join Group button to join the LinkedIn group.**

   That's it! You see a confirmation message, and you're taken back to the My Groups page with your newly added group on the list. Depending on the requirements for membership, your request will either be immediately approved or sent to the group manager for manual approval.

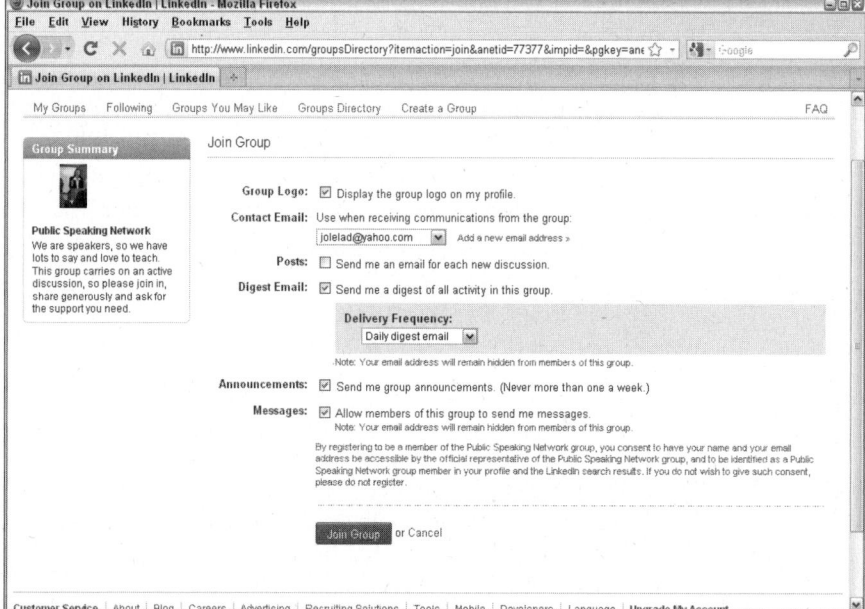

Searching a Group

After you join a group, you'll probably want to see who's in the group and how the group members are connected to you. After all, the point of these groups is to stay in touch with like-minded individuals and have them be part of your extended network.

To search a group, follow these steps:

1. **From the top navigation bar, roll your mouse over the Groups link and then click the My Groups link in the drop-down menu that appears.**

   Your My Groups page appears.

2. **Look through the list of groups on the My Groups page, scroll down to the group's header, and roll your mouse over the group's Go To drop-down arrow. Then, choose the accompanying Members option.**

   This brings up a list of members in the group, sorted by how many degrees they are away from you in your LinkedIn network.

3. **(Optional) Once you are on the Members screen, on the left-hand side of the screen, at the bottom of the Search Members box, click the Advanced Search link and add other search criteria to get a more targeted results list.**

   This brings up a Find People page, as shown in Figure 14-5. You can see that the search is automatically limited to members of your group. Now you can scroll down the page and use more of the filters provided as search requirements, such as names, companies, user types, locations, and so on.

4. **Click the Search button.**

   Your search is carried out according to the refined search criteria you entered.

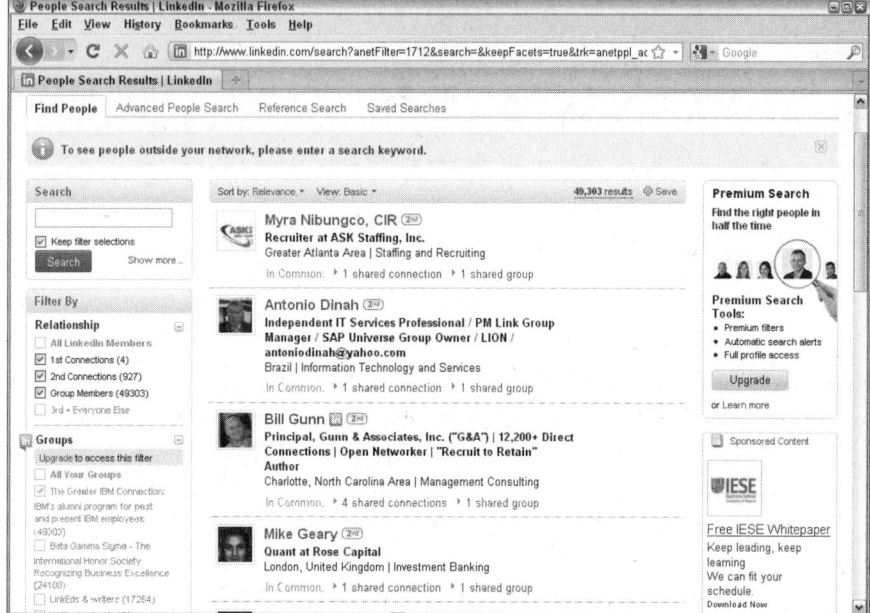

Case study: Caltech gets connected

Caltech Alumni Association launched an official alumni group on LinkedIn in 2006. Of some 20,000 contactable alumni, it now has approximately 4,250 members in the LinkedIn group — about 10 percent. Andrew Shaindlin, Executive Director of the association, is one of the early adopters of using third-party social networking sites to help alumni stay connected.

With more than a year of experience running the group, Shaindlin noticed some cool things that his alumni members were doing with this new LinkedIn group, including the following:

✔ Graduates were making connections between their alumni network members and their non-alumni network members when they were networking.

✔ Alumni group members saw higher search engine placements for their member's names and more page views for Caltech in general.

✔ The Caltech Alumni Web site saw an increase of traffic from members clicking through from LinkedIn via the LinkedIn group Web site URL link.

✔ The Caltech Alumni Association has more graduates' e-mail address on file, attributed partially to their LinkedIn group.

✔ Most importantly, there are success stories about Caltech alumni finding jobs, employees, and investors through their LinkedIn Group.

Creating a Group

When you're ready to create your own group, just follow these steps:

1. **Click the Groups link in the top navigation bar.**

   You see the Groups page, with five tabs along the top: My Groups, Following, Groups You May Like, Groups Directory, and Create a Group.

2. **Click the Create a Group tab.**

   This step brings you to the Create a Group page, as shown in Figure 14-6. This is where you input all the information about your newly requested group.

3. **Upload the logo for your group.**

   LinkedIn requires a logo. The file format must be PNG, JPEG, or GIF, and the memory size of the logo cannot exceed 100KB. Click the Browse button next to the logo box. In the Choose File dialog box that opens, locate the logo file on your computer so LinkedIn can upload it; then click Open.

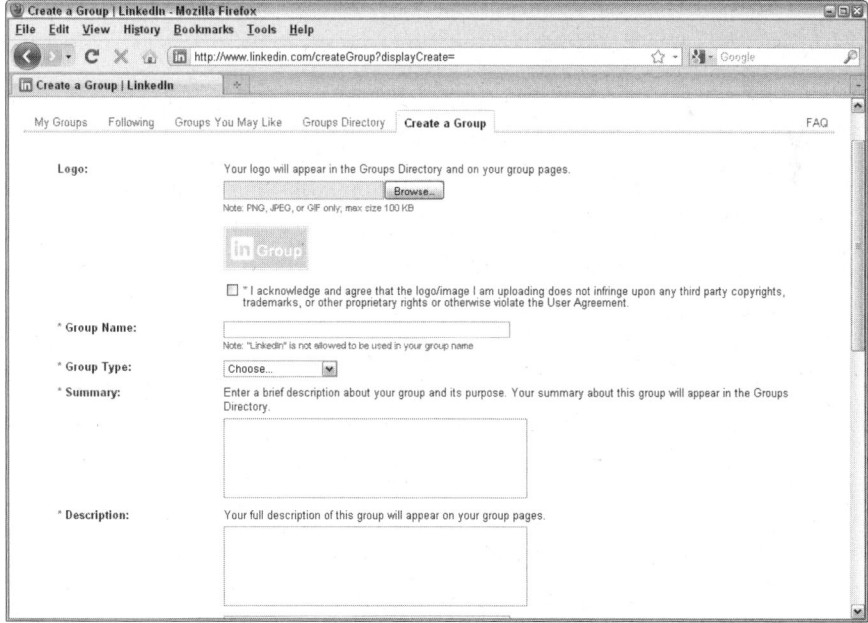

Figure 14-6: Enter your new group information here!

"But where do I get a logo?" you might ask. Well, you can design your own logo at sites like www.logoyes.com or www.logoworks.com. If a logo already exists, like for an alumni association, ask one of the administrators for a high-resolution copy of the logo, or save a copy of the logo from the group's personal Web site — as long as you know you have the rights to use that image, of course.

Your logo can't exceed 100KB, so watch that file size as you create your logo.

4. **Provide your group information and settings, including group name, description, type, Web site URL, manager e-mail, whether you want people to automatically have access to join or be pre-approved by you or another manager, and whether you want your group visible on your member's profile pages. (Refer to Figure 14-6.)**

You have only 300 characters in your group description, so choose your words wisely.

If you're wondering what to write for your group description, first click the Groups Directory tab near the top of the page (before writing anything) and read through similar groups in your group type. Then, go back to the Create Groups page and enter your description. (If you check the Groups Directory while writing your description, you'll lose whatever you typed.)

5. **If your group is located in one geographic region, select the appropriate check box.**

6. **Read through the Terms of Service and select that check box after you review it.**

At this point, your page should look something like Figure 14-7, where your logos and information are uploaded and ready for review.

7. **Click the Create Group button to create your group on LinkedIn.**

You're taken to the newly created home page for your new group, and your request is submitted.

You should see your newly created group page, as shown in Figure 14-8. Your new group is ready for members!

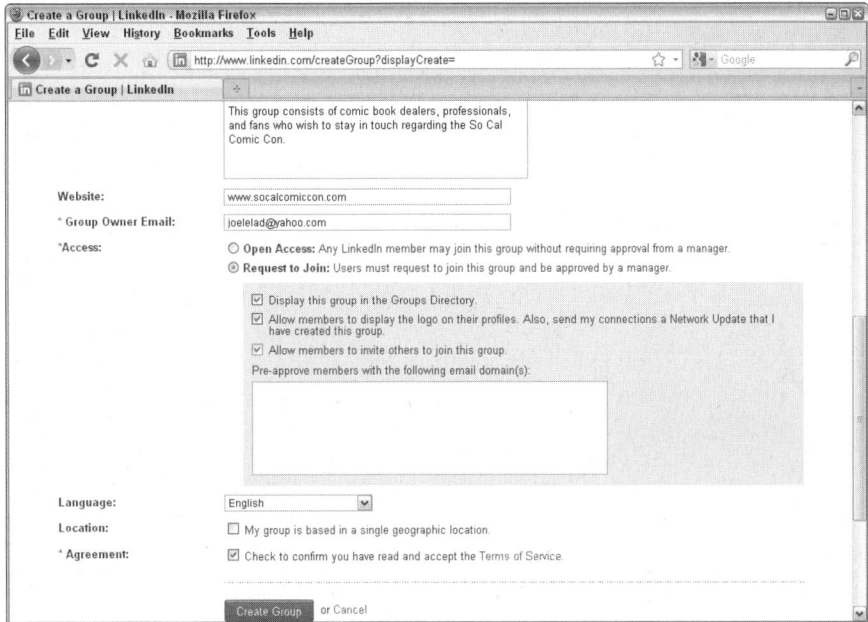

Figure 14-7:
Your group
request is
ready to be
submitted!

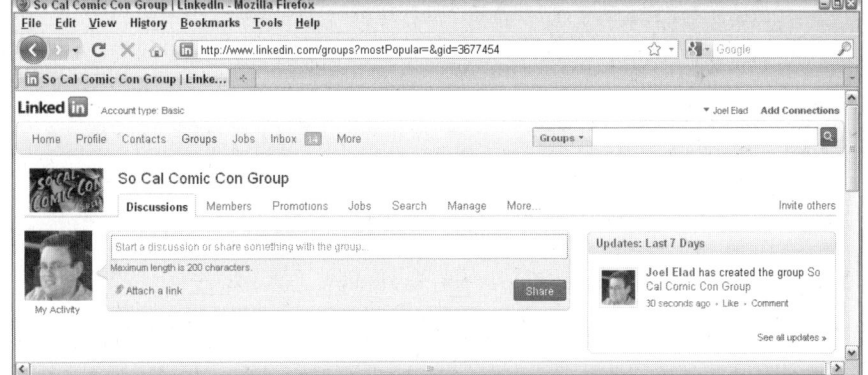

Figure 14-8:
Your group
has been
created!

Inviting Members

After you get your confirmation from LinkedIn that your new group has been created, your next step is to invite members to be a part of this group. The way this is handled with LinkedIn is actually a multi-part process:

1. You have to define a list of pre-approved members of your group, which you will upload to LinkedIn. You should do this *before* you send out any Invitations.

2. You're allowed to e-mail your prospective members with an Invitation to join your new group. LinkedIn provides you with a Web page that you can use to generate your Invitations.

3. When a new member clicks that link, LinkedIn checks to see whether that member is on your Pre-Approved list. If so, she automatically becomes a member. If not, you (the group manager) will see a member request in the Manage section of your group entry, which you will have to manually approve so the user can officially join the group. The user's status will show up as Pending on her My Groups page until you approve her membership request.

Building your member list

The easiest way to build your list of members is to use a spreadsheet program like Microsoft Excel and create a Comma-Separated Values file (`.csv` file) which is simply a text file of members and their e-mail addresses. You should definitely have your member list in front of you before starting this process.

If many of the members are already connected to you in LinkedIn, you can simply export your connections to start building your member list. See Chapter 6 for more information on how to do this.

When you're ready to build your list of members, just follow these steps:

1. **Open a spreadsheet program, such as Microsoft Excel. Choose File⇨ New from the top Excel menu to create a new blank document.**

2. **In the first row, create these entries, which will be the three column headers:**

   • First Name

   • Last Name

   • E-mail Address

3. **Starting in the second row, fill in the members' names and e-mail addresses.**

   As you fill in your list, it should begin to look like Figure 14-9.

Figure 14-9:
Use Excel
to build your
Group
member list.

4. **Choose File⇨Save As.**

   The Save As window pops up, as shown in Figure 14-10.

Figure 14-10:
Don't forget
to save your
file as CSV
(Comma
Delimited).

5. **Make sure that the Save as Type option is set to CSV (Comma Delimited) and then click OK when prompted.**

6. **Go to your LinkedIn account and click the Groups link in the top navigation bar to bring up your My Groups page.**

7. **From the My Groups page, roll your mouse over the Actions link underneath the name of your group and select Pre-approve People from the drop-down menu that appears.**

This brings up the Pre-approve People page of your group, as shown in Figure 14-11. At first, you're the only member of this new group.

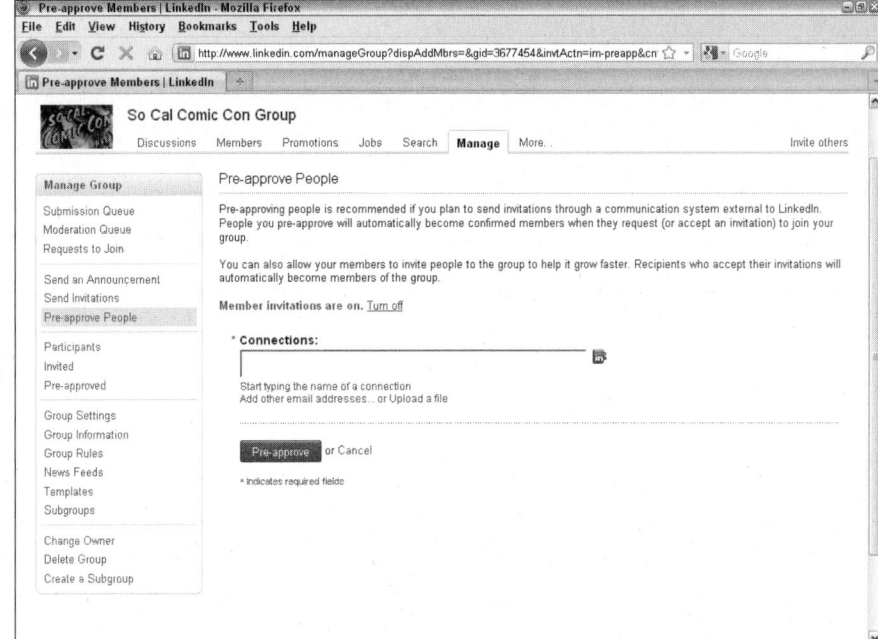

Figure 14-11:
The Pre-approve People page is one of many Manage Group tasks.

8. **Click the Upload a File link below the Connections box in the middle of the screen.**

   This brings up the Upload a File page, as shown in Figure 14-12.

9. **Click the Browse button to find the CSV file on your computer.**

10. **After you specify the file you want, click the Upload File button to upload the file (containing your list of members) into your group.**

    The next page attempts to determine whether the file was uploaded correctly. You should see your member list uploaded correctly, as shown in Figure 14-13. Here, you have two options.

    - *Finish Uploading:* If LinkedIn brought in the first few names correctly with the right text encoding — which pretty much assures everything went according to plan — click the Finish Uploading button.

    - *Try Next Encoding:* If the names shown don't display correctly, click the Try Next Encoding link.

    You're done! Your new members will appear on the Pre-Approved list for this group.

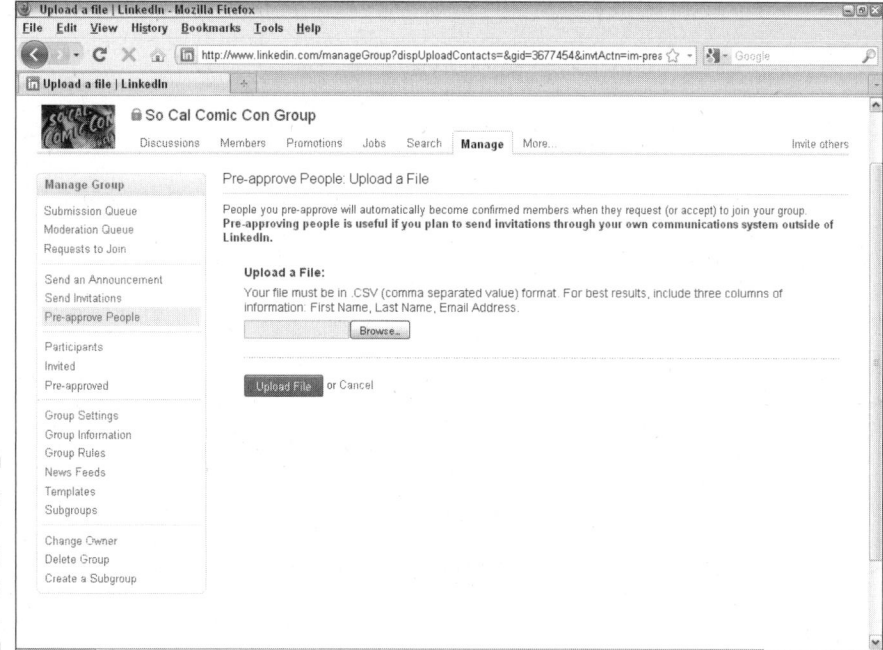

Figure 14-12:
Import your
list of
members
here.

You can always choose the Pre-approve People option from the Actions drop-down menu and use the form to manually add additional names at any time.

If the e-mail address of a member's LinkedIn profile is different from the e-mail address you put in the Pre-Approved list, this member won't be automatically approved when he clicks the link. You have to manually approve him by clicking the Requests to Join link from the Groups page.

Crafting your Invitation e-mail

LinkedIn allows you to send group Invitations from the Groups page because the folks at LinkedIn feel that the Invitations should come from the group owner — namely, you. Therefore, here are some do's and don'ts to keep in mind as you craft the Invitation:

✔ **Do relate the purpose and benefits of the group.** People are busy and need to understand why they should join this group. Explain the benefits of being connected to other people and what you hope to accomplish with this group. Remember: You're sending this to LinkedIn members, so don't worry about explaining LinkedIn — just explain your group.

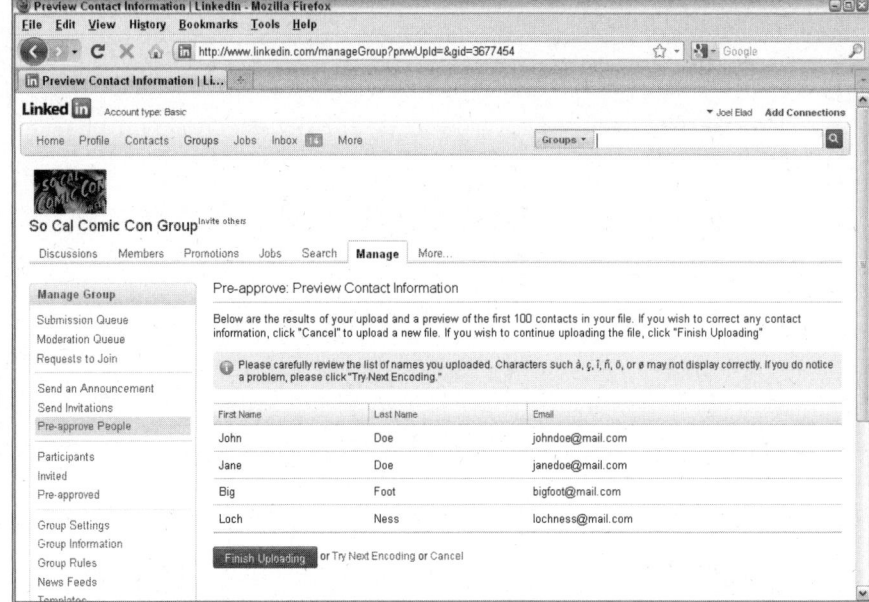

Figure 14-13:
Look through your list and add members to your group.

✔ **Don't go on forever.** One to two paragraphs is the maximum this Invitation should be. Introduce yourself, introduce the group name, give people the benefits of joining, encourage them to join, include the link to the LinkedIn group page, and sign off. No one will read a long diatribe or laundry list of reasons to join. Use bullet points and short sentences whenever possible.

✔ **Don't put other offers in the e-mail.** Some people use this as an opportunity not only to encourage folks to join one group, but perhaps to push a second group Invitation, or highlight a link to the group's non-LinkedIn Web site. The moment you start presenting multiple options for people, you lose their attention, and they won't sign up.

You can use any e-mail program to create an Invitation to your group, or you can go to the Manage tab of your group and click Send Invitations from the left-hand menu that appears. You simply type in the name of your first-degree connections (separated by commas), a Subject line, and a Welcome Message, that can look as simple as this:

Hello,

You are hereby invited to join the new UC Irvine GSM/Merage Alumni Group on LinkedIn. Joining this group will allow you to find and contact other alumni, so you can stay in touch, gain referrals, and view other alumnis' LinkedIn profiles.

Hope to see you in the group!

–Joel Elad, Class of 2002

After you send out the Invitations, as members respond, they're moved from the Pre-Approved list to the Current list of your group, and the small group logo appears on their profiles.

Approving members to your group

As more and more people find out about your new LinkedIn group, and as members start joining, you may find that some of the people who have clicked the link to join aren't on your pre-approved list. Perhaps they are people you didn't realize were on LinkedIn, perhaps you didn't realize they were valid group members, or perhaps they clicked the wrong link and/or they don't belong in your group.

Regardless, you need to go into LinkedIn and either approve or reject people's membership requests so they can be members (or non-members) of your LinkedIn group. When you need to do that, just follow these steps:

1. **From the top navigation bar, click the Groups link to bring up your list of My Groups.**

   You see the My Groups page. All the other Groups options are just a tab away, but by default, you will see the My Groups page.

2. **Scroll down until you see the name and logo of the group you are maintaining, as shown in Figure 14-14.**

3. **Click the Requests to Join link below the name of your group to bring up the Requests to Join page.**

   This step brings up the list of people waiting to be approved for your group, like in Figure 14-15.

Figure 14-14:
You can manage your LinkedIn group membership.

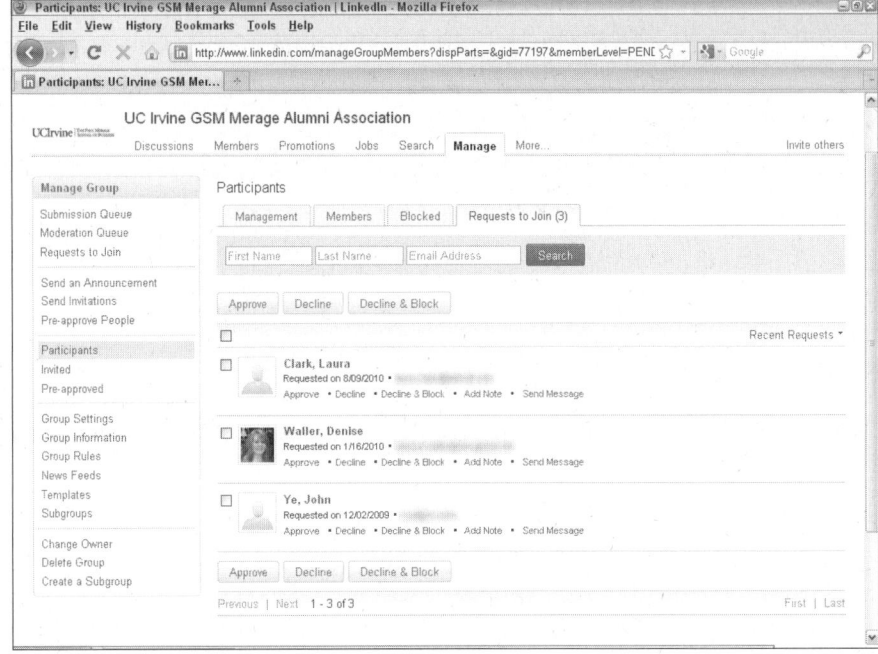

Figure 14-15:
See who is
waiting to
be approved
to your
LinkedIn
group.

4. **To accept people, first select the check box next to each person you want to approve to join your LinkedIn group. Then click the Approve button.**

   You can approve people individually or all at once if you want. You can always select the person's name on the list to read his LinkedIn profile and decide whether he belongs in the group or send him a message through his profile.

5. **To refuse membership, first select the check box next to each person you want to decline membership to the group, and then click the Decline button.**

   You can also click the Decline & Block button if you want to permanently block them from trying to join the group.

Similar to the approval process, you can decline people one at a time or all at once. (The easiest way to select everyone is to click the empty check box at the top of the list; the one with no name associated with it.) In either case (approval or decline), the user's name disappears from the Request to Join page. Lastly, remember that you can remove someone from the group membership at any time after you initially approved him.

Chapter 15

Marketing Yourself and Your Business

*I*n this part of the book, you find out how to start applying everything the previous parts cover about how to use the site for specific situations and needs. After all, every great invention needs to fulfill some sort of purpose, and LinkedIn is no exception. Its value is not just in how it allows you to network and build your brand, but also in how you can use LinkedIn to handle other tasks easier and more effectively.

I start with the age-old discipline of marketing. In this chapter, I discuss how to generate sales and how LinkedIn can affect your entire sales cycle. LinkedIn can help you "spread the gospel" of your business mission by serving as a vehicle for positive and rich marketing messages about both you and your business, whether it's a startup or a Fortune 500 company. Part of the power of LinkedIn comes from involving others in your marketing initiatives, so I cover some ways for you to do that as well.

Marketing Yourself through LinkedIn

When it comes to maximizing the benefit you receive from LinkedIn, you are your biggest advocate. Although your network of connections is instrumental in helping you grow, much of your marketing happens without your being involved; that is, after you create your profile, that and any other LinkedIn activity of yours are read and judged by the community at large — on the other members' own time and for their own purposes. Therefore, you want to make sure that you're creating a favorable impression of yourself by marketing the best traits, abilities, and features of you and your business. Because of the nature of LinkedIn, this marketing occurs continually — 24/7. So, you should look at LinkedIn as something to check and update on a continual basis, like a blog. It doesn't mean you have to spend hours and hours each day, but a little bit of time on a consistent basis can go a long way toward a favorable and marketable LinkedIn identity.

The following sections look at the different ways you interact with LinkedIn, and what you can do to create the most polished, effective LinkedIn identity possible to further your marketing message.

Optimizing your profile

In Chapter 3, I discuss building your professional profile on LinkedIn, which is the centerpiece of your LinkedIn identity and your personal brand. I refer to your profile throughout this book, but here, I focus on ways for you to update or enhance your profile with one specific goal in mind: marketing yourself better or more consistently. As always, not every tip or suggestion will work for everyone, and you might have already put some of these into action, but it's always good to revisit your profile to make sure it's organized the way you intended.

To make sure your profile is delivering the best marketing message for you, consider these tips:

✔ **Use the Professional headline wisely.** Your Professional headline is what other LinkedIn users see below your name even when they're not looking at your full profile. I've seen some users stuff a lot of text into this field, so you should have enough space to communicate the most important things about yourself. Simply put, if you have one, or even two, key phrases you want associated with your name, they should be a part of your headline.

A standard headline reads something like, "Software Development Manager at XYZ Communications," but you can write entire sentences full of great keywords for your headline. My friend Anderee Berengian's headline reads: "Growth-Stage, Results-Oriented Internet & Digital Media Professional, Advisor, and Investor." Think about how many people would want to connect with him!

✔ **Make sure you use keyword phrases that match popular keywords for you or your business.** The first step, as I just mentioned, is to put these phrases in your headline. The second step is to make sure these phrases are reflected in your Summary, Experiences, and Interests.

Be careful not to overuse your main keyword phrases. The search engines call this practice "stuffing," which is cramming as many instances of a phrase into your site in hopes of achieving a higher ranking. If the search engines detect this, you will experience lower ranking results.

✔ **If you're available for freelance work, make sure to identify at least one of your current positions as Freelance.** Remember, people aren't mind readers (Karnac excluded), so you need to let people know that you're a freelance writer, Web site designer, dog walker, or whatever. If you look at Cynthia Beale's profile in Figure 15-1, you can see that she's self-employed as a training professional, and her Experience section further details that she specializes in Management, Communication, and Personality Training.

✔ **Use the additional sections in your profile to include any relevant information that reinforces your marketing message.** For example, if you want to be seen as an expert in a given field, add the Publications section to your profile to show off the articles or books you've written, articles you've been quoted in, focus or advisory groups you belong to, and any speaking engagements or discussions you've participated in.

✔ **Make sure your profile links to your Web sites, blogs, and any other part of your online identity.** Don't just accept the standard "My Company" text. Instead, select the Other option, and put your own words in the Website title box, such as "Joel Elad's E-Commerce Education Web site." (See Chapter 3 for more information on linking from your profile to other Web sites.)

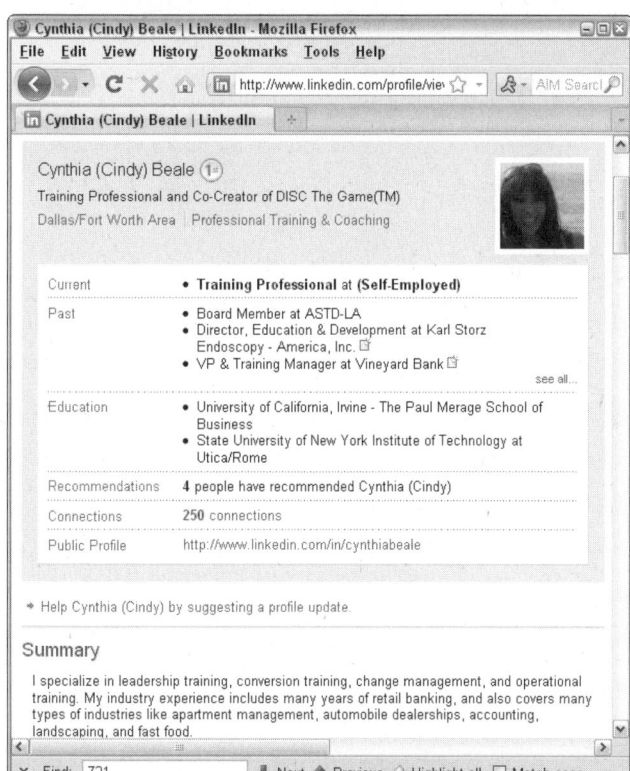

Figure 15-1:
Make sure to note if you are self-employed or freelance.

For an example of effectively linking your profile to other areas of your online presence, take a look at Scott Allen's profile, shown in Figure 15-2. His three Web site links replace the bland My Company, My Blog, and My Website with his own text — Social Media Is My Middle Name, The Virtual Handshake, and Linked Intelligence. Not only does this give more information to someone reading his profile, but search engines have a better idea of what those links represent.

Marketing yourself to your network

Optimizing your profile in the ways described in the previous section is one of the best ways to market yourself effectively using LinkedIn. Another is to be alert to how well you're communicating with your LinkedIn connections. Whether it's automatic (like when you update your profile and LinkedIn automatically notifies your network through a Network Update) or self-generated (when you use LinkedIn InMail or Introductions to send a note to someone else, which I cover in Chapter 5), this communication becomes your ongoing message to the members of your network and keeps you in their minds and (you hope!) plans.

Figure 15-2:
Give your Web site links meaningful names.

The most effective marketing occurs when people don't realize you're marketing to them. After all, the average American sees all kinds of marketing messages throughout their day. Your goal is to communicate often but not be overbearing about it so your message subtly sinks into people's minds. If you do that, people will think you're Grrrr-*eat!* (Hmm, why am I hungry for cereal?)

So when you're contemplating how to effectively communicate with your network connections, keep these points in mind:

- ✔ **Update your profile when appropriate.** Updating your profile means that you're sending an update of your newest projects to your network so that your connections know whether they might want to consider involving you in their own current or future projects. You don't need to update your profile as often as you update a blog, but you certainly don't want to leave your profile untouched for months on end, either. Useful times to update your profile include

   - Getting a new job or promotion

   - Starting a new freelance or contract job

   - Launching a new company or venture

   - Adding a missing piece of your Experiences section, like adding a new position, updating the description of an existing job, or clarifying the role of a group or interest on your profile

   - Taking on new responsibilities or duties in any of your endeavors

- ✔ **Take advantage of the Share an Update feature.** When you specify your current endeavors, several things happen. Your profile reflects what you enter here, your network connections see what you enter here when they read their Network Updates about you (see Chapter 9 for more on Network Updates), and you start to build your own microblog, in a sense, because people can follow your natural progression.

   A similar example of a microblog is Twitter. As you update your Twitter profile with 140-character messages, other people can follow your activities and even subscribe to these updates. Tie your Twitter updates to your LinkedIn account, so if you "tweet" on Twitter, those updates will automatically be reflected on your LinkedIn profile.

   Some people use the update feature to let people know that, "Joel is getting ready for his week-long vacation" or "Joel is finishing up his first draft of *LinkedIn For Dummies.*" Other people use the messages to show progression of a certain task, like "Joel is currently conducting interviews for an Executive Assistant position he is trying to fill," then "Joel is narrowing down his choices for Executive Assistant to two finalists," and then "Joel has made an offer to his top choice for Executive Assistant." See Chapter 9 for more on how to use this feature.

- ✔ **Search for, and join, any relevant LinkedIn Groups that can help you reach your target audience.** It's a good idea to participate in these groups, but whatever you do, don't immediately download a list of all group members and spam them with LinkedIn messages. When you join the group, you're indicating your interest in that group because your profile now carries that group logo. Membership in such groups gives you access to like-minded people you should be communicating with and adding to your network. Spend some time every week or every month checking out LinkedIn Groups and networking with group members to grow your network.

✔ **Ask appropriate questions of selected people rather than the whole network.** When you use LinkedIn Answers (see Chapter 7) to ask a question or gain more knowledge about something, rather than blast your entire network with your request, send a personalized invitation to only those members in your network who seem the most likely to have the knowledge you need.

Don't ask questions to the same people all the time. Change the focus of your questions at regular intervals so that you reach out to more of your network over the year. For example, you might ask some questions on software development for a few months, and then focus on project management for a while. On the other hand, when you know a question that could interest your entire network, don't hesitate to let everyone know. Do that too often, however, and people will feel annoyed by it.

✔ **Participate on a regular and consistent basis.** The easiest way to ensure a steady stream of contact with as many people as you can handle is to dedicate a small but fixed amount of time to interacting with the LinkedIn community. Some members spend 15 to 30 minutes per day, sending messages to their connections, reading through the Questions and Answers pages, or finding one to two new people to add to their network. Others spend an hour a week, or as long as it takes to create what they've set as their set number of recommendations, invite their set number of new contacts, or reconnect with their set number of existing connections. You just need to establish a routine that works for your own schedule.

Marketing Your Business through LinkedIn

LinkedIn can play a significant role in the effective marketing of your business. LinkedIn's value as a marketing tool gets a lot of buzz from most companies' finance departments, especially because they see LinkedIn as a free way of marketing the business. Although you don't have to pay anything in terms of money to take advantage of most of LinkedIn's functions, you do have the cost of the time you put in to manage your profile and use LinkedIn to the fullest.

Currently, LinkedIn offers your company promotion through its Company Profiles section. LinkedIn ties status updates, job titles, and other pertinent information from company employees' profiles directly into the Company

Profile. From each profile, you can see who you know in the company, open career positions, recent promotions and changes from their employees, and other pertinent facts.

If you're a small business, you can create your own Company page. You need to have your company e-mail address in your LinkedIn profile and be established as a current employee/manager/owner of that company in your profile as well. Click the More link from the top navigation bar, and then Companies, to learn more.

Online marketing tactics using LinkedIn

Marketing your business on LinkedIn involves working through your own network, employing both your current list of contacts as well as potential contacts in the greater LinkedIn community. Your efforts should also include making use of links from your online activities to your LinkedIn profile and promoting your business online from your LinkedIn identity. Here are some things to keep in mind as you develop your LinkedIn marketing strategy:

- **Encourage every employee to have a LinkedIn profile and to link to each other.** Extending your network in this way increases your exposure outside your company. And if anybody in your organization is nervous about preparing her profile, just tell her that even Bill Gates has a LinkedIn profile. That should do the trick! (And then buy her a copy of this book to get the profile created.)

- **Make sure your business Web sites and blogs are linked to your LinkedIn profile.** By offering your Web site visitors a direct view to your LinkedIn profile, you're allowing them to verify you as an employee of the company because they can see your experiences and your recommendations from other people. They might also realize that they share a bond with you and your business that they never would have realized without LinkedIn.

- **Make sure your LinkedIn profile links back to your business Web site and blog.** Yes, you want your visitors and potential customers to be able to verify who you are, as noted in the previous bullet in this list, but you also want them to go back to your Web site and do some business with you! Make sure that you, and every employee of your company who's on LinkedIn, includes a link to your business's Web site and, if there is one, the company blog.

If you have a search engine expert working for you, that person may complain about something called a *two-way link,* which is a link from your LinkedIn profile to your Web site and a link from your Web site to your LinkedIn profile. This practice, known as *reciprocal linking,* hurts your search engine ranking. If so, have that person identify which of the two links is more important and implement only that link.

✔ **Make sure that your most popular keyword phrases are in your company or personal profile.** Use sites such as Wordtracker (www.wordtracker.com) or Good Keywords (www.goodkeywords.com) to find the hottest keyword phrases in your field. If your business is doing any online ad campaigns, make sure those keyword phrases are the same as the ones in your profile. Presenting a consistent image to any potential customer makes you and your company look more professional.

✔ **Develop relationships with key business partners or media contacts.** When you search for someone on LinkedIn, you can be very precise about who you want to reach. So, for example, if you know that your business needs to expand into the smartphone market, you can start targeting and reaching out to smartphone companies such as Apple, Research In Motion (maker of the BlackBerry), and Palm (maker of the Pre and the Pixi). If you want to increase your visibility, start reaching out to media members who cover your industry.

Getting a Services Listing through a Recommendation

Now, you may ask, "What if I am my business?" If you provide a professional service, such as consulting or freelance writing (to name just a couple), be sure to take advantage of the LinkedIn Service Provider directory. This directory consists of categories and subcategories that range from computer-related consultants to attorneys, accountants, and real estate agents. If you roll your mouse over the word Companies in the top navigation bar, click Find Companies to bring up the Companies page, and then click the Services Provider link, you can see the list of categories along the right side of the screen. (We discuss Service Providers in more detail in Chapter 13.)

The tricky part about appearing in this directory is that you can't simply list yourself in this directory; instead, LinkedIn requires you to obtain a recommendation from another LinkedIn member. The reason for this requirement is simple: LinkedIn wants a directory of only providers who have at least one person willing to publicly validate their work.

The moment you receive a recommendation from a LinkedIn member about your services, your profile is included in the Service Providers directory. To request a recommendation from someone, just follow these steps:

1. **Click the word More in the top navigation bar, then click Companies from the menu that appears; From the Companies page, click Service Providers from the top right of the screen.**

   You're taken to the Service Providers home page, as shown in Figure 15-3.

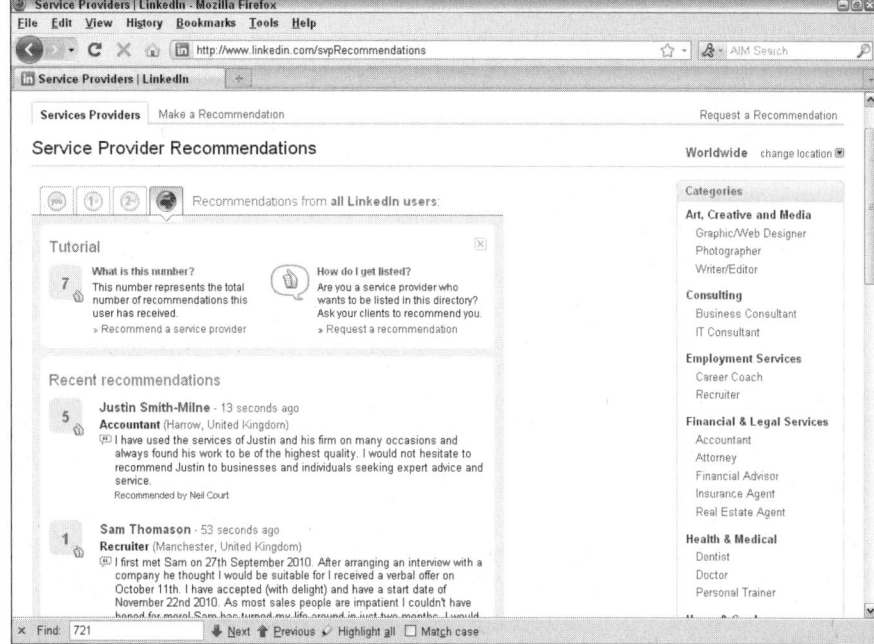

2. **Click the Request a Recommendation link (top right) to bring up the Request Recommendation page, shown in Figure 15-4.**

3. **Under Choose What You Want to Be Recommended For, click the arrow for the drop-down list to find the position you want someone to recommend you for.**

   If you want your Services recommendation to be tied to a specific role, pick one of your positions that indicates that service, such as Freelance Writer or Website Designer position. If you don't see an appropriate position in your list, click the Add a Job or School link to add a new position to your Experience section of your profile. (For more information on how to update your profile, see Chapter 3.)

4. **For the Decide Who You'll Ask section, start typing the names of people to ask for a recommendation.**

   As you type those people's names, LinkedIn prompts you with the full name of that person. Click that prompt to have LinkedIn add that person to the list.

5. **Repeat Step 4 until you add all the people you wish to ask for a recommendation.**

6. **In the Create Your Message section, write a note that will go out to each person you selected, similar to the example shown in Figure 15-5.**

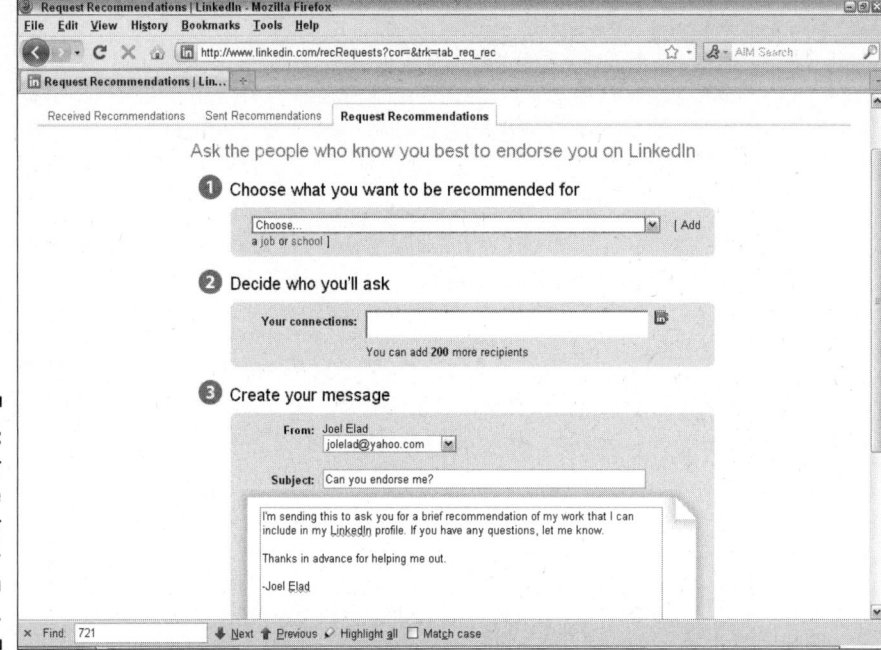

Figure 15-4:
Start your
Service
Provider
Recommen-
dation
request.

Although LinkedIn will fill in this box with canned text (as seen in Figure 15-5 below), I recommend that you change this text to make it sound as though it's coming from you.

Make sure the Subject line is appropriate, too, to help your chances of getting your intended requesters to actually open the e-mail and respond.

7. Click Send.

Your request is sent, and your selected connections receive a message from LinkedIn, asking them to come to the site and complete a Recommendation for you.

That's it! If you need information on how to complete a Recommendation for someone who requests one from you, for example, check out Chapter 8.

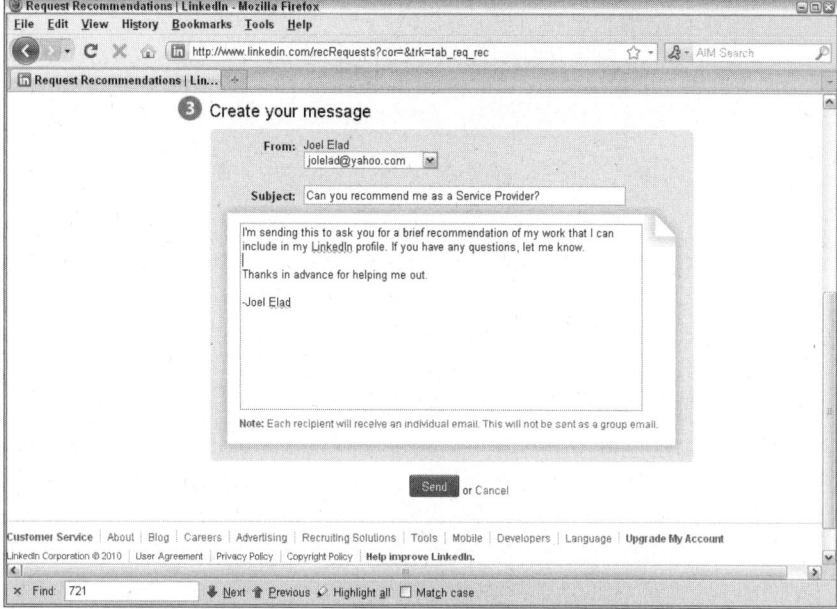

Figure 15-5:
Ask your
network
connections
for a recom-
mendation.

Finding Marketing Partners through LinkedIn

When it comes to marketing on LinkedIn, your strategy will typically involve more than just you and your business. Part of the success of marketing through LinkedIn is finding the right marketing partners to help you with your goals and take you to the next level. After all, you're connecting with like-minded professionals who have skills similar or complementary to yours, which helps you and them achieve your goals. In some cases, finding the right partner can make a big difference in the growth of your business, as I found out by interviewing Kristie Spilios. See the sidebar, "No trouble starting TrebleMakers (with the help of a LinkedIn contact)."

No trouble starting TrebleMakers
(with the help of a LinkedIn contact)

Several years ago, Kristie Spilios co-founded a company called TrebleMakers, which teaches music enrichment classes to young children. While she was building her marketing plan with her business partner, they realized that an important piece was the Web site and logo design they would be using. Given their limited preliminary budget, they were completely unable to find anyone who would address their needs. And then came salvation.

"When all hope seemed lost, I received a LinkedIn e-mail update that announced the connection of one of my contacts with an old, mutual friend from our high school days," relates Spilios. "This shared companion had just opened a consulting business and was enthusiastically eager to work with us despite our start-up woes."

Three months later, TrebleMakers received its "spectacular" Web site and "dazzling" logo for a reasonable fee that fell within their price range. The consultant even included some complementary business cards and letterhead stationery as appreciation for TrebleMakers' belief in him and his latest endeavor. Today, TrebleMakers is thriving and growing, and Spilios credits much of that success to having an informative Web site and prominent logo, saying that "We receive almost as many words of praise on our Web site and logo as we do on the music classes themselves!"

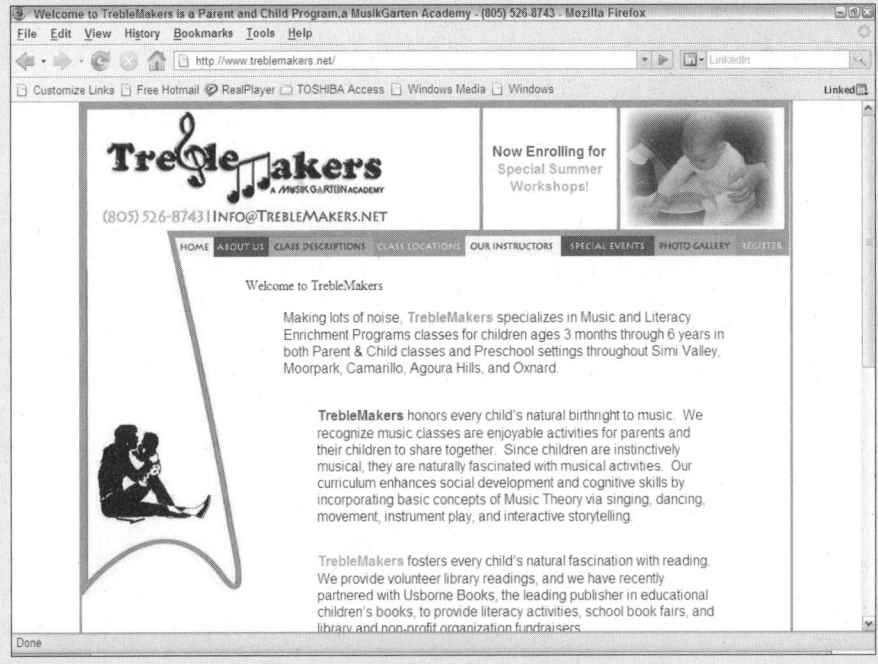

"Without LinkedIn and its awesome networking, my company would most likely still be searching for a cost-efficient marketing solution. But, instead of singing the blues, my business partner and I both have happy harmony, all thanks to LinkedIn!"

Your first order of business is to use the LinkedIn Service Providers directory to start identifying potential partners. (See Chapter 13 on how to use the Service Providers directory.) You can look for service providers who may be two or three degrees away from you or you can target people you want to meet at specific companies by seeing who in your network can arrange an introduction. Ideas to keep mind during your search include

- ✔ **Pay attention to people's titles.** In the past, you might searched for someone "who works at advertising sales for a major radio network." Today, with LinkedIn, you can look for an Advertising Sales Manager at Clear Channel Communications. Search for who you need to know, specifically, and LinkedIn will show you whether that person is connected to you by one, two, or three degrees.

- ✔ **Join the LinkedIn groups that would appeal to your business.** One of the quickest ways to signal your interest and find like-minded business-people is to join a LinkedIn group that's relevant to your industry or niche. You can then search group members to find potential partners. Also, because your groups are listed on your profile, joining a group means that you'll have a lasting reference on your profile that will let people know that you identify with this group.

- ✔ **Search LinkedIn Answers for people with similar situations as yours.** You might find someone at a similar company who looked for an SEO expert and asked the community for help. The people who responded might give you insight on whom to choose and to add to your network.

Odds are, you won't have all the answers when it comes to your strategic plan, marketing plan, or maybe even your business direction. Thankfully, when you're using LinkedIn, you're definitely not alone. LinkedIn allows you to tap the collective knowledge of its community, enabling you to performing market research on a variety of topics and get real- time answers without involving think tanks or putting out thousands of dollars in fees.

The key is to be honest, transparent, and (as odd as this might sound) grateful. After all, you are asking people's advice and thoughts, so don't expect them to write a 30-page market analysis for you for free. Share your goals and intentions, get people discussing the idea and each other's comments, and be ready to listen. The best research results from the community's exchange of ideas, with a bunch of voices chiming in to validate or discount the theorem of the moment.

✔ **Ask targeted questions on LinkedIn Answers and follow up with people who left the best answers.** As discussed in Chapter 7, LinkedIn Answers provides an excellent and free way to tap the knowledge base of the community, in an abundance of categories. Although you can post a general "Where do we go from here?" question, you can also ask a targeted or focused question concerning one element of your research and then gauge the response. Don't forget to start a dialog with your most enthusiastic responders: They already demonstrated interest and knowledge.

✔ **Watch your Question thread closely (through the My Q&A tab) and provide clarification or responses whenever needed.** Some people just throw out a question on LinkedIn Answers and then sit back and wait for the genius to flow in. More often, however, the discussion that ensues on the Answer thread may veer from your intended topic, or the responses completely miss the mark because they don't interpret your question accurately. You can add clarification to the original question, or add your own reply in when needed. If nothing else, reply with a thank you for a very good answer and encourage others to keep that answer in mind. For more details on how to accomplish this, turn to Chapter 7 and find the section on clarifying your question.

After you receive at least five to ten responses, I recommend that you pick a best answer and some good answers by selecting the appropriate check boxes next to each person's answer. Not only does this reward people who gave you a lot of great information, but it indicates to the community which responses best fit (in case someone finds this question in a search).

✔ **Keep the conversation open and continuous.** Try to leave part of your question open-ended so that the people answering it can discuss their theories and you will have a more natural reason for follow-up with them individually. Sometimes, keeping the door open is as easy as ending your post with something like, "If you think you can help with this situation, let me know."

✔ **Set up a LinkedIn Group that speaks to your target audience and your company's (or your) capabilities.** For example, to cite my tried-and-true example, say that you're trying to reach accountants for financial services companies. To get the ball rolling, you could start the Financial Services Accountants Group, spread the word to your target audience, and stay in touch with that audience via this group whenever you want to know more about your target audience.

Chapter 16

Using LinkedIn to Increase Your Sales

*W*hen it comes to "making the sale," every edge you can gain over the competition is important. LinkedIn provides several ways to help you to get more competitive, close the sale, and even help deliver the winning solution. There are ways throughout the entire sales cycle that a well-connected network and detailed profile can help you narrow the gap, identify with your potential lead, gain some trust, and make that sale.

In this chapter, I tell you about some of the ways that LinkedIn can help you in the area of sales. You find out about how generating leads means more than just coming up with a pool of potential clients; you need to zero in on the decision maker — the person who's in the position to decide to buy your product or services. Then, after you identify your target, you can research your prospects using LinkedIn and, when you succeed in setting up a meeting with your prospect, you can use LinkedIn to prepare for that crucial meeting. Finally, this chapter covers how LinkedIn can help you deliver the winning solution after you have made the sale, and how you can report a positive experience with your customer, thereby leading to even more sales!

Mining for Your Clients

It's a big world out there. In terms of clients, you need to ask yourself who you're looking for. Is everyone a potential client, or do you have a specific demographic in mind? A specific skill set? Maybe you've written the greatest plug-in tool for accountants who work in the financial services industry, and you want to sell this tool directly to your likely users. With LinkedIn, you can conduct a search to find people who match your criteria. Then after you locate those people, it's up to you to approach them and close the sale, which I talk about in "Closing the Deal," later in this chapter.

Before you start your search, ask yourself a few questions that can help you with generating your leads:

✔ Are you looking for people with a specific title or in a particular industry?

✔ Are you looking for decision makers within a company, or are you seeking a general audience? (That is, are you trying to sell into a company, or directly to people?)

✔ Besides your main target industry, can you approach related industries, and if so, what are they?

✔ Does the location of your potential contact matter? Does making the sale require an in-person visit (which means that the contact needs to live near you or you have to be willing to travel to this person)?

With your answers to these questions in mind, you're ready to start searching LinkedIn for your leads.

Generating leads with Advanced People Search

When you're ready to start looking for leads, I recommend jumping right in with the LinkedIn Advanced People Search feature, which allows you to search the database consisting of tens of millions of LinkedIn members based on the criteria you've established for the leads you want to generate.

To start a search, first make sure that People is selected in the Search drop-down menu in the top-right corner and then click the Advanced link next to the Search text box. Say, for example, that you need accountants who work in the Financial Services industry. To start such a search, you would fill in the Title and Industries fields of Advanced People Search, as shown in Figure 16-1, and then click Search.

When you begin your search of the LinkedIn database, your own network can help you identify your *best leads* (people only two or three degrees away from you who you can reach through a first-degree connection introducing you) if you select Relationship from the Sort By drop-down menu shown at the top-left corner of Figure 16-2. (The default option is Relevance, as shown in the figure.) When you see your search results, now sorted by Relationship, you first see which results are closely connected with you via your connections. You can click each person's name to read his full LinkedIn profile, see how you're connected to that person, and decide whether you have a potential lead. (This method provides much more information to you than a simple Google search, which would provide only a LinkedIn member's public profile, instead of their full profile.)

After you identify your best leads, you can use LinkedIn to find out what connections you have in common with these leads: Simply click the Shared Connections link under the name for each search result. For example, say I click the Shared Connection link for Doug S. from Figure 16-2. I see that my friend Bob R. is the shared connection between me and Mr. S., as shown in Figure 16-3, and that will help me approach Mr. S. better, because I'll most likely ask for an Introduction or ask Mr. R. for more information about Mr. S.

When doing general prospecting, surveying the market for that "perfect lead" or, at least, a lead in the right direction, try to keep these ideas in mind while filling in the appropriate Advanced Search fields in for each strategy:

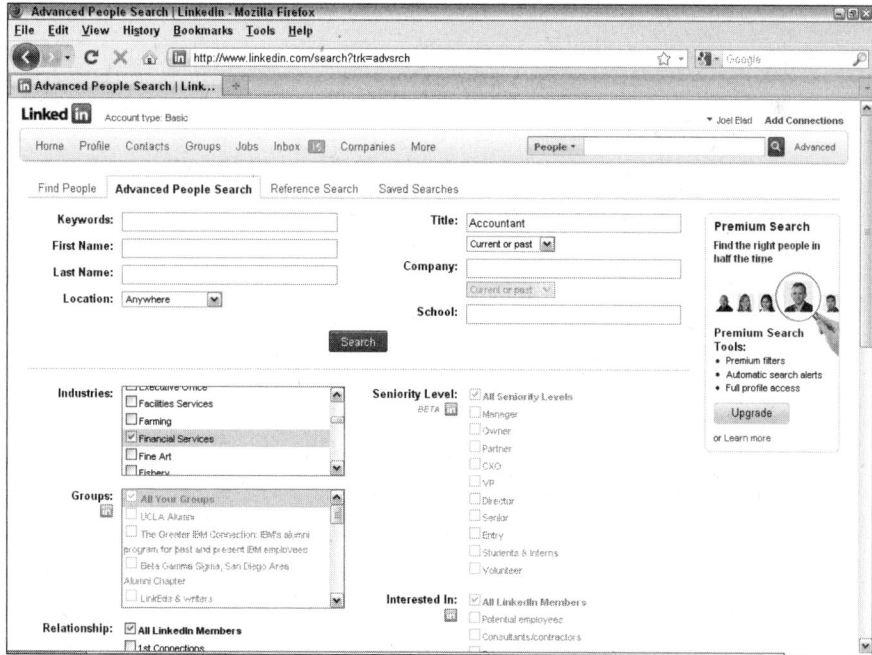

Figure 16-1: Use Advanced People Search to find your potential clients.

Sort By drop-down menu

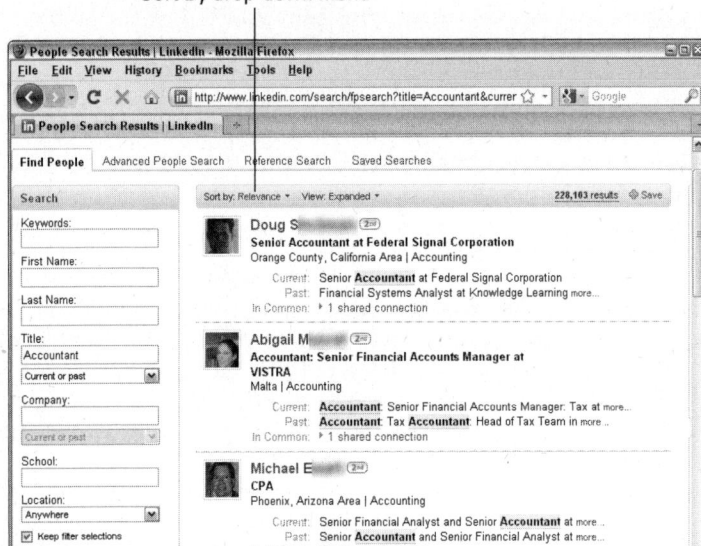

Figure 16-2:
See how
you're
connected
to your
potential
clients.

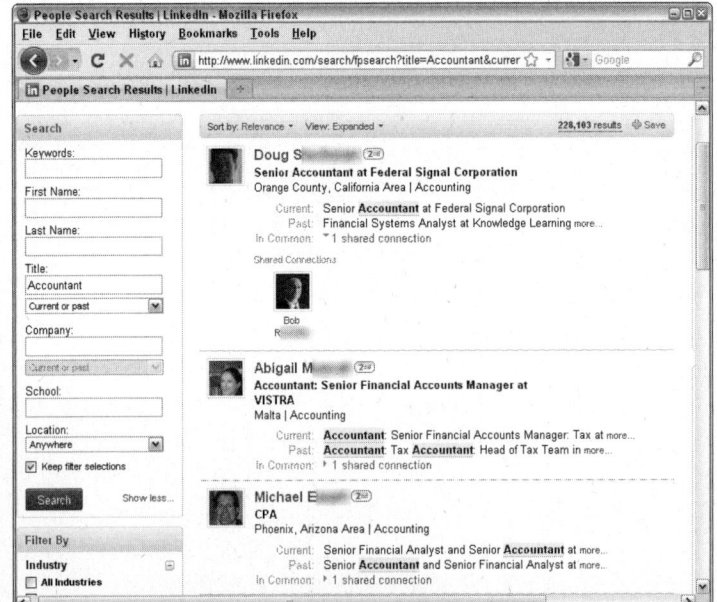

Figure 16-3:
See who
in your
LinkedIn
network is
a shared
connection
with your
target lead.

✔ **Generalize your search.** If you're looking for your ideal contacts independently of the company they work for, focus primarily on the Title and Industries fields to find your leads.

✔ **Narrow your search.** Use the Keywords field to narrow your results list when you need to reach people within a certain niche of an industry or job.

✔ **Target specific people.** Use either the Company or Keywords field, plus the Title field, to help you find specific employees in your target companies.

✔ **Refine your search by areas of knowledge.** Roll your mouse over the More link from the top navigation bar; then click Answers from the drop-down menu that appears, and look for people who answered questions in your target area to see whether you spot a potential contact there. (See Chapter 7 for more information on using LinkedIn Answers.)

✔ **Help your product sell itself.** Search for the customers of your customers. Why would you do such a thing? You want to get those people excited about your product so that they'll demand it from *your* customers, of course! This strategy is also known as *pull marketing*. (See Chapter 15 for more information about how to use LinkedIn for marketing purposes.)

✔ **Reach out through service professionals.** Search for consultants who are hired by your potential customers by using the Title and Industry fields, or by choosing Consultants/Contractors from the Interested In drop-down list. Because LinkedIn might help you discover a shared connection or bond between you and these consultants, you can ask those consultants for help in reaching your potential customers.

Finding the decision maker

Although generating a list of potential leads is a great first step in marketing your product, effective salesmanship often comes down to finding that "right person" whom you can present with an offer to buy something. This person is the *decision maker* (or the *final authority,* or even just *da boss*). You can talk to as many administrative assistants and receptionists as you'd like, but without the exact name or contact info of the person who makes the purchasing decisions, your sales effort is stalled.

LinkedIn can help you reach that decision maker in the following ways:

✔ **When you perform an advanced search, include words like Account Manager, Director, or Vice President in the Keywords field.** If your results show someone who's in your extended network, now you have a specific name to mention when you call the company. I recommend that you approach that person via LinkedIn and your mutual connections first, thereby making your first contact with her more of a "warm call" than a cold one.

✔ **Use the LinkedIn Company Profile pages to find out specific information about your target company.** If you're trying to reach someone within a company you want to target, see whether that person has a Company Profile page. To do so, click the word Companies on the top navigation bar and select Find Companies from the drop-down menu that appears so you can search through LinkedIn's company pages. Say, for example, that you need to reach someone within LinkedIn. When you bring up LinkedIn's company profile page, as shown in Figure 16-4, you get some specific information right away.

You will immediately see who in your network works for this company, so you know whom to approach to pass along your request to the decision maker, or to tell you who that decision maker is. Be sure to scroll down the rest of the page, too, to see other useful information, such as new hires, recent tweets, blog updates, promotions and changes, and open job listings for the company. (See Figure 16-5.) You can then follow that company to see all its new updates and information as part of your LinkedIn News Feed, for example. At the top right of every company page is a button you can click that reads Follow Company. In Figure 16-4, you can click the Follow Company link to stay in touch with that company's activities.

✔ **Use your existing network to ask for an Introduction or to point you in the right direction.** Using your network in this manner was basically the original intent of LinkedIn: You contact someone who works at your target company and ask that contact to introduce you to the decision maker. The decision maker is much more likely to receive an Introduction than a cold call. Your network connection might also serve as a recommendation of you to the decision maker, which will carry some weight when you try to close the deal.

✔ **Use InMail to contact people close to the decision maker.** You may find that, in some cases, the decision maker may not be on LinkedIn yet, or his or her profile is closed to Introductions and InMail. In such a case, you can use LinkedIn to find the closest person to the decision maker and ask that person for help, a connection, or information to help you reach the next level.

✔ **Use InMail to contact the decision maker, if she is on LinkedIn.** You may not have the time or opportunity to get introduced to your decision maker, and if you're using InMail to approach the decision maker, why not just go for the gusto and make your introduction directly? This is a faster option than waiting or asking for an Introduction, but there is the chance the decision maker will ignore your message. You have to decide what's best for your situation.

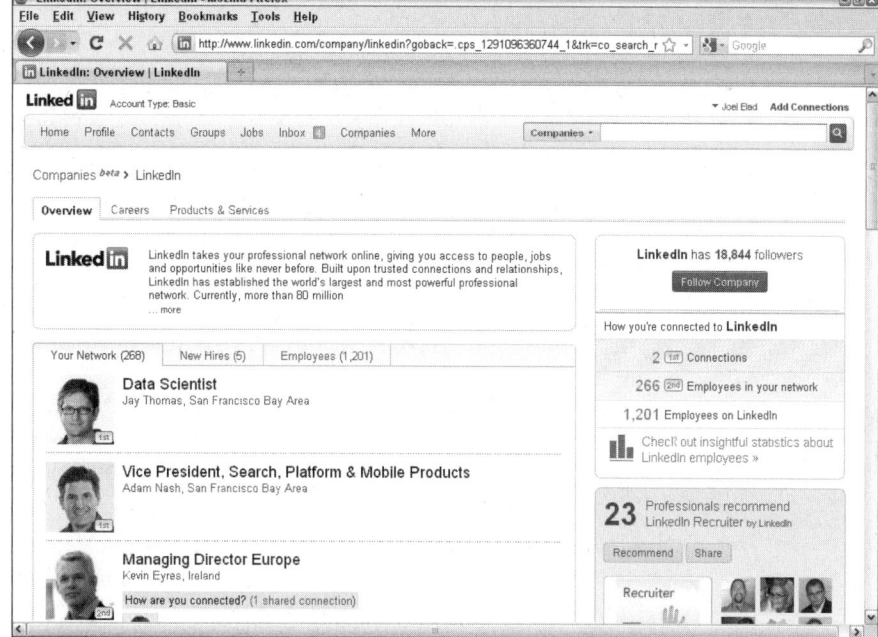

Figure 16-4:
Get specific information about your target company through its profile.

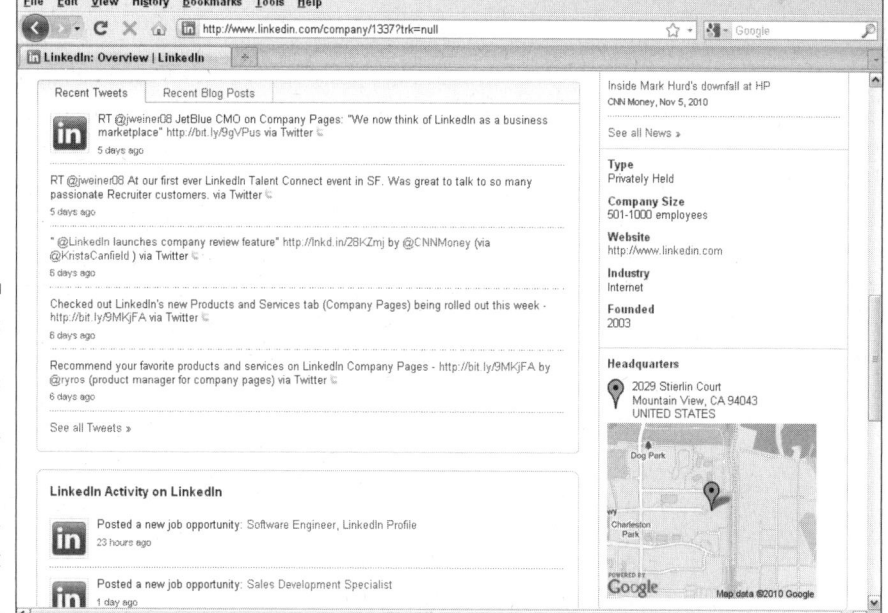

Figure 16-5:
Use a company's LinkedIn Company page to find out more about your target company.

Closing the Deal

Establishing a connection to the right person (the one who makes the purchasing decisions) is half the battle of getting your product sold. However, you still have to convince the person and close the deal, of course. In this section, I give you some pointers on how to put LinkedIn to work for you for the final phase of a sales effort: completing it successfully!

The key to getting the most out of LinkedIn for closing the deal is knowing that LinkedIn has more than just names — it has information in the form of detailed profiles of its tens of millions of users, and in the form of knowledge sharing through LinkedIn Answers, associations made through LinkedIn Groups, and corporate information through LinkedIn Company Profiles.

Researching prospects

After you identify your prospects, spend some time familiarizing yourself with them before you contact them. Gleaning some insight about your potential buyers can go a long way toward getting the person to respond, taking the time to listen to your pitch, and buying your product. Following are some tips concerning specific ways to research your prospective clients:

- **Read the prospect's *full* profile to discover all you can about his or her interests, likes, dislikes, and so on.** You can do far more than simply scan a person's profile looking for past jobs and maybe her education to see whether she shares an alma mater with you. A person's LinkedIn profile can be or lead to a gold mine of information about that person. For instance, people may include links to their own Web sites, blogs, or company Web sites. Follow those links, especially to blogs or personal Web sites, and see what you can find out. In the prospect's profile, look over the Interests section and the Additional Information section. And don't forget the Contact Settings section — here's where you can find out under what circumstances this person wants to be contacted. Be sure to respect those wishes.

- **Read your prospect's recommendations for other people.** You can gain a lot of insight by seeing what qualities a person likes to praise in other people, especially if your prospect has left multiple recommendations. In this way, you also gain insight into the people they trust, so check those people who received a recommendation to see whether you have a connection to any of *them*. If so, ask that person first for an Introduction to your prospect.

- **Read any questions or answers your prospect wrote for LinkedIn Answers.** If you pull up someone's profile, look for a section on her profile page in the right sidebar called Q&A and click one of the three links to view either the questions that person asked or the answers that person gave, or the see the entire Questions & Answers page. The page that opens (shown in Figure 16-6) contains all the questions and answers this person has contributed to LinkedIn. When you read these contributions, you might gain some insight into this person's preferences and "hot button issues" — what motivates or annoys her.

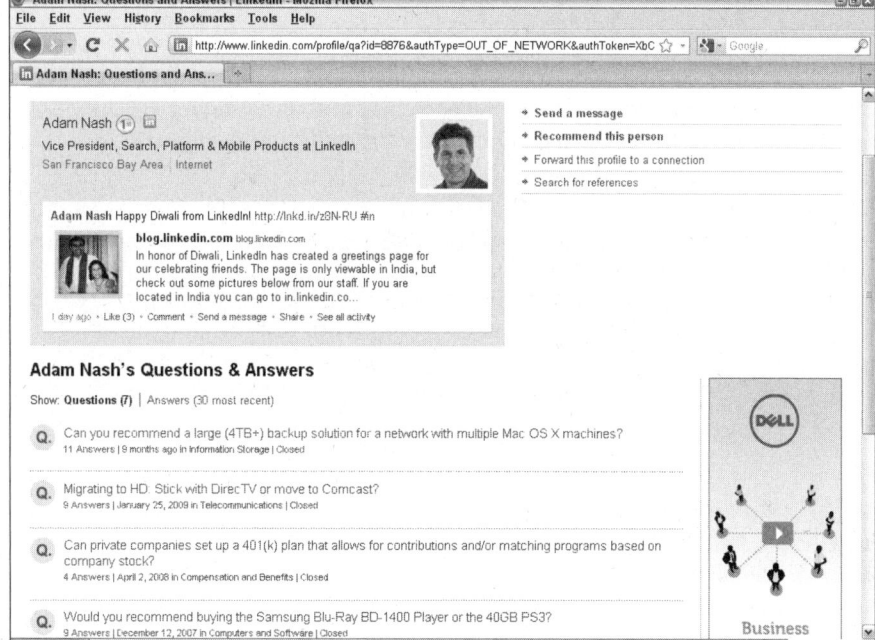

Figure 16-6:
Read through any questions or answers your prospect has contributed to LinkedIn.

Preparing for the client meeting

Say that your initial conversations with your prospects have gone well and you have been granted a meeting with a potential client to make your pitch. Whereas you may have already used LinkedIn to gain more information about the specific person, you can now turn to discovering details about the specific industry, the company, and the company's potential response to your business pitch. Here are ways to go about gathering information about the company:

✔ **Try to get an informational interview with someone at the target company, preferably with someone you know.** Check your LinkedIn network to see whether you have a first- or second-degree contact at the company you're planning to pitch to. Ask that person to spend some time with you for the purpose of gathering information about the company, and try to get some insights into company priorities and culture. Also see what you can learn about the company's top motivation in purchasing decisions — what priorities or issues the company considers before buying something from a vendor.

✔ **Visit the LinkedIn Company Profile page to review all the recent company activities.** As mentioned earlier in this chapter in the "Finding the decision maker" section, when you look at the Company Profile page, you see sections such as New Hires, Recent Tweets, or Recent Blog Posts. Peruse these sections before your meeting with your potential buyer to find out who has been promoted or hired, the key statistics of that company, open job listings at the company, and even the most popular profiles of employees at that company. By doing so, you'll have more background information and therefore more confidence; also, this type of knowledge helps you identify interests or commonalities to enhance your sense of connection with your buyer (and hers with you).

✔ **Use LinkedIn Answers to get advice from the community at large or your network.** Search LinkedIn Answers to see whether other people have already asked questions about your target company, or to find out how to approach companies in your industry. If you don't find anything directly related to what you're searching for, you can pose a question yourself and see what recommendations you get from other LinkedIn members.

All these efforts are meant only to prepare you and get you closer to your prospect or target company so that you can make your pitch. Obviously, to complete the sale, you still need to have a compelling product, pitch, and offer for this company. Have all that ready *before* you approach your prospect.

When all else fails, ask for help!

Michael Goodman is a sales professional from Phoenix, Arizona, with more than 30 years of sales experience. But even he admits that with all the new technologies out there, he was a bit lost when trying to figure out exactly how to use LinkedIn and other Web 2.0 technologies to help him make that next sale. So, he went to LinkedIn Answers and posed the following question:

"With all the social media available, including LinkedIn, blogs, Twitter, Plaxo, Second Life, et al., what is the best way to utilize all this stuff, stay ahead of the techno-bleeding edge, and really just find another customer to tell my story to?

I can't keep up with all the social media, Web 2.0 marketing movement. Really, all I want to do is find the next customer. I am hoping someone has figured out the magical answer to taking advantage of technology and simply finding new people interested in what I have to offer. Anyone?"

Goodman received more than 25 responses, some of which were detailed, multiparagraph essays that helped point him in the right direction on how to use LinkedIn. The answers included links to articles about using LinkedIn and references to LinkedIn experts who could fully answer his question.

Using LinkedIn to Help You Complete the Sale

At this stage you have, to borrow a famous phrase, "gotten to yes," meaning that you've contacted your prospect and she has agreed to buy your product or service. Congratulations! You made the sale, and now it's time to deliver. Your membership in LinkedIn can continue to provide value by giving you some resources to help you deliver what you promised and ensure future sales success.

Getting help to deliver the solution

After you make the sale, go back to your company with the contract in hand and determine the resources and personnel necessary to deliver on your contract. In some cases, you may not have everything you need to deliver the order. As it can in earlier stages of the sales process, LinkedIn can assist you in this stage as well. Here are some of those ways:

- **Find partners to create the winning team.** You've done the hard part: You got the contract. The customer trusts you to deliver on that contract, so it's your job to build the winning team, and your company may not employ full-time all the people you need or you may have agreed to additional items to make the sale that require something where your business has to speed up development. In such a case, you can use your LinkedIn connections to find people who have the missing skill sets you need. (See Chapter 11 for tips on finding an employee.) You can also perform an Advanced People Search or Service Providers search for a consultant or part-time employee who has the skills you need to build your products or consult on your service offering.

- **Get some direction from the LinkedIn community.** You can create a question in LinkedIn Answers that polls your network and the greater LinkedIn community in the problem area you've been hired to solve. Get an idea of how other people would tackle this problem, and use the answers to identify potential partners or contacts you can use to deliver your solution. For example, polling the community about a part of your service offering (a part that isn't client-specific) may result in a LinkedIn member providing a new way of approaching the problem.

- **Search LinkedIn Answers for past responses that can help you.** Odds are that the solution you were hired to deliver is not the very first time since the world began that someone had to solve that problem. Therefore, you should try your luck and search through past answers in LinkedIn Answers; you're likely to get lots of ideas by seeing how other people handled similar situations.

- **Hire the skills you need.** If you can't find a part-time person or tap the skills you're seeking from someone in your LinkedIn network, it's time to post a job listing on LinkedIn Jobs. See Chapter 11 for the steps on how to post a job listing.

Reporting a positive sale

Reporting the completion of a sale is my favorite part of the business sales process. You made the sale, developed the solution, and delivered it to the customer. At this point, many people think, "Whew, I'm done. Nothing to do now but enjoy the happy hour!" This is a common and natural response, but as a member of the LinkedIn world, your job isn't really done. You want to demonstrate your growth (and your company's growth) that resulted from handling this project to encourage future contracts to come your way. Here are some actions to consider after you complete the sale and deliver the solution:

- ✓ **Invite your customer to your network.** You worked hard to earn this customer's trust and to meet (or exceed) the customer's expectations by completing the sale. As a result, you should feel comfortable enough to send that person an Invitation to join your network. Doing so could keep you in contact with this customer for future opportunities. Studies have shown that it's six times cheaper to sell to an existing customer than to acquire a new customer.

- ✓ **Leave your customer a recommendation.** After you add a customer to your network, post a recommendation for him on the system if you feel it's deserved. Doing so gives your customer a sense of "reward" for being a positive contributor, but more important, it informs the community that you did a project for this person, which can help you in the future. Also, the customer may reciprocate by leaving you a recommendation, which strengthens your profile and makes you more appealing to future prospects.

- ✓ **Stay in touch with your customer.** You can keep track of your customer's activities by monitoring your Network Updates (if he or she is a part of your network). Routinely keep in touch about the solution you delivered, perhaps to open the conversation for selling additional products or services or maintenance contract work.

- ✓ **Update your profile with the skills you acquired or demonstrated through this sale.** To be ready for future prospects who search the LinkedIn database, it's important to have the right keywords and skill sets on your profile so that these prospects can identify you as someone who can provide a similar solution. If you're a consultant or freelance worker, you can add the project you just completed as experience on your profile as well. (See Chapter 3 on how to update your profile.)

- ✓ **Tap the customer's network by asking him for referrals.** After you connect with your customer, keep an eye on his network. If you think you see a future prospect, consider asking your customer for an Introduction or a Recommendation. Usually, if you provided a quality solution, the customer will readily oblige your request.

Chapter 17

Venture Capital and Angel Funding

· ·

In This Chapter

▶ Finding investors

▶ Asking the right questions

▶ Building your management team

▶ Using LinkedIn to get an investor

▶ Searching for investments

▶ Evaluating your potential investments

· ·

*W*hen you put bunches of Internet-savvy, knowledgeable professionals who like to network on a growing social networking site like LinkedIn, you're bound to have a community of people who are involved and interested in venture capital (VC), where specific firms provide millions (or tens of millions) of dollars in funding as well as support and board members for emerging companies that want to grow. Or you might run across professionals involved in *angel funding,* where wealthy investors invest up to a few million dollars of their own money in exchange for ownership percentages of emerging companies. You could say that LinkedIn has VC at its roots. LinkedIn founder Reid Hoffman is an angel investor who has invested in more than 60 companies besides LinkedIn, including such famous companies as Facebook, Digg, Flickr, Technorati, Tagged, and Ning.

LinkedIn has become an important tool for everyone involved in the VC or angel funding industry, from the casual observer to the hyper-extended dealmaker, for many reasons:

✔ LinkedIn can help entrepreneurs figure out how to connect with a VC firm.

✔ Entrepreneurs can use LinkedIn to build their management team before a proposal is made.

✔ Business owners can test their business ideas on fellow first-degree connections.

✔ LinkedIn Answers can help entrepreneurs fill in the blanks on their proposals.

✔ VC firms can monitor LinkedIn Answers to get a perspective on up-and-coming trends.

✔ Experienced business veterans can use LinkedIn Answers to give advice, encouragement, and a new perspective to first-timers.

In this chapter, I talk about how you can benefit from using LinkedIn when it comes to VC or angel funding, regardless of your role or position in the process. I cover different cases and stories on how entrepreneurs have benefited from LinkedIn, as well as how VC firms or angel networks have used LinkedIn to find, evaluate, or advance their deals.

Finding Potential Investors

So, you have a great idea for a company, you want to be the next great thing in your industry, and all you need is a blank check to make your dreams come true, right? Although LinkedIn can't guarantee that you'll find the right funding partner, get the money you need, and build your business with a great return on investment, the site can help you improve your chances of success when dealing with the funding and growth of your business.

No matter what stage your business is in, whether you just thought of a new business idea or invention, you're building a prototype, you earned your first dollar of revenue, or you just hit $1 million in sales, LinkedIn can be an invaluable resource for reaching the next step and beyond. The following sections take a look at some of the ways LinkedIn can assist you in the quest for an investor.

Asking questions and getting LinkedIn Answers

Although you may be an expert in your field, you could probably use some good advice from existing venture capitalists, angel investors, or successful entrepreneurs when it comes to obtaining financing. LinkedIn Answers allows you to tap a vast network of knowledgeable folk who are experts in that field and gladly give general and specific tips. (See Chapter 7 for more information about how to use LinkedIn Answers.) And although LinkedIn Answers has a special category for Startups and Small Business, I focus on the areas of VC and angel funding here. If you're not ready for that big investment, definitely check out the Startups and Small Business category for advice.

When you're ready to use LinkedIn Answers to get answers to your specific questions regarding VC or angel funding, just follow these steps:

1. **Roll your mouse over the More link from the top navigation bar; then click the Answers link from the drop-down list that appears.**

   You are promptly brought to LinkedIn Answers.

2. **Scroll down the LinkedIn Answers home page, locate the Browse section on the right side of the page, and then click the link for Finance and Accounting to find the Financing subsection.**

3. **Select Financing, which expands the view to reveal the Venture Capital and Private Equity category.**

   When you go to that category, as shown in Figure 17-1, you see a targeted list of questions for this area.

You can pose a question from a very general perspective or target a highly specific topic. Sample questions people have asked include:

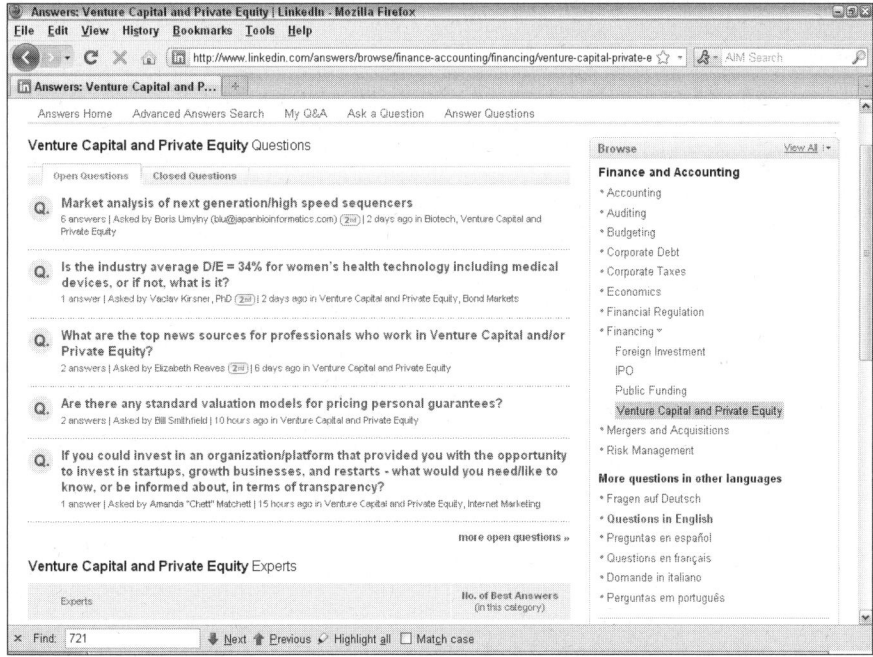

Figure 17-1:
See what questions and answers LinkedIn has for VC and equity.

✔ What's the difference between a venture capitalist and an angel investor?

✔ What are some good venture capital Web sites?

✔ Who should I go to for nontraditional funding of a startup?

✔ Who are the venture capitalists who invest in scalable open source ventures?

✔ What is the best way to seek interim funding during a period of heavy VC negotiations?

✔ How do venture capitalists view venture debt before, during, and after different funding rounds?

LinkedIn members have used the Financing subsection of LinkedIn Answers to get critiques or reviews of their executive summaries, directly ask for a VC or angel investor to consider their venture, or ask other entrepreneurs how their experience was with a particular VC or angel investor. Most questions, pleas for help, and advice solicitation have received multiple responses, from the one- or two-sentence reply to the pages-long exposition of precise advice and list of accompanying Web sites or contact information.

If you're thinking of using LinkedIn Answers, here are some of the best ways to do so:

✔ **Before you post, search the database.** Believe it or not, you might not be the first person with your particular question to approach the LinkedIn community. Take the time to search LinkedIn Answers to see whether someone has asked your question or a variation of it. If you find your question, look over the answers given and see whether you get the information you needed. If the answers aren't specific enough, rewrite the question in your own words and post it yourself.

✔ **Get the information you're missing.** If you're writing your business plan to get funding and you need some more information to supplement one of your sections, ask the LinkedIn community for the facts. Perhaps you need to know the size of a potential customer market or the top Web sites used by consumers to perform price comparison searches.

✔ **When asking for advice, be as specific as possible.** Your question can gauge people's experiences and ask for advice, instead of a fact or figure. When asking for advice, though, help your audience by being as specific with your request as possible. Asking for help is one thing, but asking for three ways to strengthen your proposal will probably generate more replies. If you're in the middle of a situation, spell out the scenario, terms and all, as much as you are legally allowed to do.

Build your dream team

When you're looking for funding of any amount, one of the top things that any investor will want to see is your management team. No matter how great your idea is, the execution of that idea will determine your success. Investors see one way to mitigate the risk of their investment by rewarding strong management teams that have the skill to weather unexpected turns. If your management team is lacking in at least one key area, consider LinkedIn as a source to find that missing person.

Here are some things to keep in mind when doing a search on LinkedIn for your next team member:

- ✔ **Experience is key.** Although desire, motivation, and interest are important, the way to improve your chances of getting funding is to have experienced personnel. This means that when searching for potential candidates, you should study each person's profile to gauge her documented experience at past positions first; then see whether her interests match your company's interests.

- ✔ **Pick complements, not carbon copies.** It's very tempting for an entrepreneur to seek out like-minded individuals with similar backgrounds to build a business. However, companies with the strongest growth had a diverse management team that could handle different situations because the team's skills complemented each other. Put your business needs ahead of your personal preference. Look for LinkedIn members whose profiles indicate strengths that aren't yet represented in your startup.

- ✔ **Gauge the strength of the candidate's network.** Any time you look to add someone to your organization, you should be asking what value the person could bring through his existing network. (After all, who you know can make the difference.) When you connect with someone, see who's a part of his network, if possible. See what groups and affiliations, Web sites, and Q&A are on the candidate's profile, because that indicates his overall reach into the greater network.

Putting it all together

Suppose that you have your business plan, management team, market analysis, prototype or working model, and you've built up a customer set. You've done some research and are ready to start shopping around and looking for investment. You've perfected your 30-second elevator pitch so you can quickly and accurately describe your business to anyone who's interested, and you can quote the facts and figures you need for any presentation. It's time to seek out a funding partner.

Although this is not the exhaustive list of what you can do, here are some tips that can help you find that partner using LinkedIn:

- ✓ **Gather leads.** Use LinkedIn Answers to post a question to either your network or the general community about the best firms or investors to consider. (You can find out more about LinkedIn Answers in Chapter 7.)

- ✓ **Do research on your leads.** Look up potential investors on LinkedIn and read their profiles. See what interests they have, what group affiliations they maintain, and what information they share or gather using LinkedIn Answers. Follow through on any Web sites, blogs, or profiles they link to from their profiles. See what you have in common or which benefit of your company might interest them the most.

- ✓ **Work your network and get them working.** Do advanced searches to see how your network can connect you with the right person. Maybe someone in your network knows a VC or someone at the same firm as a VC or angel investor. Perhaps someone in one of your groups has the right connection in one of her other groups. Let your network know what you're looking for and ask, respectfully, for help, advice, or a push in the right direction.

- ✓ **Get introduced or reach out yourself.** If you have a second- or third-degree connection to a potential investor, use LinkedIn Introductions to ask your contacts to introduce you. If you have no direct connections, consider using InMail to make your own Introduction. (Chapter 5 has more on Introductions and InMail.)

- ✓ **Do your homework before any meeting.** Use LinkedIn to prepare before you meet any potential investor. Study her profile and check the LinkedIn Company Profiles for information about her company. If she's in your extended network, ask your connections (who know her) for advice and information on your potential investor. See what companies they have invested in and research those companies as well.

Finding Potential Investments

Maybe someone in your VC firm needs to connect with someone in a particular industry, or perhaps your organization wants to invest in an emerging market or new technology. LinkedIn is a great place for you as a potential investor to look for your next investment.

It's all in the network

One of the benefits of a good investor is the network he brings with him to the investment. Although some VCs recommend their own executive and/ or board structure to their investments, other investors simply offer advice as to any new hires or support personnel a new company may need in its growth phase. Sometimes, the right investor is someone who knows a new company's customer base well and can help this new company land a key account. This is all possible through a strong network. Therefore, LinkedIn is one of the best ways an investor can grow and strengthen his network. Here are some ways that LinkedIn can help:

- **Monitor your Network Activity.** Your network is always working, and this point is clearly demonstrated in your Network Activity. Spend some time every day or week to look through your Network Activity to see which contacts of yours have moved companies, started new projects, or participated in questions you may find relevant. (See Chapter 9 for more information on Network Activity.)

- **Monitor LinkedIn Answers.** See what questions people are asking in your particular industry, and what answers are being posted by other people. Pay attention to question categories like Starting Up, Venture Capital and Private Equity, and Business Plans. (Chapter 7 has much more on LinkedIn Answers, in case you're dying of curiosity.)

- **Identify thought leaders.** As you watch your network, LinkedIn Answers, and any relevant LinkedIn Groups, pay attention if certain names keep popping up over and over again. These people could be *thought leaders* in your intended industry — people who everyone respects as the authority in their given subject matter — and they are worth connecting to in order to stay ahead and scope out the best opportunities. Reach out to these parties through Introductions or InMail (see Chapter 5) to see whether you can create a meaningful connection now and in the future.

- **Strengthen your network.** Build good contacts in your field through regular networking, and avenues like LinkedIn Answers. Identify people in your network who are a part of your desired industry and expand into their networks by getting to know their connections.

Do your due diligence

As new proposals for investments come your way, or you meet an entrepreneur in one of your industries who could come to you later with an investment proposal, you have to evaluate these proposals and decide how to proceed. Here are some ways that LinkedIn can help you filter all this incoming information:

- ✓ **Evaluate your entrepreneurs.** When you're evaluating a proposal, do some research by seeing whether the requester has a LinkedIn profile. Compare notes between his business plan and his actual profile. See how he contributes to LinkedIn through Q&A. Evaluate the entire management team.

- ✓ **Ask for endorsements.** If you're evaluating a proposal or contemplating adding someone to your network, see who in your network knows this person (or company). If you find a connection, ask your connection whether she would endorse or recommend this person.

- ✓ **Get a sense for your intended market.** Ask questions about the intended market on LinkedIn Answers. Search previous questions to see whether the requesting company has been mentioned or profiled. If so, take a close look at the information.

Chapter 18

Miscellaneous Creative Uses of LinkedIn

*W*hen you think of a business networking site such as LinkedIn, the most obvious applications spring to mind pretty quickly: finding a job, finding an employee, getting to meet new people, building a new business, getting funding and partners for that new business, and so on. But LinkedIn has acquired even more uses than the obvious ones. The power of the Internet and tens of millions of LinkedIn members have encouraged people to use this large community to accomplish other goals, both close to home and reaching around the world.

In this chapter, I give you a look at the some of the "creative" uses that people have found for LinkedIn. Some people use LinkedIn in combination with other services, such as Google News Alerts. Other people use LinkedIn as a gathering place to find recruits to help mold a new venture. Yet others have been using LinkedIn to meet each other in person! I describe these endeavors as well as provide several case studies with some points to keep in mind if you feel like doing something similar.

Mashing LinkedIn with Other Services

One of the hotter trends on the Internet in recent years has been the creation of mashups. No, I'm not talking potatoes here. A *mashup* is created when somebody takes data from more than one application and puts that data together into a single new and useful application. For example, say you combine real estate sales data from a database application with the Google Maps application, enabling a search result of the real estate data to be mapped onto a satellite image on Google. The satellite image represents a mashup because it's a new, distinct service that neither application provided on its own.

Something similar to the concept of mashups occurs with creative uses of LinkedIn. As LinkedIn continues to evolve and its members use more and more of LinkedIn's functionality, new uses for LinkedIn continue to emerge, especially as part of a user's Internet exploits. The following sections describe a smattering of these mashups.

LinkedIn and Google News Alerts

LinkedIn + Google News Alerts = Better-informed communication

I got this tip from Liz Ryan, a workplace expert, author, and speaker, as one of her top ten ways of using LinkedIn. It has to do with using both sites as a business tool when you're trying to reach out to an important potential business contact who you do not know. It works like this:

1. **Click the Advanced link next to the search box on the top-right corner of any LinkedIn page to bring up the Advanced People Search page.**

2. **Fill in the appropriate fields to search for the name of a person at a company who is relevant to your situation, and with whom you would like to connect.**

3. **Armed with the name that turned up in the results, set up a Google News Alert with the person's name and the company name so that Google will notify you when that person is quoted or in the news.**

When you go to Google's Alerts page (as shown in Figure 18-1), you simply enter the person's name and company name in the Search Terms box, and then configure how you want Google to alert you by setting the Type, How Often, and Volume filters below the Search Terms box. Finally, you set the e-mail address you want the alerts to be sent to with the Deliver To drop-down list. Then when you click the Create Alert button, you're good to go!

When you receive a notice from Google News Alerts, you'll have a much better idea of what the person is working on as well as his impact at the company. This knowledge gives you an icebreaker by which to strike up a conversation. Rather than send a random connection request, you can reference the person's speech at the last XYZ Summit or agree with his last blog post.

Don't overuse all this information you get when you contact the person, or, as Liz Ryan warns, he might think you're a business stalker.

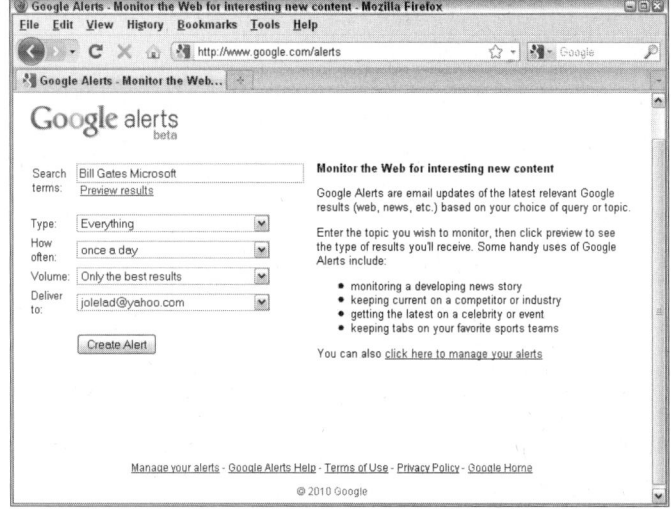

Figure 18-1:
Google can
automatically
send you
specific
alerts.

LinkedIn Answers and RSS feeds

LinkedIn Answers + RSS feeds = Searchable targeted information

Millions of people are asking, answering, and reading information through LinkedIn Answers, and sometimes you may want one thread containing every mention of a certain company, person, or concept, instead of having to search through Answers all the time. Well, now you can subscribe to a live RSS feed and get automatic updates when someone asks or answers a question around a given keyword or category.

But exactly what is an RSS feed? Imagine if someone regularly sent you a file that contained only the newest updates to a Web page, instead of seeing every version of the Web page without knowing what was changed. An RSS feed is simply a file that only contains the changes that have been made to a file, like a Web page. Think of it as getting a stream of updates instead of hearing every version of the same story.

To benefit from this feature, just do the following:

1. **Log in to your LinkedIn account. Roll your mouse over the More link from the top navigation bar, and then click Answers from the drop-down menu that appears.**

   Doing so takes you to the LinkedIn Answers home page.

2. **Pick the category you want to subscribe to by choosing it from the right column, under the Browse header.**

   For this example, I choose the Startups and Small Business category, as shown in Figure 18-2.

3. **Look for the header Subscribe to New Questions In on the right side of the screen. Click the drop-down arrow next to the category name to bring up a choice of RSS feed readers (as shown in Figure 18-2).**

   The *feed reader* is basically the software program that will receive your RSS feed file and display it to you so you can read it. You can either choose from the preprogrammed choices, like Google Reader or My Yahoo, or cut and paste the link offered in the bottom of this window into your own RSS feed reader.

4. **Set up the news reader to handle the newly subscribed RSS feed(s) so that you can read all this information as it gets fed to you.**

   A popular RSS reader is Google Reader, which you can set up by going to `http://reader.google.com` and following the instructions there.

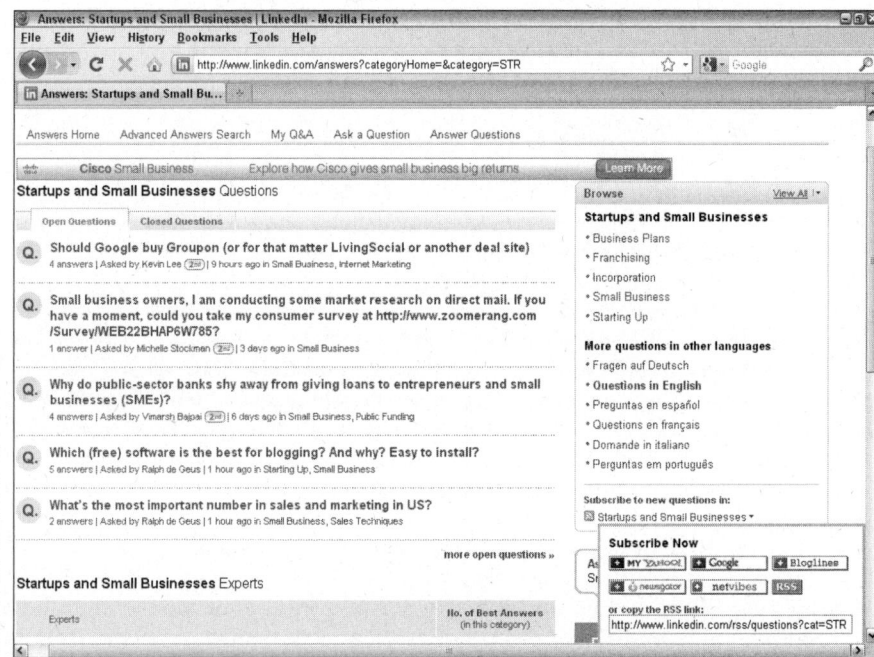

Figure 18-2:
Subscribe to RSS feeds from LinkedIn's Answers feature.

LinkedIn and the Xobni e-mail plug-in

LinkedIn + Xobni e-mail plug-in = More precise sender information

If you use Microsoft Outlook for your e-mail and you're constantly being deluged with e-mail from people you don't remember well, Xobni may be the tool for you. Xobni is an Outlook plug-in tool that gives you a window of summary information for each sender of an e-mail you receive. Say that you got an e-mail from Adam Smith, but you can't remember exactly what Adam does, when and how often Adam e-mails you, and so on. With Xobni, the plug-in window shows you who Adam is and how you interact with him. Figure 18-3 shows an example of the kind of information Xobni can display.

Xobni has now integrated LinkedIn information into its plug-in window, so now when someone's summary window is displayed, Xobni displays that person's employer, job title, and profile photo, and also offers a direct link to the person's complete profile on LinkedIn. To add this functionality to your Microsoft Outlook program, just follow these steps:

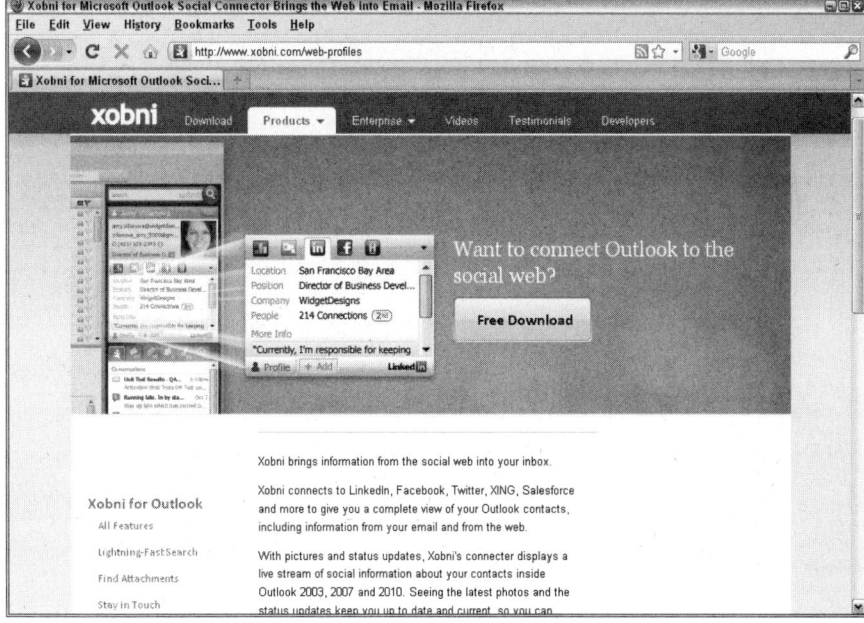

Figure 18-3:
Xobni displays precise information about an e-mail sender.

1. **Go to the Xobni site at www.xobni.com/download and download its newest plug-in application setup file.**

   The download window should start up automatically when you go to the site's download page, shown in Figure 18-4.

2. **Run the downloaded file and follow the set-up wizard that opens to install Xobni on your system.**

   The next time you run Microsoft Outlook, you should see the Xobni plug-in on the right side of your Outlook window.

If you use another e-mail program besides Outlook, there are tools that can help you as well. As an example, for those of you who use Google's Gmail service, you should consider a program called Rapportive, which includes a rich profile of your contacts within the Gmail interface (as the example shows in Figure 18-5). Simply go to www.rapportive.com for more information.

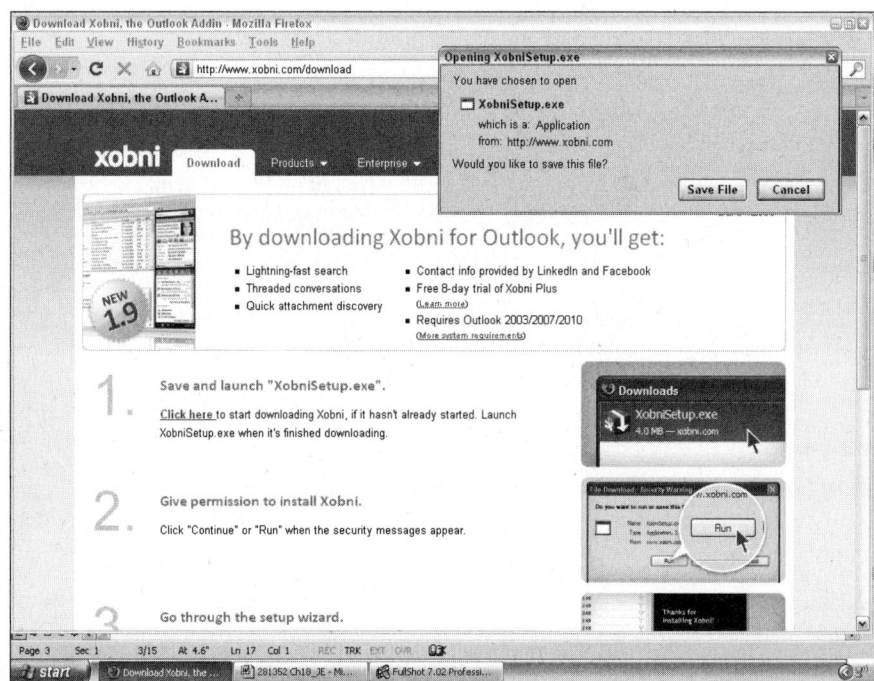

Figure 18-4:
Download
the Xobni
application.

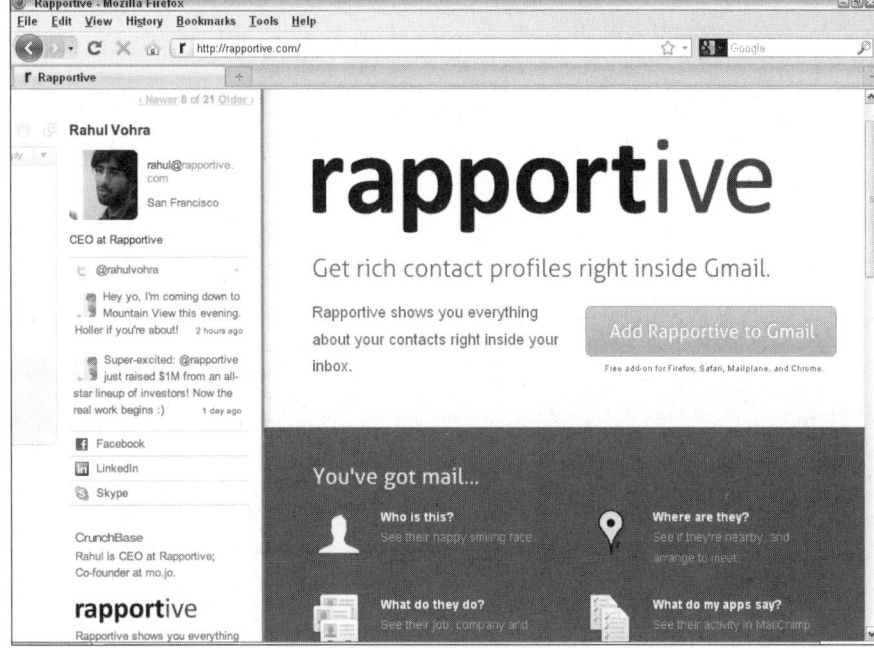

Figure 18-5:
Get rich
contact
profiles
in your
Gmail with
Rapportive.

Building Your Focus Group

In other chapters, I tell you about the potential for finding qualified partners and customers using LinkedIn, and how LinkedIn Answers can help you perform market research and gauge reactions to a new product. Here, I want to take these ideas one step further and discuss how LinkedIn can help you build a focus group for your new or next project.

Here are some ideas to keep in mind if you want to build your own focus group using LinkedIn:

- **Start by building your network.** Your best participants in this group are first-degree connections of yours (or of another employee of your company) because those people are most likely to join based on your recommendation and how well they fit your group's purpose. Try to network and invite potential candidates right away.

Who's ready to play DISC?

Cynthia (Cindy) Beale heard about LinkedIn the way most people do: She got an invitation from an old contact — a former high school classmate, in her case. After she joined, Beale at first used the site for typical purposes, but eventually she took her use of LinkedIn to the next level after co-founding her consultancy business, Stecin Leadership Solutions.

Beale and her co-founder, Steve Settimo, started Stecin as a consulting and training company focused on management and leadership training. The business partners spent two years developing an exclusive curriculum that can be customized for any size company. Recently, they created a brand-new board game called DISCFunctional to demonstrate the power of understanding the DISC Quadrant behavior system (see the following figure for the layout). This game became a popular training tool, and Stecin's co-founders decided to use the power of their LinkedIn networks to help advance the game.

Beale explains, "Suddenly, we had a way to communicate information about our training and consulting business to a group of people that we already identified as knowing." They added the game to their profiles and included a Web site link in each of their profiles so that potential customers could actually order the game. They updated their network with progress reports on how the game was doing, and then they created a special DISCFunctional group on LinkedIn for contacts who wanted to learn more.

This LinkedIn group became a focus group for Stecin Leadership Solutions, as they invited first-degree connections who expressed interest and potential customers who learned about the product elsewhere. Beale and Settimo were very careful about how they invited people to this focus group, doing research on each potential invitee, asking for Introductions through their own personal LinkedIn networks whenever possible, and crafting a polished invitation.

Stecin has built a growing community that has been very influential in the game's development. Beale is happy to report that their first training contract came from a LinkedIn connection! She concludes by saying, "We are always looking for more ways to utilize LinkedIn to reach people who will benefit from our business offerings."

- ✔ **Build your accompanying Web site before building the group.** Your focus group participants will want to see something before deciding to join and participate, so make sure you've spent some time building an informational Web page, e-mail, FAQ, or other system that is available for viewing before you start to build your group.

- ✔ **Use your first-degree connections to expand your network.** After you've rustled up some involvement there, expand your group by asking for referrals or Introductions to potential second- and third-degree network members or general LinkedIn members who might get some value and add some insight to your process.

- ✔ **Continually send out updates.** You always should be sending out some form of update, whether you do so by filling out the status update option, using LinkedIn Messages, or going through your own e-mail system. (See Chapter 9 for more information about these options.) Don't deluge people with messages — but also don't ask them to sign up and then be silent for weeks or months at a time. Keep your group members informed and ask for input when needed.

- ✔ **Ask for recommendations.** As group members get introduced to your product, ask them for a recommendation on your profile if they liked or approve of the product. Getting their feedback or recommendations will help to build future involvement when your product is live and ready for the mass market.

Location-Based LinkedIn Ideas

It's easy to forget the importance of location when you have easy access to such a resource-rich community as LinkedIn. After all, you can communicate with your contacts through LinkedIn Messages, send Recommendation requests or post questions, or grow your network without leaving your computer. When you're done using your computer, however, you need to interact in the real world, whether your interaction amounts to shoveling snow or catching a plane to a far-flung convention. When it comes to what I call "location-based" situations, meaning that the problem or situation is tied to a physical spot, you can discover solutions with the help of LinkedIn.

The best use of LinkedIn for location-based problems is this: Your network is typically spread out across the country and across the world. Therefore, not only can you tap someone's professional experience, you can also tap their knowledge or presence in a specific geographical area to help you solve a problem. Take a look at three different location-based situations.

Building your network before moving to a new city

These days, when you have to move to a new city, you can do a lot of planning for it on the Internet. You can research the neighborhoods, look into the school systems, and shop for homes online. You can take this one step further if you plan to move to a different country, and you need information on local customs, cultures, and practices. But what about the questions you can't seem to answer through a Web browser? What about the "local knowledge" of where to go and where to avoid? LinkedIn can help.

Every LinkedIn user has defined her location, so you can do a search and figure out which LinkedIn users live in your target area. If nobody in your network is from your target area, start networking and expand that network to include people who reside (or used to reside) in that area who can help.

Here are some specific actions you can take through LinkedIn to help you with the big move:

Hello? Any opportunities out east?

Chuck Hester had a problem. He had to relocate his family from California to Raleigh, North Carolina, and he didn't have a job for himself when he would arrive. In fact, he didn't know anyone in Raleigh — but what he *did* have was a rich LinkedIn network. Hester quickly saw the value of LinkedIn and started contacting people and building relationships, driving his number of connections into the thousands.

Hester started networking with everyone he could who was located in Raleigh. He tapped his existing network to put him in touch with like-minded individuals who lived in the area and kept searching for contacts. One of the contacts he made was the chief executive of iContact, an e-mail marketing company. Hester turned this contact into a job interview, and today he's the corporate communications manager for iContact. Even virtual persistence can pay off! Today, Hester continues to grow his LinkedIn network, for himself and for iContact, and he even encourages his local contacts in Raleigh to network "Live," or use LinkedIn Live, to be specific — a feature that I cover later this chapter.

✔ **Use LinkedIn Answers to ask the community.** Not every question on LinkedIn Answers is directly related to software development or venture capital. You can post your dilemma on LinkedIn Answers (see Chapter 7 for more information on how to do this), notify your network of your question, and see what the community says in response. Take a look at Figure 18-6, which shows how a young Australian looked for advice about moving to New York City by posting a detailed question. After he posted that question, he received 12 different responses filled with general and specific information to help him out.

When you post your question, be sure to select the My Question is Focused around a Specific Geographic Location check box and enter the ZIP code of your destination in the newly enabled text box next to the check box you just selected.

✔ **Start as early as possible.** Building a region-specific network will take time as you recruit new members, ask your existing contacts for referrals, and search for specific people who match the location and either an industry or job title. As soon as you sense that a move is necessary, or maybe when you're mulling over whether to move, start building your network so that you can tap those people for location-specific information before you actually move.

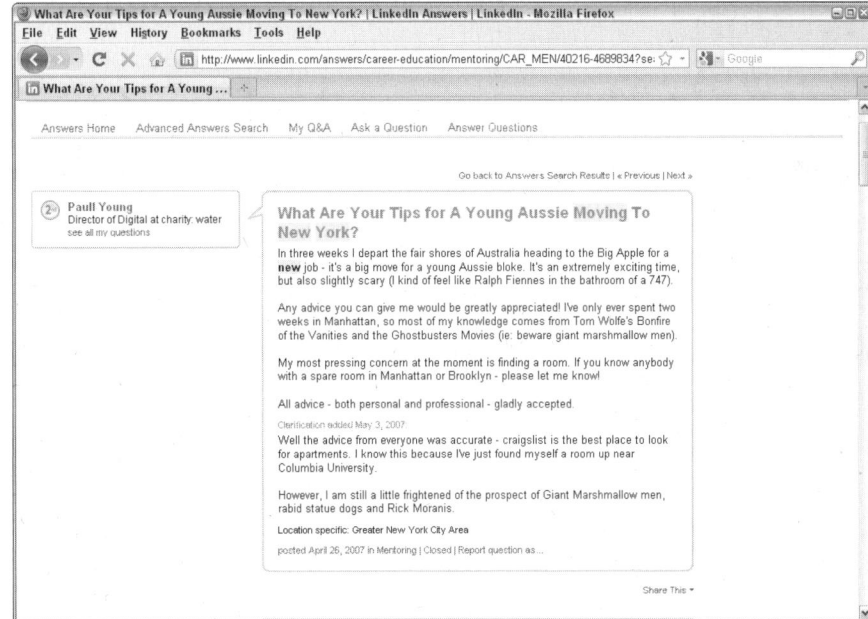

Figure 18-6:
Ask the community for advice on your move.

✔ **Look for contacts who used to live in your new city.** You might try entering the location of your new city in the Keyword search field rather than the Location field. By doing so, you might find first- or second-degree contacts who used to live in your target area but have since moved; they might reference their past locations in their profiles. Contact those people and see whether they can introduce you to any contacts they may still have in that target area, regardless of whether those contacts are on or off LinkedIn.

Arranging face-to-face meetings when traveling

LinkedIn can serve as a wonderful resource even when you're not moving to another city but are just traveling for business, a convention, or even personal reasons. Say that you know you have some extra time on your trip, or you want to make some local connections to reinforce your business trip. Why not tap your LinkedIn network and visit your contacts in person?

A growing practice of busy LinkedIn professionals who travel is to arrange face-to-face visits with other LinkedIn members on a business trip. This way, the traveler can meet with someone she is familiar with who could share similar interests and goals. Also, both people get a chance to expand their networks by creating a stronger connection. To bring about in-person meetings, most people either post something to LinkedIn Answers or send a message to targeted members of their networks.

If you're interested in making your next trip more of a LinkedIn adventure, keep these tips in mind:

✔ **Provide enough notice to attract people's attention.** If you're putting up a post on Monday night that you're available for Tuesday lunch, you probably won't get many responses in time to set up anything meaningful.

✔ **Give too much notice, and your visit will be forgotten by the time you arrive.** Some notice is necessary to get on people's calendars, but too much notice will make people forget when your visit gets closer. More than two to four weeks in advance is probably too much notice.

✔ **Be specific with your availability.** It's great that you want to get together, but you probably have other plans when you're visiting. Therefore, when you contact other members, offer a few choices of when you can get together — and be specific. For example, you could say, "Hey, I'm going to be in San Jose for most of next week. Who's available either Monday night or Wednesday lunchtime to get together?"

✔ **Use your get-together to help prepare for business.** Your get-togethers with people in other cities don't have to be purely social. Say that you know you're traveling to that city for an interview. Perhaps you want to send a targeted message to a few contacts who used to work for your target company and ask to meet them in person before your interview so that they can help you prepare. Or maybe you want to practice your sales presentation on a knowledgeable person before you go into someone's office to do the real thing.

LinkedIn networking . . . in person!

Social networking is definitely a great way to stay connected, grow your personal and professional contact list, and learn about new opportunities. But after lots of e-mails, Instant Messages, and discussion boards, sometimes you just want the experience of meeting someone face to face. Lots of LinkedIn members have felt this way and have used the virtual power of LinkedIn to bring together people in the real world.

You can find all sorts of "chapters" of in-person networking groups inspired by people first meeting on LinkedIn and then connecting in-person with people from their network at a live event. Besides LinkedIn Live in Raleigh, I've discovered LinkedIn Live or LinkedIn Face-to-Face events in Phoenix, Chicago, and Philadelphia — and there may well be more.

LinkedIn Live

If you use LinkedIn and you're in the Raleigh-Durham area of North Carolina, odds are you've heard of Chuck Hester. "I'm known as the Kevin Bacon of Raleigh," he smiles. "If I don't know a person, I probably know someone who does." He's the creator of LinkedIn Live Raleigh, an informal networking group formed in July 2007 and dedicated to having Hester's virtual connections meet up with each other in person so that they could increase their own networking. By that time, Hester had built up more than 700 connections in the Raleigh area alone, so he sent out an invitation, and 50 people showed up to the event. The event was such a success that meetings are now held every other month, and attendance has grown exponentially, more than tripling in the first six months. In fact, Hester doesn't have to worry about the costs because he gets sponsors to donate the food, meeting space, and even door prizes!

Hester receives calls from more than a dozen other similar LinkedIn groups, each asking for advice on how to set up and maintain these live networking events. He's proud of the results from all this live networking, saying "At least 20–30 people have found new jobs from meeting someone at a LinkedIn Live." Of course, he has used the opportunity to build brand recognition for his company, iContact, which he found by networking on LinkedIn. (See the "Hello? Any opportunities out east?" sidebar, earlier this chapter.) The LinkedIn Live Raleigh networking has also earned him mentions in the Fast Company blog, the *Wall Street Journal, Inc.* magazine, and *The New York Times.* You can find out more by reading Hester's blog at: `http://thepayitforward chronicles.blogspot.com`. And if you're in Raleigh, check out a LinkedIn Live event!

To find or organize a LinkedIn Live group from your network, here are some tips to keep in mind:

✔ **Search LinkedIn Answers to see whether anyone's tried to organize a group.** Do an Advanced Answers search and put in the word LinkedIn and a word such as Live, Face to Face, or In Person; also, include the city or region where you live. You might find a posting from someone like Chuck Hester, who started LinkedIn Live in Raleigh and helped someone else start LinkedIn Live in New York City by posting something and alerting his network, as shown in Figure 18-7.

✔ **Search LinkedIn Groups to see whether a group exists in your area.** Click Groups and then Groups Directory to see whether a Networking or Professional group of LinkedIn members shows up in your area. For example, when I looked at Networking Groups, I saw LinkedIn groups in places as diverse as San Diego, Houston, and Charlotte, as shown in Figure 18-8.

✔ **Use the Internet to look for social networking meetings.** You may have to go outside LinkedIn to find an eager group of LinkedIn members. If you do a search with a networking site like Meetup.com, you will find a number of LinkedIn groups already established in cities around the world, as shown in Figure 18-9.

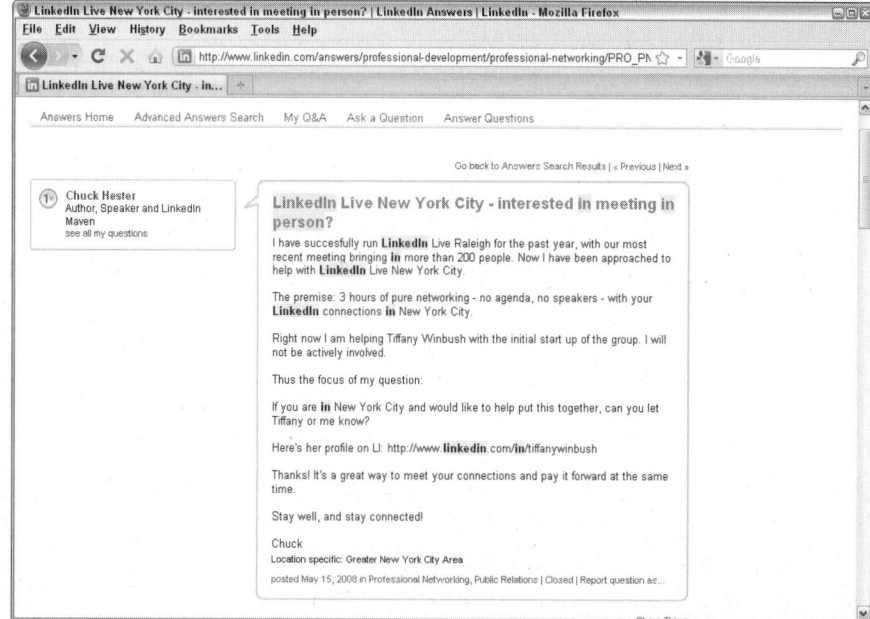

Figure 18-7: Hester started another LinkedIn Live group using LinkedIn Answers.

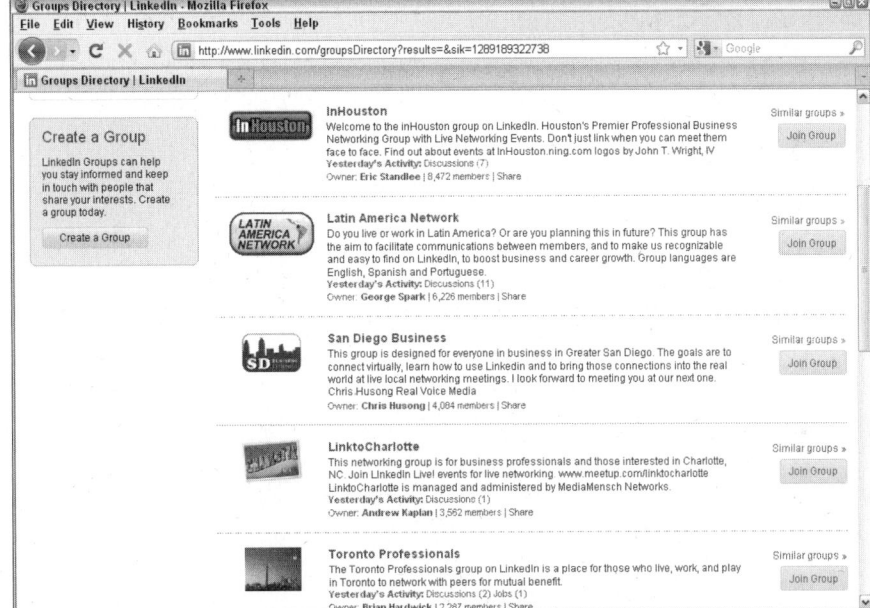

Figure 18-8:
Look for a
LinkedIn
group in
your area.

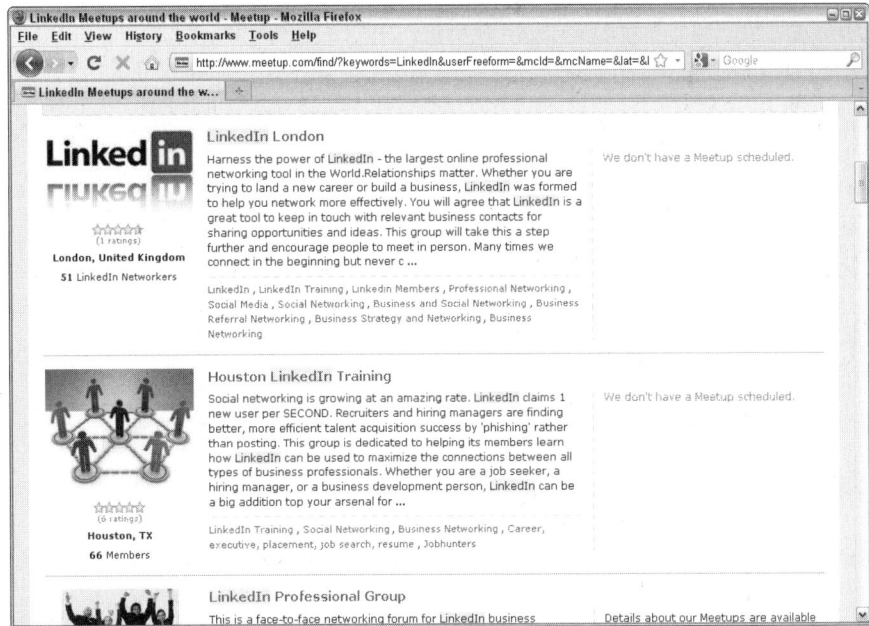

Figure 18-9:
Read about
LinkedIn
in-persons
on the
Internet.

✔ **If nothing exists, start your own live group.** Post something on LinkedIn Answers and try to build a core group to start the first event. Send an update or message to your network members who live in the area and encourage them to pass along the message to their local friends who are LinkedIn members.

Andrew Warner turned to LinkedIn to help find interest for a regular get-together of technology folks known as Lunch 2.0, for which companies involved in Web 2.0 technologies open their doors to hungry technology workers who then learn about their host company over lunch. He posted a question on LinkedIn Answers to find a host company (see Figure 18-10) and got several responses, which led to some great meetings!

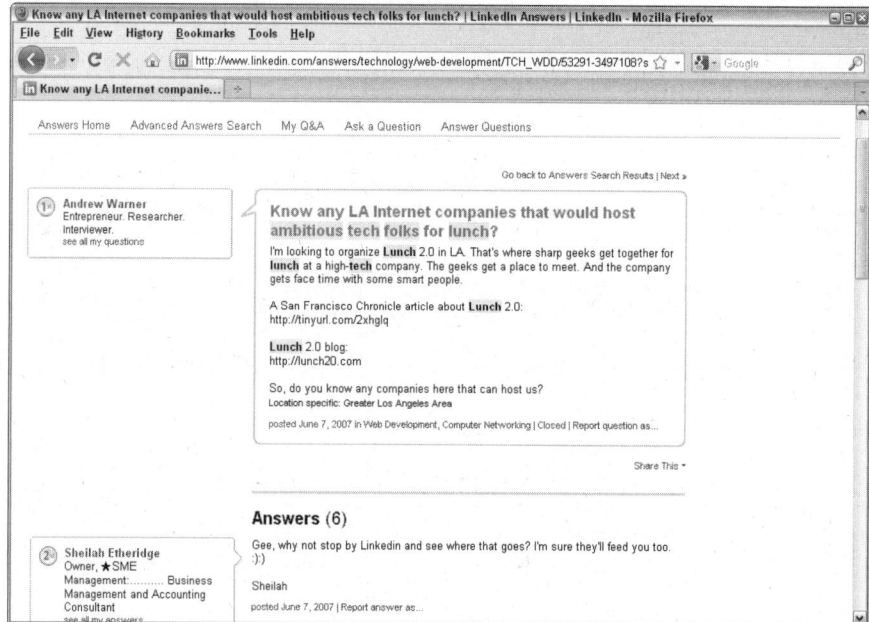

Figure 18-10:
Lunch 2.0
was looking
for a home.

Part VI
The Part of Tens

"Hold on, Barbara. Let me post this question and see what my connections have to say."

In this part . . .

You made it! In this final part of the book, I present a beloved tradition in the *For Dummies* world: the Part of Tens. I created a great list of ten do's and don'ts, as well as a list of ten useful resources you can find on the Internet to make your LinkedIn experience that much richer. Use them wisely, for while the right tips will bring you lots of success, the wrong tips will . . . eh, probably just slow you down a bit.

Chapter 19

Ten LinkedIn Do's and Don'ts

In This Chapter

▶ Managing setup and maintenance to get the most out of LinkedIn

▶ Following netiquette to keep from alienating contacts

▶ Keeping your LinkedIn activity more personal and less mechanical

I cover a lot of ground in this book — so much that it might be hard to remember it all as you're going about your daily use of LinkedIn. So here are ten essential do's and don'ts to help you build relationships and get the most value out of LinkedIn.

Keep Your Profile Complete and Current

Even though LinkedIn has many features, your profile is still one of the most compelling reasons to use the Web site, which is why LinkedIn is one of the best searchable databases of businesspeople available. And if you want to be found by others, you need to make sure that your data is complete and current. Here are a few of ways to do that:

✔ **List all your former employers and schools.** Several features help users find and connect with former colleagues and classmates (see Chapter 6). Including your complete work and educational background in your profile can help you reconnect.

If you've had a lengthy career, you don't necessarily need to include details about positions early in your career — just the companies and titles will suffice. A good guideline is to include details on just the past 7–10 years. Additionally, consider including only those positions relevant to your current work. I seriously doubt that my first job at a McDonald's is relevant to my current work as an author (except if I want to write the sequel to *Fast Food Nation*).

✔ **Update your profile (and headline) any time you achieve a new position or complete a major side project.** Your direct connections will be notified (assuming they haven't turned off the feature) of the change. This is a subtle, unobtrusive way to notify your network of your career changes. And you never know when someone is going to be looking for what you have to offer. Make sure that if you have a new position, you update your e-mail address with your new corporate e-mail address so people can still reach and invite you.

Don't Use Canned Invitations

There is never ever a good situation in which to use one of the default Invitation text messages LinkedIn provides when you send someone an Invitation to join your network on LinkedIn. Nothing says, "You're not really worth a few extra seconds of my time," quite like the all-too-familiar "I'd like to add you to my professional network" message.

That doesn't mean every Invitation has to be a lengthy personal epistle. Here are a few tips for keeping Invitations efficient but personal.

✔ **Keep it short when you can.** With people you know well and have been in recent contact with, the canned messages are actually too long. The message can be as simple as this:

Great to see you last night, Jerry — let's connect.

✔ **Make sure you know whether the person is already a LinkedIn member.** Someone who's already a member doesn't need to be convinced of LinkedIn's benefits. Maybe it shouldn't be annoying to them that you're explaining something they already know, but it's just an indication that you didn't really put any thought into making the connection.

✔ **If the contact isn't already a member, offer to help with the registration process.** You can try to explain the benefits of joining LinkedIn in an e-mail, but almost no matter what you do, it's going to come across as a sales pitch, or at least a bit evangelistic. The best way to persuade people is to offer to spend a few minutes on the phone explaining it and how you're using it. That also turns the Invitation into an opportunity to strengthen your relationship with that person by offering your time to bring them something of value.

✔ **You can still personalize a batch of Invitations.** You can give the Invitation a personal touch even if you're sending it to multiple people. For example, you can send the same Invitation to all the people you met or ran into at an event. Or you can write one Invitation to everyone in your chamber of commerce. Just remember to write it as if it were going to one person, not the whole group.

For more on Invitations, see Chapter 2.

Don't Expect Everyone to Network Like You Do

Setting rigid networking expectations can be a source of needless frustration and can actually prevent you from building relationships with some pretty great people. Here are some of the common issues that arise:

- **Different people have different standards for connecting.** Some people use LinkedIn to connect only with people they know very well. Some connect only with people with whom they share some common points of interest. Others connect with anybody. None of these approaches are wrong. If some people don't have the same standard for a connection that you do, don't take it personally, and don't judge them — they're doing what's right for them.

- **People might have perfectly good reasons not to allow other people to browse their LinkedIn connections list.** Don't hold anything against people who don't enable it. People may be concerned about client confidentiality, and thus be required to keep their connections secret. Or they may be connected to a competitor and not want their bosses and co-workers to know about it. Or they may just be concerned about their time commitments and not want to handle a growing number of Introduction requests if all their friends see their long list of connections. However, even if a person has disabled connections browsing, you can still get Introductions to people they know. Frankly, if you're just browsing other people's networks, maybe you should think about a more focused approach.

- **Not everyone responds in a timely manner.** If your request doesn't get forwarded or your InMail hasn't been replied to after a couple of weeks, don't take it personally. It doesn't mean that you're unimportant; it just means that the people you're trying to contact are busy. If it's really urgent, pick up the phone.

- **Some people are bad with names.** Just because you remember somebody's name doesn't mean that she remembers yours. Unless you're 100 percent certain that she will recognize your Invitation, contact her via e-mail or phone or a LinkedIn Introduction request before sending a connection request. Otherwise, don't be surprised when she declines your Invitation or clicks the I Don't Know button.

- **Relationships aren't always symmetrical.** For example, if you were someone's client, you might be able to provide a great recommendation for him. That doesn't mean that he can do the same for you, so don't expect it.

- **Not everyone networks just to network.** Some people are extremely busy and not receptive to "I'd just like to meet you" requests. It's nothing personal, and it doesn't mean they're bad networkers. It just means that the demands on their time exceed the supply.

Do Your Homework

People provide you all kinds of guidance, both direct and implicit, regarding what to contact them about and how. If you're the one initiating the communication, it's your responsibility to communicate on their terms. And showing that you took the time to do your homework about them demonstrates a certain level of commitment to the relationship right from the outset.

The most basic rule of good conversation is to listen. In the context of LinkedIn, that rule means simply this: Pay attention to what's on a person's profile. Any time you contact somebody, review her profile first as well as her contact settings. Respect what you see in her profile and contact settings.

For example, suppose you have a business deal or a job inquiry that you want to contact John Smith about, but his profile says he's not accepting such inquiries right now. Don't think that you know better than John does about whether he might be interested, and definitely don't try to pass off your deal or job inquiry as a mere "expertise request" or a "request to reconnect" and then tell him why you're really contacting him.

When you send an Introduction request or an Invitation to someone you don't know very well, don't put the burden on her to figure out what the common areas of interest or potential opportunities are. You took the time to read her profile and determine that it's a worthwhile connection. Save her the trouble of figuring out what you already know and put your common areas of interest in your Introduction request or Invitation.

Give LinkedIn Messages Equal Importance

Many people have a tendency to treat LinkedIn communications as less important or less time-sensitive than an official e-mail or phone call.

Nothing could be further from the truth. People get jobs, hire employees, gain clients, and make deals as a result of LinkedIn-based communications. They are every bit as much a part of your essential business correspondence as the rest of your e-mail. (If they're not, you're connecting with the wrong people!)

Here are some tips for managing your LinkedIn communications:

✔ **Don't turn off e-mail notifications.** Missing time-sensitive communications is one of the worst things you can do. If the volume of e-mail seems overwhelming, you can use e-mail rules to move LinkedIn requests into a separate folder, but as a general productivity practice, you want as few different inboxes as possible.

To make sure you have e-mail notifications set up correctly, log in to your LinkedIn account and go to this URL:

```
www.linkedin.com/secure/settings?msgdelivprefs
```

You see the Receiving Messages screen, as shown in Figure 19-1. Here, you can set up what will come to you as an individual e-mail, a digest e-mail, or no e-mail (by setting Web Only) so you can decide what is most important.

✔ **Handle your LinkedIn inbox every day.** Or at least every couple of days. You wouldn't go a week without checking your e-mail at work — don't treat LinkedIn messages any differently. (See Chapter 9 on how to manage your LinkedIn inbox.)

✔ **Do it, delegate it, defer it, or delete it.** This technique from David Allen's book *Getting Things Done: The Art of Stress-Free Productivity* (Penguin) will help you keep your inbox organized. As you're going through your inbox, if you can handle a request in under two minutes, go ahead and do it. Or you can delegate it by passing on the Introduction request or recommend one of your contacts as an expert to answer the person's question. If it will take a little more time, you can defer it by putting it into your work queue to handle later.

For additional tips on e-mail organization and productivity, check out David Allen's book *Getting Things Done,* and also take a look at 43 Folders' Inbox Zero collection at www.inboxzero.com.

Figure 19-1: Set your e-mail notifications so you don't miss an important message.

Don't Spam

One person's networking is another person's spam. Better to err on the side of caution. There are plenty of ways to use LinkedIn productively without getting a bad rep as a spammer. Some basic rules of etiquette are

- ✔ **Don't post marketing messages, job listings, job search queries, or connection-seeking messages on Answers.** All these will get your message flagged and fairly quickly removed. Don't waste your effort. There's a fine line between an advertisement and market or product research that calls attention to your company, which I cover in Chapter 7.

- ✔ **Don't automatically subscribe your connections to your newsletter.** This is admittedly a gray area. Connecting with someone indicates a certain level of receptivity to receiving communication from him, and it's reasonable to assume that should include something more than just LinkedIn Introduction requests. After all, he's supposed to be someone you know and trust, right? Well, that's not necessarily the same thing as signing up for a regular bulk newsletter.

  I think it's better to be safe than sorry, so I don't recommend auto-subscribing folks to your newsletter. People can get ticked off if they suddenly start getting some newsletter they didn't subscribe to.

  The best approach is simply to ask permission to subscribe your individual contacts to your newsletter. If you get their permission, even if they do complain later, you can politely point out that you asked first.

- ✔ **Don't send connection requests to people you don't know.** Unless they've given some kind of explicit indication that they're open to receiving Invitations (for example, announcing it on a forum, stating it in their profiles, or being a member of an open networking group), you have to assume that most people don't want to receive LinkedIn connection Invitations from strangers. LinkedIn has taken measures to curb such rampant inviting behavior, and it will get you suspended soon enough. Again, there's a simple solution: *Ask permission first.* Send an Introduction request, or contact the person via e-mail or his Web site, and ask whether it would be okay for you to send him a connection Invitation.

Be Proactive about Making New Connections

If you just set up a profile, connect with a few of your contacts, and then expect business to come your way, you're setting yourself up for disappointment. That's not to say that it can't happen, but being a little bit proactive goes a long way.

✔ **Search for people who can help you with your goals.** If you want to meet people in a particular city, industry, or target market, search for them specifically and make Introduction requests. Some people will be receptive to corresponding or talking just for networking purposes, but you'll get a better response if you have a specific need or opportunity as the basis of your contact.

✔ **Introduce people to each other.** LinkedIn's basic Introduction paradigm is reactive. For example, an Introduction is made when person A wants to connect with person C via person B. But an essential practice of a good networker is identifying possible connections between people in your network and introducing them to each other. You can do this by forwarding one person's profile to the other and Cc'ing the first person (see Chapter 5). You can send a LinkedIn message to both connections introducing them and telling them why you think they should get to know each other. You can also recommend someone in your network as an expert resource when answering questions in LinkedIn Answers.

✔ **Seek out questions to answer.** Your direct connections can send you questions that they think you may have a good answer for, but that won't help you meet new people. However, answering a single question in the Answers section allows you to interact with dozens, hundreds, or even thousands of people. Find the Answers categories that are related to your business and either check them regularly, or better yet, subscribe to them via RSS (see Chapter 18).

✔ **Ask questions.** The Answers section is the main form of public group interaction on LinkedIn. You can ask questions for highly focused activities like market research, or you can aim for more general relationship building by posing thought-provoking questions on relevant topics. One question can make dozens of new contacts for you and initiate private conversations around a topic currently relevant to your business.

Cross-Promote

Your LinkedIn profile is just one Web page of your total Web presence. It should connect people to your other points of presence, and you probably want to direct people to your LinkedIn profile from other venues as well. Here are some good cross-promotion practices:

✔ **Customize your LinkedIn profile links.** As described in Chapter 3, you can create up to three links on your profile that you can use to lead people to your business site(s), personal site, blog, your book, an event, and so on.

✔ **Include a link to your LinkedIn profile in your signature.** You can use this both in your e-mail signature and also on discussion forums. If you don't have a centralized personal professional Web site, your LinkedIn profile is a good alternative. I even cover how LinkedIn can help you create your e-mail signature in Chapter 10.

✔ **Link to your LinkedIn profile in your blog's About page.** Why rehash your entire bio? Put a couple of paragraphs that are relevant to the blog and then refer people to your LinkedIn profile for more details.

✔ **Put your LinkedIn URL on your business card.** More and more people are starting to do this.

Add Value to the Process

LinkedIn is based on the idea that existing relationships add value to the process of people meeting each other. If all you're doing is just passing the Introduction "bucket" down the virtual bucket brigade, you're actually getting in the way of communication, not adding value.

To add value, you have to give those Introduction requests some thought. Is it an appropriate fit for the recipient? Is the timing good?

Add your comments to the Introduction request. Do you know the sender? Saying, "I worked with Michael Bellomo for several years as a co-author, and he was hard-working, trust-worthy, and ambitious" goes a lot further than saying, "Hey, Francine, here's this guy Michael to check out." For additional guidance on how to handle this tactfully, see Chapter 5.

Don't Confuse Quantity with Quality

Just because you're doing a lot of something doesn't mean you're doing something well. And when you think about it, is *more networking activity* what you really want? Or do you really want *more results with less activity?*

If you want to track your real progress using LinkedIn, don't measure it by meaningless metrics like number of connections, endorsements, or questions answered. Use metrics that you know directly tie to business results, such as

✔ Leads generated

✔ Joint venture/strategic partner prospects generated

✔ Qualified job candidates contacted

✔ Qualified employers successfully contacted

✔ Interviews scheduled

✔ Speaking opportunities

✔ Publicity opportunities

Chapter 20

Ten LinkedIn Resources

As you continue building your LinkedIn presence, you might want to take advantage of additional Web sites that keep you up to date on new features and possibilities on LinkedIn, as well as explore common and uncommon uses for the Web site and make you think about how to properly take advantage and enjoy some benefits from LinkedIn and social networking in general. I rounded up a list of ten Internet resources that can provide extra information or functionality regarding your LinkedIn activities. Whether you use one or use them all, I'm sure you can find the resources that best match the way you like to learn and grow online.

The Official LinkedIn Blog

http://blog.linkedin.com

Mario Sundar, previously a LinkedIn "evangelist" who promoted the company on his own blog, was hired by LinkedIn to run its official company blog. Every week, Mario and various LinkedIn employees put up fun, informative, and timely blog posts about new functions or changes to the site as well as success stories, case studies, and practical information to make your LinkedIn experience that much more rewarding.

In addition, the blog posts live on forever, and you can search them to find out valuable information or post your own comments to give your own feedback!

You can also follow the official LinkedIn Twitter feed (@LinkedIn) and on Facebook at www.facebook.com/linkedin.

LinkedIn Labs

www.linkedinlabs.com

As LinkedIn employees think up new functions and possibilities to add to the LinkedIn Web site, there is the need to test those ideas, see whether the community finds them as valuable or relevant as first conceived, and understand how the user community would implement these new functions. LinkedIn Labs is the special site that hosts these new ideas.

LinkedIn employees post a small number of new projects or features and share them with the user base to find beta test users and gain feedback on these projects. Some projects may be promoted to become an official LinkedIn feature, while others disappear after a short time. Don't expect to find a lot of technical support for these new functions; they are here for you to play with and possibly gain your support. Keep an eye on this site to see the future of LinkedIn first-hand.

LinkedIn Applications Directory

www.linkedin.com/static?key=application_directory

LinkedIn launched an impressive suite of applications designed to enhance your profile, allow you to share information and collaborate more efficiently with your network, and help you make your career more productive. These applications are added to your LinkedIn profile home page and deliver specific functionality. For example, you can add the SlideShare application and offer PowerPoint presentations embedded in your LinkedIn profile. You enable the controls to see who has access to what information. Also, new applications are being added, such as LinkedIn Polls, which allow you to create and administer polls to your LinkedIn network or the community at large.

MyLinkWiki

http://linkedin.pbworks.com/MyLinkWiki

A *wiki* is an Internet technology that allows multiple people to collaborate on gathering and presenting information. On a wiki site, anybody can create, add, or edit information, and those changes are then reviewed by other users, and ultimately those changes are approved or rejected. The best known example of this technology is Wikipedia, one of the fastest growing repositories of information on the Internet. This online encyclopedia has rapidly become a broad source of information because of the collaborative knowledge gathering it has fostered.

One great LinkedIn wiki is MyLinkWiki, where users comment on and update the width and breadth of LinkedIn's functionality and usefulness. As you become more familiar with LinkedIn, you can contribute to this growing community as well.

RSS Feeds with Google Reader

`http://reader.google.com`

The Web technology known as RSS (commonly referred to as Really Simple Syndication) works as follows: If you want to follow all the changes, additions, and updates of a Web site, blog, or profile page, the easiest way to do that is to read a list of just the changed or added information rather than combing the entire site over and over again. An RSS feed does precisely that by providing subscribers with this list of new information.

Many active LinkedIn users maintain an RSS feed for their profile so their friends and connections can get a list of the changes and updates. You can create an RSS feed of your Network Updates to keep track of your first-degree connections on LinkedIn. In addition, LinkedIn Answers provides RSS feeds for the growing number of categories that contain questions and answers from the community. To get these updates, you need an RSS feed reader. I cover LinkedIn RSS feeds in more depth in Chapter 18.

Google makes a great tool — Google Reader — that you can use to handle all the RSS feeds you subscribe to, whether related to LinkedIn or not. You can install this free tool on practically any system. And a quick Google search for "RSS feed readers" can help you track down other feed readers to try.

Linked Intelligence Blog

`www.linkedintelligence.com`

When LinkedIn was growing in size and popularity during its earlier days, blogger Scott Allen put together the LinkedIntelligence site to cover LinkedIn and its many uses. Over the years, he built up a healthy amount of blog posts, links, and valuable information from himself and other bloggers regarding LinkedIn and how to use it.

One of his more ambitious projects started in May 2007, simply dubbed 100+ Smart Ways to Use LinkedIn. Allen had bloggers compete to provide valuable information and tips across all of LinkedIn's functions, and he created a table of contents of the best entries on his blog site. You can still find this handy resource at `www.linkedintelligence.com/smart-ways-to-use-linkedin`

The large repository of links and information can be helpful to new, intermediate, or power users of the site. The blog posts are divided into dozens of helpful categories, from LinkedIn News to Training & Coaching.

Podcast Network Connections

`http://connections.thepodcastnetwork.com`

The staggering popularity of the Apple iPod gave rise to a new way of broadcasting audio information to eager listeners — the podcast. Think of the podcast as a recorded audio broadcast that you can download to your iPod, computer, MP3 player, or other device. You can subscribe to engaging and unique podcasts, regardless of where in the world they're recorded and played.

At The Podcast Network (`http://thepodcastnetwork.com`), you can find the Connections show, where show host Stan Relihan prepares a weekly audio podcast about the art of business networking. This 20-minute podcast features interviews that Relihan does with other members of his network of connections to discuss how different social networks (like LinkedIn and Facebook, as well as new Web applications) can be used to provide a benefit to any business. You can subscribe to this show and hear great interviews, tips, and stories of how other people and companies connect online.

Digsby Social Networking/IM/E-Mail Tool

`www.digsby.com`

As you monitor your LinkedIn activity, you're most likely using other tools and networks as part of your overall experience, such as Facebook and Twitter. Rather than go to each site individually, you can use an *aggregator* — a special software tool you use to group all the information generated in all your social networks, and then present them in one tool.

One such application is Digsby, which promises to integrate your e-mail, Instant Messaging, and social networking accounts in one clean interface. After you download and set up Digsby, you can view a live newsfeed of all your friends and connections based on their events or activities on sites like LinkedIn, as well as manage chat sessions and see e-mail notifications. In the era of information overload, a tool like Digsby can help you make sense of all the messages and updates zooming to your computer screen.

Add Your LinkedIn Profile to your Facebook Page

```
www.facebook.com/apps/application.php?id=6394109615
```

For many Internet users, their LinkedIn profile is simply one aspect of their overall online identities. However, some users have built up impressive LinkedIn profiles, and rather than duplicating the information on other Web sites (like their Facebook profile) would rather display their LinkedIn profiles dynamically so any changes to their LinkedIn profiles will ripple out automatically to Facebook — without lots of work.

The My LinkedIn Profile Facebook application is the solution. You can install this dedicated Facebook application on your Facebook account that will read your LinkedIn profile, create a new Facebook Page tab, and display your LinkedIn profile as part of your Facebook Page.

One Update for Multiple Sites with Hellotxt

```
http://hellotxt.com
```

If you're active on LinkedIn and other social networking sites (Facebook, MySpace, Twitter, and others), you probably hop from site to site to provide up-to-the-minute information about what you're doing and what you want others to know. Well, instead of site hopping, you can use one function to update your status across all your social networking pages and microblogs: Hellotxt.

Hellotxt works like this: You log on to the site and enter your text message into the dashboard. You then select the sites you want to update with your new status message, and Hellotxt does the rest, reaching out to your various pages to add your new status message. It's a great centralized way to keep all your various profiles as up to date as possible and it is designed to update your LinkedIn status by answering the question, "What are you working on?"

Index

● **F** ●

• Q •

• S •

Notes

Notes

Notes

Apple & Macs

iPad For Dummies
978-0-470-58027-1

iPhone For Dummies,
4th Edition
978-0-470-87870-5

MacBook For Dummies, 3rd
Edition
978-0-470-76918-8

Mac OS X Snow Leopard For
Dummies
978-0-470-43543-4

Business

Bookkeeping For Dummies
978-0-7645-9848-7

Job Interviews
For Dummies,
3rd Edition
978-0-470-17748-8

Resumes For Dummies,
5th Edition
978-0-470-08037-5

Starting an
Online Business
For Dummies,
6th Edition
978-0-470-60210-2

Stock Investing
For Dummies,
3rd Edition
978-0-470-40114-9

Successful
Time Management
For Dummies
978-0-470-29034-7

Computer Hardware

BlackBerry
For Dummies,
4th Edition
978-0-470-60700-8

Computers For Seniors
For Dummies,
2nd Edition
978-0-470-53483-0

PCs For Dummies,
Windows
7 Edition
978-0-470-46542-4

Laptops For Dummies,
4th Edition
978-0-470-57829-2

Cooking & Entertaining

Cooking Basics
For Dummies,
3rd Edition
978-0-7645-7206-7

Wine For Dummies,
4th Edition
978-0-470-04579-4

Diet & Nutrition

Dieting For Dummies,
2nd Edition
978-0-7645-4149-0

Nutrition For Dummies,
4th Edition
978-0-471-79868-2

Weight Training
For Dummies,
3rd Edition
978-0-471-76845-6

Digital Photography

Digital SLR Cameras &
Photography For Dummies,
3rd Edition
978-0-470-46606-3

Photoshop Elements 8
For Dummies
978-0-470-52967-6

Gardening

Gardening Basics
For Dummies
978-0-470-03749-2

Organic Gardening
For Dummies,
2nd Edition
978-0-470-43067-5

Green/Sustainable

Raising Chickens
For Dummies
978-0-470-46544-8

Green Cleaning
For Dummies
978-0-470-39106-8

Health

Diabetes For Dummies,
3rd Edition
978-0-470-27086-8

Food Allergies
For Dummies
978-0-470-09584-3

Living Gluten-Free
For Dummies,
2nd Edition
978-0-470-58589-4

Hobbies/General

Chess For Dummies,
2nd Edition
978-0-7645-8404-6

Drawing
Cartoons & Comics
For Dummies
978-0-470-42683-8

Knitting For Dummies,
2nd Edition
978-0-470-28747-7

Organizing
For Dummies
978-0-7645-5300-4

Su Doku For Dummies
978-0-470-01892-7

Home Improvement

Home Maintenance
For Dummies,
2nd Edition
978-0-470-43063-7

Home Theater
For Dummies,
3rd Edition
978-0-470-41189-6

Living the
Country Lifestyle
All-in-One
For Dummies
978-0-470-43061-3

Solar Power Your Home
For Dummies,
2nd Edition
978-0-470-59678-4

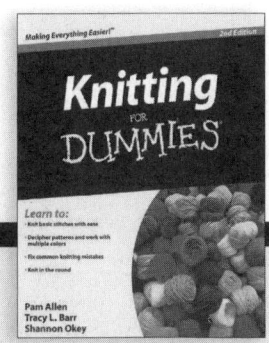

Internet

Blogging For Dummies,
3rd Edition
978-0-470-61996-4

eBay For Dummies,
6th Edition
978-0-470-49741-8

Facebook For Dummies,
3rd Edition
978-0-470-87804-0

Web Marketing
For Dummies,
2nd Edition
978-0-470-37181-7

WordPress
For Dummies,
3rd Edition
978-0-470-59274-8

Language & Foreign Language

French For Dummies
978-0-7645-5193-2

Italian Phrases
For Dummies
978-0-7645-7203-6

Spanish For Dummies,
2nd Edition
978-0-470-87855-2

Spanish
For Dummies,
Audio Set
978-0-470-09585-0

Math & Science

Algebra I
For Dummies,
2nd Edition
978-0-470-55964-2

Biology For Dummies,
2nd Edition
978-0-470-59875-7

Calculus For Dummies
978-0-7645-2498-1

Chemistry For Dummies
978-0-7645-5430-8

Microsoft Office

Excel 2010 For Dummies
978-0-470-48953-6

Office 2010 All-in-One
For Dummies
978-0-470-49748-7

Office 2010 For Dummies,
Book + DVD Bundle
978-0-470-62698-6

Word 2010 For Dummies
978-0-470-48772-3

Music

Guitar For Dummies,
2nd Edition
978-0-7645-9904-0

iPod & iTunes For
Dummies, 8th Edition
978-0-470-87871-2

Piano Exercises
For Dummies
978-0-470-38765-8

Parenting & Education

Parenting For Dummies,
2nd Edition
978-0-7645-5418-6

Type 1 Diabetes
For Dummies
978-0-470-17811-9

Pets

Cats For Dummies,
2nd Edition
978-0-7645-5275-5

Dog Training For Dummies,
3rd Edition
978-0-470-60029-0

Puppies For Dummies,
2nd Edition
978-0-470-03717-1

Religion & Inspiration

The Bible For Dummies
978-0-7645-5296-0

Catholicism For Dummies
978-0-7645-5391-2

Women in the Bible
For Dummies
978-0-7645-8475-6

Self-Help & Relationship

Anger Management
For Dummies
978-0-470-03715-7

Overcoming Anxiety
For Dummies,
2nd Edition
978-0-470-57441-6

Sports

Baseball
For Dummies,
3rd Edition
978-0-7645-7537-2

Basketball
For Dummies,
2nd Edition
978-0-7645-5248-9

Golf For Dummies,
3rd Edition
978-0-471-76871-5

Web Development

Web Design
All-in-One
For Dummies
978-0-470-41796-6

Web Sites
Do-It-Yourself
For Dummies,
2nd Edition
978-0-470-56520-9

Windows 7

Windows 7
For Dummies
978-0-470-49743-2

Windows 7
For Dummies,
Book + DVD Bundle
978-0-470-52398-8

Windows 7 All-in-One
For Dummies
978-0-470-48763-1

DUMMIES.COM®

Wherever you are in life, Dummies makes it easier.

From fashion to Facebook®, wine to Windows®, and everything in between, Dummies makes it easier.

Visit us at Dummies.com

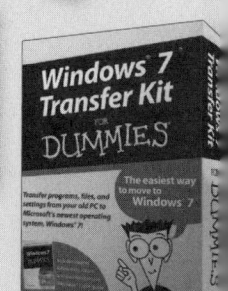